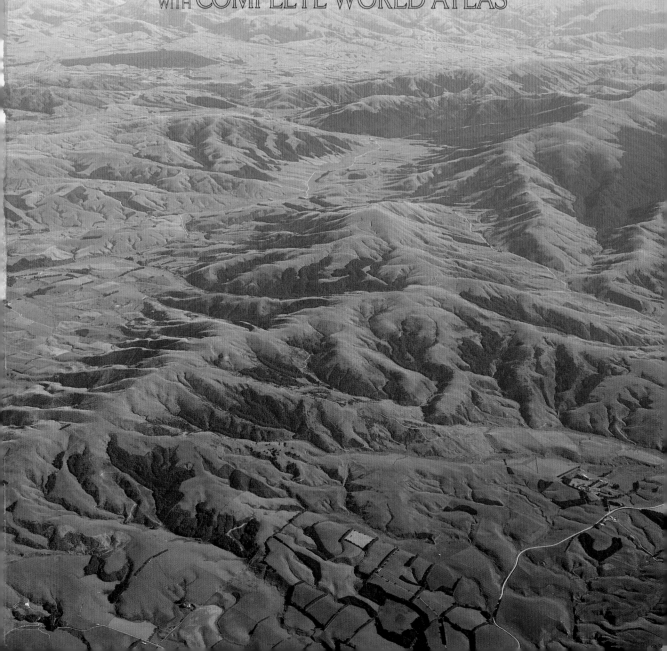

The USBORNE GEOGRAPHY ENCYCLOPEDIA

WITH COMPLETE WORLD ATLAS

The USBORNE GEOGRAPHY ENCYCLOPEDIA
WITH COMPLETE WORLD ATLAS

Gillian Doherty, Anna Claybourne and Susanna Davidson

Designers: Laura Fearn, Keith Newell, Stephen Moncrieff,
Katrina Fearn, Melissa Alaverdy and Linda Penny
Project editor: Gillian Doherty

Additional contributors: Nathalie Abi-Ezzi,
Kamini Khanduri, Rebecca Treays and Stephanie Turnbull
Consultant cartographic editor: Craig Asquith
Cartography by European Map Graphics Ltd

Consultants:
Dr. Roger Trend, Senior Lecturer in Earth Science
and Geography Education, University of Exeter
Professor Michael Hitchcock, University of North London
Dr. William Chambers
Dr. Uwem Ite, Department of Geography, University of Lancaster
Susan Bermingham, Senior Lecturer, Institute of Education,
Manchester Metropolitan University
Dr. Stephanie Bunn, University of Manchester
Dr. Susan Pfisterer, Menzies Centre for Australian Studies,
King's College, University of London
Dr. Vivien Miller, Senior Lecturer in American Studies, Middlesex University
Dr. Francisco Dominguez, Head of Latin American Studies, Middlesex University
Dr. Elizabeth Bomberg, Department of Politics, University of Edinburgh
David Harrison, Professor of Tourism, Culture and Development,
University of North London

CONTENTS

USBORNE QUICKLINKS

The Usborne Quicklinks website is packed with links to all the best websites on the internet, along with free downloadable pictures that you can use for homework or school projects.

At Usborne Quicklinks, there are over 500 recommended websites for this book. To find links to the websites, and the downloadable pictures, go to **www.usborne.com/quicklinks** and type the keyword **geography**.

Internet links

For links to all the websites recommended for this book, and for free downloadable pictures, go to **www.usborne.com/quicklinks** and enter the keyword "**geography**".

Downloadable pictures

Pictures with a ★ symbol can be downloaded at the Usborne Quicklinks website and printed out for your own personal use. To print out these pictures, go to the Usborne Quicklinks website at **www.usborne.com/quicklinks** and enter the keyword **geography**. Please note downloadable pictures must not be copied or distributed for any commercial purpose.

★

Pictures marked with a symbol like this can be downloaded free of charge from the Usborne Quicklinks website at **www.usborne.com/quicklinks**

What you can do

Here are some of the things you can do at the websites recommended for this book:

- Take virtual tours of the Solar System, the underwater world of the Great Barrier Reef, and other distant places.
- Watch video clips of erupting volcanoes, Antarctic icebergs and extreme weather events around the world.
- Explore interactive maps and satellite images of the Earth.
- Get the latest information about climate change and endangered animals and environments.
- Meet people from every continent and find out about their everyday lives.
- Discover the world's population when you were born and learn about megacities with populations over ten million people.
- See animals in the wild, from grassland and rainforest habitats, to oceans and deserts.
- Look up weather forecasts for worldwide locations and try to predict the weather.

Internet safety

When using the internet, please make sure you follow our three basic rules:

• Always ask an adult's permission before using the internet.

• Never give out personal information, such as your name, address, the name of your school or telephone number.

• If a website asks you to type in your name or email address, check with an adult first.

• For links to websites with more advice for children on staying safe on the internet, go to the Usborne Quicklinks website and click on 'Help and advice'.

Site availability

The websites described in this book are regularly checked and reviewed by Usborne editors and the links at Usborne Quicklinks are updated. If a website closes down, we will replace it with a new link. Sometimes we add extra links too, so when you visit Usborne Quicklinks, the links may be slightly different from those described in your book.

Please note that the content of a website may change at any time and Usborne Publishing is not responsible for the content or availability of any website other than its own.

Computer not essential

If you don't have use of the internet, don't worry. This book is a complete, self-contained reference book on its own.

Notes for parents

We recommend that children are supervised while using the internet, and that you ensure they read and follow our three basic rules for internet safety shown on this page.

There are also ways you can help keep children safe online. Here are our top tips for parents:

• Play and explore online with your children so you know which websites they like to visit and can talk about them together.

• It's a good idea to keep all devices that have access to the internet in a family space so you can be involved and talk about what your child is doing.

• Impress on your children that they should not give out personal information without checking with you first.

Tools to protect children

As well as educating your child about the internet, you may also wish to use the parental controls provided in most web browsers and search engines, and by Internet Service Providers. These can help you restrict access to particular websites, set time limits and monitor where a child is going.

For more information about using the internet, go to the 'Help and advice' area at the Usborne Quicklinks website.

The Earth and its moon

PLANET EARTH

OUR SOLAR SYSTEM

The Solar System is made up of the Sun and all the objects that travel around it, from planets and moons, to chunks of rock and ice and huge amounts of dust. At the moment, scientists know of eight planets that travel around the Sun.

This is a picture of the planet Saturn and some of its moons. Saturn is the one with the rings around it.

Planets

A planet is a large spherical object that travels around, or orbits, a particular star. As each planet moves, it also spins around on its axis (an imaginary line running through the planet).

Stars

Stars are huge balls of hot gas which give off heat and light. The stars we see in the night sky only look tiny because they are far away. Our closest star is the Sun. It is about 146 million km (93 million miles) away. Light takes eight minutes to travel from the Sun to Earth.

Moons

Most of the planets in our Solar System have moons. A moon orbits a planet in the same way that a planet orbits a star. Earth has just one moon, but some planets have several. Saturn, for example, has at least 53 moons.

The Sun

Internet links

To learn more about the Solar System and find fun games and quizzes to help you discover more about the stars and planets, follow the links at **www.usborne.com/quicklinks**

Uranus

Neptune

Jupiter

Saturn

Mars

This picture shows the eight planets in our Solar System in the order they are from the Sun, though they are not to scale.

Space rocks

Asteroids and comets are pieces of rock, ice, dust and grit that whizz around our Solar System. Scientists believe that they are pieces left over from when the Solar System formed. The Solar System is also full of much smaller pieces of space debris called meteoroids. These may be grains of dust from comets, large chunks of rock or even shattered asteroids.

Galaxies

A galaxy is a group of many millions of stars. Galaxies are so big that it can take light thousands of years to travel across one. There are many millions of known galaxies in the universe, all of different shapes and sizes, but there could be many, many more. Galaxies are separated from each other by vast, empty spaces. Our Solar System is part of the Milky Way galaxy.

This picture shows stars in the southern part of the Milky Way galaxy.

THE EARTH

Earth is the third planet from the Sun. It is the only planet in our Solar System with the right conditions to support living things. The closest natural object to the Earth is the Moon, which is about 384,400km (240,250 miles) away.

Factories like this one release harmful chemicals into the air, polluting the Earth's environment.

Life on Earth

The Earth's distance from the Sun means that it has just the right amount of heat and light for life to flourish. Its combination of gases enables plants, animals and people to breathe, and it is warm enough for water to exist as a liquid. All of these things are essential for life on Earth.

This is a satellite photograph of the Earth taken from space. You can see the shapes of North America and the north of South America.

Earth in danger

As the number of people on Earth grows, we use more land, and our motor vehicles and industries release an increasing amount of waste, or pollution. This damages the environment: the land, oceans and the air we breathe. It is essential that we start taking more care of the Earth, before it is too late.

The Moon

Earth has only one moon. Most moons are very small compared with the planets they orbit, but our Moon is unusually large. It is about a quarter of the Earth's size.

The Moon does not make its own light, but it reflects the Sun's rays, so it can look very bright in the night sky.

Pulling power

Between objects in the Solar System there is an invisible force called gravity, which attracts, or pulls, things together. It is the Earth's gravity that holds the Moon in orbit around it.

The Moon's gravity affects the Earth too. It pulls on the water in the Earth's oceans and seas, making the sea level rise and fall. These changing sea levels are called tides.

Satellites

Today, scientists are able to monitor vast areas of Earth from space. Devices called satellites orbit the Earth and send back information about our planet. The first satellite ever to go into space was launched by the U.S.S.R.* on October 4, 1957, to study the gases surrounding our planet. It was officially named "Satellite 1957 Alpha 2", but became better known by its nickname "Sputnik", which is a Russian word meaning "little voyager".

The Moon's surface is covered in craters. On a clear night, you can see the larger craters with your naked eye.

This is RADARSAT, Canada's first Earth observation satellite. It was launched in November 1995.

RADARSAT can produce high quality images of Earth's surface. It is used to monitor Earth's natural resources and the environment.

Internet links

For links to websites where you can view satellite images of the Earth and find fascinating facts about our planet, go to **www.usborne.com/quicklinks** and enter the keyword "geography".

*U.S.S.R., 204

THE SEASONS

The Earth takes just over a year to orbit the Sun. As it makes its journey, different parts of the world receive different amounts of heat and light. This causes the seasons (spring, summer, autumn and winter).

Tilting Earth

The Earth is tilted at an angle as it travels around the Sun. This means that one half, or hemisphere, is usually closer to the Sun than the other. The hemisphere that is closer receives more heat and light energy than the one that is tilted away. So in this half it is summer, while in the other it is winter.

As the Earth orbits the Sun, the half that was closer to the Sun gradually moves farther away, so that eventually it becomes winter in this hemisphere and summer in the other. In June the Sun's rays are most concentrated at the Tropic of Cancer and in December they are most concentrated at the Tropic of Capricorn.

In June, it is summer in the Arctic. The warmer weather only lasts for six to eight weeks.

In autumn in Maine, northeast U.S.A., the leaves on the trees turn red and golden.

The diagram below shows how the seasons change as the Earth orbits the Sun.

March: Neither hemisphere is tilted toward the Sun.

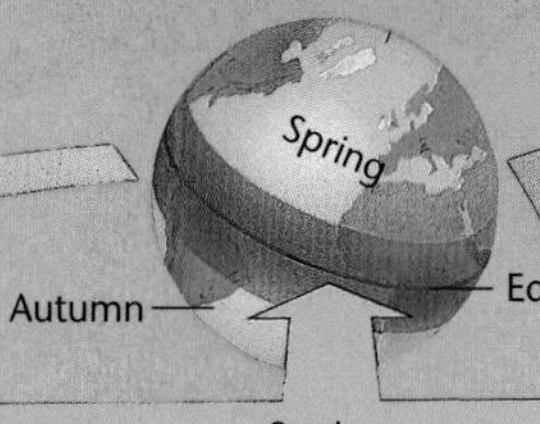

Autumn

Equator

Sun's rays

Summer

Winter

June: When the northern hemisphere is tilted toward the Sun, it is summer there. In the southern hemisphere, it is winter.

September: As in March, neither hemisphere is tilted toward the Sun.

December: When the northern hemisphere is tilted away from the Sun, it is winter there. In the southern hemisphere, it is summer.

The heat and light that the Sun gives out are essential for life on Earth.

Leap years

The time it takes for the Earth to orbit the Sun is called a solar year. A solar year is 365.26 days, but as it is more convenient to measure our calendar year in whole days, we round the number down to 365. In order to make up the difference, every four years we have to add an extra day to our calendar year, making it 366 days. These years are called leap years*. The additional day is February 29th. However, this does not make up the difference exactly, so very occasionally the extra day is not added.

Equatorial seasons

The Earth is hottest where the Sun's rays hit its surface full on. But because the Earth's surface is curved, in most places rays hit the ground at an angle. This causes them to spread out over a larger area, which makes their effect less intense.

Temperatures are also affected by the distance the Sun's rays have to travel through the Earth's atmosphere. Over greater distances, the Sun's rays lose more heat energy to the atmosphere, which makes temperatures cooler.

This picture shows how the Sun's rays spread out as they reach the Earth's surface.

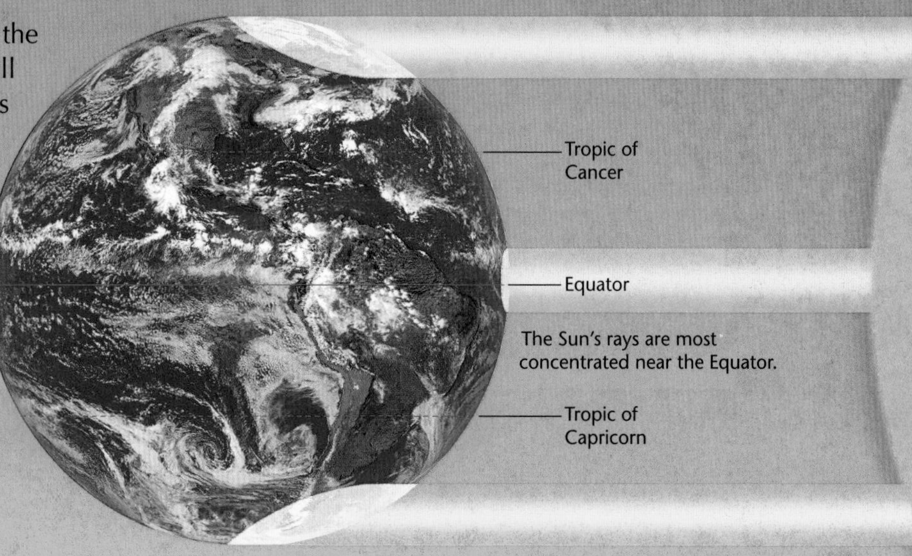

The Sun's rays are most concentrated near the Equator.

The Sun's rays spread out at the poles and have farther to travel through the Earth's atmosphere.

Internet links

For links to websites with animations and online activities that show how the seasons change as the Earth travels around the Sun, go to **www.usborne.com/quicklinks**

At the poles, the midday Sun is low on the horizon even in summer, making it cool.

At the Equator, the midday Sun is high in the sky all year round, so it is very hot.

*Leap years, 340

DAY AND NIGHT

When it's daytime in Australia, it's night-time in South America. This is because the Earth spins around on its axis as it orbits the Sun, so the part of the Earth that faces the Sun is constantly changing.

Rotating Earth

It takes 24 hours, or one day, for the Earth to spin around once on its axis. As it rotates, different parts of the world turn to face the Sun. The part of the Earth that is turned toward the Sun is in the light (daytime), but as it turns away from the Sun it becomes dark (night-time).

This diagram follows the change from day to night in one place (marked by the flag) as the Earth spins.

Path of orbit around the Sun

Sunrise and sunset

In the morning, you see the Sun "rise" in the sky. This is only an illusion. What is actually happening is that as your part of the Earth is turning to face the Sun, the movement of the Earth makes it seem as though the Sun is rising. When your part of the Earth turns away from the Sun at night, it looks as if the Sun is sinking in the sky until eventually it disappears over the horizon. This is called a sunset.

In the morning, the Sun looks as though it's rising, as your part of the Earth gradually turns to face it.

In the evening, the Sun seems to sink down in the sky, as your part of the Earth turns away from it.

Daylight hours

Everywhere in the world, apart from places that are on the Equator, days are longer in the summer than in the winter. This is because the hemisphere where it is summer receives more sunlight than the hemisphere where it is winter.

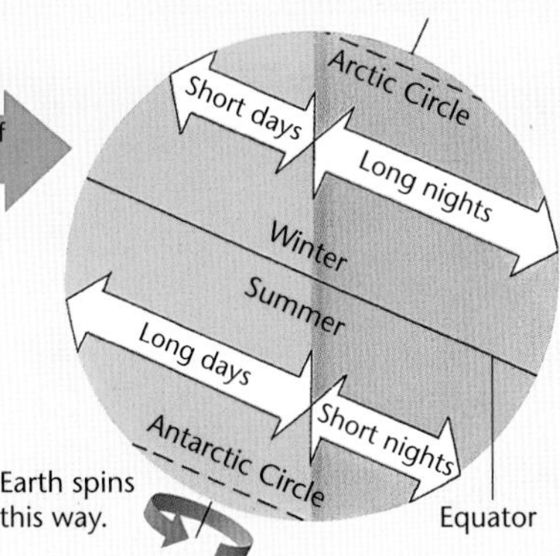

This diagram shows how the length of day and night varies depending on the time of year and where you are on the Earth.

Midnight Sun

In summer, when the northern hemisphere tilts toward the Sun, the regions north of the Arctic Circle don't turn away from the Sun, even at night. For this reason it is known as the Land of the Midnight Sun.

Internet links

Follow the website links at **www.usborne.com/quicklinks** to see the regions of the Earth where it is day and night at this moment, and to find out more about day and night and the different phases of the Moon.

Moon shapes

The Moon doesn't give out any light of its own. It looks bright to us because we see the Sun's rays reflected off its surface.

As the Moon orbits the Sun and we see different amounts of its sunlit side, its shape seems to change as shown in these diagrams.

The pictures below show what the Moon looks like from the northern hemisphere when it is in each of the positions numbered above. When the Moon is visible from the southern hemisphere, the sequence is reversed, so that a southern waxing Moon looks like a northern waning Moon. On the Equator, a crescent Moon may appear to lie on its back.

1. New Moon
2. Waxing crescent
3. First quarter
4. Waxing gibbous
5. Full Moon
6. Waning gibbous
7. Last quarter
8. Waning crescent

This shows the Sun in the Arctic Circle in the middle of the night.

INSIDE THE EARTH

The Earth is mainly solid. It has a rocky surface, but inside it has different layers, some of which are partly molten (melted). If you sliced through the Earth, you would see four main layers: the crust, the mantle, the outer core and the inner core.

This diagram shows the Earth's structure, though the layers are not drawn to scale.

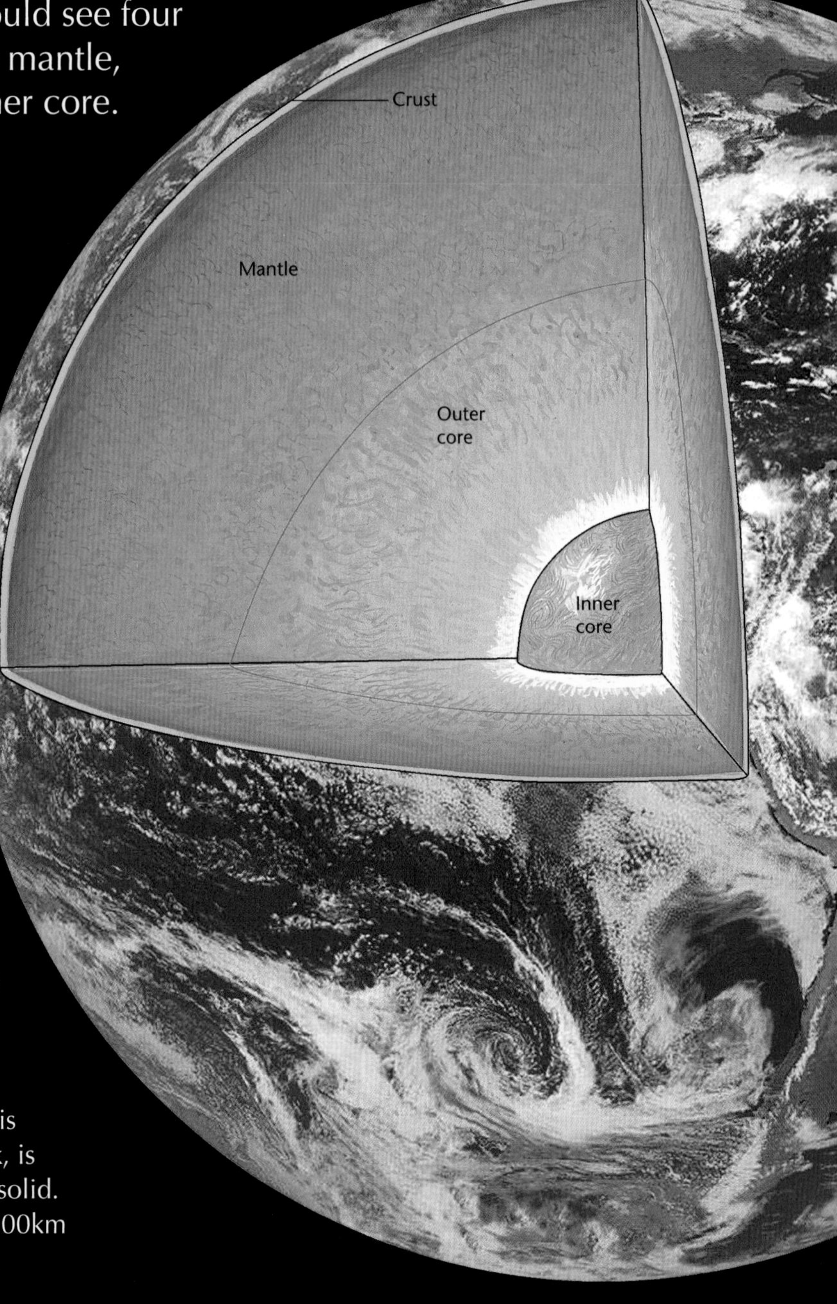

> **Internet links**
> Find out more about the structure of the Earth, magnetism and how compasses work by following the links to websites suggested at **www.usborne.com/quicklinks**

Earth's layers

The crust is the thinnest layer. It is between 5km (3 miles) and 70km (43 miles) thick. Beneath the crust is the upper part of the mantle, and together these make up the lithosphere.

The mantle is made of silicon and magnesium. The region in the mantle at the bottom of the lithosphere, about 100km (62 miles) down, is partly molten. This layer flows very slowly.

The core is probably made of iron and nickel. The outer core, which is about 2,200km (1,400 miles) thick, is molten, whereas the inner core is solid. The inner core, which is about 1,300km (800 miles) thick, is extremely hot (about 6,000°C, or 10,800°F).

The Earth's crust

There are two different types of crust. Thick continental crust forms land, and much thinner oceanic crust makes up the ocean floors. Continental crust is made of granite and similar light rocks. Oceanic crust is made of a heavier rock called basalt.

The Earth's crust is made up of oceanic and continental crust.

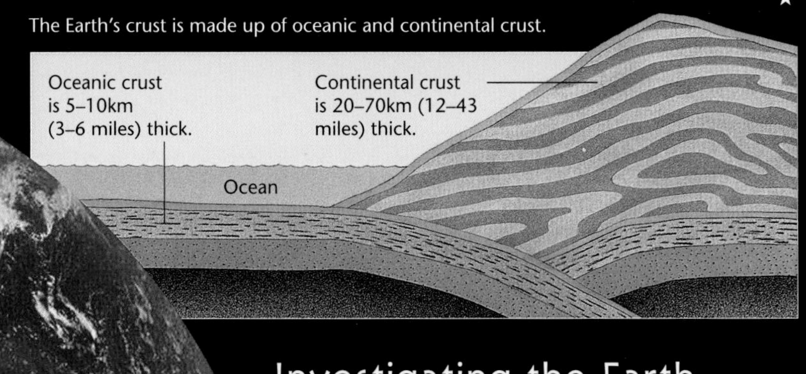

Investigating the Earth

It's difficult to find out about the inside of the Earth. Geologists, who study rocks, find out about areas near the surface by drilling holes into the crust and collecting rock samples. But they can only drill a short distance below the surface.

Volcanic eruptions provide some information about material deep inside the Earth. But the main way that geologists find out about the Earth's structure is by studying earthquakes. During an earthquake, vibrations called seismic waves travel through the Earth. As they pass through different materials, they change speed and direction. By studying records of earthquakes, called seismograms, geologists try to determine what rocks are found at different depths.

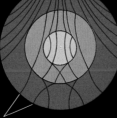

Earthquake

Paths of waves

This diagram shows how seismic waves change direction as they pass through the Earth.

Magnetic Earth

The Earth is magnetic, as if it had a huge magnetic bar inside. This may be caused by molten iron circulating in its core. The ends of this "magnet" are called the magnetic poles. These are not in exactly the same place as the geographic North and South Poles.

This diagram shows the Earth's magnetic field: the field of force surrounding it. The lines show the direction of the magnetic field.

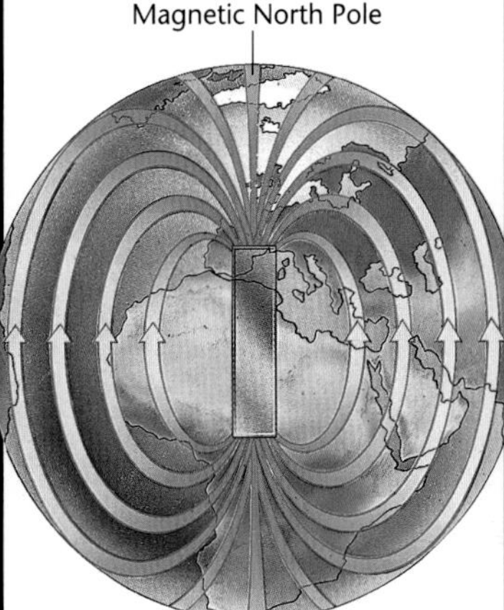

You can see the Earth's magnetism at work when you use a compass. The compass needle, which is magnetic, always points north. This is because it is pulled, or attracted, by the magnetic North Pole.

A compass's magnetic needle always points north.

THE EARTH'S CRUST

The solid surface of the Earth is broken up into large pieces called lithospheric plates, which are made up of the Earth's crust and upper mantle. Many of the Earth's most spectacular features have been formed by the movement of these plates.

North American plate
Cocos plate
Caribbean plate
Plate boundaries
Nazca plate
Mantle

A moving surface

There are seven large plates and several smaller plates. The edges of the plates are called plate boundaries. The plates move on the partly molten layer of the mantle at a rate of about 5cm (2in) a year. As all the plates fit together, movement of one plate affects the others. The study of these plates and the way they move around is called plate tectonics.

> **Internet links**
> Visit the websites recommended at **www.usborne.com/quicklinks** to learn more about plate structure and see how the Earth's plates have changed position over time.

Ocean features

As plates on the ocean floor move apart, molten rock, or magma, from the mantle rises and fills the gap. Boundaries where this happens are called constructive boundaries. As the magma reaches the surface, it hardens to make new oceanic crust. The new crust sometimes forms islands or underwater mountain ranges, called ridges.

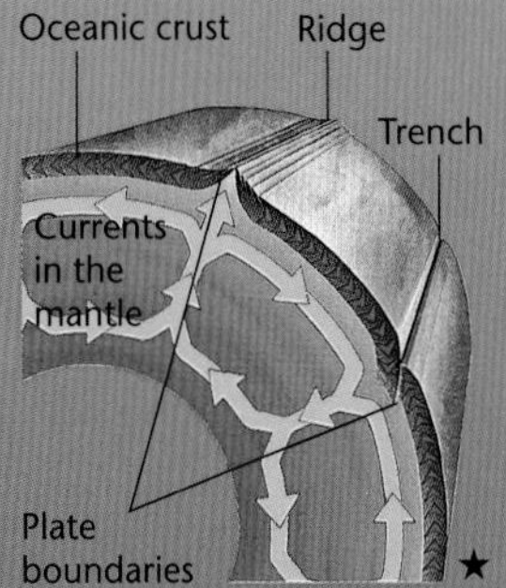

When plates push together, underwater trenches form as one plate is forced below another. These boundaries are called destructive boundaries. The deepest trench, the Mariana Trench in the Pacific Ocean, is deeper than Mount Everest is tall.

This diagram shows how ridges and trenches form.

Shifting continents

As plates shift, the position of the oceans and continents on the Earth's surface changes. The maps on the right show how geologists think the continents may have shifted.

Geologists think that there was once a single supercontinent, which we call "Pangaea".

As new rock formed at plate boundaries, the floor of the Atlantic Ocean probably widened.

Today, South America and Africa are drifting apart at a rate of 3.5cm (1.5in) each year.

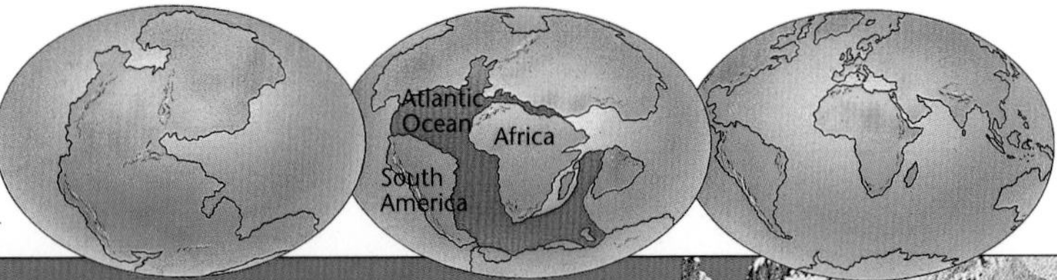

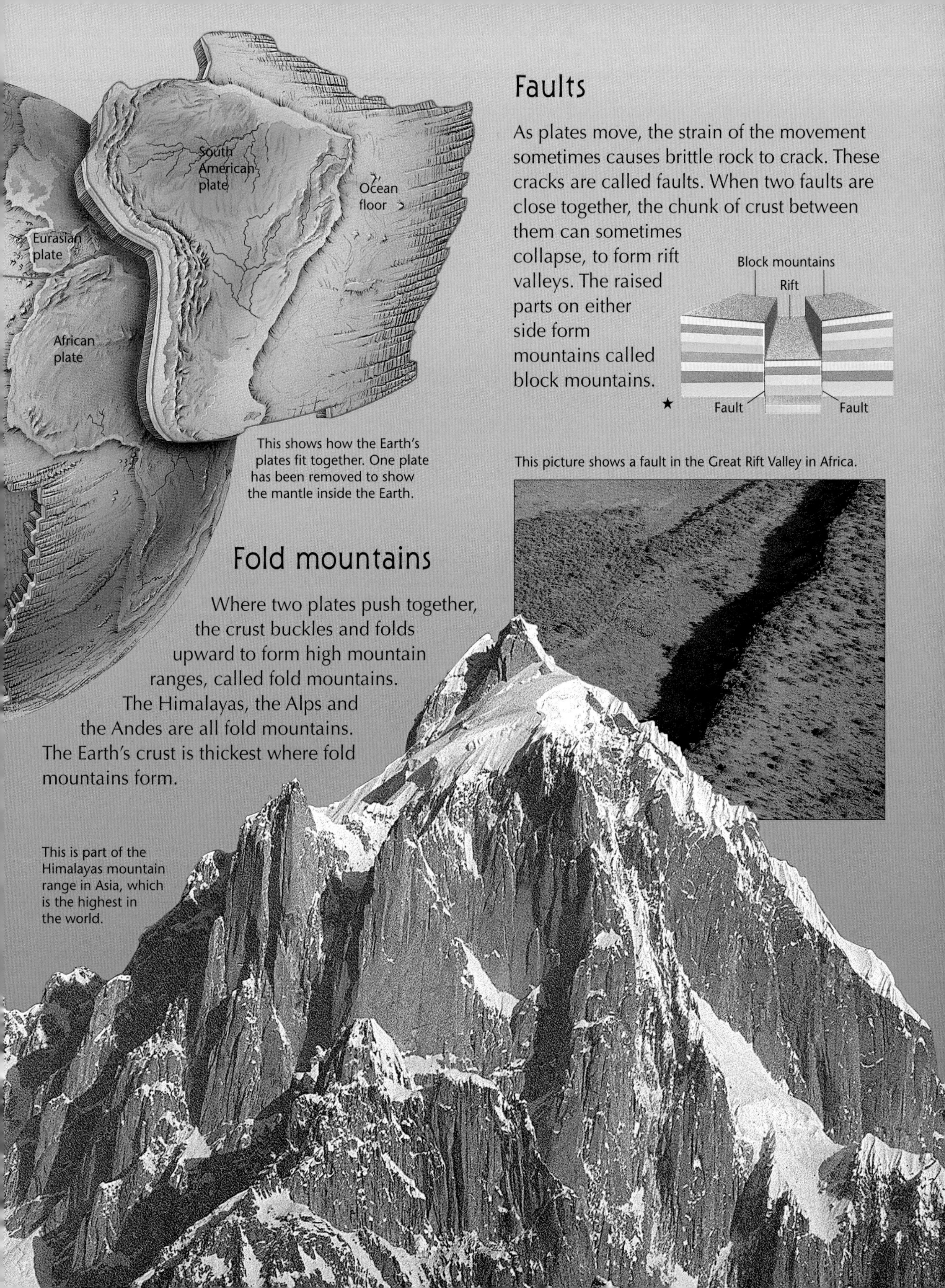

This shows how the Earth's plates fit together. One plate has been removed to show the mantle inside the Earth.

Faults

As plates move, the strain of the movement sometimes causes brittle rock to crack. These cracks are called faults. When two faults are close together, the chunk of crust between them can sometimes collapse, to form rift valleys. The raised parts on either side form mountains called block mountains.

★

This picture shows a fault in the Great Rift Valley in Africa.

Fold mountains

Where two plates push together, the crust buckles and folds upward to form high mountain ranges, called fold mountains. The Himalayas, the Alps and the Andes are all fold mountains. The Earth's crust is thickest where fold mountains form.

This is part of the Himalayas mountain range in Asia, which is the highest in the world.

ROCKS, MINERALS AND FOSSILS

The Earth's crust is made up of rock. There are three kinds of rocks: igneous, sedimentary and metamorphic. Over many years, rocks are sometimes transformed from one kind to another.

Igneous rock

Igneous rock gets its name from the Latin word for "fire", because it is formed from magma from inside the Earth. When the magma cools, it forms solid igneous rock. The way that the magma cools determines the hardness and appearance of the igneous rock that is formed.

Tuff is an igneous rock made from pieces of volcanic rock and crystals compressed together.

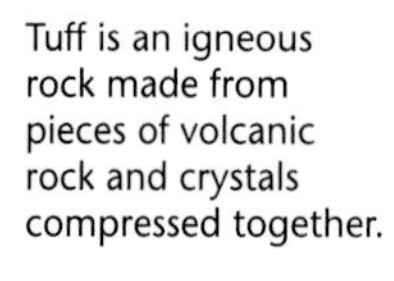

Obsidian is a shiny igneous rock formed when magma cools quickly.

Sedimentary rock

Sedimentary rock is made from tiny pieces of rocks and the decayed remains of plants and animals. These fragments, called sediment, are usually blown by winds, or carried by rivers, glaciers or landslides, to the sea, where they sink. The water and upper layers of sediment press down on the lower layers until, eventually, they form solid rock.

Chalk is a sedimentary rock made from tiny sea creatures.

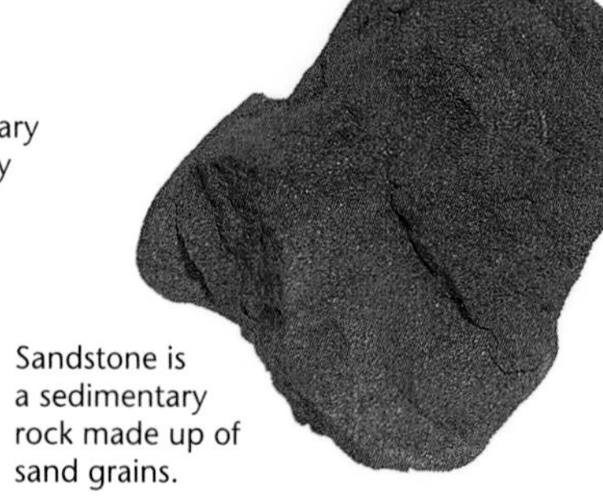

Sandstone is a sedimentary rock made up of sand grains.

The Grand Canyon, in the U.S.A., is a gorge formed by the Colorado River. You can see the layers of sandstone. Layers of rock like these are called strata.

Metamorphic rock

Metamorphic rock is rock that has been changed – for example, by heat from magma, or pressure caused by plate movements or very deep burial. It can be formed from igneous, sedimentary or other metamorphic rocks.

Marble is a metamorphic rock formed from limestone.

Mica schist is a metamorphic rock that tends to split into layers.

Minerals

Rocks are made from substances called minerals, which in turn are made up of simple chemical substances called elements. Some minerals are cut and polished to be used as gemstones.

These pictures show minerals in rocks and as gemstones.

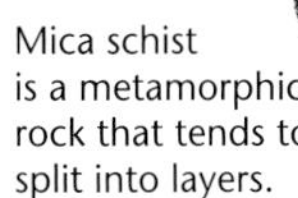

Opal can be milky white, green, red, blue, black or brown.

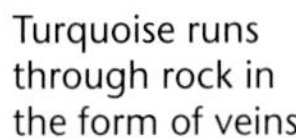

Turquoise runs through rock in the form of veins.

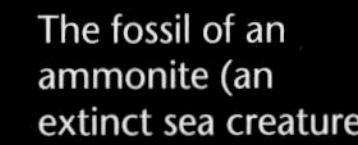

Carnelian is a dark red stone.

Internet links

You can explore more about how rocks are created, changed and worn away by following the links at **www.usborne.com/quicklinks**

Fossils

The shapes or remains of plants and animals that died long ago are sometimes preserved in rocks. They are called fossils. Fossils are formed when a dead plant or animal is buried by sediment which then turns to sedimentary rock. Usually the remains decay, although hard parts such as teeth, shells and bones can sometimes survive. The space left by the plant or animal fills up with sediment or minerals which preserve its shape.

The fossil of an ammonite (an extinct sea creature)

THE EARTH'S RESOURCES

The Earth provides all sorts of useful rocks, minerals and other materials. We quarry stone and sand for building and glassmaking, extract over 60 types of metals, and mine hundreds of useful chemicals and compounds such as salt, talc and silicon.

Metals and minerals

Metals are among the most important materials we get from the Earth. They are strong, yet they can be beaten out into flat sheets or drawn out to make wire. They also conduct electricity and heat well. Some metals even have medical uses.

Most metals are found in ores, types of rocks that contain a metal in the form of a chemical compound. Metals are extracted from ores by mixing them with other chemicals to cause a reaction or by heating them strongly.

As well as metals and stone, the Earth also provides many other chemicals and elements. Their uses often depend on how hard they are.

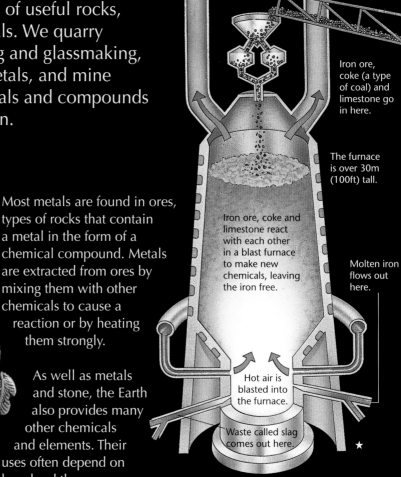

Iron is extracted from its ore in a blast furnace.

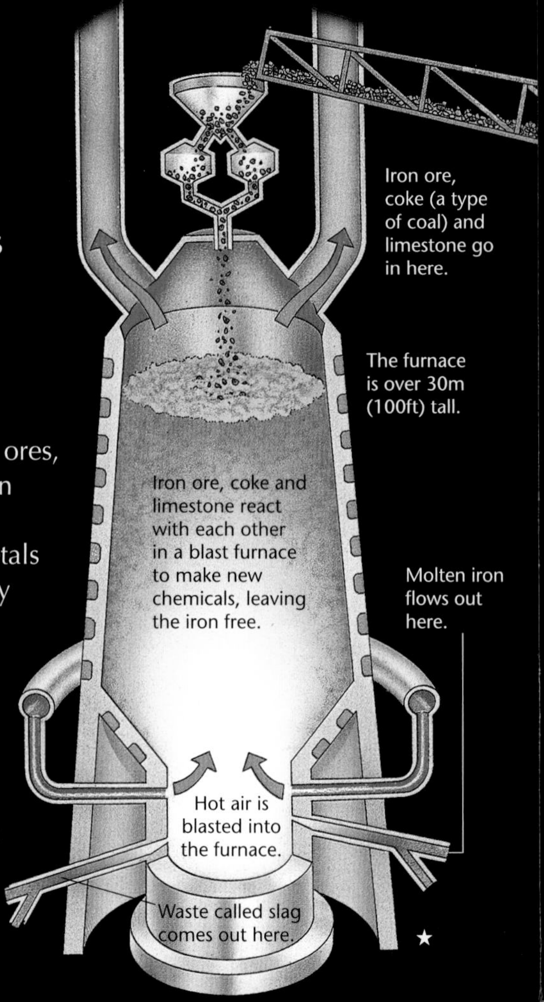

Iron ore, coke (a type of coal) and limestone go in here.

The furnace is over 30m (100ft) tall.

Iron ore, coke and limestone react with each other in a blast furnace to make new chemicals, leaving the iron free.

Molten iron flows out here.

Hot air is blasted into the furnace.

Waste called slag comes out here.

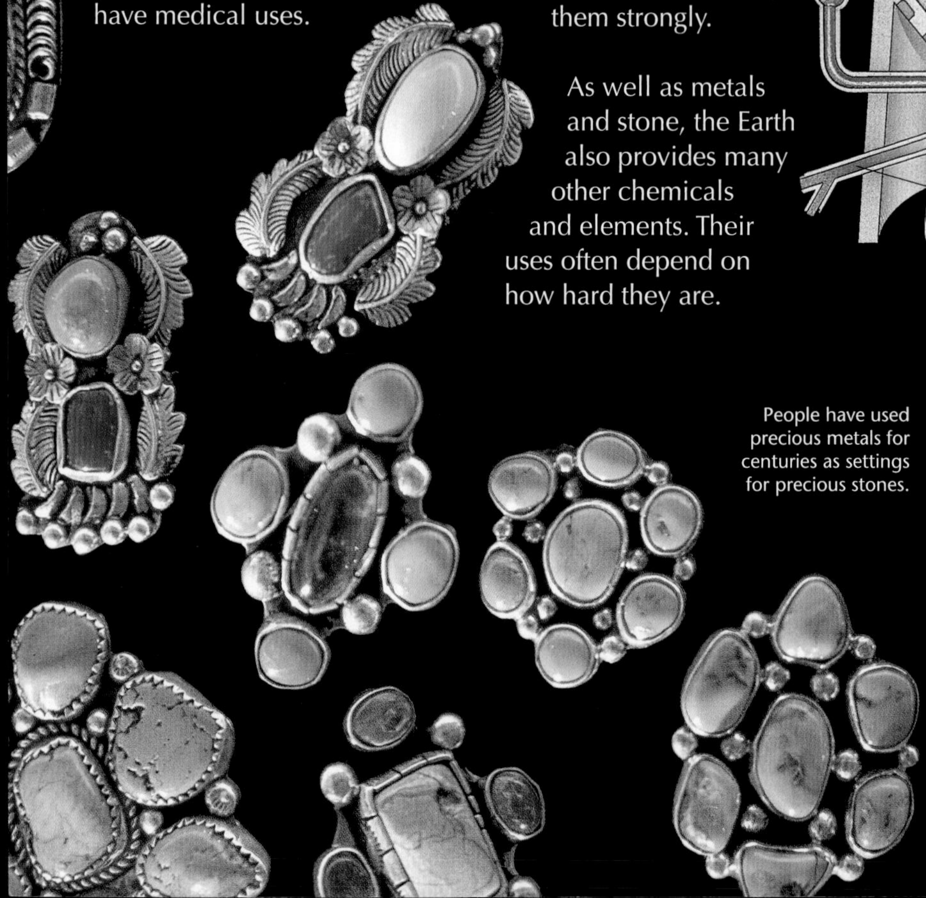

★

People have used precious metals for centuries as settings for precious stones.

Internet links

Follow the links at **www.usborne.com/quicklinks** to find out more about metals and minerals and how we use them, with activities and quizzes and a recipe for growing your own crystals.

The Mohs scale

The hardness or softness of minerals is measured on a scale of 1 to 10, called the Mohs scale. Soft minerals, such as talc, crumble easily into powder. At the other end of the scale are the hardest minerals, such as diamonds, which are used in cutting tools.

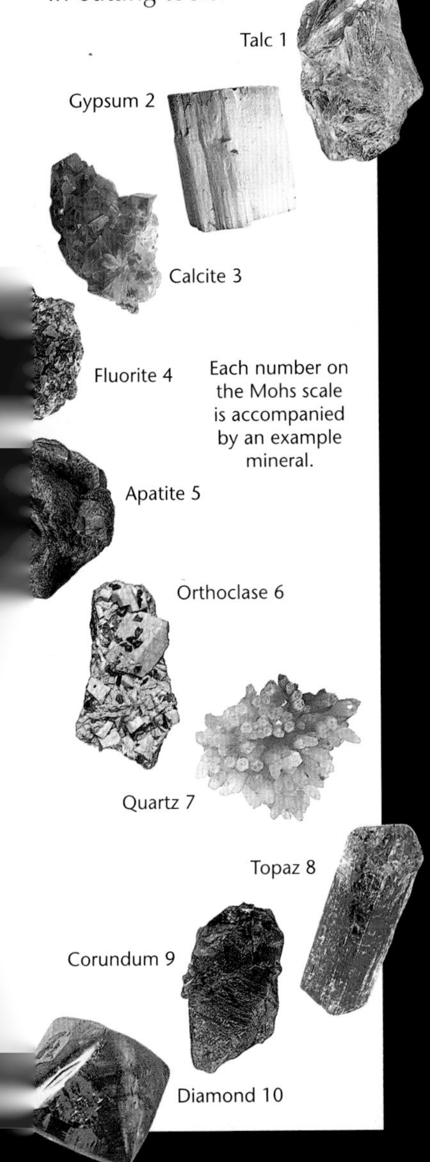

Each number on the Mohs scale is accompanied by an example mineral.

Silicon chips

Silicon comes from a mineral called quartz. It has become very important in modern society, because it is used to make the electronic chips that run computers, digital watches, mobile phones and millions of other everyday appliances.

A silicon chip

Building materials

Rocks and minerals from the Earth are used to make bricks, cement, glass and other building materials. Stone for building is usually extracted from the ground in quarries. It's often so hard and heavy that explosives have to be used to blast it apart.

Sand is made of rocks, minerals and sometimes seashells, ground down to fragments by the action of water (which is why it is usually found near the sea). Concrete and glass are both made using sand.

The Taj Mahal is a huge Indian tomb. Its exterior is white marble.

ENERGY FROM THE EARTH

The Earth's rocks, minerals and fossils contain energy which we can extract and use. Oil, gas and coal, which can be converted into heat and electricity, all come from the Earth. So do other forms of energy, such as nuclear energy.

This huge structure is the top part of an oil platform, which sticks out above the sea's surface. It contains equipment for processing the oil, and living quarters for the workers.

Fossil fuels

Coal, oil and natural gas are fossil fuels. They are called this because, like fossils*, they form in the ground over a very long period of time from the bodies of dead plants and animals.

Coal is formed from trees and other plants. Layers of sand and clay gradually settled on top of them, and compressed them slowly into thick, underground layers, or seams, of coal.

Coal being extracted from a mine at the surface of the ground, called an opencast mine.

Oil is formed from the bodies of tiny sea creatures. It is usually found in rocks under the seabed but may be found under land. Under certain conditions, natural gas is formed from dead plants and animals. Gas and oil are often found close together.

Extracting fuels

The coal we use comes from underground mines or opencast mines, which are huge, open holes dug in the ground. To extract oil and gas, a drill, supported by a structure called a rig, bores a hole into the ground or seabed. Sometimes the fuel flows out naturally, but usually water is pumped into the hole to force the oil or gas out.

*Fossils, 23

Using fossil fuels

When a fossil fuel is burned, it releases energy, which is used to heat buildings and to run vehicle engines. In power stations, heat from fossil fuels is converted into electricity.

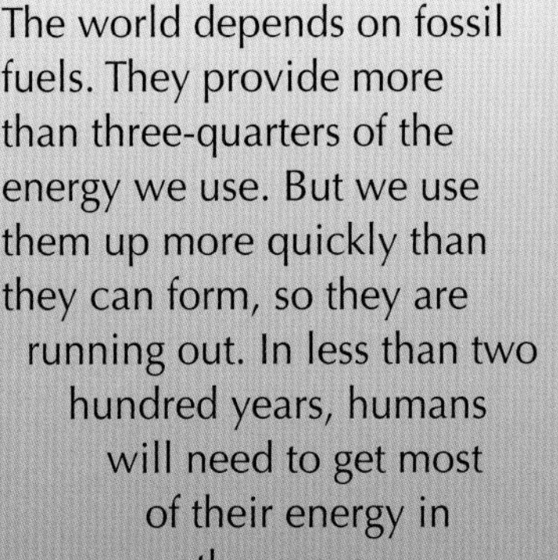

The world depends on fossil fuels. They provide more than three-quarters of the energy we use. But we use them up more quickly than they can form, so they are running out. In less than two hundred years, humans will need to get most of their energy in other ways.

As well as providing energy, oil is used to make plastic, which is made into thousands of things, from bottles to polyester clothing.

Radiation

Some minerals found in the ground are radioactive. This means their atoms (the tiny particles they are made of) are unstable.

Instead of staying as they are, unstable minerals break up and send out particles or rays, known as radiation. As they break up, a type of energy called nuclear energy is released. Uranium, a metal, is the main radioactive mineral used to produce nuclear energy.

Internet links

Visit the websites suggested at **www.usborne.com/quicklinks** to find out more about fossil fuels and take a tour of an oil platform.

This diagram shows how atoms of uranium produce nuclear energy.

A tiny particle called a neutron is fired at the uranium nucleus.

This is the nucleus, or middle, of a uranium atom.

The nucleus splits, giving off energy.

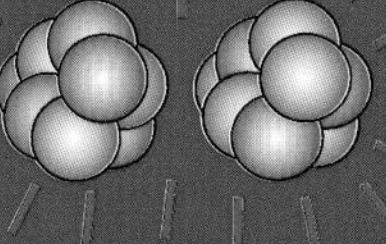

More neutrons fly off the nucleus and split other uranium atoms.

SOIL

Soil covers over half of the Earth's land surface. It is vital to life on Earth, because it provides the food and conditions plants need to grow.

Internet links

To take a closer look at soil and find out about different soil types and the important work of earthworms, visit **www.usborne.com/quicklinks** and follow the links.

As they burrow through the soil, earthworms drag dead leaves and other organic matter down to the lower levels, and break them down into humus.

What's in the soil?

Soil is made up of particles of rocks and minerals, dead plant and animal matter, tiny living organisms, gases and water. The particles of rocks and minerals range from big chunks of stone to tiny mineral particles which get dissolved by the water in the soil. Some minerals are taken in by plants and used as food. These are called nutrients. The dead plant and animal matter is gradually broken down into a substance called humus, by all the tiny creatures, bacteria and fungi in the soil.

Humus is what makes soil fertile (easy for plants to grow in). Living things are a vital part of the soil. If they weren't there to break down dead plants and animals, the remains of things that have died would keep piling up on the Earth's surface.

The water in the soil comes from rain, and gases come from the air and from plants and animals. Plants absorb water and gases through their roots.

This earwig and her babies are among the thousands of insects and other small animals that live in soil.

Soil layers

If you looked at a slice of soil under the ground, you would see that it has several different layers, called horizons.

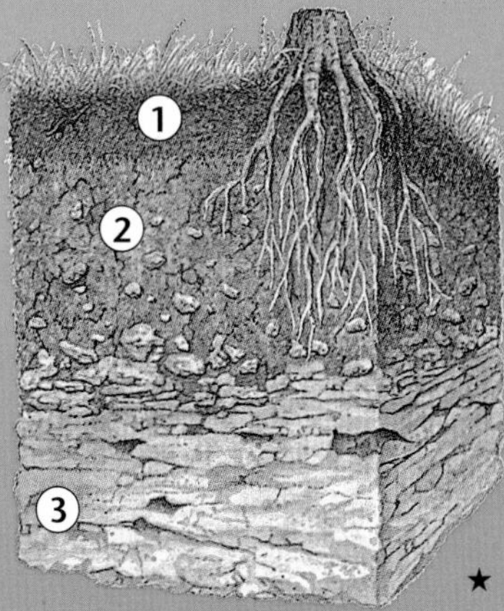

① The topsoil contains a lot of humus and is full of tiny living creatures.

② Subsoil is made up of humus, rocks and minerals. Cracks and holes, or pores, in the subsoil help water to drain away, preventing the soil from getting too wet.

③ The rock that lies underneath the soil is called bedrock. Chunks of it sometimes break off into the soil.

Types of soil

There are thousands and thousands of different types of soil. Some are more fertile than others, but different plants prefer different soils. Farmers can choose what to grow, depending on the type of soil they have on their land.

There are three main soil textures: sand, silt and clay. Sandy soil is rough and grainy. Silt has small particles, which are hard to see, while clay soil is made of fine particles, which bind together with water to form a thick, creamy mud. Clay is used to make pottery and china.

This picture shows parsnip roots reaching into the soil for water and minerals. Parsnips grow well in sandy and clay soils.

This hand contains sandy soil. Its grainy texture allows moisture to drain through it easily.

A handful of fertile soil contains up to six billion bacteria.

This hand contains loam soil. It is a very fertile soil containing a mixture of clay and sandy soils.

PROTECTING SOIL

Why do we need to take care of soil? The answer is that pollution, farming and cutting down trees can all damage soil and upset its natural balance. If we want to keep using the soil to grow food, we have to protect it, and replace all the chemicals that farming takes away.

This farmer in Minnesota, U.S.A., is loading up manure to spread over his land as a fertilizer.

The soil cycle

Where there is no farming, soil is part of a continuous cycle. Minerals are gradually dissolved into the soil. Dead plants and animals fall onto the ground, begin to rot, and are broken down into humus*. The minerals and the humus provide nutrients (food) for new plants, and the cycle starts again. This means that the nutrients that are taken out of the soil eventually get put back in.

But, when soil is used for farming, the crops are taken away to be sold, instead of rotting back into the ground. This causes the soil to become gradually less fertile* as it loses its nutrients.

Fertilizing

The best way to replace the nutrients in soil is to add a fertilizer. Fertilizers contain chemicals, such as nitrates, which plants need in order to grow. Manure (animal dung) is a natural fertilizer, but many farmers use specially made chemical fertilizers. Sometimes, if farmers use too much fertilizer, the chemicals can leak out of the soil into rivers, causing pollution.

Crop rotation

Crop rotation means changing the crop grown on a piece of land each year. It helps to keep the soil fertile, especially if the land is sometimes left to "lie fallow". This means the farmer doesn't harvest the crop, but lets it rot back into the soil. Plants such as legumes (peas and beans) and clover make good fallow crops because they put nitrates into the soil instead of taking them out.

Bright yellow oilseed rape is used to make cooking oil and as food for animals. Oilseed rape crops are often rotated with other crops on farms in Europe.

Fertile, 28; humus, 28

Soil erosion

In the natural environment, plants and trees hold soil together and stop it from being washed away by the rain or blown away by the wind. But when people chop down trees for firewood and farmers dig up the land to plant crops it leaves the bare soil exposed.

However, there are some ways to protect the soil. In some places, farmers can grow crops among the trees without cutting them down. If a main crop leaves bare patches of soil, a second crop called a cover crop can be planted in the gaps to stop it from eroding. In hilly areas, farmers build steps called terraces into the hillside to hold soil in place.

This cover crop protects the soil between rows of rubber trees. It also lets farmers grow two crops on the same land.

Internet links

Visit the websites suggested at **www.usborne.com/quicklinks** to find out more about the importance of protecting the soil and the dangers of soil erosion.

Lost forever

Ancient ruins show that there were once busy towns in places that are now desert, such as parts of Egypt and Saudi Arabia.

7,000-year-old pottery jars from an ancient civilization called Mesopotamia. The area where they were found is now desert.

The people who lived there may not have known how to look after soil and stop it from eroding. This may be why their civilizations died out.

With the trees cut down, the soil on this hillside could soon be washed away.

WEATHERING

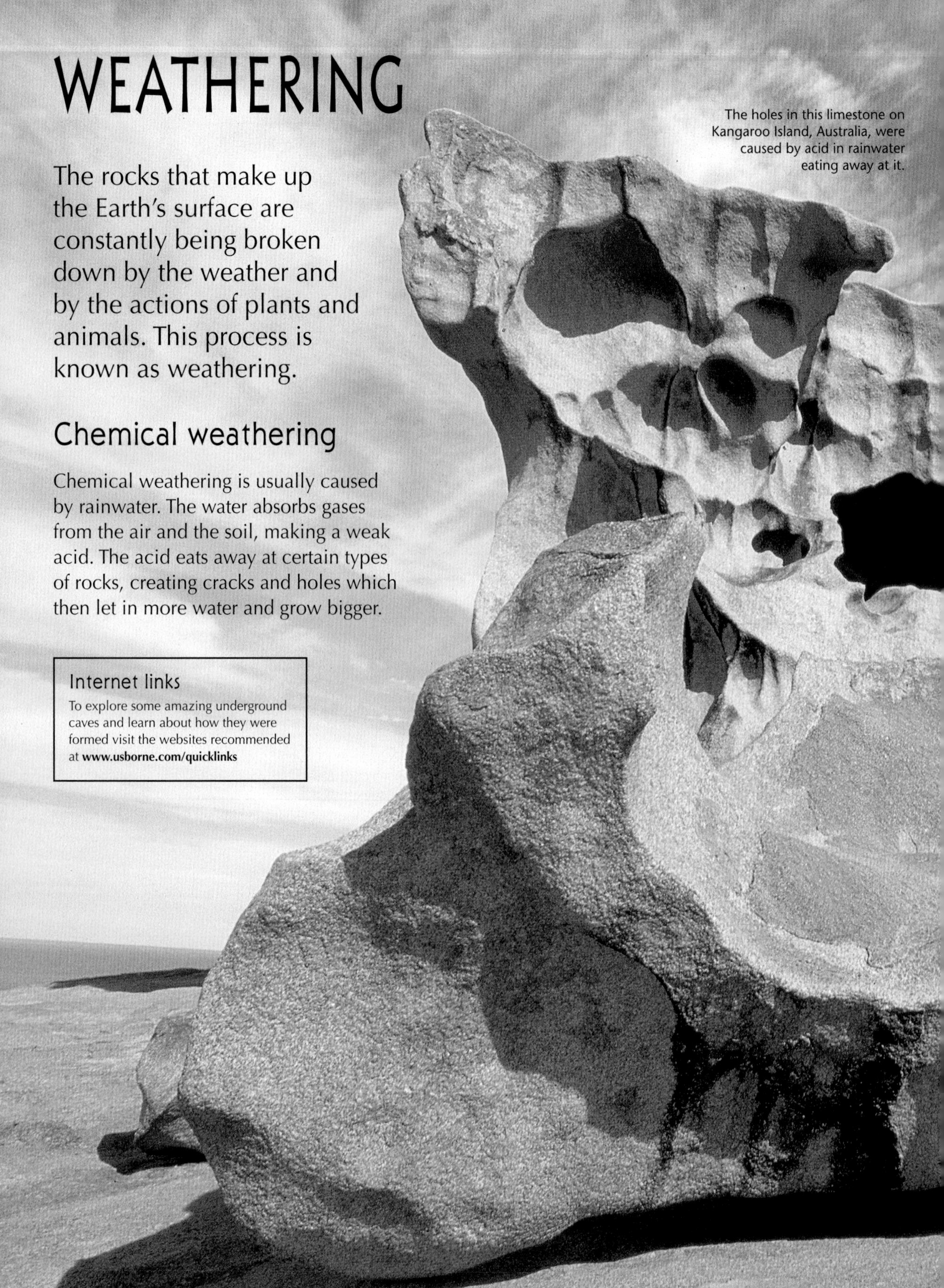

The holes in this limestone on Kangaroo Island, Australia, were caused by acid in rainwater eating away at it.

The rocks that make up the Earth's surface are constantly being broken down by the weather and by the actions of plants and animals. This process is known as weathering.

Chemical weathering

Chemical weathering is usually caused by rainwater. The water absorbs gases from the air and the soil, making a weak acid. The acid eats away at certain types of rocks, creating cracks and holes which then let in more water and grow bigger.

Internet links

To explore some amazing underground caves and learn about how they were formed visit the websites recommended at **www.usborne.com/quicklinks**

Physical weathering

Heat makes most substances get bigger, or expand. When rocks are warmed by the Sun, they expand, and when they cool down at night they shrink, or contract. The outer layer of the rock expands more, because it is directly exposed to the Sun's heat. Eventually it separates from the rock and peels off. This is called exfoliation.

A type of weathering called freeze-thaw action occurs when water seeps into cracks in rock and then freezes and expands.

★

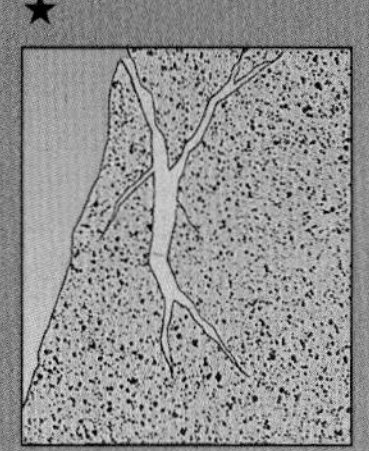

The process of freeze-thaw action begins when rain seeps into a small crack in rock.

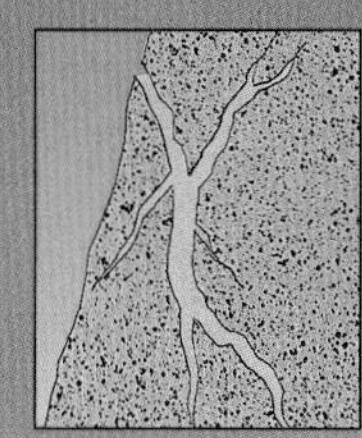

The water freezes, expands and widens the crack. When the ice thaws, more water can seep in.

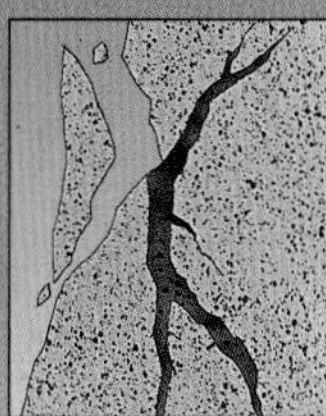

As the temperature rises and falls, the crack gradually grows until the rock breaks apart.

Biological weathering

Weathering caused by plants or animals is called biological weathering. For example, lichens, which are small organisms that grow on rocks, give out acidic chemicals which eat away at the rock surface. Animals burrowing and roots growing in the ground can also contribute to rocks breaking down.

As well as being dissolved by acidic rainwater, the Kangaroo Island rock on the left is being eaten away by lichens – the red areas on its surface.

Shaping the landscape

Because some rocks are harder and more resistant to weathering than others, they wear away at different rates. Harder rocks get left behind as outcrops, which stick up out of the surrounding land, or as long ridges. Over many years, weathering can produce amazing rock shapes, jutting mountain peaks and deep limestone caves*.

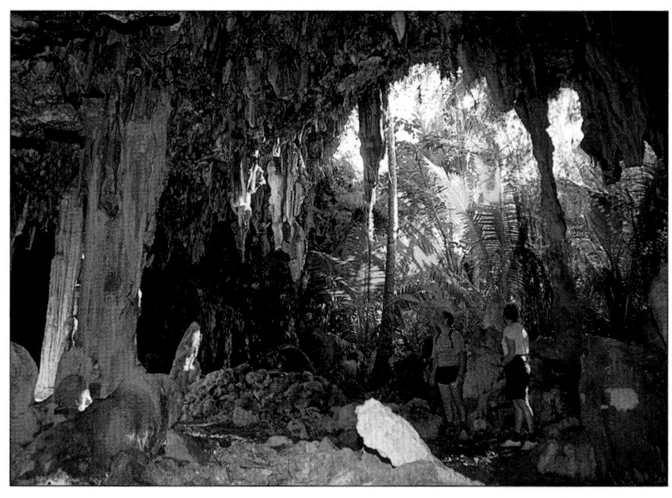

This cave is still being shaped by chemical weathering, as acidic water eats away at cracks in the rock.

*Limestone caves, 65

EROSION

Erosion happens when wind, water, ice and gravity carry away particles of rock and soil that have been worn down by weathering*. Gradually, eroded material is carried downhill and into rivers, and most of it ends up being washed into the sea.

You can sometimes tell old mountains from younger ones by how worn and flattened they are.

K2 in the Himalayas is 8,612m (28,253ft) high. It is relatively young and still has pointed peaks.

Mount Baker in Washington, U.S.A., is 3,285m (10,778ft) high. It has a flatter, worn shape, showing it was formed earlier in the Earth's history.

Wind and rain

Over hundreds of years, wind gradually blows away tiny particles from the surface of rocks. Many rocks contain different minerals, some harder than others. The wind wears them away at different rates, carving the rocks into wind sculptures.

Rain splashing onto rocks and soil washes away bigger particles and carries them into rivers. Farmers have to protect the soil* to prevent it all from eroding away in the rain.

These pinnacles in Arizona, U.S.A., are striated, which means the wind has carved their surfaces into narrow grooves.

Moving mountains

On mountains, particles of rocks and soil are pulled downhill by gravity. Chunks of rock that break off near the top of a mountain fall down the slopes, knocking off other chunks as they go. Often a covering of loose stones, called scree, collects at the bottom of a slope.

Humans can add to this kind of erosion. Rock climbers sometimes dislodge scree and set off rockfalls, and walkers can slowly wear mountain paths away.

Wearing flat

As erosion carries particles of rocks and soil away from mountains and high ground toward the sea, the Earth's land masses become lower and smoother. However, new islands and mountains are sometimes formed by volcanoes* erupting and by the plates* that make up the Earth's crust grinding together. So as old land is worn away, new land rises up to replace it.

This photo shows the bare hillside left behind after a landslide in North Carolina, U.S.A.

Preventing erosion

A certain amount of erosion is normal, and we could never stop it completely. In some places, though, we can try to slow it down.

On mountains that are popular with walkers, stone or wooden paths help to protect the land from being worn away by feet. In hilly areas, trees help to keep the soil in place and prevent landslides, so people have learned not to cut down hillside trees.

A worker planting vegetation to prevent erosion near a roadside

Internet links

Learn more about erosion, and try an experiment to find out how rain shapes the Earth, by following the links at **www.usborne.com/quicklinks**

Landslides

A landslide is a mass of soil and rock suddenly slipping down a steep slope. Many landslides are caused by rainwater soaking into the soil and making it heavier. Landslides are particularly likely if water soaks into a layer of shale (a type of slippery rock made from compressed clay).

*Plates, 20; soil erosion, 31; volcanoes, 38; weathering, 32

Lava flowing from the Kilauea volcano, Hawaii

EARTHQUAKES AND VOLCANOES

THE EXPLODING EARTH

An erupting volcano is one of the most dramatic sights in the natural world. Bubbling hot lava spews out of a hole in the Earth's crust and engulfs the land. Ash, dust and poisonous gases pour into the air and chunks of rock are hurled high into the sky.

Volcanoes

Volcanoes erupt when red-hot molten rock, called magma, from the Earth's mantle rises toward the surface. Eventually it builds up enough pressure to burst through the Earth's crust. Once magma has reached the surface of the Earth it is called lava.

A cross-section through a cone volcano

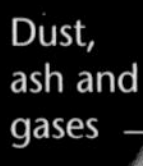

Growing

When a volcano erupts, the lava and ash it throws out eventually set as a solid layer of volcanic rock. As the layers build up, the volcano grows. Thick lava flows only a short way before setting, so it forms steep-sided cone volcanoes. Thinner lava flows farther before setting hard, so it forms shield volcanoes that have gently sloping sides.

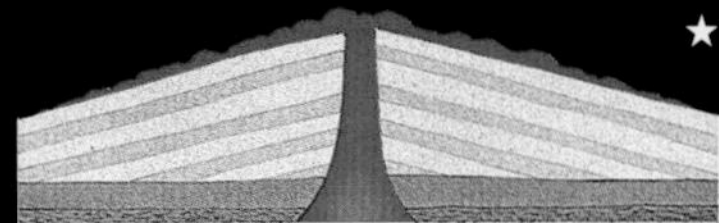

A cross-section through a shield volcano

Bombs and blocks

Volcanic bombs and blocks are thick lumps of molten lava which are blasted into the air as a volcano erupts. They start to cool and harden as they travel through the air. Blocks tend to be angular whereas bombs are more rounded.

Some blocks are the size of trucks.

As they twist through the air, some bombs form a "tail".

Tiny bombs shaped like drops form from very runny lava.

Dead or alive?

Volcanoes that erupt regularly are known as active volcanoes. Volcanoes that won't ever erupt again are called extinct volcanoes. Sometimes, people think a volcano is extinct when actually it is only dormant (sleeping). Volcanoes can lie dormant for thousands of years.

Internet links

For links to websites with animations of volcanoes erupting and information on some recent eruptions, go to **www.usborne.com/quicklinks**

Danger

Lava destroys everything it engulfs but, because it usually flows quite slowly, it rarely kills people. There is more danger from the hot gas, bombs and ash which can sweep down a volcano's slopes at speeds of 200kph (120mph). In AD79, when Mount Vesuvius in Italy erupted, the people of Pompeii were wiped out by poisonous gas and ash.

A plaster cast made from the hollow of a body left in the ash in Pompeii.

VOLCANIC VARIATIONS

Most volcanoes occur at weak spots on the Earth's crust where magma bursts through. Volcanoes erupt in different ways, depending on the thickness of the lava.

Volcanoes with runny lava, like this, erupt gently.

Spreading ridges

Whole mountain ranges of volcanoes can form at underwater boundaries where two plates* are moving apart. These are called spreading ridges. As the plates move apart, magma from the mantle rises to the surface. Most of it solidifies on the edge of the plates to make new crust, but some works its way up to the seabed, where it erupts as volcanoes.

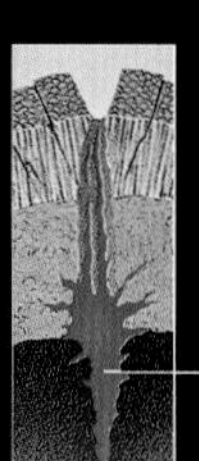

Spreading ridges form when plates move apart.

Hot spots

Some volcanoes form in the middle of plates. They may be caused by hot zones deep in the Earth's mantle. Scientists think that currents of warm rock called plumes rise slowly through the mantle and make magma which burns through the Earth's crust to make a hot spot volcano.

Hot spot

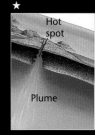

Plume

A diagram showing a hot spot volcano in the middle of a plate

Subduction zones

Volcanoes also occur at subduction zones. These are places where two plates collide head on and one plate is pushed down beneath the other. As the plate is forced deeper and deeper underground, it begins to melt, forming magma. This newly formed magma rises up through cracks in the surface and explodes in a volcano.

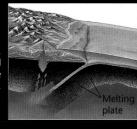

At subduction zones, one plate is forced underground where it starts to melt.

Melting plate

*Plates, 20

Lava

Not all volcanoes erupt in the same way. Some throw clouds of ash high into the air, while others have gentle lava fountains. The thicker and stickier the lava, the more gases are trapped within it. These gases create the pressure which makes a volcano erupt explosively. When lava is thin and runny, gases can escape more easily. They just bubble out of the top of the volcano.

Internet links

To examine different types of volcanoes around the world, follow the links at **www.usborne.com/quicklinks**

Hawaiian-type eruptions are usually gentle. They occur when lava is runny, so trapped gases bubble out easily.

Plinian-type eruptions are the most explosive. Trapped gases cause massive explosions as they escape, and huge amounts of volcanic ash are thrown high into the air.

NATURAL HOT WATER

In areas where volcanoes are found, there are often other dramatic natural features. Hot springs, jets of hot water and underwater chimneys that belch out black water can also be caused by volcanic activity.

Internet links

Follow the links at **www.usborne.com/quicklinks** to watch video clips of the geysers in Yellowstone National Park, U.S.A.

Hot rock

In volcanic areas, when magma rises into the Earth's crust, it heats the rock around it. This rock might contain groundwater, which is rain or sea water that has seeped down into the Earth's crust through cracks in the surface. As the rock heats up, so does the groundwater around it, producing a natural supply of hot water.

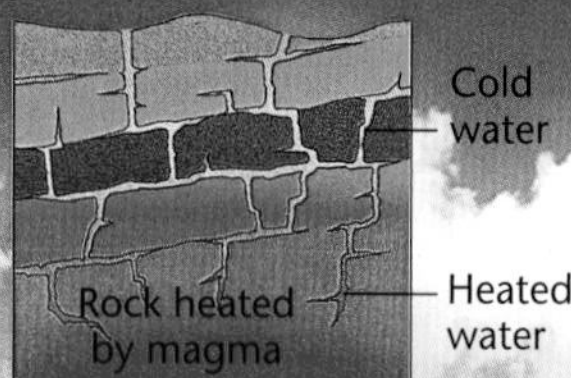

Hot rock heats up groundwater. ★

Hot springs

Groundwater heated by hot rock sometimes bubbles to the surface as a hot, or thermal, spring. The water usually contains minerals which have been dissolved from the rock below. Minerals from the water often build up around the edge of the spring.

This is the Morning Glory pool, one of many hot springs in Yellowstone National Park, U.S.A. The park has over 10,000 features, such as hot springs and geysers, that have been caused by hot, volcanic rock.

Black smokers

Black smokers form on the seabed and puff out clouds of hot, black water. Some are as tall as 6m (20ft).

Around volcanic mountain ranges under the sea, hot springs sometimes emerge through holes in the seabed called hydrothermal vents.

Some vents, called black smokers, look like chimneys and puff out plumes of hot, cloudy black water. The water is cloudy because of the minerals it has dissolved from the hot rock. As minerals are deposited around the vent, the sides of the chimney build up. Some unusual creatures, such as tubeworms and blind spider crabs, live near black smokers. They feed on bacteria that live on the minerals given out by the vents.

Geysers

A geyser is a jet of hot water and steam that shoots into the air from a hole in the ground. Geysers occur when heated groundwater gets trapped in a network of cracks under the Earth's surface. Because the water is trapped, it continues to heat up until it boils and forms steam. The pressure builds up until it forces the water to find a way out of the ground. This results in occasional bursts of hot water.

"Old Faithful" is a geyser in Yellowstone National Park, U.S.A. A fountain of hot water like this spurts out once every hour or so.

VOLCANIC ISLANDS

A volcanic island called White Island, off the coast of New Zealand

If a volcano on the seabed erupts enough times, it may become tall enough to reach the surface of the sea and begin to form an island. As ash and lava from repeated eruptions pile up around the vent, the island grows.

Hot spot islands

Hot spot volcanoes* under the sea sometimes grow into volcanic islands. Over thousands of years, a hot spot can produce a chain of volcanic islands. Scientists think that the rising plume remains in a fixed position inside the Earth's mantle, while the plate above moves. Over a long period of time, a volcanic island is carried away from the plume that caused it.

When an island moves away from a hot spot, the volcano becomes extinct as it loses its supply of magma. A new volcano then forms on the part of the plate lying above the plume. Eventually a chain of islands is formed.

The Hawaiian island chain is made up of hot spot volcanic islands.

★

*Hot spots, 40

Internet links

View photo galleries and video clips of volcanic islands by following the website links at **www.usborne.com/quicklinks**

An island is born

This picture shows steam and ash billowing from Surtsey, a volcanic island near Iceland.

In 1963, fishermen off the coast of Iceland saw smoke rising from the sea. They thought it must be a boat on fire. In fact, it wasn't smoke, but ash and steam from a volcano just below the water's surface.

During the next four years, the volcano erupted many times. As it emerged above the water, the eruptions became more explosive as the water pressure decreased. Lava and ash built up, until eventually they formed a volcanic island. The island was named Surtsey after Surt, the Nordic giant of fire.

Black beaches

Some volcanic islands have black sandy beaches. This is because they are formed from basalt lava which is black. When the lava runs down to meet the sea, it cools instantly. The change in temperature makes the lava shatter into tiny pieces which form the grains of sand.

A black sandy beach in Tahiti

LIVING WITH VOLCANOES

Despite the danger that active volcanoes present, many people choose to live on their slopes. Scientists are sometimes able to predict eruptions and warn those at risk.

> **Internet links**
> Read more about Mount St Helens and other volcanoes that threaten nearby villages by following the links at **www.usborne.com/quicklinks**

Monitoring volcanoes

Before a volcano erupts, the ground may change shape. This kind of change can be measured by instruments such as tiltmeters and geodimeters. The ground may also begin to tremble. This is known as volcanic tremor. It can be detected by seismometers.

Such instruments were used to monitor the Mount St. Helens volcano, Washington, U.S.A., in early 1980. They recorded a bulge swelling by 1.5m (5ft) per day. The area around the volcano was evacuated shortly before it erupted.

A group of experts monitoring the Mount St. Helens volcano were in a plane flying over it when the volcano began to shudder. This photograph of the eruption was taken as the pilot turned the plane to escape the blast.

The area around Mount St. Helens after the eruption. Despite the evacuation of the area, 61 people died.

A bulge on the side of Mount St. Helens swelled to 90m (295ft) before a massive eruption blasted away the side of the volcano.

Using volcanoes

Although volcanoes are usually a destructive force, they can also be put to productive uses.

The ash from volcanoes contains minerals which make soil very fertile. As a result, the land around volcanoes is very good for farming. This is one of the reasons why people choose to live in such dangerous places.

Engineers have discovered how to use the heat energy in volcanic rock to produce electricity. When groundwater seeps into the cracks in volcanic rock, it gets hot. (Sometimes cracks are created artificially to produce the same effect.) The hot water is then pumped up to the surface where it is converted into steam. The steam is used to turn machines called turbines which make electricity.

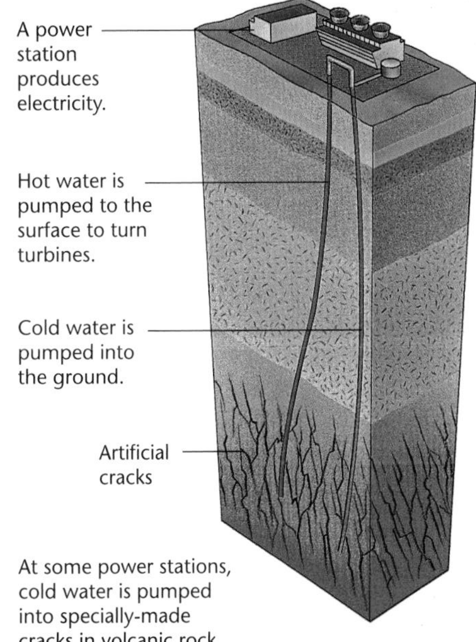
A power station produces electricity.
Hot water is pumped to the surface to turn turbines.
Cold water is pumped into the ground.
Artificial cracks

At some power stations, cold water is pumped into specially-made cracks in volcanic rock.

EARTHQUAKE EFFECTS

An earthquake is a sudden release of energy that makes the ground tremble. The effects of a large earthquake can be devastating: the ground lurches violently and buildings sway from side to side, or may even collapse. However, earthquakes only occur in certain parts of the world and most earthquakes are not felt by people at all.

An apartment block in San Francisco, U.S.A., which has been damaged by an earthquake

Damaging effects

Earthquakes cause most damage when they occur in large towns and cities. During severe earthquakes, buildings and bridges collapse, and cracks called fissures may appear in the ground. There are also threats from hazards such as fire and flooding. These may be caused when underground gas pipes or water pipes crack during an earthquake.

The power of earthquakes

Over 800,000 earthquakes occur each year, but only around a hundred of these cause serious damage. Their power and effects are measured by seismologists, scientists who study earthquakes.

There are two scales for measuring earthquakes: the Richter scale and the Mercalli scale. The Richter scale measures the power of vibrations called seismic waves that travel through the ground when an earthquake happens. These tremors are registered using a device called a seismometer. Then a chart of the vibrations, known as a seismogram, is produced.

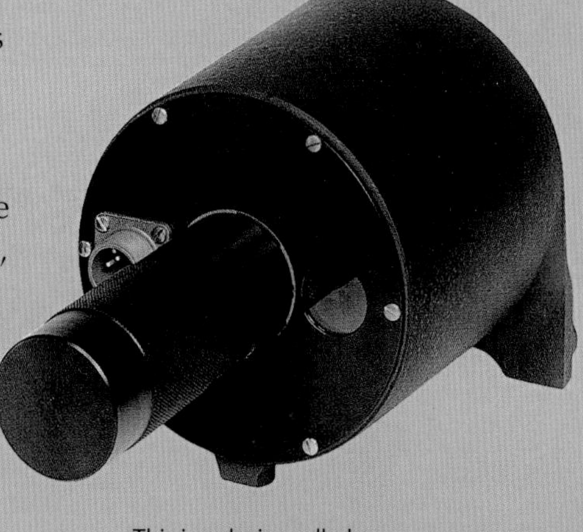

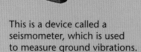

This is a device called a seismometer, which is used to measure ground vibrations.

A survivor views the devastation caused by an earthquake in Sichuan, China, in 2008.

Internet links

Go to **www.usborne.com/quicklinks** for links to websites with pictures, video clips and eyewitness accounts of earthquakes.

Mercalli scale

The Mercalli scale rates earthquakes from I to XII according to the effects of the shaking, including the damage caused in different places. It is based on information from eyewitnesses.

These pictures show how earthquakes are rated using the Mercalli scale. Ratings below IV indicate very slight vibrations.

IV
People indoors may notice plates and windows start to rattle.

V
Small objects move and liquids in glasses and bowls splash around.

VI
Books and ornaments fall off shelves. Vibrations are felt indoors and outdoors.

VII
Walls crack and tiles and bricks fall from buildings.

VIII
Some weaker buildings collapse.

IX+
Many larger buildings collapse.

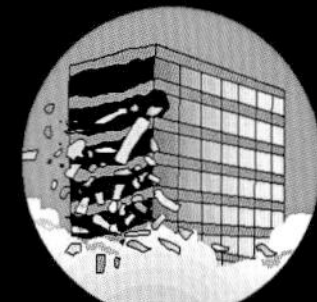

HOW EARTHQUAKES HAPPEN

Earthquakes are most common near plate boundaries*. The movement of the plates causes stress to build up in certain areas of rock. When this stress is suddenly released, the surrounding rock vibrates, causing an earthquake.

Fault lines

Earthquakes occur along cracks in the Earth's crust called faults. Faults can be tiny fractures or long cracks stretching over vast distances. They often occur when plates slide against each other, causing the rock to be twisted, stretched or squeezed until it splits. Boundaries where plates slide past each other in the same or in opposite directions are called conservative margins.

San Francisco
San Andreas fault
The North American plate moves 1cm (0.4in) a year.
Los Angeles
San Diego
The Pacific plate moves 6cm (2.4in) a year.

Earthquakes regularly occur along the San Andreas fault, on the west coast of North America. These plates slide in the same direction, but move at different speeds.

This diagram shows how some plates slide past each other in opposite directions.

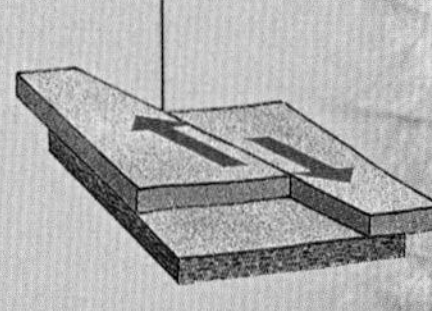

An overhead view of the San Andreas fault

Releasing energy

If the jagged edges along a fault become jammed, energy builds up as the two edges strain against one another. Eventually, the stress becomes so great that one side is suddenly forced to give way, causing a jerking movement. The energy that has built up is released, making the surrounding rock vibrate in an earthquake.

A fault running through rock

Energy builds up at the point where the rocks become jammed.

*Plate boundaries, 20

The focus

The point where the rock gives way is called the focus. This is where the earthquake starts, usually about 5–15km (3–9 miles) underground. The point on the surface directly above the focus is called the epicentre*.

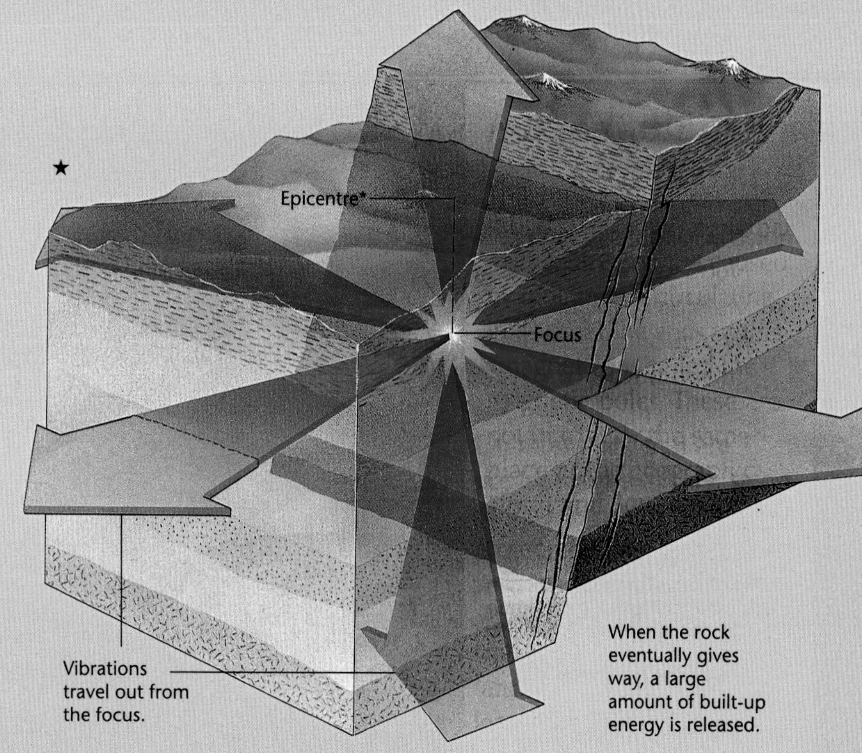

When the rock eventually gives way, a large amount of built-up energy is released.

> **Internet links**
> For links to websites with animated guides to why earthquakes happen and a closer look at California's San Andreas Fault, go to **www.usborne.com/quicklinks**

Seismic waves

Seismic waves are at their strongest nearest the focus and become weaker as they travel out. There are different types of seismic waves, each of which makes the rock it travels through vibrate in a different way.

Different types of seismic waves travel by distorting rock in different ways.

 Direction of waves

 Vibrations of the rock particles as the waves pass through

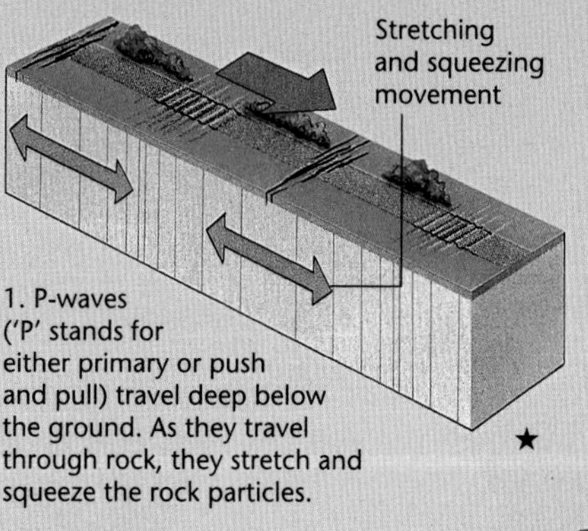

1. P-waves ('P' stands for either primary or push and pull) travel deep below the ground. As they travel through rock, they stretch and squeeze the rock particles.

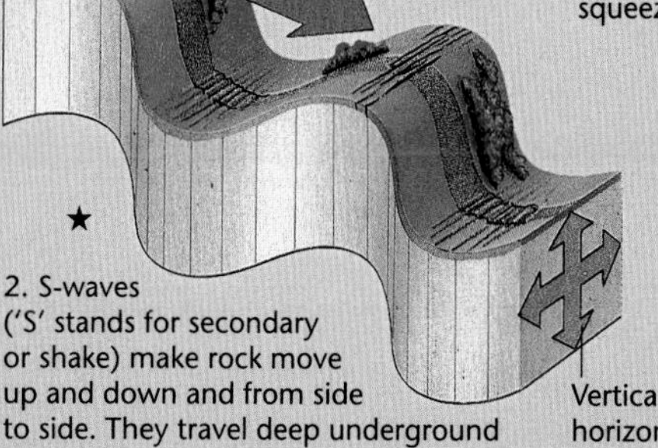

2. S-waves ('S' stands for secondary or shake) make rock move up and down and from side to side. They travel deep underground and can't move through liquid.

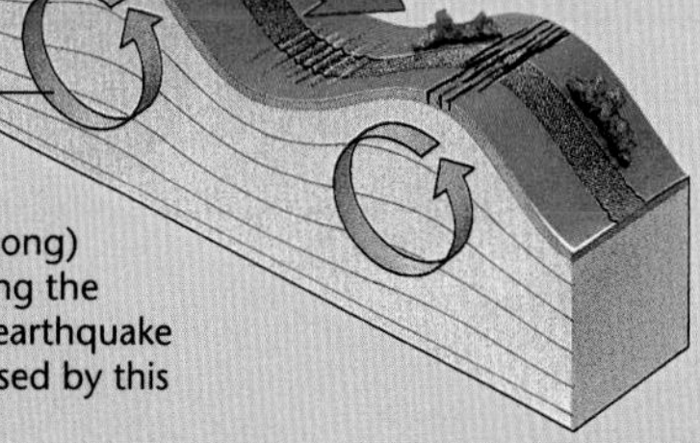

3. L-waves ('L' stands for long) only travel along the surface. Most earthquake damage is caused by this type of wave.

Aftershocks

Sometimes, not all of the energy that has built up is released during an earthquake. This may mean that after the main earthquake there are smaller tremors, known as aftershocks, as the remaining energy is released. Small amounts of energy may also be released before an earthquake occurs. This produces tremors known as foreshocks.

*Epicenter (U.S.A.)

EARTHQUAKE SAFETY

By monitoring faults, scientists can sometimes predict when and where earthquakes are likely to occur. This means that they can take steps to limit the damage caused by an earthquake or even prevent an earthquake from happening.

Seismic gaps

Stress that builds up at fault boundaries is often released gradually by slow movement known as fault creep. Earthquakes are less likely to happen in areas where fault creep occurs, because stress is being released. They are most likely to occur at sections of a fault where there has been no movement for many years. These sections are known as seismic gaps.

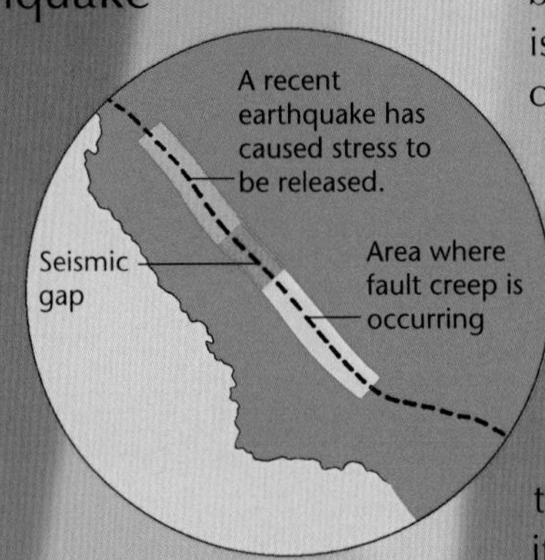

By identifying seismic gaps, scientists can carefully monitor areas where earthquakes are most likely to occur.

Monitoring faults

If the surface of the Earth suddenly starts to tilt, it may be a sign that an earthquake is about to happen. Devices called tiltmeters can measure tiny changes in the level of the ground. Horizontal movement along faults can be monitored using lasers. A laser beam from one side of the fault is bounced off a reflector on the other side, which reflects it back. A computer records the time it takes the beam to travel this distance. If the time changes, it shows that movement has taken place.

Scientists use lasers like these to detect ground movements. They can detect shifts as slight as 1mm (0.04in).

Preventing earthquakes

Earthquakes can be prevented by releasing jammed plates before too much stress builds up. This can be done by conducting a small explosion to shift the plates. Alternatively, drilling deep holes and injecting water into rocks reduces friction, enabling smoother movement along a fault.

Keeping safe

During an earthquake, if you are indoors, the safest place to be is under a solid table or desk. You should cover your eyes to protect them from flying glass and hold on tightly to the leg of the table. If you are outside, it's better to be in an open space, away from buildings, trees and power lines.

Internet links

For links to websites where you can find fascinating earthquake facts, pictures and animations, and learn how to stay safe during an earthquake, go to **www.usborne.com/quicklinks**

Animal instincts

Scientists think that animals' highly developed senses may alert them to earthquakes before they happen. It is possible that they can detect slight vibrations, changes in electrical currents in rocks, or the release of gases. In San Francisco, U.S.A., zoo animals are monitored in case the way they behave gives warning of an earthquake.

If animals become unusually agitated, it may be a clue that an earthquake is about to happen.

Safe buildings

In areas where there is a high risk of earthquakes happening, more buildings are being designed so that minimum damage is caused if there is an earthquake. The foundations of some buildings are constructed to absorb vibrations and reduce the effects of shaking. Steel frames can be used to strengthen buildings, so that a building may sway but will not collapse when the ground trembles.

The Transamerica skyscraper in San Francisco, U.S.A., is designed to withstand tremors.

GIANT WAVES

An earthquake or a volcanic eruption under the sea or near the coast can cause giant waves called tsunami. These waves surge across the sea in all directions. Just before a tsunami crashes onto the shore, it may swell to an enormous height.

In 1998, a tsunami caused incredible devastation in Papua New Guinea. This is a still from a video taken there. It shows steel roofing wrapped around a tree by the force of the water.

Tsunami

Tsunami begin when an earthquake or volcano causes the water to shift and waves to form. Out at sea, tsunami are a similar height to ordinary waves, but the distance between one tsunami and the next can be more than 100km (62 miles). What makes tsunami so dangerous is their speed. They race across the sea at speeds of up to 800kph (500mph). Normally tsunami do not break like ordinary waves. As a tsunami enters shallow water, its height increases and it surges over the land. This is what causes the devastating flooding of coastal regions.

> **Internet links**
>
> Visit the websites recommended at **www.usborne.com/quicklinks** to see animated diagrams of how tsunami form and to learn about the devastating Indian Ocean tsunami of December, 2004.

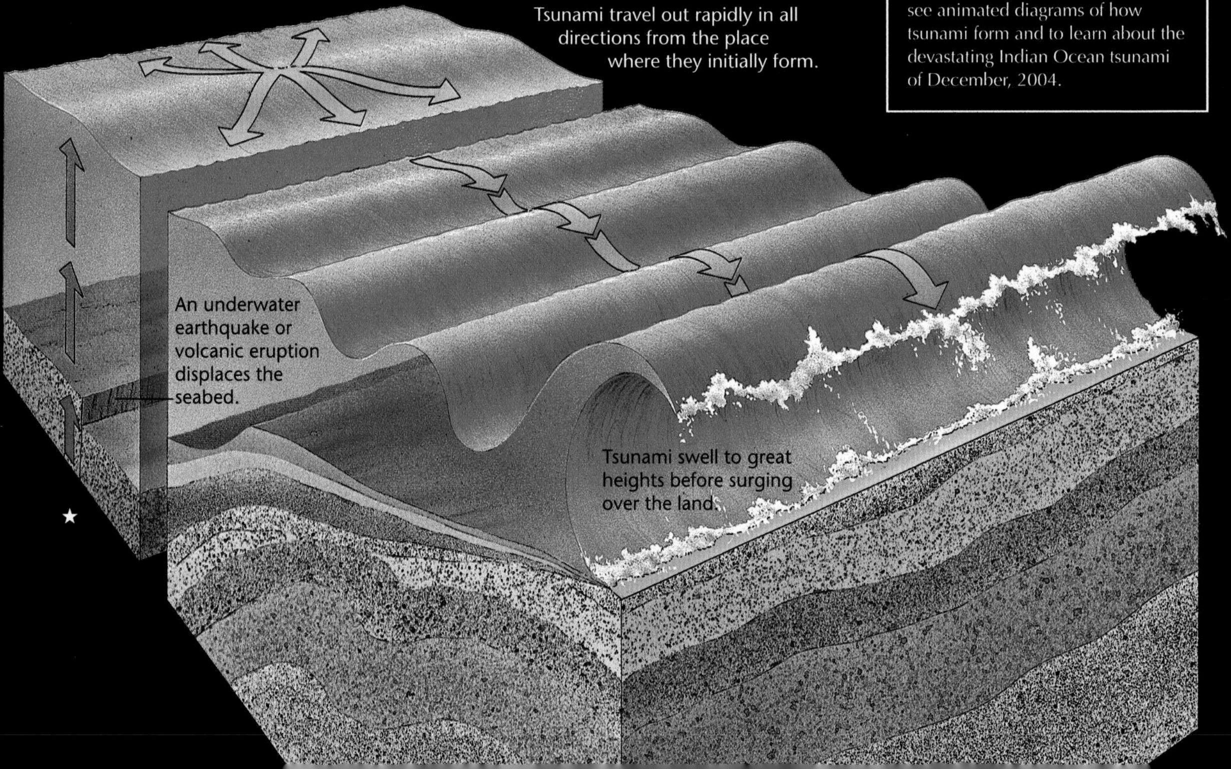

Tsunami travel out rapidly in all directions from the place where they initially form.

An underwater earthquake or volcanic eruption displaces the seabed.

Tsunami swell to great heights before surging over the land.

Tsunami warning system

Most tsunami occur in the Pacific Ocean. For this reason, there are observation stations throughout the Pacific to monitor earthquakes. If an earthquake is large enough to generate tsunami, warnings are issued to coastal towns, so that they can prepare for it. Tide stations along the coast then monitor the arrival of the tsunami.

Observation and tide stations in the Pacific monitor tsunami.

Tsunami look like a huge wall of water. They can reach heights of up to 50m (165ft).

A group of Atlantic salmon swimming

RIVERS AND OCEANS

RIVERS

The water in rivers comes from rainfall, from snow and ice melting, and from water inside the Earth, called groundwater. Rivers carry this water downhill to lakes and oceans.

Hippopotamuses live in and around slow, muddy rivers in Africa. This one has an egret on its head.

A river's course

A river changes as it flows downhill along its path, or course. Many rivers begin in mountain areas, where rain and melting ice run into steep, clear streams. Mountain streams cut narrow, deep valleys and join together as they flow downhill. Smaller streams and rivers that flow into a bigger river are called tributaries.

Mountain streams, like this one in Connecticut, U.S.A., form series of mini waterfalls as they tumble down over the steep, rocky slopes.

Away from the mountains, the water flows more smoothly in broader channels and larger valleys. As the land levels out, the river starts to form large bends, or meanders.

Finally, the river widens out into a broad estuary, or sometimes splits to form a delta*, before flowing into the sea (or sometimes into a large lake). The part of a river where it meets the sea is called the river mouth.

Internet links

Follow the links at **www.usborne.com/quicklinks** to discover more facts about rivers, see aerial photographs showing the different stages of rivers and find out more about river creatures.

Stonefly larvae live in mountain streams. They cling to stones with their claws so they don't get swept away by the water.

Drainage

The area of land from which a river collects its water is called its drainage basin. When water drains into streams and rivers, it forms different patterns, depending on the shape of the land and the type of rock it is made of.

When there is only one type of rock, streams form a tree-like pattern like this. It is called a dendritic drainage pattern.

River records

The Manu River, a tributary of the Amazon, winding its way through the rainforests of Peru

The longest river in the world is the River Nile in Africa. It travels northward for 6,671km (4,145 miles) from its source in Burundi to its delta in Egypt, where it flows into the Mediterranean Sea. However, the world's biggest river, or the one that holds the most water, is the Amazon in South America. It is about 6,440km (4,000 miles) long, and flows across South America from west to east. Every single second, it pours about 94 million litres (20 million gallons) of water into the Atlantic Ocean. At its mouth, the Amazon is 240km (150 miles) wide.

A Nile crocodile stalks its prey by swimming silently along in the river, with most of its body underwater.

*Deltas, 60

RIVERS AT WORK

Rivers can carve through solid rock and move huge boulders hundreds of miles. Over many years, rivers have eroded deep gorges and huge waterfalls, and carried vast amounts of rock, sand, soil and mud to the sea.

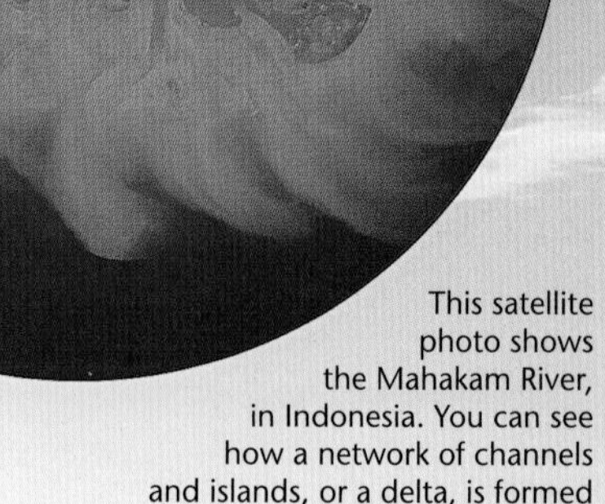

This satellite photo shows the Mahakam River, in Indonesia. You can see how a network of channels and islands, or a delta, is formed where the river runs into the sea.

How rivers erode

As a river flows, the water sweeps along any loose soil, sand or rocks in its way. As they roll, slide and bounce along, the rocks and pebbles chip away at the riverbed, making it deeper and wider. They also grind against each other, which wears them down and breaks them into smaller pieces.

The river forces water and air bubbles into cracks in the riverbed, breaking off more chunks of rock. Another reason that rivers erode is that river water is slightly acidic, because it comes from rain*. It gradually wears away some types of rocks by dissolving them.

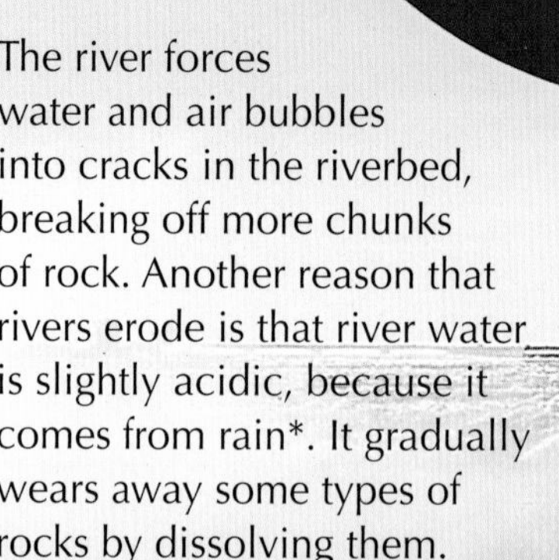

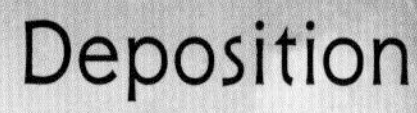

These rocks have been smoothed and rounded by the action of the water in the river.

Deposition

In its upper stages, a river is very turbulent and has lots of large boulders and pebbles on its bed. As it flows downstream the riverbed becomes smoother, so the water flows slightly faster. It starts to drop, or deposit, sand, silt and then mud. This is why the lower sections of a river have muddy beds. Near the sea, the deposited sediment may build up to form whole islands. The river splits up and forms a network of channels called a delta. The rest of the sediment flows into the sea.

*Meander, 58; rainwater, 32

Changing course

Rivers flow faster around the outside of a meander* than on the inside. The outside edge is slowly eroded, while the river deposits debris on the inside edge. Eventually the two sides of the meander meet, and the river cuts through to form a new course.

> **Internet links**
> Learn more about different river features, river erosion and how rivers change over time by visiting the websites recommended at **www.usborne.com/quicklinks**

★

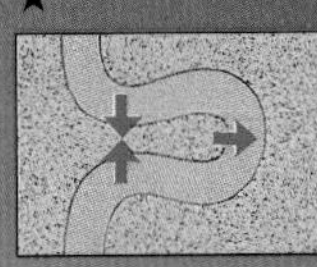

A river erodes the outside of a meander and deposits sediment on the inside, making a loop.

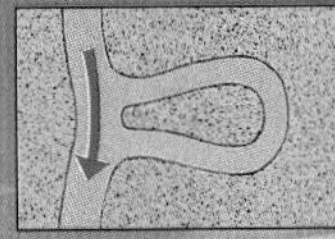

The loop grows longer and narrower until the river finally breaks through.

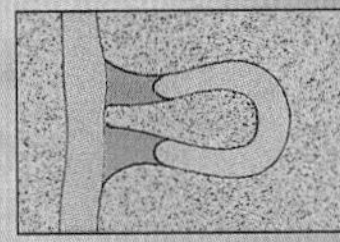

The river flows past the ends of the loop and they slowly become silted up.

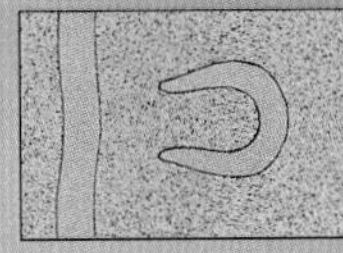

Eventually the loop gets cut off completely and forms a lake called an oxbow lake.

This is the Horseshoe Falls, part of Niagara Falls, which is a huge waterfall on the border between Canada and the U.S.A. The waterfall moves upstream by around 3m (11ft) per year.

Waterfalls

Waterfalls begin when a river flows from an area of hard rock onto soft rock. The river wears away the soft rock more quickly and creates a ledge. Water falling over the ledge erodes a hollow at the bottom called a plunge pool. The action of the water and pebbles churning in the plunge pool can undercut the hard rock, creating an overhanging ledge. Chunks of the overhanging rock break off and very gradually, over hundreds of years, the waterfall moves backward, cutting a deep valley called a gorge.

This diagram shows how a waterfall is formed.

Waterfall cutting back

Falling water cuts away at the soft rock below.

Hard rock

Plunge pool

Softer rock

Spray undercuts here.

USING RIVERS

Rivers are central to the way human civilization has developed. They have been used for thousands of years for drinking and washing and as transport routes. Farming and industry depend on the water they provide and we can convert their flowing force into useful energy.

This engraving shows London, England, in 1631, with large ships plying their trade up and down the River Thames.

Amsterdam in the Netherlands is not on the sea, but is an important port, with over 80km (50 miles) of canals dividing it into over 80 islands.

River ports

A port is a city where ships can load and unload. When most international transport was by sea, many large ports, such as Montreal in Canada, Manaus in Brazil, and London in England, grew up near navigable rivers, that is rivers that can be used by ships. For example, most of the Amazon is navigable, because it is so wide and deep.

Canals

Canals are artificial waterways built to replace or extend rivers. Irrigation canals divert water from rivers onto fields. Navigational canals are built for boats or ships to travel on. For example, the Suez Canal joins the Mediterranean Sea to the Red Sea, so that ships can take a short cut between Europe and the Indian Ocean. The beds and banks of canals are usually built of brick or concrete, so they suffer less erosion* than rivers.

Internet links

To find out about the world's most famous canals and waterways, and learn how dams and hydroelectric power plants affect communities, follow the links at **www.usborne.com/quicklinks**

*River erosion, 60

Clean energy

Electrical energy from water power is called hydroelectric power or HEP. An HEP plant usually consists of a dam built on a river to create a large reservoir or lake. High-pressure jets of water are released from the lake through narrow channels, and used to spin turbines which produce electricity.

Water power is increasingly important as an energy source. Unlike fossil fuels, it is renewable (it won't run out). It also causes little pollution. But there can be problems when hydroelectric reservoirs take up precious land, or when dams collapse.

This small waterwheel generates electricity for a rural area of Washington State, U.S.A.

Water power

The energy in a river can be converted into electricity or other useful forms of energy. The earliest water power systems used a river or stream to turn a waterwheel. The turning force of the wheel was then used to drive machines, such as mills for grinding flour. Simple waterwheels like this are still used in many countries.

Dam disasters

The present-day ruins of the Malpasset Dam, in France, which burst in 1959.

In the past, several large dams have caused disaster by breaking or overflowing. One example is the Malpasset Dam in Frejus, France. It collapsed in 1959, causing a flood which killed over 500 people. The dam failed because it was built on rock called schist, which cracks easily.

Part of the Shasta Hydroelectric Dam in California, U.S.A. The spillway in the picture releases water to stop the dam from overflowing.

WATER IN THE GROUND

Water doesn't just flow over the surface of the Earth; it flows under it too. As well as the rivers and lakes that we can see, there is a huge amount of water, called groundwater, stored underground in rocks and caves.

Bottling mineral water and spring water to sell as drinking water is a major industry in some areas.

Groundwater

Many types of rocks are permeable, which means that water can soak through them. Water that has soaked into the ground and then been soaked up, or absorbed, into a layer of permeable rock is known as groundwater. Underground, the upper layers of rock press down on the lower layers, compressing them so that they are less permeable. So the amount of groundwater decreases farther down. The top level of the water-soaked layer is known as the water table.

Aquifers are layers of rock that can hold water. Some stretch for thousands of miles under the ground. In some places they are an important source of fresh water.

Springs

A spring is a stream of fresh water springing out of the ground. Springs form where a layer of water-filled rock meets the surface of the Earth, especially on a hillside. The groundwater flows out of the rock and forms a small pool or stream.

Spring water is often clean and sparkling because it has been filtered through layers of rock. Sometimes the water dissolves minerals from the rocks. Some of these minerals are thought to be good for your health.

★

Rain and snow seep through permeable rock.
Water table
Saturated rock
Aquifer
Mountain rivers
Rivers, lakes and springs may appear where an aquifer meets the surface.
A spring emerges where saturated rock meets the surface.
Lake
Impermeable rock

Rivers under the ground

Water can also be found in underground rivers, waterfalls and even large lakes in caves and tunnels. These usually form in limestone. The water eats away at the rock through chemical weathering*.

Internet links
For links to websites about different cave formations and to read about how they developed over time, visit **www.usborne.com/quicklinks**

Stalactites and stalagmites

In some caves, long columns of stone, called stalactites, hang from the ceiling, and columns called stalagmites rise up from the floor. They are formed when water full of dissolved minerals drips from the cave roof. With each drop, a tiny deposit of rock is left behind and over time this grows into a long column. As the drips hit the ground, they deposit more minerals, which build up into stalagmites.

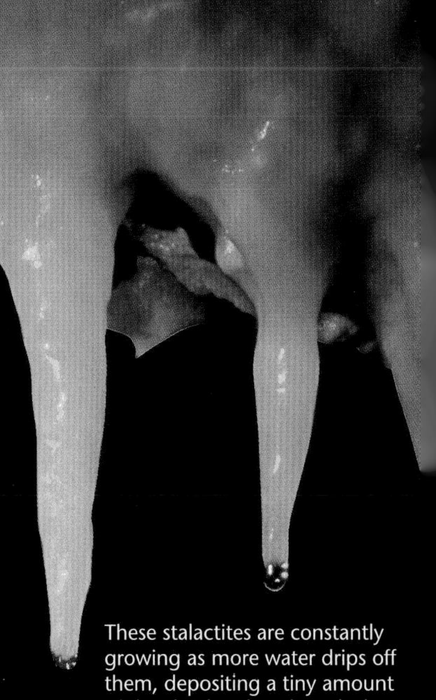

These stalactites are constantly growing as more water drips off them, depositing a tiny amount of dissolved rock with each drip.

Inside this cave in Mexico, long stalactites have grown down from the ceiling, while water has gathered to form a still underground pool.

RIVERS OF ICE

A glacier is a huge mass of ice that flows downhill, a little like a river. Glaciers flow much more slowly than rivers. But, because they are solid, they cut through the landscape more easily, gouging deep U-shaped valleys as they carry rocks and soil along with them.

This is a glacier in Glacier Bay National Park, Alaska, U.S.A.

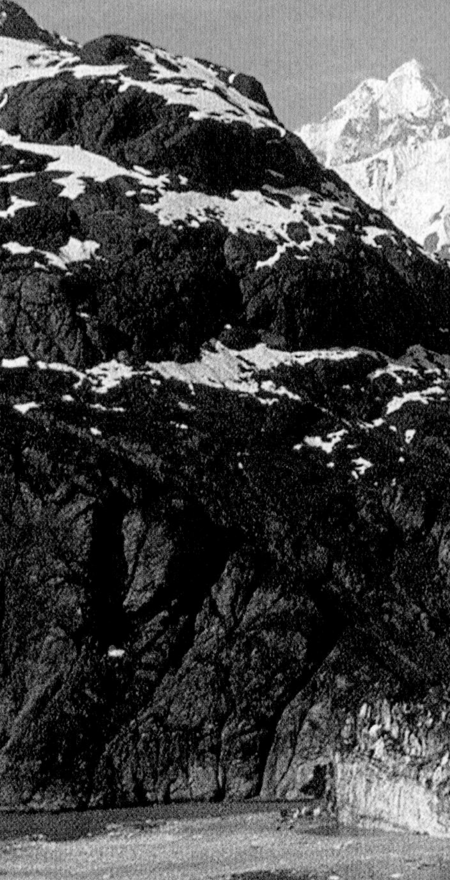

How glaciers form

Glaciers are found in cold places, such as high mountains. At the top of a glacier, known as the accumulation zone, layers of snow collect and become packed down into hard, solid ice. As more snow falls on top, the mass of ice gets heavier and heavier, until it starts to move down the mountain.

As the ice gradually flows downhill, it gets warmer, because the air is warmer lower down. At the lower end, called the ablation zone, the glacier melts and the icy-cold water, known as meltwater, flows into streams and rivers.

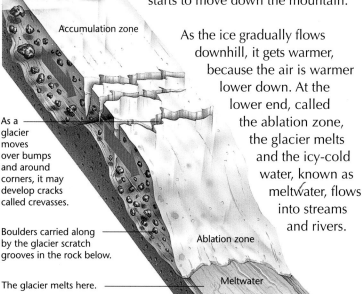

Fresh snow falls here.

Accumulation zone

As a glacier moves over bumps and around corners, it may develop cracks called crevasses.

Boulders carried along by the glacier scratch grooves in the rock below.

Ablation zone

The glacier melts here.

Meltwater

This diagram shows the different parts of a glacier and the way it moves downhill. ★

Internet links

To learn more about the stages of a glacier's life by taking a quick online tour with historical photographs, follow the links at **www.usborne.com/quicklinks**

Ice force

Glaciers are very heavy and powerful. As a glacier flows along, the ice and rocks caught in it scrape soil and rock from the sides and floor of the valley, carving a deep channel. When the ice melts, it deposits thick layers of debris, called moraine, and boulders, known as erratics, on the valley floor.

Glacial clues

If the climate gets warmer, glaciers sometimes melt, leaving behind a glacial valley. You can recognize a glacial valley by its deep, rounded U-shape and by debris, such as boulders and moraine hills, or drumlins, left on the valley floor. Sometimes, valleys called hanging valleys, that once joined the glacier, are left high above the main valley. At the coast, some glacial valleys are filled with seawater. They form narrow inlets called fjords.

This diagram shows some of the features that will help you to recognize a glacial valley. A glacial valley filled with seawater, like this, is called a fjord.

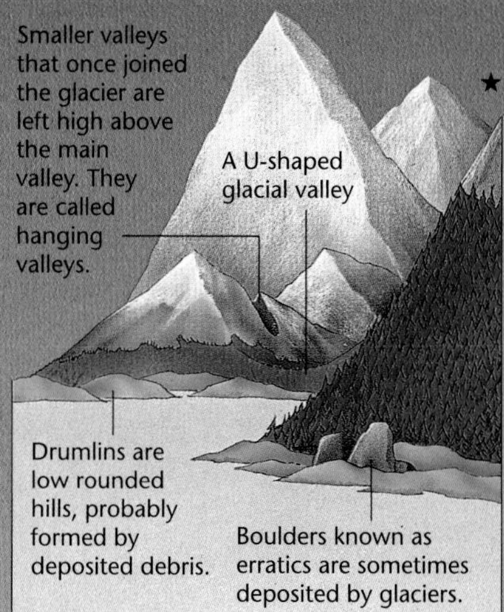

Smaller valleys that once joined the glacier are left high above the main valley. They are called hanging valleys.
A U-shaped glacial valley
Drumlins are low rounded hills, probably formed by deposited debris.
Boulders known as erratics are sometimes deposited by glaciers.

Ice sheets

Not all glaciers are found on mountains. They also form in very cold places near the poles, such as Greenland and Antarctica. There, ice collects in huge sheets, called continental ice sheets. The ice flows outward at the edges as more snow falls and more ice forms in the middle. Parts of the glacier can be pushed right into the sea and break off, forming icebergs.

Icebergs float away into the ocean, gradually melting as they reach warmer areas.

THE EDGE OF THE SEA

The coast, where the land meets the sea, is constantly being broken down and built up by the action of waves. The ebb and flow of the tide means that the environment at the seashore is always changing. Specially adapted animals and plants make their homes there.

Internet links

Follow the links at **www.usborne.com/quicklinks** to find out more about beach and coastline formations, how erosion changes the shoreline and why tides happen.

Waves

Waves are formed far out at sea by the wind. Although they travel through water, they do not move the water itself forward. They make water particles move in circles under the surface. When a wave reaches shallow water, these circles are interrupted at the bottom and the wave breaks.

Out at sea, wind blows the surface of the ocean into waves.

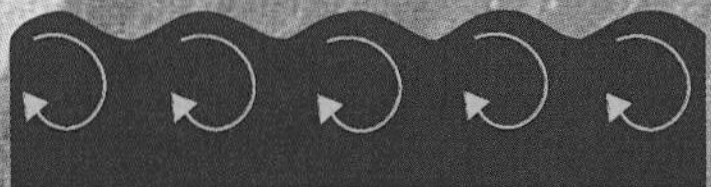

The waves make particles of water move in circular patterns under the surface.

On a shallow, flat beach, waves break before they reach the shore.

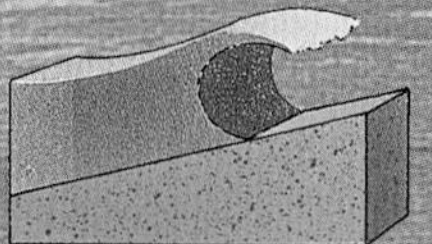

On a sloping coast, waves break at the shore and crash onto the beach.

On a very steep slope, waves do not break, but surge against the shore.

★

Coastal erosion

This archway in Dorset, England, is called Durdle Door. It was created over many years by the destructive action of waves. It started as a headland with caves on either side. The waves gradually eroded the caves until, eventually, they broke through, creating an arch.

Waves that crash onto the shore are known as destructive waves, because they gradually wear away, or erode, the coast. When they break onto beaches, they drag sand, pebbles and other debris out to sea. When they crash onto rocky cliffs, any debris they are carrying is flung against the rock, wearing it down. Waves force water and air into cracks in cliffs, carving out caves.

Destructive waves erode the coastline at different rates. Soft rock wears down quite fast, and is worn away into curved bays. Hard rock is left behind, forming cliffs and jutting pieces of land called headlands. Sometimes two caves form on either side of a headland, and the sea breaks through, leaving an arch. The arch may collapse, leaving a tower of rock called a stack.

*Tides, 341

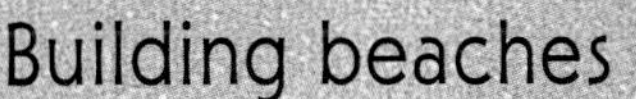

Building beaches

While destructive waves wear away parts of the coast, other waves, called constructive waves, wash up debris onto the shore, forming beaches. When a wave breaks gently onto a flat coast, it slows down and loses energy. This makes it drop any debris it may be carrying, such as pebbles and grains of sand previously broken off into the sea from cliffs and rocky shores. Over time, this deposited material builds up into a beach.

Stones and pebbles in the sea are polished and rounded by the action of the waves.

Tides

Tides* are caused by the gravity, or pulling force, of the Moon. The Moon pulls the sea slightly towards it. So, as the Earth spins, the part nearest the Moon has a high tide. There are roughly two high tides each day.

Animals and plants that live on the seashore have to be able to survive in the water at high tide, and in the air at low tide. They also have to find ways to avoid being smashed to pieces or swept away by crashing waves.

Crabs, like this rock crab, can breathe in both water and air. They have hard shells to protect them from the sea, and can burrow into the sand to hide from predators.

Coastlines

Over many years, the action of the sea changes the shapes of countries, as it builds up the land in some places and wears it away in others. Buildings near the sea sometimes fall in or get washed away as the land is gradually eroded.

For example, the coast of Holderness in Lincolnshire, England, has worn away quickly. Over 50 coastal villages listed in a national survey of towns and villages called the Domesday Book in 1086 have since been washed into the sea.

SEAS AND OCEANS

More than two-thirds of the Earth's surface is covered with salt water. The Earth's five oceans and its seas are all connected, so sea water flows freely among them. The seas and oceans, and the creatures that live in them, still hold many mysteries for scientists to explore.

The ballan wrasse fish is found mainly near rocky shores in Europe.

Under the sea

Near the land, the seabed slopes gradually downhill, forming a wide shelf called the continental shelf. At the edge of the shelf, a cliff called the continental slope drops away to the deeper part of the ocean floor, which is called the abyssal plain.

A 3-D map of part of the floor of the Atlantic Ocean

Just like the land, the abyssal plain has valleys, hills, mountains and even volcanoes. It also has ridges* where new rock is pushed out from inside the Earth, and trenches* where the Earth's crust is swallowed up again.

Exploring the sea

By studying the seabed and the creatures that live there sea scientists, called oceanographers, can find out about how the Earth was formed and how life began. Oceanographers visit the seabed in mini-submarines called submersibles, or explore it from the surface using unmanned robots called remote operated vehicles (ROVs). They also map the seabed using sonar. This sends out sounds which are bounced back as echoes, showing how deep the seabed is.

This diver is retrieving a rock from a remote operated vehicle (ROV). The ROV has returned to shallow waters after collecting rock samples from the seabed.

*Ridges, 20; trenches, 20

Life in the oceans

Seas and oceans contain a huge variety of plant and animal life, from the surface all the way down to the deepest trenches.

The loggerhead turtle lives in warm, shallow seas and comes ashore to lay its eggs.

The main food source in the sea is phytoplankton, a type of microscopic plant. Billions of phytoplankton drift near the surface of the sea, making food from sunlight, water, gases and minerals.

Part of a coral reef in the Red Sea, which lies between Egypt and Saudi Arabia

Coral reefs

Coral reefs are amazing undersea structures made of the skeletons of tiny animals called coral polyps. When old polyps die, new ones grow on top of their bodies, and over many years a huge reef builds up.

Internet links

You can explore interesting sites filled with information about the diverse life in the world's oceans by following the links at **www.usborne.com/quicklinks**

Ocean zones

The deeper down you go in the ocean, the darker and colder it is, and the fewer plants and animals are found.

Sunlit zone
Sea plants and many animals live here.

Down to 200m (650ft)

Twilight zone
Many fish, such as swordfish, survive here.

Down to 1,000m (3,300ft)

Sunless zone
Animals feed on dead food that falls from above.

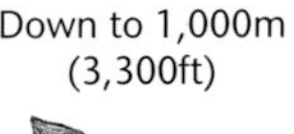

Down to 4,000m (13,100ft)

Abyssal zone
The water is cold and dark. Few creatures live here.

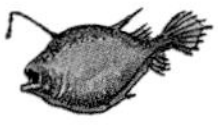

Down to 5,000m (16,400ft)

USING SEAS AND OCEANS

For thousands of years, the sea has provided people with food. We also carry passengers and goods by sea and go on trips to the coast. But the oceans are often used as a place to dump waste, which causes pollution and may endanger wildlife.

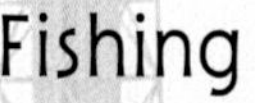

Fishing

Most sea fish are still caught using nets. There are three main types of nets. Purse seine nets are drawn closed around schools of fish that swim near the surface. Otter trawl nets are dragged along the seabed to catch fish that live there, while drift or gill nets can be used near the surface or on the seabed. Fishing boats now find schools of fish by using sonar* and satellite* technology.

Above and top right: sea bass are the most common fish caught and eaten around the world. These were caught in Tokyo Bay, Japan.

Overfishing

Because of advances in fishing technology, fishing boats are now able to catch more fish than ever before, and the number of fish in the sea is falling rapidly. International laws have now been passed to restrict the areas where fishing boats can fish and the numbers and types of fish that can be caught.

A Japanese fishing boat at work in Tokyo Bay, Japan, drawing a large net behind it.

Internet links

For links to websites to help you understand the causes of ocean pollution, go to **www.usborne.com/quicklinks**

*Satellites, 252; sonar, 70

Container ships carry all kinds of goods in large metal boxes called containers. Cranes lift the containers off the ships and transfer them to trucks or trains.

World travel

A century ago, if you wanted to travel across the sea, you had to go by boat. Huge ocean liners carried people around the world, and travel could take months.

Today, most people go long distances by plane, but boats such as ferries, hovercrafts and hydrofoils are still used for shorter distances. The only ocean liners left are cruise ships, which take people on long, relaxing sea journeys on vacations.

Shipping

Millions of different products, from oil and bananas to books and computers, are transported around the world on cargo ships. Ships travel more slowly than planes, but they can carry a lot more goods at once and are much cheaper to use.

Sea pollution

The seas and oceans are huge and can absorb and break down a lot of the waste we pump into them. For example, a lot of sewage (waste from drains and toilets) goes into the sea and is broken down naturally into harmless chemicals.

However, some waste and litter doesn't break down fast enough, and ends up polluting the seas. Plastic, for example, dropped from ships or washed off beaches, can take up to 80 years to be broken down by the sea. Chemical and radioactive waste from factories, farms and nuclear power stations* can also end up in the sea and may poison plants, fish and other animals.

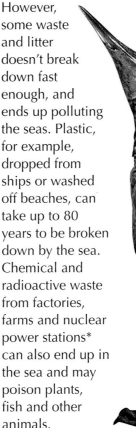

Oil tankers occasionally sink and spill the oil they are carrying. It can harm plants and animals, such as this seabird, by poisoning them or by coating them in oil so that they cannot breathe or move properly.

*Nuclear power, 27

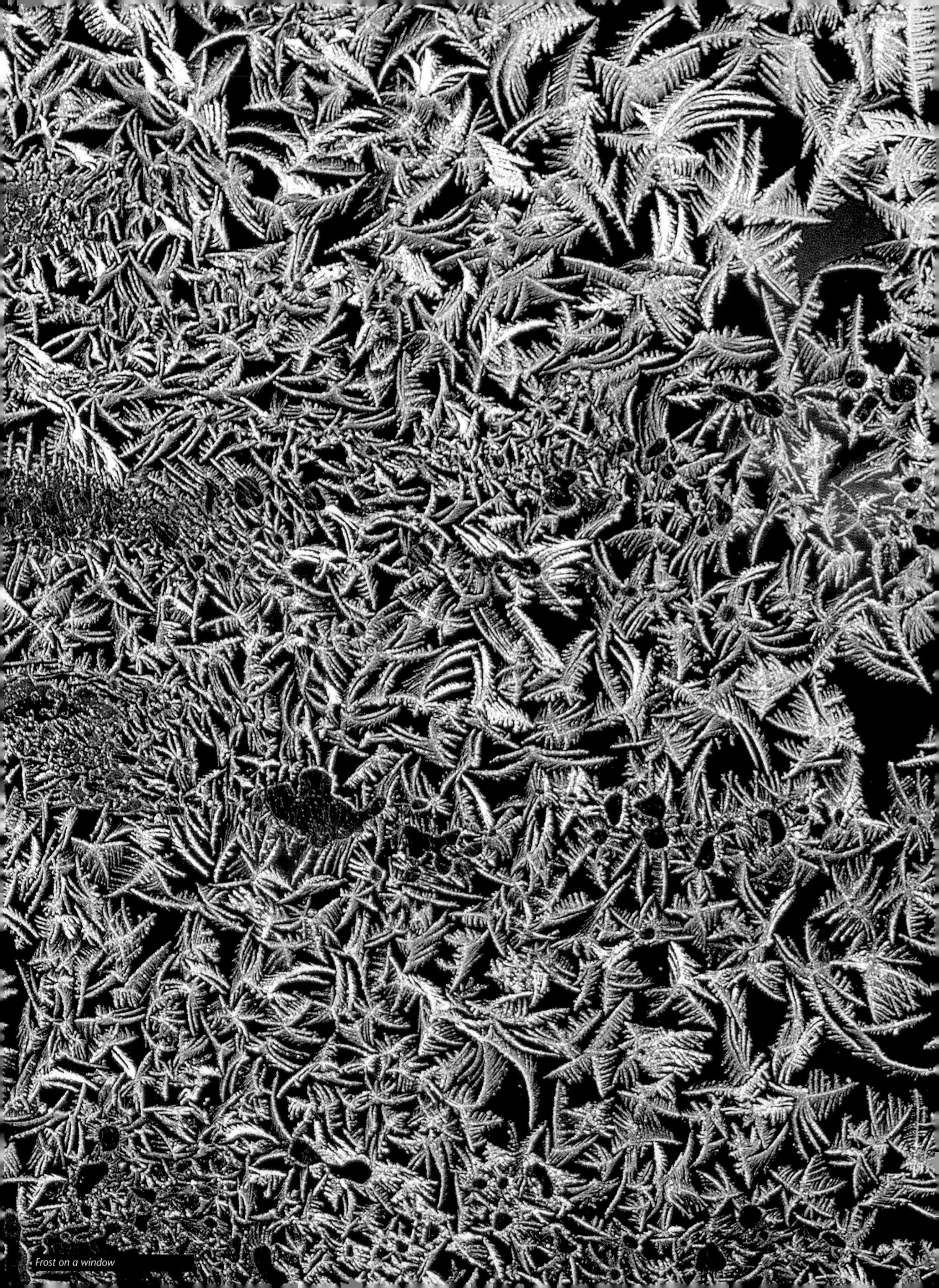

Frost on a window

WEATHER

WHAT IS WEATHER?

Weather is the way the Earth's atmosphere* behaves, whether it is hot or cold, windy or still, raining, snowing or hailing. Climate* means the overall temperature and patterns of weather in a particular place.

The importance of weather

Weather affects everyone's life. Anything from crops to summer vacations can be ruined if the weather behaves unexpectedly. Weather is also a factor in many of the world's worst disasters, such as floods, droughts and famines.

For thousands of years, people have worshipped weather gods and used rituals to try to affect the weather. But, even with modern technology, it is almost impossible to control.

Internet links

Follow the links at **www.usborne.com/quicklinks** to websites where you can learn more about different types of weather. You can also find fact files, photographs and video clips of weather around the world.

This Japanese dancer wears a special costume as part of a traditional dance which is meant to make the rain fall.

*Atmosphere, 94; climate, 100; cumulus clouds, 79; evaporation, 78

What weather is

Weather is made up of three main ingredients: temperature, the movement of the air, and the amount of water in the air.

Hot weather is caused by the Sun heating up the land and the atmosphere*. If the Sun is hidden by clouds, or if a cold wind is blowing, the temperature is cooler.

Wind is also caused by the Sun. As air gets hotter, it expands, gets less dense, and rises. A mass of colder, heavier air rushes in to replace it, making wind.

Finally, the Sun's heat makes water from plants, soil, rivers and seas evaporate* into the air. High up, this condenses into water droplets which form clouds, and may then fall as rain, snow or hail.

These factors are always changing and affecting each other. They combine to make complicated patterns, known as weather systems.

The way bees behave could help us predict the weather.

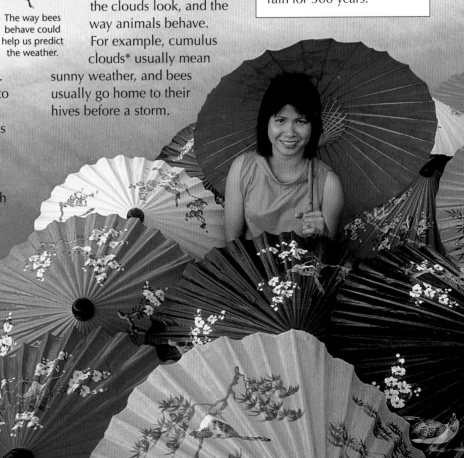

Umbrellas have been used for hundreds of years to protect people from the weather. These paper umbrellas, called parasols, help to protect people from the Sun.

Traditional signs

Cumulus clouds usually appear when the weather is warm and sunny.

Today, scientists can predict the weather using satellites and computers. But before these were invented, people predicted the weather by observing signs, such as the way the clouds look, and the way animals behave. For example, cumulus clouds* usually mean sunny weather, and bees usually go home to their hives before a storm.

Weather facts

- The heaviest hailstones, weighing up to 1kg (2lb 2oz), fell in Gopalganj, Bangladesh, in 1986.
- The wettest place in the world is Mawsynram, India. It gets nearly 12m (40ft) of rain a year.
- The biggest recorded snowflakes were 38cm (15in) across and fell on Montana, U.S.A., in 1887.
- The driest place in the world is the Atacama Desert, Chile. In some spots, there has been no rain for 500 years.

WATER AND CLOUDS

The amount of water on Earth doesn't change, but water changes its state as it moves in a cycle. It exists as a liquid (water) in seas, rivers and cloud droplets, it freezes into a solid (ice) as snow and hail, and it exists as an invisible gas in the air.

Snowflakes form when water droplets freeze into ice crystals. These snowflakes have been tinted so you can see their six-sided shapes more clearly.

The water cycle

When water is heated up, it changes from a liquid into an invisible gas. This process is called evaporation.

The Sun's heat causes water to evaporate from rivers, lakes and seas. Plants suck up water from the ground and it escapes from their leaves as a gas. Similarly, people and animals breathe out water as a gas.

As the gas molecules rise, they get cooler. This makes the water condense, or turn into liquid again, to form tiny droplets which can be seen as clouds. As the cloud droplets move around they collide with each other and grow bigger. When they are heavy enough, they fall as rain, and the water flows back into rivers, lakes and seas. This process is known as the water cycle.

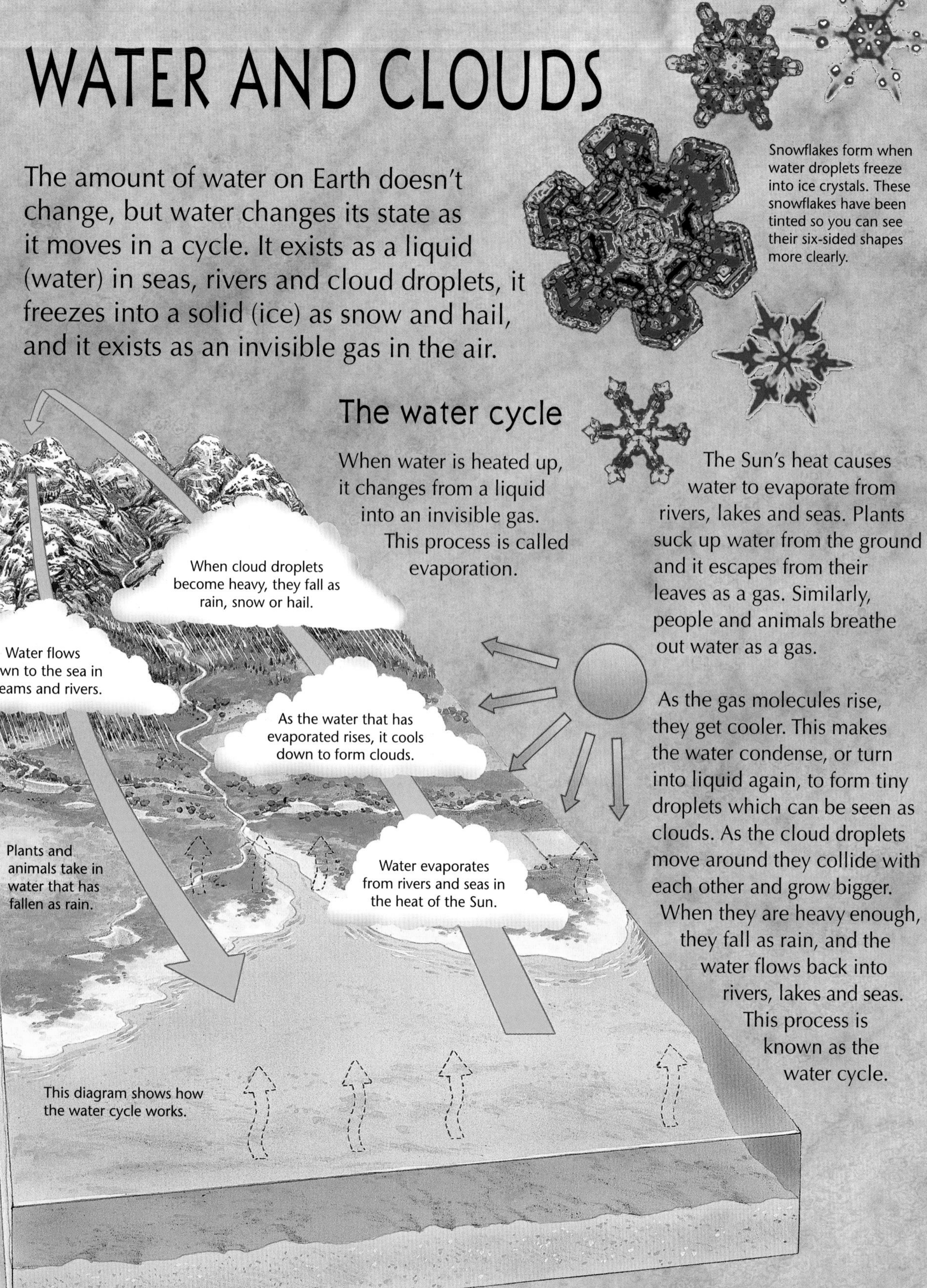

When cloud droplets become heavy, they fall as rain, snow or hail.
Water flows down to the sea in streams and rivers.
As the water that has evaporated rises, it cools down to form clouds.
Plants and animals take in water that has fallen as rain.
Water evaporates from rivers and seas in the heat of the Sun.

This diagram shows how the water cycle works.

Clouds

The way clouds look depends on how much the air is moving up and down and how much water is in them. When clouds form in calm air, they spread out in sheets. On hot days, they puff up into heaps, following the rising air. Clouds full of big droplets look darker.

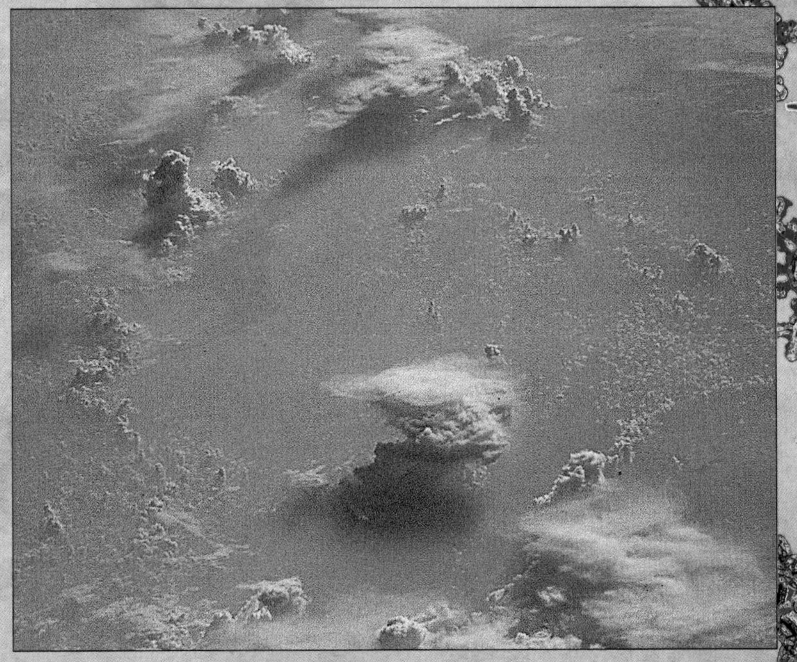

These tall, piled-up cumulonimbus clouds were photographed over the Gulf of Mexico. A cumulonimbus cloud is freezing at the top, but warmer at the bottom.

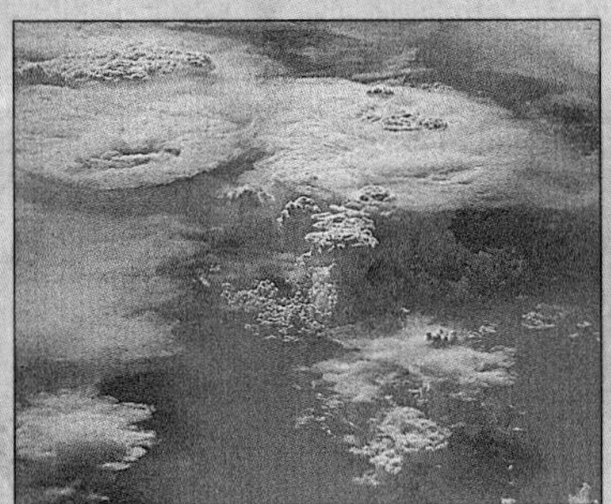

Cumulus clouds look like white, puffy heaps. They often form high in the sky in warm sunny weather.

Stratus clouds form low, flat layers and often block out the sunshine.

Cirrus clouds are high and wispy. (The word cirrus means "like wispy hair" in Latin.)

Precipitation

Water that falls onto the Earth's surface is called precipitation. Rain is the most common kind. There are many types of rain, from light drizzle to monsoon rains*. In freezing weather, precipitation sometimes takes the form of snow or hail instead of raindrops.

This diagram shows how hailstones are formed.

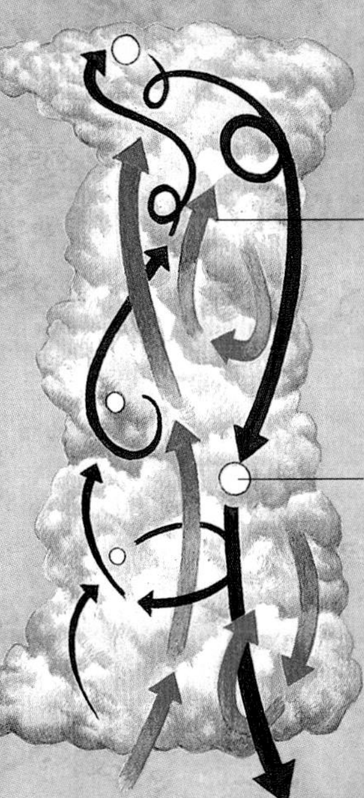

Hail begins as ice crystals in giant cumulonimbus clouds.
Air currents push the crystals up and around inside the cloud.
As they move, the crystals bump into water droplets, which freeze around them in layers, like the layers of an onion.
The layers of ice build up until they form heavy hailstones, which fall to Earth.

Internet links

Follow the links at **www.usborne.com/quicklinks** to read descriptions of different types of clouds.

*Monsoons, 120

THUNDERSTORMS

Sometimes in warm weather, huge storm clouds form very quickly. These clouds are full of water and fast-moving air currents. They can build up a store of electricity powerful enough to make lightning and thunder.

Internet links

For links to websites with animations that explain why lightning happens and what causes the bright flash, go to **www.usborne.com/quicklinks**

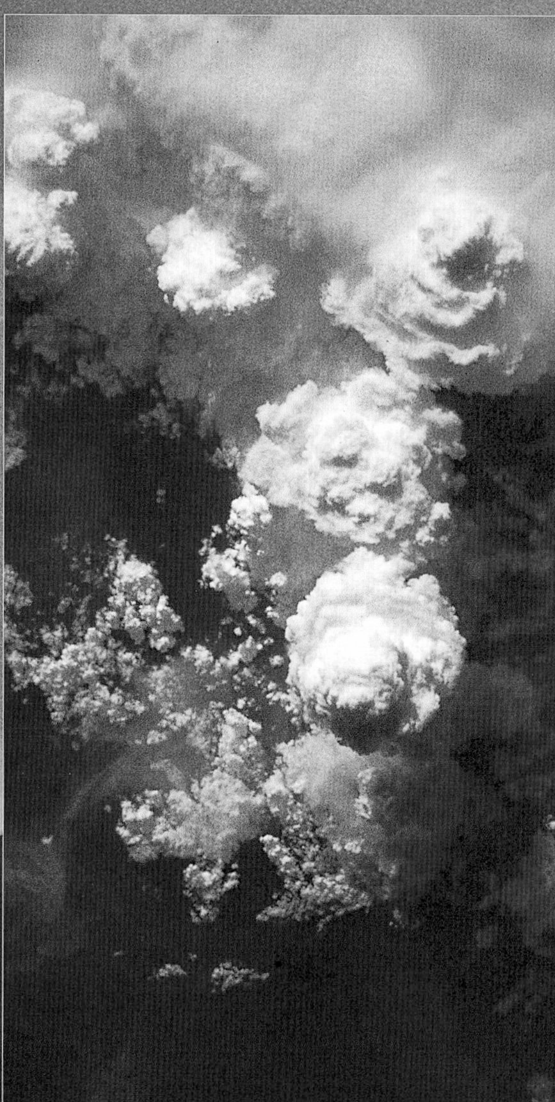

Electric clouds

In hot, damp weather, the evaporated water in the air rises very fast. When it hits the colder air above, tall, piled-up clouds called cumulonimbus clouds form.

Inside the cloud, water droplets and ice crystals rub together in the swirling air. This rubbing causes the crystals and droplets to build up a strong electric charge. Some have a negative charge (-) and some have a positive charge (+). Negative charges collect at the bottom of the cloud, making a huge energy difference between the cloud and the ground, which has a positive charge.

The difference builds up so much that it has to be equalized. A giant spark jumps between the bottom of the cloud and the ground, allowing the different charges to even out. The spark appears as a flash of lightning.

The satellite photograph on the left shows piled-up cumulonimbus storm clouds viewed from above.

Lightning zigzags through the air as it finds the easiest path from the cloud to the ground.

Ball lightning is a very rare kind of lightning which appears as a small, floating ball of bright light. It can travel through walls and has been seen inside buildings and aircraft.

Lightning

When lightning strikes, it travels first downward, then upward. The first stroke, called the leader stroke, is invisible. It jumps from the cloud to the ground. This creates a path for the main stroke, which sparks from the ground back up to the cloud.

The main stroke contains so much energy that it heats up the air around it. The heat makes the air expand quickly, causing an explosion. This is the loud noise of thunder.

Struck by lightning

Lightning always travels the shortest distance it can between a cloud and the ground. So it usually strikes high places, tall buildings or prominent objects such as trees or people.

Lightning quickly heats up whatever it strikes. When a tree is struck, the water in the tree boils instantly and turns into steam, which makes the trunk explode. But although lightning is dangerous, being struck is very rare. You can stay safe by avoiding trees and open spaces during storms.

WINDSTORMS

Because of the way the world spins, wind doesn't flow in straight lines, but swirls into spirals. Sometimes, wind spirals grow into terrifying storms, such as hurricanes and tornadoes, which contain the fastest wind speeds on Earth.

A satellite picture of the hurricane Typhoon Odessa

Coriolis effect

Winds are caused by high-pressure air rushing toward low-pressure areas, called cyclones. But instead of moving straight into the cyclone, the air circles around it in a spiral. This is called the Coriolis effect, and it happens because the spinning of the Earth always pushes winds to one side.

Hurricanes

Hurricanes are very powerful windstorms that can be hundreds of miles wide and last up to ten days. They only form in warm, wet conditions, usually over the sea in tropical areas near the Equator. No one knows exactly what makes a hurricane start.

The warm, wet air has a very low pressure, so cooler winds spiral toward it.

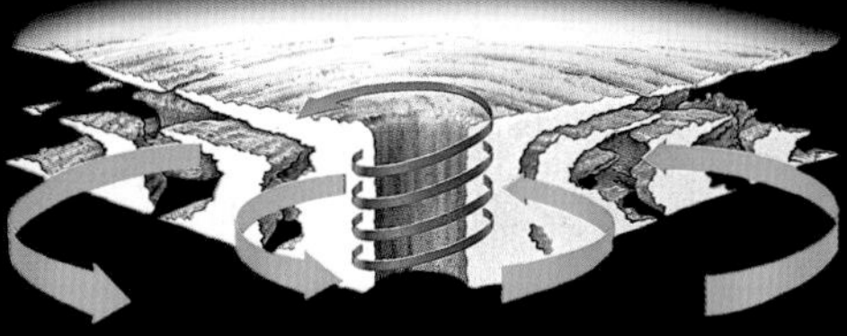

The damp air rises higher and condenses into thick clouds. They are blown into a spiral by the wind.

After hurricanes form, they sometimes hit land and cause massive damage. Winds of up to 240kph (150mph) destroy buildings and rip trees out of the ground. But hurricanes die down soon after they hit land, as there is not enough moisture to keep them going.

Tornadoes

Tornadoes are much smaller than hurricanes, but they can be even more dangerous. Tornadoes form during violent thunderstorms, when a hot, fast-moving upward air current meets a cold, downward air current. Because of the Coriolis effect, the hot and cold currents spiral around each other into a tight funnel of clouds.

The wind inside a tornado's funnel can be as fast as 480kph (300mph), the fastest wind speeds measured on Earth. Where the funnel touches the ground, it can be up to 500m (1,640ft) wide. It roars across the land, dragging people, animals and even cars into the air. Most tornadoes only last a few minutes.

Internet links

Visit the sites suggested at **www.usborne.com/quicklinks** to watch video clips of hurricanes and tornadoes, find out how they form and how they are tracked by satellites.

A tornado looks like a huge black or grey trunk, twisting from the thunderclouds down to the ground.

Tornado Alley

Some places have frequent thunderstorms and lots of tornadoes. Part of the U.S.A., between Texas and Illinois, has so many that it is known as Tornado Alley. The worst tornado ever recorded there hit Ellington, Missouri, on March 18, 1925. It lasted 3½ hours, destroyed four towns and killed 689 people.

Waterspouts

When a tornado moves over the sea a narrow column of swirling water droplets reaches into the clouds above. These tornadoes are called waterspouts (though not much water is actually sucked up from the sea). Sailors used to think they were sea monsters.

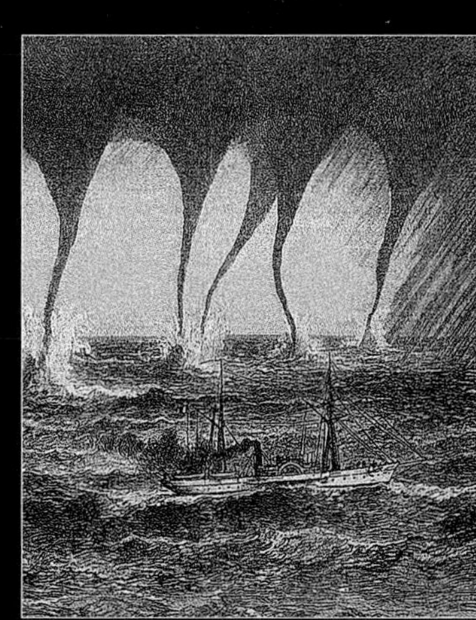

This 19th-century engraving shows monstrous waterspouts.

FLOODS AND DROUGHTS

Plants, animals and people need water to survive, and they rely on the weather to bring it to them. If there is too little rain, rivers dry up and crops fail. On the other hand, too much rain causes floods, which can damage crops and buildings and wash away precious soil.

Wet and dry

Some parts of the world always have more rain than others, and many places have wet and dry seasons. Rainy and dry periods like these are not usually a problem if they are regular, but too much or too little rain can be dangerous when unexpected weather changes take people by surprise.

This picture shows terrible flooding in Vietnam. People are forced to use boats to get around.

Too much rain

Normally, rainfall soaks into the ground or flows away in streams and rivers. Floods happen when there is suddenly too much water for the ground to hold, and streams, rivers and drains overflow. The extra water can come from rain, brought by heavy storms, from ice and snow on mountains melting and flowing into streams and rivers, or even from the sea spilling onto the land.

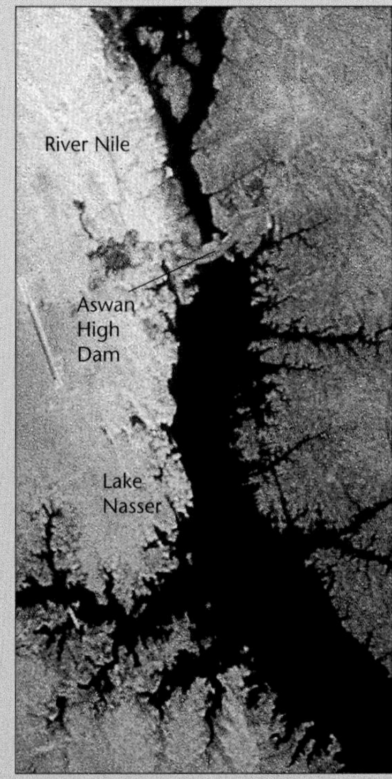

The Aswan High Dam enables people to control the flooding of the River Nile. When the river floods, it waters the land, making it fertile (good for growing crops) without causing destruction.

Dirt and disease

Floods are very dangerous. As well as drowning people and animals and destroying homes and crops, floods can actually cause water shortages. They cover the land with dirty water, contaminating clean water supplies and helping diseases to spread.

Lack of rain can make soil harden, crack into lumps, and eventually crumble into dry dust.

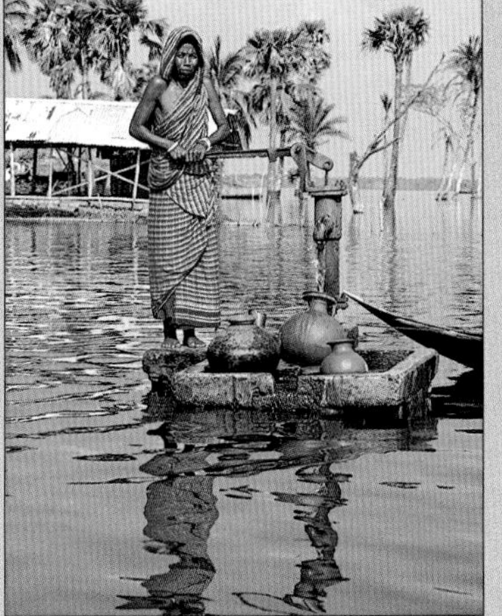

This pump is an important source of clean water, but the dirty floodwater surrounding it could contaminate the water supply.

Not enough rain

A drought happens when there is less than the expected amount of rain. Droughts are often hard to predict, but they usually happen when winds change direction and no rain clouds are blown over the land. Droughts can happen in almost all climates. A bad drought may last several years and make the land completely infertile. The effects of drought can be much worse if the land has not been used carefully.

Internet links

You can read about the disastrous effects of drought and flood in different areas of the world by visiting the websites suggested at **www.usborne.com/quicklinks**

FREEZING AND FRYING

This woman is carrying frozen milk home. It is so cold in Siberia, where she lives, that there's no danger of the milk melting.

The temperature on Earth can range from a bone-numbing -88°C (-127°F), measured at Vostok in Antarctica, to an unbearably hot 56.7°C (134°F), recorded in Death Valley, California, USA. Extreme hot and cold weather can be deadly, and often has strange effects on people and places.

World of ice

Ice storms are caused by rain falling onto very cold surfaces. They happen when a mass of warm air passes through a cold area in winter, bringing rain that falls in the form of liquid raindrops, instead of snow or hail. But when the drops of water hit cold surfaces, they immediately freeze into a coating of solid ice. Ice storms are beautiful, but lethal. If enough rain falls, outdoor surfaces can get covered in a layer of ice up to 15cm (6in) thick. It makes roads hazardous to drive on and builds up on rooftops until they cave in. The ice also weighs down power lines until they snap. People can freeze to death in their homes.

This branch was caught in an ice storm that hit Kingston, Canada, in 1998.

Blizzards

Blizzards are a combination of heavy snow, strong winds and cold temperatures. They are especially dangerous because blizzard victims are blinded by the swirling snow, and they can be caught in the freezing cold.

Internet links

Find links to websites where you can learn more about the hottest and coldest places on Earth and what everyday life is like there, by visiting **www.usborne.com/quicklinks**

Heatwaves

A heatwave is a period of extra-hot weather. Heatwaves are caused by a combination of factors. Usually, a lack of wind and cloud allows the Sun to heat up the land and the atmosphere much more than normal. The hotter the air is, the more moisture it can hold as a gas. This makes the air very humid, which makes it feel "sticky".

In some hot places, people have siestas – they sleep during the hottest part of the day to avoid the Sun.

This Egyptian boy's white clothes reflect the Sun's rays and help to keep him cool in hot weather.

Heatstroke

Heatstroke is usually caused by staying out in the sun too long. Normally, if you get too hot, your body sweats. The sweat evaporating from your skin helps you cool down. But heatstroke stops your body from sweating so that you get much too hot, and may go into a coma.

Heatstroke can happen quickly, especially inside a car, where the windows act like a greenhouse and stop heat from escaping. This is why animals and babies should never be left inside cars on hot days.

Sun and skin

Although the Sun provides warmth and energy, direct sunlight can be bad for you. It can cause wrinkles, sunburn and even skin cancer.

This poster advises Australians to slip on T-shirts, slop on sunscreen and slap on hats

Hot and bothered

Hot weather can affect how we behave. For example, statistics show that in New York, U.S.A., the murder rate rises as the temperature goes up, and most big riots start on hot, humid nights. No one is sure why heat makes people angry.

This riot took place in the hot city of Los Angeles, in western U.S.A., in 1992.

Unusual, extreme weather, often called freak weather, can take people by surprise. Sometimes it can be so odd it doesn't seem like weather at all. Strange lights in the sky, clouds that look like UFOs, and even showers of frogs, are all natural weather phenomena.

Lenticular clouds are shaped by waves of wind blowing around mountaintops. This one was seen at Mauna Kea, Hawaii, U.S.A.

Weather beliefs

When strange weather strikes, people often think they're seeing something magical or supernatural. Weather may lie behind many traditional beliefs in fairies and ghosts, and also behind sightings of UFOs. One type of cloud, called a lenticular cloud, looks exactly like a flying saucer.

Strange lights

The aurora borealis and aurora australis light up the sky around the poles with blue, red, green and white patterns. They are caused by streams of electrical particles which come from the Sun. When they interact with the gases in the Earth's atmosphere, they release energy which lights up the sky.

A solar flare is a storm on the Sun that sends electrical particles out into space, causing auroras on Earth.

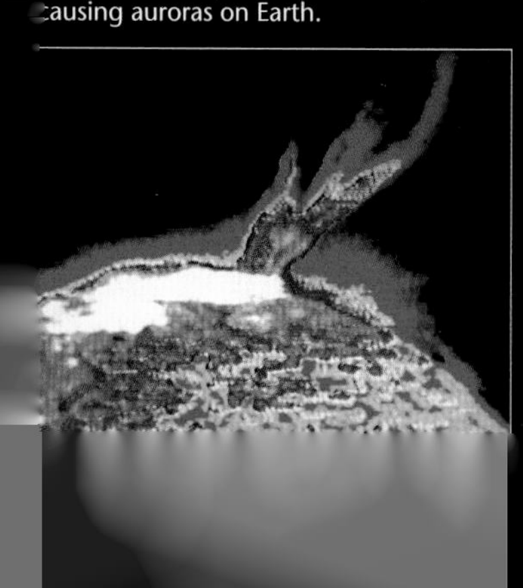

The aurora borealis appears in the northern skies, and is sometimes called the Northern Lights

Raining frogs

"Rain" consisting of animals, fish or other objects has been reported many times through the centuries. The Roman historian Pliny reported a shower of frogs almost 2,000 years ago and in the fourth century, fish fell on a town in Greece for three days. During a storm in England in 1939, so many frogs fell that witnesses were afraid to walk around in case they squashed them.

Showers like this, also known as "skyfalls", are probably caused by tornadoes* sucking up animals from ponds and rivers. Frogs are most often reported, but there have also been showers of snails, maggots, worms, pebbles and even sheep.

The common frog, a species seen falling from the sky.

This magazine from May 1958 shows a skyfall of frogs which had recently been reported.

> **Internet links**
> To see clips of auroras and find out about weather folklore and legends, follow the links at **www.usborne.com/quicklinks**

Big waves

Freak waves are one of the most dangerous types of unusual weather, though not all big waves are freak waves. Freak waves can appear from nowhere, even in calm conditions. Scientists think big waves like this may form when several smaller waves merge together. These waves are especially dangerous because people are not prepared for them.

*Tornadoes, 83

WEATHER FORECASTING

Weather often seems random but, by careful observation, meteorologists (weather scientists) can learn how weather behaves and how to predict it. Radar and satellites* help them to track clouds and watch weather patterns from space.

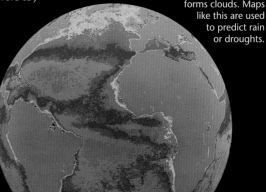

This satellite image shows the temperature of the sea. Water evaporates from warm areas (shown in pink) and forms clouds. Maps like this are used to predict rain or droughts.

Measuring weather

Meteorologists measure different aspects of the weather, such as temperature, atmospheric pressure* and the amount of rainfall, at weather stations around the world. Weather balloons and weather planes carry instruments into the sky, where they can track the movements of clouds and high-altitude winds.

Weather technology

Weather satellites have been used since about 1960 to record the Earth's weather from space. From their positions in orbit above the Earth, satellites can take photographs and measure the temperature of the Earth's surface.

Geostationary satellites, like the weather satellite shown here, hover 36,000km (22,370 miles) above the Equator.

On the ground, radar equipment is used to detect cloud patterns. Radar waves are sent out, bounce off raindrops and are collected by giant radar dishes. Computers collect the signals and create maps which show where rain clouds are heading.

*Atmospheric pressure, 96; satellites, 252

Predicting weather

To forecast weather, readings from weather stations and satellites are stored in powerful computers. The data can then be examined to detect patterns and make predictions. At the moment, meteorologists can only predict weather a few days in advance. Weather can change so quickly that the forecasts are sometimes wrong.

Internet links

You can look up weather forecasts for places all around the world by visiting the websites suggested at **www.usborne.com/quicklinks**

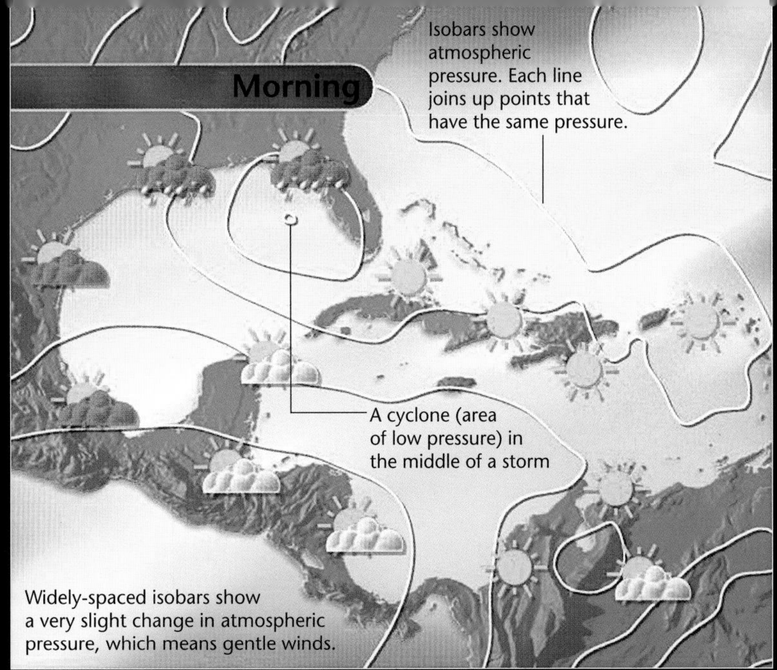

Morning
Isobars show atmospheric pressure. Each line joins up points that have the same pressure.
A cyclone (area of low pressure) in the middle of a storm
Widely-spaced isobars show a very slight change in atmospheric pressure, which means gentle winds.

Weather maps use lines called isobars to show differences in atmospheric pressure*, and symbols to indicate sunshine, rain and snow.

A digital photograph of Hurricane Gordon taken by a crewmember aboard the Space Shuttle Atlantis, in September 2006.

Autumn in the Cache National Forest, Idaho, U.S.A.

CLIMATE

THE EARTH'S ATMOSPHERE

Surrounding the Earth is a blanket of gases which makes up its atmosphere. The atmosphere contains the air we need to breathe. It also affects weather and climate and protects us from extremes of temperature and from the Sun's harmful rays.

The atmosphere's structure

The gases surrounding the Earth are held by its gravity, a force which attracts things to Earth. The atmosphere is divided into layers according to the temperature of these gases. The diagram below shows the different layers.

This diagram shows some of the layers in the Earth's atmosphere. The outermost layer, the exosphere, is not marked; it is around 500km (310 miles) from Earth.

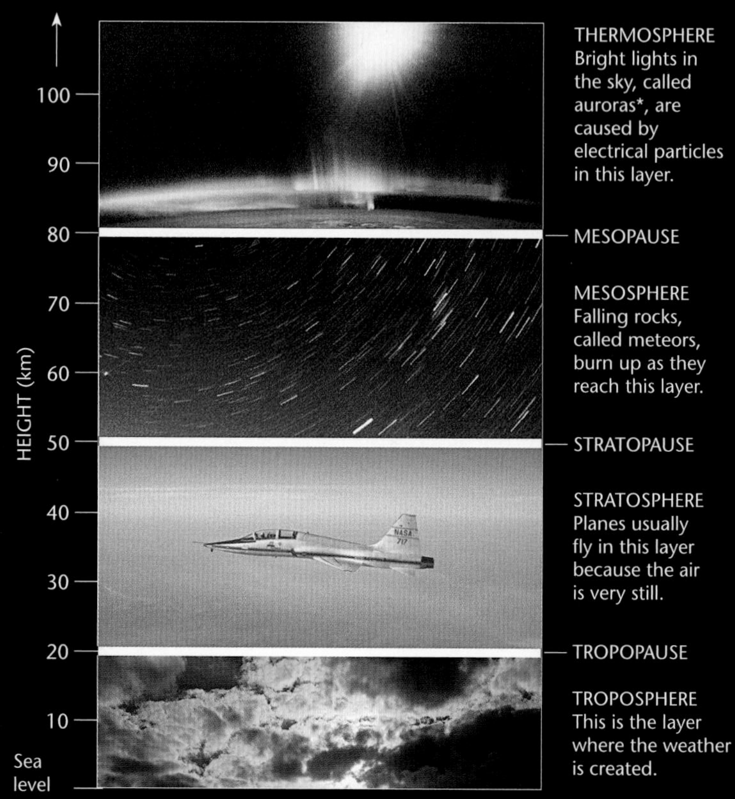

HEIGHT (km)
100
90
80
70
60
50
40
30
20
10
Sea level
THERMOSPHERE Bright lights in the sky, called auroras*, are caused by electrical particles in this layer.
MESOPAUSE
MESOSPHERE Falling rocks, called meteors, burn up as they reach this layer.
STRATOPAUSE
STRATOSPHERE Planes usually fly in this layer because the air is very still.
TROPOPAUSE
TROPOSPHERE This is the layer where the weather is created.

The troposphere

The troposphere is the layer of the atmosphere nearest to the Earth's surface. As well as a mixture of gases, this layer contains clouds, dust and pollution. It extends to between 10km (6 miles) and 20km (12 miles) from the Earth. Temperatures are high near the Earth because the air is heated from below by the Earth's surface, which is warmed by the Sun. Higher up, the air is thinner and can't hold as much heat, so temperatures decrease.

The troposphere is the layer where the weather is produced. It gets its name from the Greek word *tropos* which means "a turn". This is because the air there is constantly circulating*.

KLM

*Air currents, 96; auroras, 88

The stratosphere

The upper limit of the stratosphere is around 50km (30 miles) from the Earth's surface. The stratosphere contains a concentration of ozone gas. This layer of ozone gas is very important, as it absorbs ultraviolet rays from the Sun which can cause skin cancer.

The mesosphere

The mesosphere reaches to a height of around 80km (50 miles). Temperatures there are the coolest in the atmosphere because there is very little ozone, dust or clouds to absorb energy from the Sun. It is warmer at the bottom as there is more ozone there.

The thermosphere

Temperatures in the thermosphere can be extremely high, reaching up to 1,500°C (2,732°F). This is because there is a high proportion of a gas called atomic oxygen. This gets warmed as it absorbs energy from the Sun.

The ozone layer

The layer of ozone gas in the stratosphere is being damaged by chemicals called chlorofluorocarbons (CFCs), which are used in some spray cans and refrigerators. At certain times of year, a hole in the ozone layer appears over Antarctica, and in other areas the ozone layer becomes very thin. This damage means that more of the Sun's harmful ultraviolet rays reach the Earth's surface.

The bright pink areas in this picture show a hole in the layer of ozone gas over Antarctica.

Internet links

To find out more about the ozone layer, why we need it and how we can stop damaging it, follow the links at **www.usborne.com/quicklinks**

When you fly in a plane in the stratosphere you can often see the clouds in the troposphere below.

AIR AND OCEAN CURRENTS

As the Sun heats the Earth, it causes air and water to move around in the form of currents. As particles of air and water are heated, they first expand and rise and then they cool and fall, producing patterns of circulating air and water, which are crucial in determining climate.

The circular shapes on the satellite image in the background are called spiral eddies. They are swirls of water that have separated from the main band, or current, of water.

Moving air

The air around us is constantly pushing in every direction. The force that it exerts is known as atmospheric pressure.

The movement of air is affected by temperature. The Sun heats up the land and oceans, which in turn heat the air directly above in the troposphere*. As the air is heated, it rises and so leaves behind an area of low pressure. When the air cools, it sinks down on the Earth's surface in a different area, causing high pressure.

Because the Sun doesn't heat up the world evenly, there are differences of pressure. Where there is a difference, air flows from high to low pressure areas in order to even out the pressure. This moving air is wind. As the air moves, the spinning of the Earth causes it to be deflected sideways. This deflection is known as the Coriolis effect*.

Global winds

Air is constantly circulating between the tropics and the poles as global winds. Warm air flows from the tropics and displaces the cold air at the poles, which then flows back toward the tropics. Global winds form because areas near the Equator receive more heat from the Sun than other areas. As the air is heated, it rises and spreads out. When it cools, it sinks at around 30° north and south of the Equator. This increases pressure at the Earth's surface and air at the base of the atmosphere is forced outward in the direction of both the Equator and the poles. The surface air currents moving toward the Equator are called the trade winds.

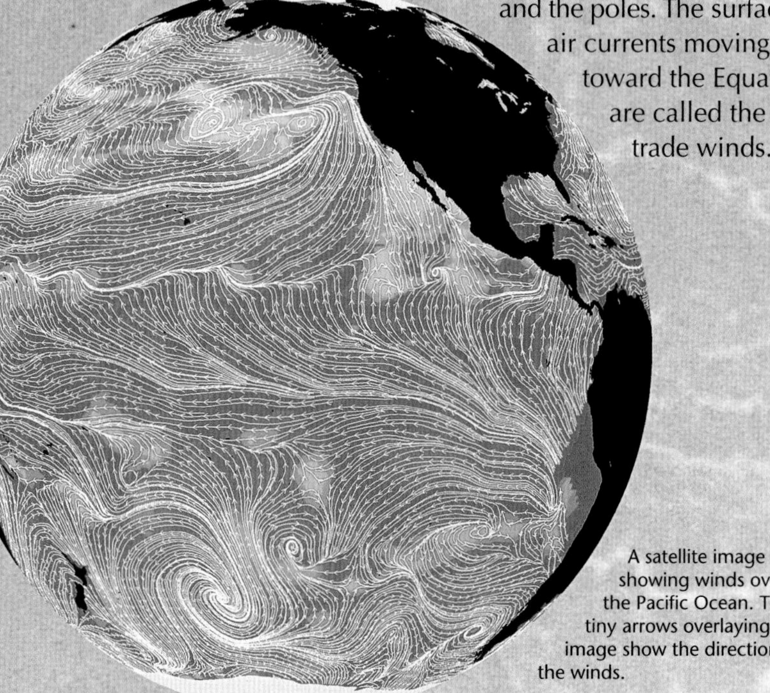

A satellite image showing winds over the Pacific Ocean. The tiny arrows overlaying the image show the direction of the winds.

Coriolis effect, 82; troposphere, 94

Moving water

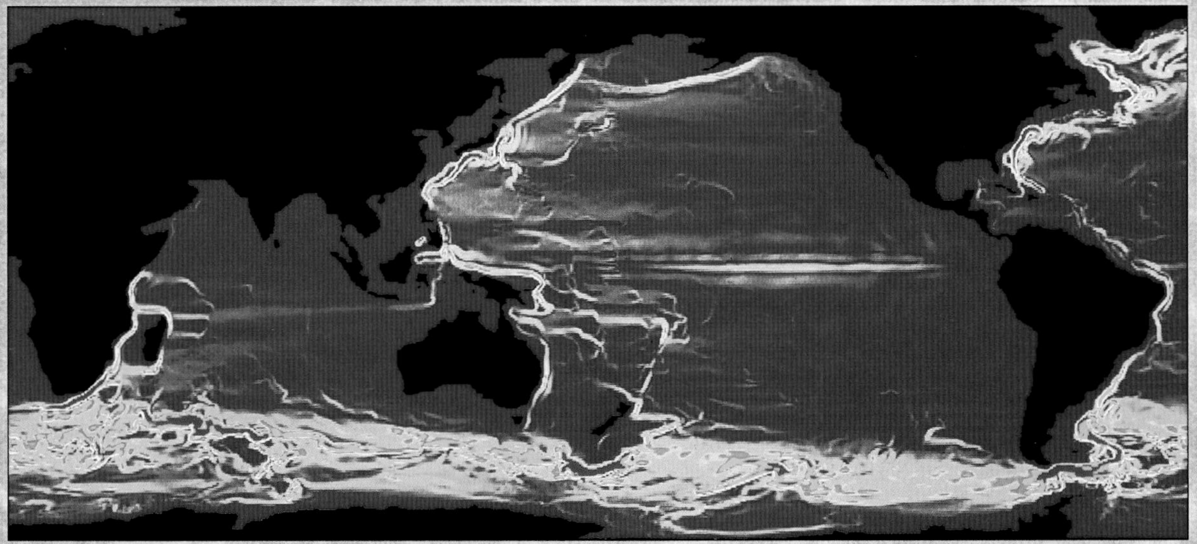

This image shows ocean currents around the world. The red areas are fast currents and the light blue areas are slow currents.

Ocean currents are wide bands of water, like rivers that flow in the world's oceans. They sweep around the oceans, moving water between hot and cold places.

Heat from the Sun also causes the movement of water in the form of currents. However, in the oceans, the temperature difference between the poles and the Equator is greater than it is on land. Near the Equator, the Sun's rays penetrate far below the ocean's surface. At the poles, the Sun's rays hit the water at a shallow angle. This causes the water to act like a mirror, reflecting rather than absorbing the Sun's rays.

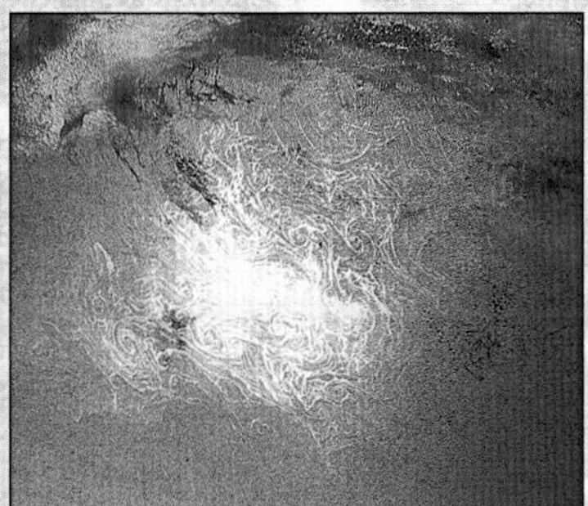

A satellite picture of part of the Gulf Stream, a current of warm water that flows in the Atlantic Ocean

Internet links

You can learn more about different air and ocean currents, and about El Niño and how it could affect the area where you live, by visiting the websites recommended at **www.usborne.com/quicklinks**

Effects of currents

Currents vary in temperature and move at different speeds. If a current is much warmer or cooler than the surrounding water, it can dramatically affect the climates of the nearby coastal areas. A warm current called the Gulf Stream, which runs between the Gulf of Mexico and Europe, brings a mild climate to northwest Europe.

El Niño

The incredible effect that the warming of the ocean can have on weather and climate is illustrated by a phenomenon known as El Niño. Every few years, a current of water in the Pacific, off the northwest coast of South America, suddenly becomes warmer. Scientists are not sure why it happens, but it causes a chain of climatic changes around the world, including floods and severe storms.

NATURAL CYCLES

Some substances, such as nitrogen and carbon, are constantly changing form as they move around in huge cycles. This exchange of substances is essential to life on Earth. The air, land, water, plants, animals, and even your own body, all form a part of these cycles.

This magnified part of a pea plant contains bacteria which convert nitrogen from the air into a form the plant can use.

Keeping a balance

Living things take in substances such as oxygen, nitrogen, carbon and water from the world around them through food, soil and air. They use them to live and grow. When a plant or animal dies and decays, its body is broken down and gases are released into the air. The cycle continues, with these substances being used again and again. This process maintains the balance of gases in the air.

The nitrogen cycle

This diagram shows some of the different forms that nitrogen takes.

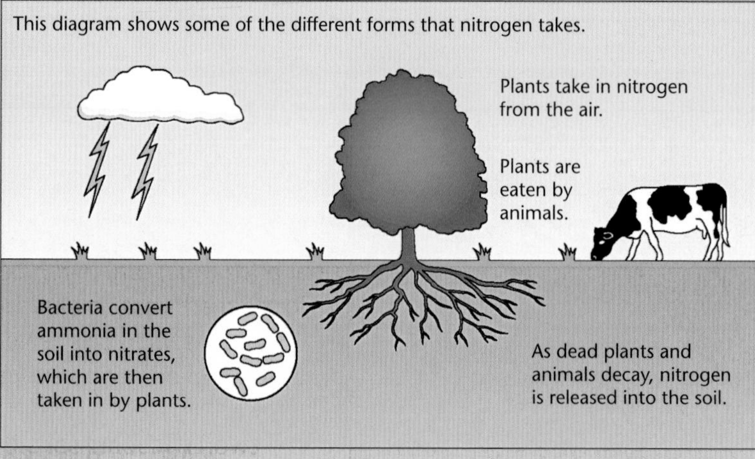

Plants take in nitrogen from the air.
Plants are eaten by animals.
Bacteria convert ammonia in the soil into nitrates, which are then taken in by plants.
As dead plants and animals decay, nitrogen is released into the soil.

Nitrogen (chemical symbol – N) makes up 78% of the air. Plants and animals need it for growth. Plants take in nitrogen from the air and the soil. Bacteria convert the substance into a form the plants can use. Animals obtain nitrogen by eating plants or by eating animals that have eaten plants. When plants and animals die and decay, fungi and bacteria break down their remains and nitrogen is released back into the soil.

This dung beetle is feeding on animal dung. Insects like this help to break down plant and animal matter.

One form that carbon can take is charcoal, as shown here. Charcoal can be burned as a fuel. When it is burned, it gives out carbon dioxide.

The carbon cycle

Carbon forms part of the gases in the air, mainly as carbon dioxide (chemical symbol – CO_2), which is a compound of carbon and oxygen. Plants take in CO_2 from the air and use it to make food. At night, they give out CO_2.

Animals obtain carbon by eating plants. They release carbon in their waste and when they breathe out. CO_2 is also released when plants and animals die and decay. Carbon can be stored in the form of fossilized remains. Eventually these form fossil fuels* such as coal and oil, which release CO_2 when burned.

This diagram shows some of the different forms that carbon takes.

When fossil fuels are burned, carbon dioxide is released.

Plants take in carbon dioxide from the air to help them make food. At night, they give out carbon dioxide.

When dead plants and animals decay, carbon dioxide is released into the air.

Animals take in carbon when they eat plants. They breathe out carbon dioxide.

Upsetting cycles

Left alone, these cycles create a natural balance of gases. However, human activities interfere with this balance by adding waste and pollution to the atmosphere. The effects of human disruption on the carbon cycle are described on pages 102 to 103.

When farmers harvest crops, they break the nitrogen cycle because the plants are not allowed to decay naturally. Farmers often use a chemical fertilizer* to replace nitrates in soil. If too much is added, it can seep through the soil into rivers, where it can affect plants and animals.

The algae in this canal are thriving because of excess nitrates running into the canal from fertilizer used on nearby farmland.

Internet links

Visit **www.usborne.com/quicklinks** and follow the links to find out more about the importance of the nitrogen cycle.

*Fertilizer, 30; fossil fuels, 26

WORLD CLIMATES

The long-term or typical pattern of weather in a particular area is known as its climate. Climates vary enormously in different parts of the world. They determine the character of an area, affecting the plants, animals and people that live there.

This map of the Earth's surface contains information from several different satellites*. It shows some of the main climate types around the world.

Maple trees grow in temperate regions.

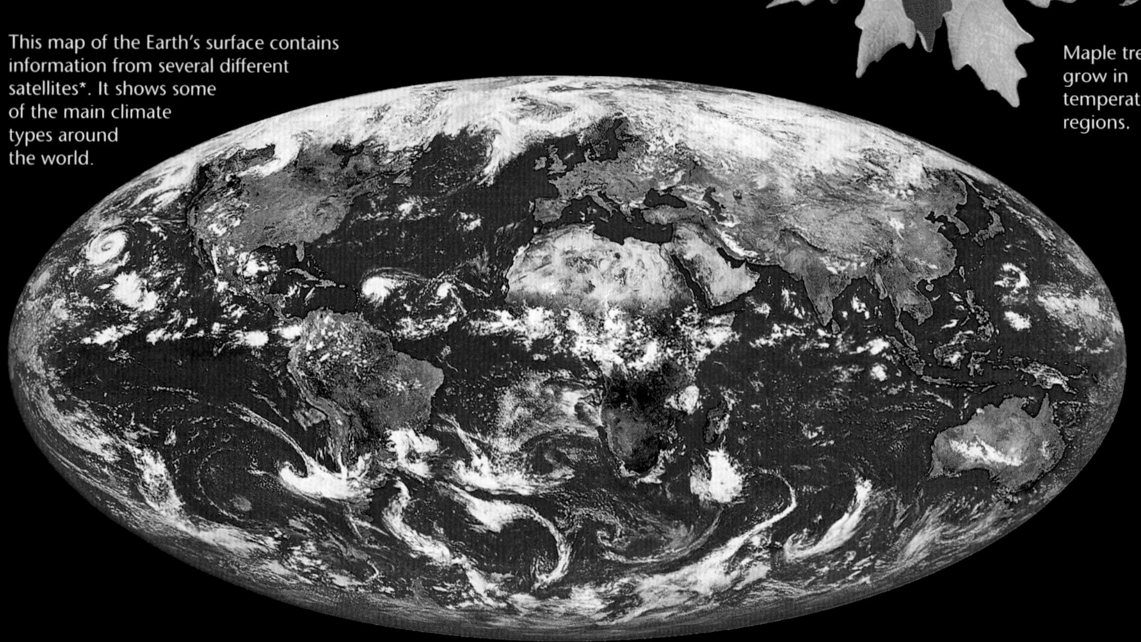

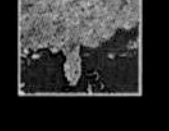

Temperate and tropical regions are green. They contain lots of vegetation.

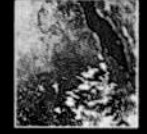

Tropical grasslands and deserts are yellow and brown. They are dry, with little vegetation.

Snowy regions are light blue or white. The swirling white masses are clouds.

Climate types

Areas can be grouped into several main climate types, such as polar, temperate and tropical. These are also known as biomes*. The most important factor in determining an area's climate is its latitude*, because this affects the amount of heat received from the Sun. This in turn has a crucial effect on the vegetation and animals which give each climate zone its distinctive characteristics.

The map above shows how areas at the same latitude share broadly similar climates. The different climate zones are described in more detail on pages 116–131.

Other factors, such as height and distance from the ocean, are also very important in determining the climate of a particular area.

*Biomes, 113, latitude, 250, satellites, 252

High places

Mountain regions have a different climate from the surrounding lowland areas. It rains and snows frequently, as the mountains force clouds to rise higher. Temperatures can be extremely cold because mountain air is thinner and can't hold as much heat.

> **Internet links**
>
> For links to websites where you can learn about the different climates around the world, go to **www.usborne.com/quicklinks**

Land and sea

Climate is affected by the oceans. Places near the sea have a maritime climate, a milder and wetter climate than areas farther inland. Temperatures there are not usually so extreme as inland areas at the same latitude. This is because ocean temperatures change less than land temperatures and this affects the climate of areas nearby. The climates of inland areas are known as continental climates.

Moose live in forests in cool temperate regions.

Land surfaces

Different land surfaces absorb the Sun's rays differently. Light surfaces, such as snow-covered land or deserts, reflect the Sun's rays, whereas dense forests and dark soils absorb them. Where a higher proportion of the rays is reflected, clouds are less likely to form. This means that areas with lighter land surfaces will have less rainfall. Clouds also reflect the Sun's rays, affecting the amount of energy reaching the Earth's surface.

GLOBAL WARMING

Some of the gases in the atmosphere help to keep the Earth warm. They trap heat from the Sun in the same way that a greenhouse traps heat. This process is known as the greenhouse effect. But, as these gases increase, the Earth might be getting too warm.

A magnified picture of pollen from the ragwort plant. As the Earth warms up, pollen from plants may increase. This could cause problems for people with allergies.

Greenhouse gases

The Earth's surface absorbs much of the heat from the Sun. This is then given off as heat energy into the atmosphere. It gets trapped there by gases, such as carbon dioxide, which are known as greenhouse gases. As the amount of greenhouse gases increases, more heat is trapped.

Most greenhouse gases occur naturally, but industrial processes and other pollution are increasing the amount of greenhouse gases in the atmosphere. Scientists think that this may be causing the Earth to become warmer. This process is known as global warming.

Plants are important for the balance of greenhouse gases because they take in carbon dioxide.

Balance of gases

Whenever we burn oil, coal or wood, carbon dioxide is released. For example, when forests are burned to make room for farming, they release carbon dioxide. This also reduces the number of plants available to absorb carbon dioxide, upsetting the natural balance of the carbon cycle*. Factories, power stations and cars also give out pollution which may contribute to global warming.

Huge roads, like this one, are useful for car drivers, but the pollution from cars could be contributing to global warming.

Venice, Italy, is a city built on over 100 tiny islands in the Lagoon of Venice. If the sea level rises, it may eventually disappear under the sea.

Rising sea level

As atmospheric temperatures rise, so does the sea level. This will eventually result in the flooding of low-lying areas. Scientists estimate that the sea level is rising at a rate of 1–2mm (0.04–0.08in) each year. It may rise by another 0.25–1m (0.8–3.3ft) by the year 2100. There are two main reasons for the increased volume of water. First, as the oceans heat up, the water expands. The sea level rises because the water takes up more space. Secondly, the higher temperatures may cause glaciers and icecaps on land to melt. This water will then flood into the sea.

Changing climate

Scientists predict the average atmospheric temperature will increase by around 2°C (3.6°F) this century. Extreme weather may become more common. Climate change will affect the habitats* of plants and animals. Some species may thrive, but others may struggle to survive.

Internet links

To find out more about global warming and the greenhouse effect and to learn how you can make a difference, visit the websites recommended at **www.usborne.com/quicklinks**

Shifting the balance

People have already begun to take steps to reduce the emission of gases that contribute to global warming. The main ways that this can be achieved are by looking at alternative energy sources and reducing pollution levels.

*Carbon cycle, 99; habitats, 112

CHANGING CLIMATES

Ever since the Earth was formed, its climate has been changing. Volcanic eruptions, collisions with asteroids, and the path of the Solar System through space may all have caused climate changes that affected the atmosphere, the landscape and living things.

The red outline on this map shows the areas of the Earth that were covered in ice during the last Ice Age. The white areas are those places that are still covered in ice today.

Long ago, widespread volcanic activity could have caused fires which damaged habitats, wiping out various species.

Ice ages

Throughout its history, the Earth has gone through several ice ages, when the climate was colder than it is now, and glaciers* and ice sheets spread across much of the globe. Sea levels were lower as well, because so much of the water was frozen into ice on land.

Ice ages have several causes. As the galaxy spins, the Earth may enter the magnetic fields which shield it from the Sun's heat. Earth may also sometimes change its orbit, move away from the Sun and get cooler. There may be another ice age in the future.

Internet links

Visit the websites recommended at **www.usborne.com/quicklinks** to explore climate timelines and to find out what fossils can tell us about the past. You can also learn about mass extinctions, such as the disappearance of dinosaurs

Explosions

Long-term climate patterns can be affected by sudden events, such as huge volcanic eruptions, or asteroids* hitting the Earth. Events like this in the past could have filled Earth's atmosphere with smoke and dust which blocked out the sunlight, making the climate cold and dark and killing plants and animals.

*Asteroids, 11; glaciers, 66

Geological evidence

We can tell the Earth's climate has changed by looking at rocks and fossils. Many rocks form gradually in layers. These layers provide a record of what happened, called the fossil record. In warmer periods of the Earth's history, more plants and animals were alive and more fossils were preserved. Layers with fewer fossils show colder periods, when there were fewer living things.

Landscapes also hold clues about the past. For example, a U-shaped valley shows where a glacier gouged out a huge channel during an ice age.

Fossils found in stone, such as this well-preserved bird fossil, can reveal which types of animals lived in which places long ago.

As well as blocking out vital sunlight with smoke and ash, volcanic eruptions can destroy plant life by smothering the land with lava, hot molten rock that burns everything in its path.

Moving continents

As the plates* that make up the Earth's crust have slowly changed position, the climate of each continent has altered. For example, what is now West Africa was once at the South Pole. As it got nearer the Equator, its climate warmed up as it received more sunlight. Climates are also affected by ocean currents*. As the continents separated from each other, currents could flow between them, bringing cold or warm water from other parts of the Earth.

*Ocean currents, 97; plates, 20

WORLD ECOSYSTEMS

A red-eyed tree frog

PLANT LIFE ON EARTH

The Earth is the only planet known to support living things, or organisms. There are millions of different kinds of living things on Earth. They fall into two main groups: animals and plants. To survive, nearly all of them need light and heat from the Sun, food, water and air.

The Earth is the only planet so far discovered whose land looks green from space.

The green planet

Most plants are green because they contain a green substance called chlorophyll, which helps them to make their food. From space, the Earth's land looks mainly green, because of the billions of plants on its surface.

Plant food

Plants feed themselves by using sunlight to produce food chemicals. This process is called photosynthesis, which means "building with light". For this to happen, plants also need water and nutrients* from the soil, and carbon dioxide from the air. They then use all these things to make glucose, a kind of sugar, which they can feed on.

The Sun provides energy, in the form of light.
A plant's flowers contain parts that make seeds. These grow into new plants.
This part of the underside of a leaf has been magnified.
Leaves convert water and carbon dioxide into glucose and oxygen.
The stalk carries water and nutrients from roots to the leaves and flower.
Leaf stalk
Tiny holes called stomata let carbon dioxide in, and water and oxygen out.

Internet links

Visit the websites suggested at **www.usborne.com/quicklinks** to explore why we need plant life. You can also learn more about photosynthesis and how to identify plants.

*Nutrients, 28

Why we need plants

Plants are essential for life on Earth. Without them, the planet would look totally different, and there would be no people or animals. Animals – even meat-eaters – need plants, because plants form the basis of all food chains*. Plants also give out oxygen and water, which animals and people need; and their roots hold the soil together. Without them, much of the soil would wash away into the sea. We use plants to make medicines, food, fabrics and perfumes, and we get wood from trees.

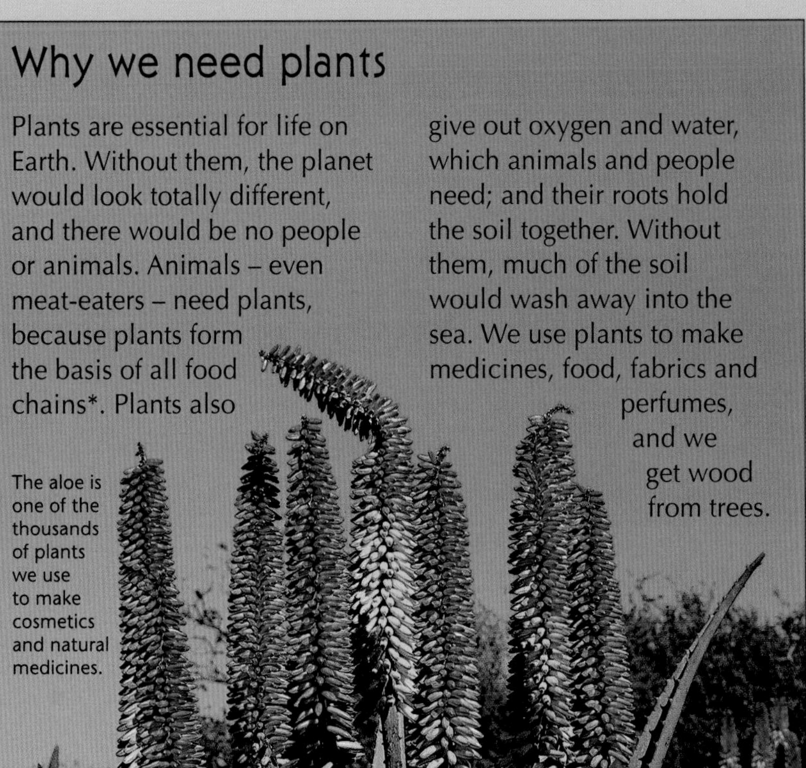

The aloe is one of the thousands of plants we use to make cosmetics and natural medicines.

Plant babies

Like all living things, plants reproduce (make new versions of themselves). Most do this by making seeds. The seeds usually form inside the flower. They may then be carried a long way by the wind before falling to the ground and beginning to grow.

A sunflower contains hundreds of seeds like these. Like the seeds of many plants, they are an important source of food for people and animals.

Types of plants

Different types of living things are called species. There are millions of species of plants, from tiny flowers to enormous trees called giant sequoias, which are the biggest living things on Earth. Different species are suited, or adapted, to living in different parts of the world. In deserts, for example, where water is scarce, cactuses grow thick stems for storing water.

A giant sequoia tree. These are found mainly in California, U.S.A.

*Food chains, 112

ANIMAL LIFE ON EARTH

There are millions of types, or species, of animals living on Earth. They include insects, fish, birds, reptiles, amphibians and mammals, such as humans. Unlike plants, animals can move around to find food and water.

The bald eagle is a carnivore. It feeds mainly on fish, swooping down and snatching its prey from lakes and rivers.

How animals live

All animals have to eat in order to survive. Herbivores eat plants and carnivores eat animals. There are some animals, such as giant pandas, that eat both plants and animals. These are called omnivores. Most humans are also omnivores.

Honeyeaters are herbivores. They feed on nectar, a sweet juice found inside flowers.

Many animals have to watch out for predators, which are other animals that want to eat them. Their bodies have to be adapted for running fast or hiding. Some animals, such as zebras, are camouflaged, which means they are patterned so that they blend in with their background and are harder for predators to see. But some predators are also camouflaged, so they can creep up on their prey.

Tools for eating

Animals' bodies are adapted to suit the kind of food they eat. Herbivores usually have flat, broad teeth designed for munching plants, while most carnivores have sharp teeth to help them grab and grip their prey (the animals they eat) and tear raw flesh.

You can see the long, sharp teeth in this badger's skull. They are good for gripping and slicing through flesh.

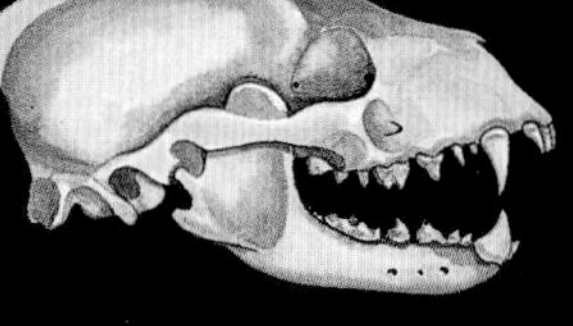

In this roe deer's skull, you can see the long front teeth which are suited to biting off pieces of plants and flat molar teeth which are good for chewing plants.

Natural selection

Why are animals and plants so well adapted to their way of life? One answer might be that they have gradually changed, or evolved, over a very long time to suit the places they live in and the food that is available to them. In the 19th century, a scientist named Charles Darwin (1809–1882) put forward a theory, which he called "natural selection", to explain how these changes might happen.

According to Darwin, individual animals and plants sometimes have qualities that help them to survive. For example, in a green forest, a green bug would probably survive longer than a brown bug, because its appearance would help it to avoid being seen and eaten.

The individuals that survive the longest are likely to have more babies, and will pass on their useful qualities to them. Over a very long time, each species will gradually develop all the most useful qualities for surviving in its own habitat.

Internet links

For links to interactive websites where you can find out more about some of the amazing animals around the world, go to **www.usborne.com/quicklinks**

Breathing

As well as eating food, animals need to breathe oxygen, a gas which is found in air and water. All animals take oxygen into their bodies, in a variety of different ways.

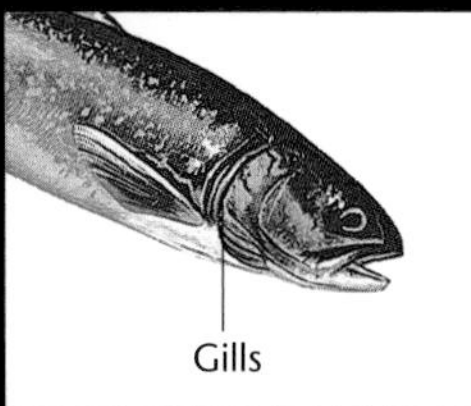

Fish have gills, which filter oxygen from the water as it flows through them.

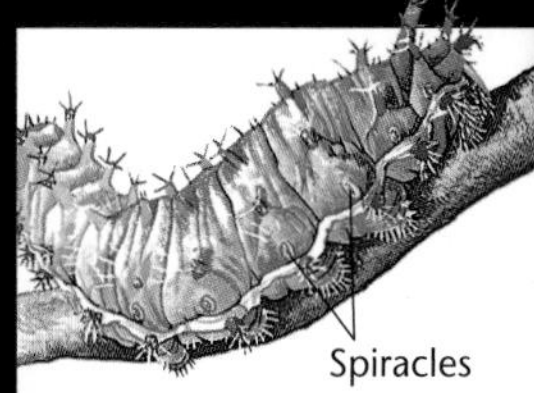

Insects take in oxygen through tiny holes in their bodies, called spiracles.

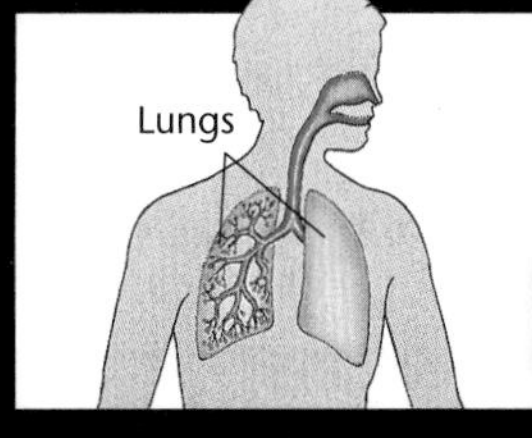

Humans and many other animals have lungs, which extract oxygen from the air.

Useful animals

Animals are very useful to humans, providing meat, milk, eggs, wool, silk, leather and even medicines. Many animals are farmed carefully, but some species are in danger of dying out and becoming extinct, because humans have killed too many of them. You can find out about these endangered species on page 115.

Guanacos are hunted for their long, thick wool.

ECOSYSTEMS

A place where a plant or animal lives is called its habitat. For example, seas, rivers, mountains, forests and deserts are all habitats. Together, a habitat and the group, or community, of plants and animals that live in it form a whole system, called an ecosystem.

Snowy owls and lemmings are part of the ecosystem in the Arctic.

Meat-eaters survive by eating other animals found in their habitat. These cheetahs are chasing a Thomson's gazelle.

Food webs

In an ecosystem, many different food chains intertwine to make up a complicated system known as a food web. Each animal in the web may eat many different species and be hunted by several others. The diagram below shows part of a food web in a mountain forest in a northern country, such as Canada. Each blue arrow points from a species that is eaten to a species that eats it. (This is a simplified diagram. In fact, there would be many more species than this in one ecosystem, and the whole food web would be too complicated to fit on the page.)

Food chains

The animals and plants in an ecosystem depend on each other for food. One species eats another, and is in turn eaten by another. This is called a food chain. Plants form the first link in a food chain, because they make their own food from sunlight, using a process called photosynthesis*. Plant-eating animals (herbivores) eat plants, and meat-eating animals (carnivores) eat herbivores and other carnivores.

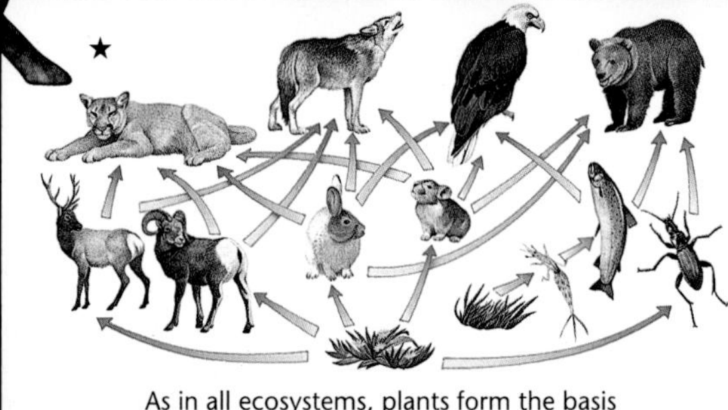

As in all ecosystems, plants form the basis of this food web.

*Photosynthesis, 108; soil, 28

Trophic levels

A food web has several layers, known as trophic levels. There are different kinds of plants or animals on each level.

The Sun provides light and energy for plants.

Tertiary consumers
Animals that eat other meat-eating animals

Secondary consumers
Animals that eat plant-eating animals

Primary consumers
Animals that eat plants

Producers
Plants that use the Sun's energy to manufacture food

Decomposers
Organisms that feed on dead plants and animals and break them down in the soil*

The energy cycle

Plants and animals use food to make energy, which helps them grow, move, keep warm, make seeds and have babies. When plants or animals die, they are broken down by decomposers, such as fungi, and the energy goes back into the soil in the form of chemicals. These help plants to grow, and the cycle begins again.

Internet links

You can read about the major biomes of the world, find out more about ecosystems and learn about the science of ecology by going to the websites suggested at **www.usborne.com/quicklinks**

Competition

Each type of plant or animal has a unique place in its ecosystem, known as a niche. If two different species try to compete for the same food, the stronger one survives, and the other dies out or has to move away. Different species in an ecosystem can survive side by side by eating slightly different types of food. For example, in African grasslands, elephants reach up to eat the higher branches of trees and bushes, gerenuks eat leaves lower down and warthogs nibble grasses on the ground.

Biomes

The Earth has several climate types, or biomes, such as rainforests and deserts. Each biome supports many ecosystems, but can also be seen as one big ecosystem. Together, all the biomes combine to form the biggest ecosystem of all, the Earth itself.

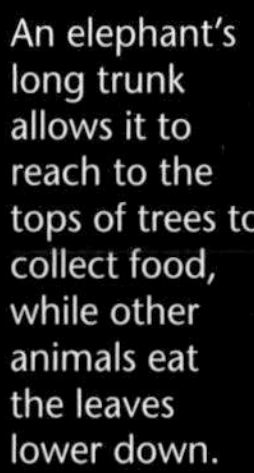

An elephant's long trunk allows it to reach to the tops of trees to collect food, while other animals eat the leaves lower down.

PEOPLE AND ECOSYSTEMS

Like every other plant and animal on Earth, you are part of an ecosystem. But there are now so many humans that we need more energy and make more waste than our ecosystem can deal with.

Using up energy

The first humans were suited to the ecosystems of the places they lived in. They ate the food that was available and used only as much energy as they needed to survive.

Now, though, we use up lots more energy than we really need to survive, because of all the things that modern humans do, such as running factories, getting around in cars and planes, and using electric lights and machines. We get most of our energy by burning fossil fuels*. This creates waste gases which can't be broken down quickly enough, so they build up around us as pollution.

Pollution

Pollution is any waste product that nature can't easily process and recycle. Things such as exhaust from cars, smoke from factories, and plastic packaging are all pollution.

Some pollution is just ugly, but some can be dangerous. For example, exhaust fumes that build up in the air can cause asthma, and chemicals that leak from farms into rivers can kill fish and upset the local food web*.

Smog is a kind of pollution caused when fossil fuels* are burned and give off waste gases.

Upsetting ecosystems

Each part of an ecosystem depends on all the other parts, making a natural balance. If one part is damaged or destroyed, it affects all the others.

If the plants in this food chain* were destroyed, the animals farther up the chain might starve.

*Food chains, 112; food webs, 112; fossil fuels, 26

Using up space

Our farms, cities, roads and airports all need space. We use space that used to be the habitats of plants and animals. Without its habitat, an ecosystem can't work, and animals and plants die. If this happens too often, some species become extinct, which means they die out completely.

Extinction is sometimes caused by natural disasters, such as volcanic eruptions, but often it is brought about by people. Pollution, hunting and introducing animals into new areas can all cause extinctions. For example, several species of flightless birds were wiped out when humans brought dogs and cats to Australia and New Zealand.

Wind turbines like these convert the energy of the wind into electricity. This causes less pollution than burning fuel.

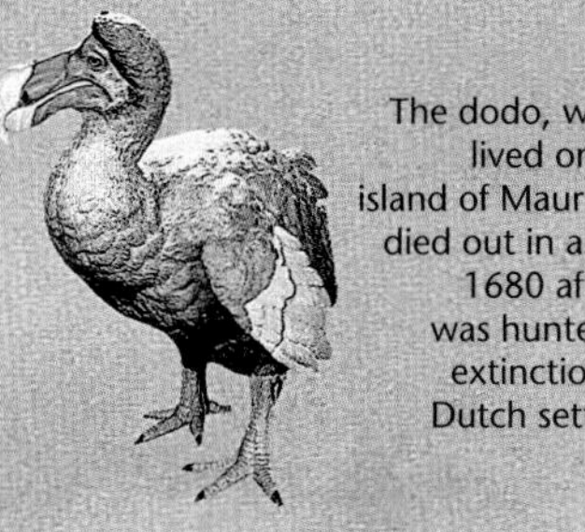

The dodo, which lived on the island of Mauritius, died out in about 1680 after it was hunted to extinction by Dutch settlers.

Internet links

Learn about endangered ecosystems, the effects of pollution and explore some important conservation projects, by going to the websites suggested at **www.usborne.com/quicklinks**

Conserving the Earth

Conservation means trying to reduce the damage done to the Earth and its species by pollution and other human activities. We can begin to conserve the Earth by using less energy, making less waste, and replacing as much as possible of the resources we use up. This is sometimes called sustainable living.

We cannot bring back plants and animals that are already extinct, but endangered species (those that are in danger of dying out) can be protected. Conservationists work to save natural habitats and protect rare wild animals from being hunted, so that they can build up their numbers.

Snow leopards are an endangered species. They are now protected by laws and bred in zoos to try to save them.

RAINFORESTS

In the tropics*, it rains nearly every day and is hot throughout the year. Large areas are covered in thick, lush forests called tropical rainforests.

Rainy places

Tropical rainforests receive more than 2,000mm (80in) of rain each year. The intense heat causes water to evaporate quickly, making the air very moist, or humid.

Internet links

Visit the recommended sites at **www.usborne.com/quicklinks** to discover the threats to the rainforests of the world and read some of the strategies used to protect them.

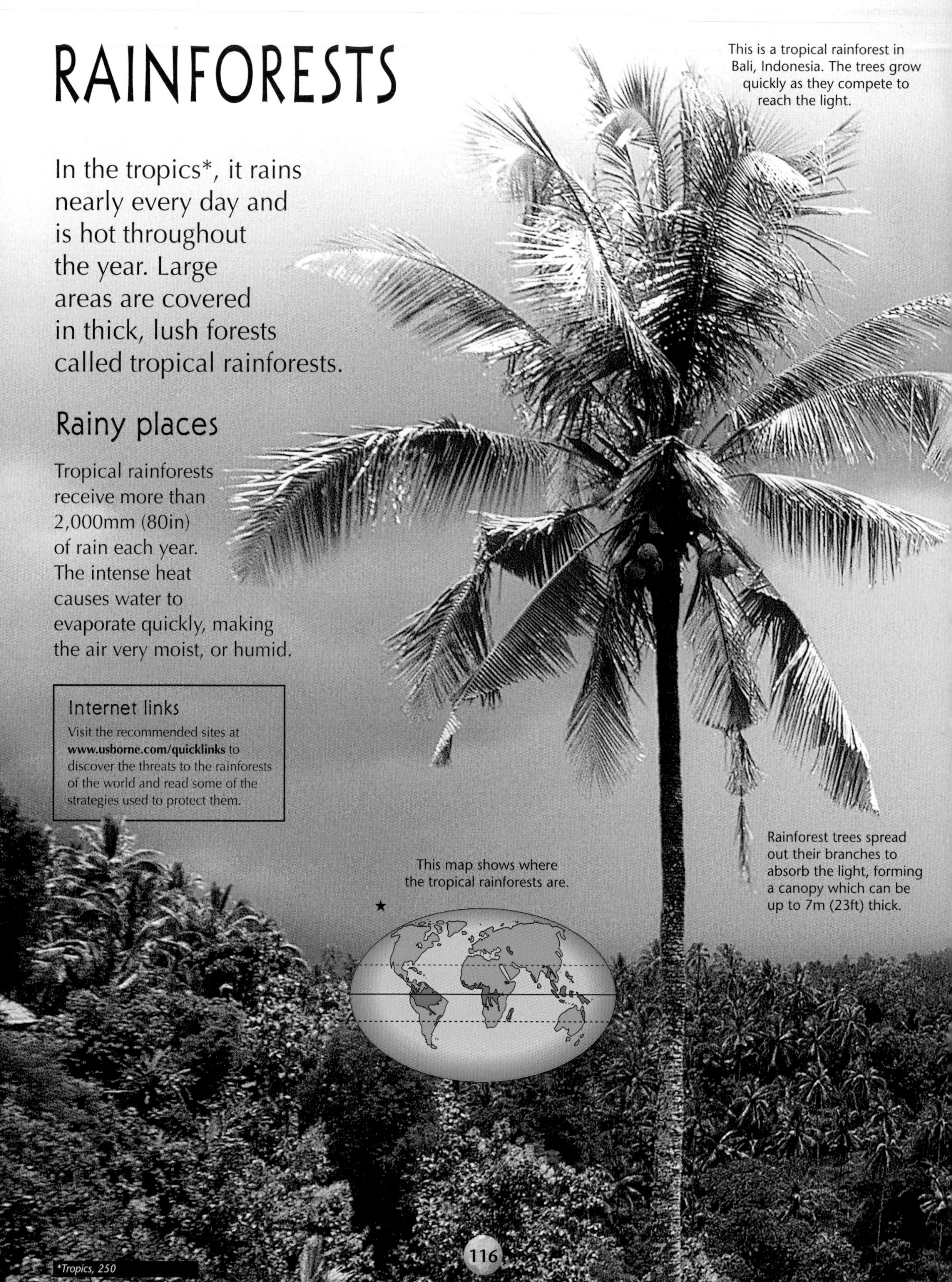

This is a tropical rainforest in Bali, Indonesia. The trees grow quickly as they compete to reach the light.

Rainforest trees spread out their branches to absorb the light, forming a canopy which can be up to 7m (23ft) thick.

★ This map shows where the tropical rainforests are.

*Tropics, 250

Rainforest people

Many small ethnic groups living in tropical rainforests survive by hunting animals and gathering plants, or by small-scale farming. However, their lifestyle has been threatened by people who have moved to these areas for commercial reasons. They chop down trees and burn them in order to clear land for farming and mining.

These rainforest trees are being burned to create space for farming.

Animal life

Rainforests are home to over half the world's plant and animal species. Different kinds of animals have adapted to living at different levels in the rainforest. Many animals live in the branches of trees. They need to be good at climbing and able to move easily from tree to tree by swinging, jumping or gliding.

On the forest floor, it is dark and the tangled vegetation makes it difficult for some animals to move around. The larger animals tend to be sturdy so they can easily force their way through. There are also many insects.

Colugos climb trees for food. They use the flaps of skin between their arms and legs to help them glide between trees.

Forests in danger

Every year, huge areas of rainforest are chopped down or burned. The disappearance of so many trees affects the balance of gases in the atmosphere. This may cause an increase in global warming*. Due to the destruction of their natural habitat, many rainforest plants and animals have died out and many others are endangered.

Golden lion tamarins are an endangered species of monkey.

*Global warming, 102

TROPICAL GRASSLANDS

The tropical grasslands are flat, open plains in the central parts of continents. They occur between 5° and 15° north and south of the Equator and get their name from the grasses that make up the majority of their vegetation.

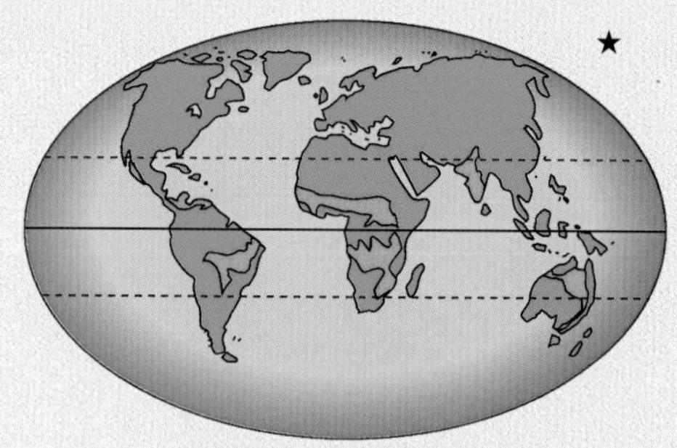

This map shows where the tropical grasslands are.

Two seasons

The tropical grasslands have two seasons: a dry season, when the vegetation is dry and brown, and a rainy season, when the grasses become tall and green.

The rainy season occurs when the Sun is directly overhead and the trade winds* meet and cause rainfall. As the Sun moves, so does the point where the trade winds meet until the dry season begins.

Vegetation

Only a few trees grow in the tropical grasslands, for example the acacia tree whose thick trunk is resistant to the fires that sometimes rage during the dry season. However, there are around 8,000 species of grasses, which are suited to dry conditions. They have long roots which can reach downward and sideways in search of water.

Acacia trees in the Taragire National Park, Tanzania, Africa. Acacias are among the few trees that can survive in the dry tropical grasslands.

Internet links

To read more about grassland vegetation and find information on grassland animals, follow the links at **www.usborne.com/quicklinks**

*Trade winds, 96

During the dry season, wildebeest move away, or migrate, to find food and water. Many thousands of wildebeest migrate together for protection.

Grassland animals

The tropical grasslands are home to large numbers of herbivores (plant-eating animals). These attract large hunting animals, such as lions and cheetahs, that feed on them. Because the land is so exposed, many animals live in large groups, so that some animals can watch out for predators while others feed or rest.

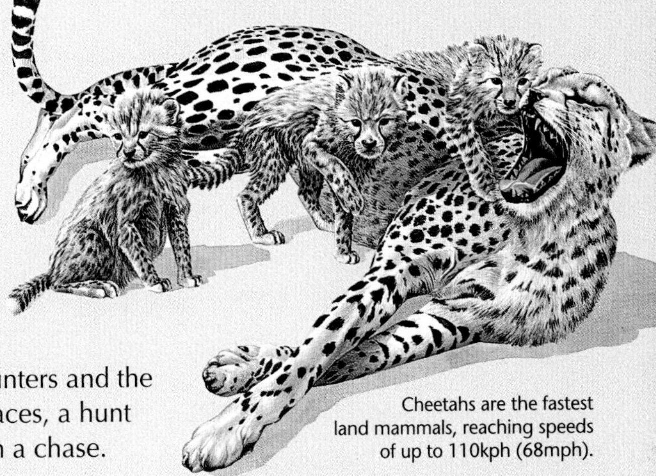

Cheetahs are the fastest land mammals, reaching speeds of up to 110kph (68mph).

Some of the fastest animals, such as cheetahs, gazelles and ostriches, live in grasslands. Speed is important for survival, both for the hunters and the hunted. With so few hiding places, a hunt for food often results in a chase.

The tsetse fly

Many grassland areas are now used for farming. However, the largest grasslands, in Africa, are almost untouched. This is because of a parasite, carried by an insect called the tsetse fly, which infects humans and animals. In humans, it causes sleeping sickness, the effects of which are sluggishness, fever and sometimes death. In animals, it causes a similar disease called nagana.

A close-up of a tsetse fly feeding on a human arm

MONSOONS

At certain times of year, some areas of the tropics have a period of torrential rain and another period of drier weather. This strong seasonal change is known as a monsoon. The rain can cause severe flooding, but people also rely on it for survival.

Three seasons

Monsoons occur in certain parts of the tropics, particularly in Southeast Asia. Monsoon regions have three seasons – a long, cool dry season, a hot humid season when the land is very dry and a rainy season when there are thunderstorms on most days.

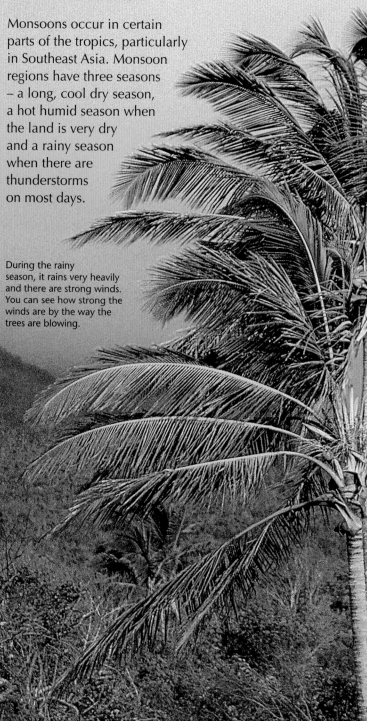

During the rainy season, it rains very heavily and there are strong winds. You can see how strong the winds are by the way the trees are blowing.

Changing winds

The word *monsoon* is from an Arabic word meaning "season". It refers to the seasonal reversal of the wind direction. During the cooler season, the land is cooler than the ocean, and so winds blow from the land to the ocean, giving dry weather over the land. The warm season occurs when the midday Sun is almost directly overhead. The land is hotter than the ocean, so moist winds rush in from the ocean and shed their moisture on the land as heavy rain.

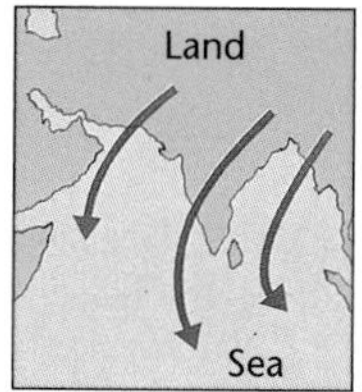

In the dry season, winds blow from the land to the sea.

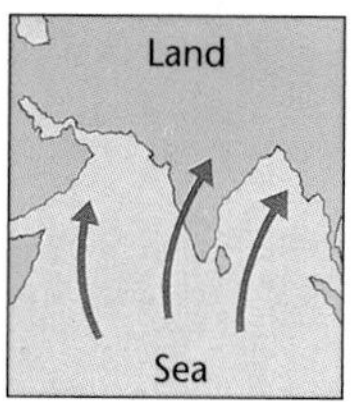

In the rainy season, moist winds rush in from the sea.

Farming

Around a quarter of the world's people live in monsoon areas. Many of them rely on growing their own food. The main crops are rice and tea, which grow well in wet conditions.

Rice in particular needs lots of water to grow. The seedlings are planted during the wet monsoon season in flooded fields called paddy fields. Rice is an important food for many poor nations, because it can be grown cheaply and in large quantities. If there is too little rain, it can be disastrous, resulting in crop failure which may in turn cause famine.

A rice farm in China. The field has been flooded with water, as rice plants grow well in waterlogged soils.

Internet links

For links to websites where you can find out more about monsoons and see how they affect people's lives, go to **www.usborne.com/quicklinks**

Diseases

A mosquito magnified. These insects thrive in monsoon regions.

A number of serious diseases spread easily after the monsoon season, because stagnant floodwater provides an ideal breeding ground for the bacteria that cause them. Typhoid and cholera are particularly common. Mosquitoes, insects which can carry diseases such as malaria and yellow fever, also thrive in the warm, wet conditions of monsoon regions.

TROPICAL DESERTS

The tropical deserts are the hottest and driest places in the world. With so little water or shelter, only a few animals and plants are able to survive in the burning heat of the day. Very few people live in tropical deserts.

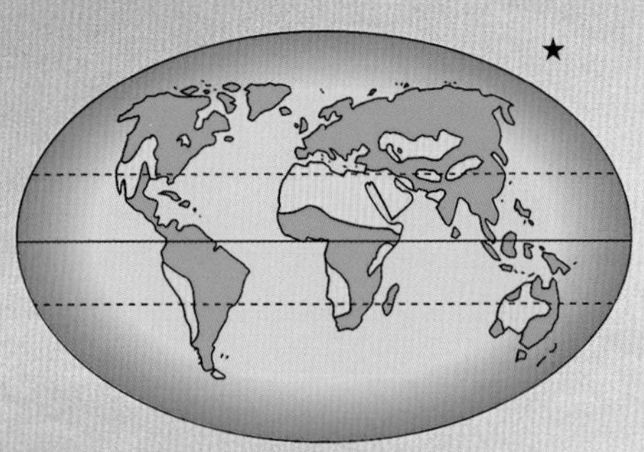

Tropical deserts exist mainly between 15° and 30° north and south of the Equator.

This is a fertile area, called an oasis, in the Thar Desert, Rajasthan, India. The people are collecting water.

Desert climate

Most deserts are hot during the day and cold at night. During the day, the heat is intense because the Sun is high in the sky and there are few clouds to block the Sun's rays. Temperatures can reach over 52°C (126°F). At night, the lack of clouds allows heat to escape, so temperatures can drop to below freezing. Less than 250mm (10in) of rain falls on deserts each year. When it rains, it is usually in short, violent storms. If the land has been baked by the heat of the Sun, these brief rainstorms can cause floods because the rain is not absorbed quickly enough by the dry ground.

Oases

There is water in the desert, but most of it is located underground in rocks that are porous, which means they can hold water like a sponge. In a few places, where these rocks are at the surface, moist areas called oases are formed. Birds, animals and people gather at oases to drink.

Desert landscapes

Only 25% of the world's deserts are sandy. Most deserts consist of bare rock or stone. Some even have dramatic rocky mountains. In sandy deserts, sand often collects together to form hills called dunes, which move and change shape as the wind blows the sand across the desert.

Strong winds sometimes sweep across deserts, causing sand-storms which can wear away the rocks in their path. Over many years, this sand-blasting effect can produce some unusually-shaped rocks. The process of wearing away rocks in this way is a type of erosion*.

This is a sand dune in the Sahara Desert, Africa, the biggest desert in the world. The man is one of the Tuareg, a group of people who live in the Sahara.

Internet links

Explore the climate and geography of some of the world's deserts, and find out about their wildlife, landscape and peoples, by visiting the suggested websites at **www.usborne.com/quicklinks**

Adaptation

In order to survive in the desert, those plants and animals that live there have adapted so that they are able to cope with the heat and limited supplies of water. Some desert plants can store water in their stems or can access water deep in the ground through long roots. Many desert animals have dry droppings to help them save water.

Camels can drink gallons of water in a few minutes and then last days without any.

Desert expansion

The world's deserts are increasing in size. This process, known as desertification, is caused by the destruction of the vegetation near the edges of deserts. People living in these dry areas need grass for their animals to eat and wood from trees to burn as fuel. This destruction of vegetation means that the soil is easily washed or blown away and the water cycle* is disrupted. Once this has happened, it is very difficult for vegetation to grow there.

*Erosion, 34; water cycle, 78

MEDITERRANEAN CLIMATES

Mediterranean climates are warm temperate* climates. They get their name from the regions bordering the Mediterranean Sea. However, other parts of the world, such as small areas around Cape Town (South Africa), Perth (Australia), San Francisco (U.S.A.) and Valparaiso (Chile) also have Mediterranean climates.

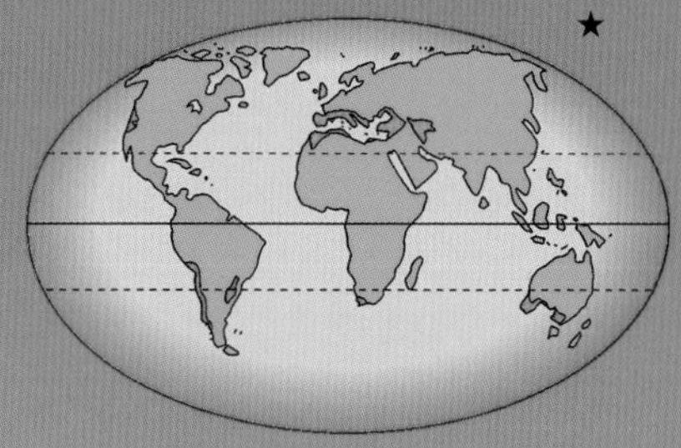

This map shows those areas with a Mediterranean climate.

Warm and dry

Mediterranean climates cover only a small part of the world. They are found on the west coasts of continents between 30° and 40° north and south of the Equator.

In summer in the Mediterranean, descending air usually causes hot, cloudless weather. In winter, the westerly winds bring moist air from the Atlantic, causing wetter weather.

In the Mediterranean region itself, the Mediterranean Sea (an inland sea with a narrow link to the Atlantic Ocean) has a moderating influence on the climate of the surrounding countries, making the winters milder than they would be otherwise.

In other parts of the world that have Mediterranean climates, cold offshore currents* have a similar effect on the local climate as the Mediterranean Sea has on southern Europe.

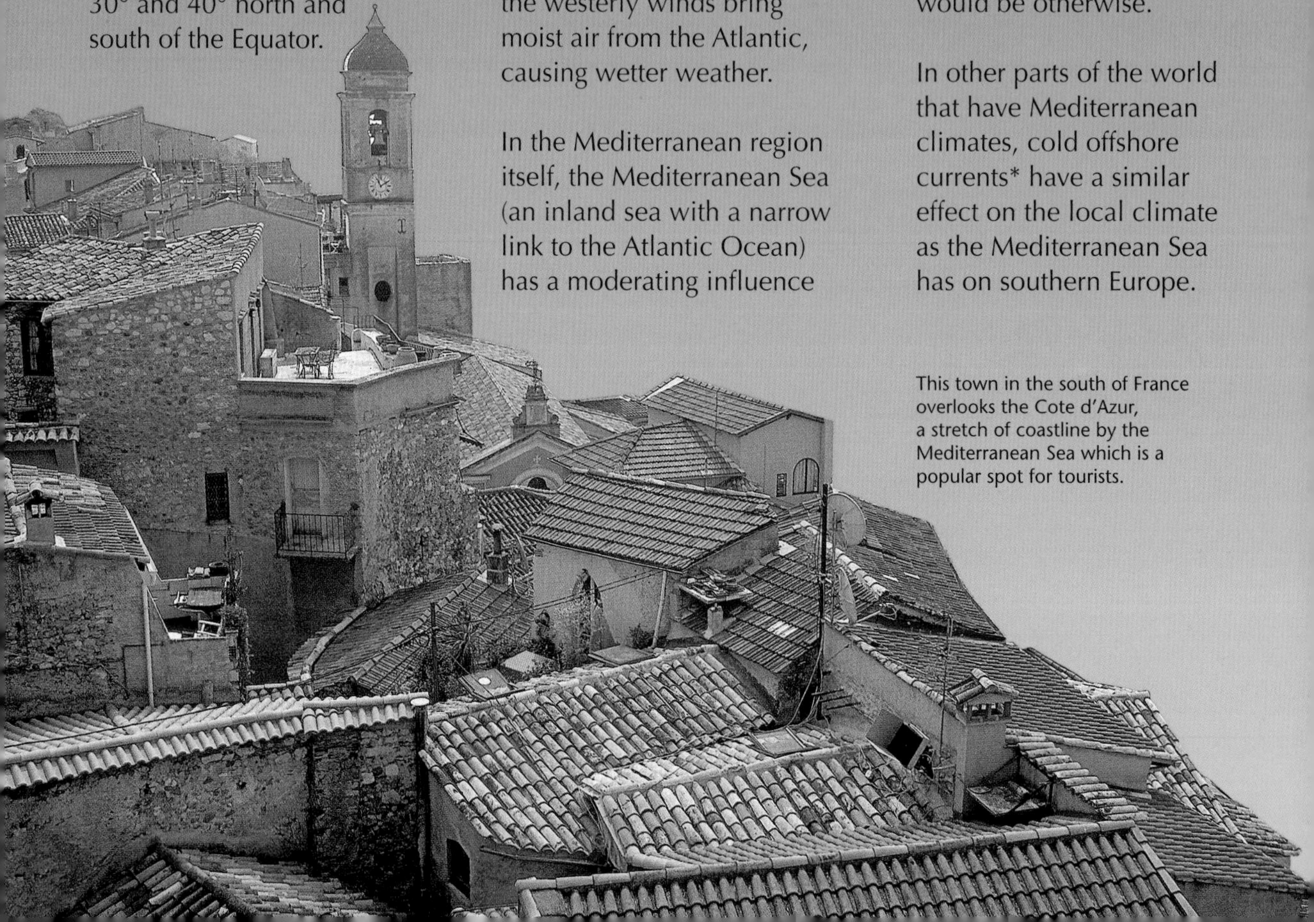

This town in the south of France overlooks the Cote d'Azur, a stretch of coastline by the Mediterranean Sea which is a popular spot for tourists.

Oranges grow well in Mediterranean climates.

Vegetation

There are two main types of vegetation in Mediterranean regions: trees such as cork oaks and olives, and low woody plants, or scrub. The vegetation is well adapted to the dry summer climate. Plants have thick, waxy leaves which reduce the amount of water they lose, and long roots which enable them to reach water deep underground.

Tourism

People sunbathing on a beach in the Cote d'Azur, southern France

The hot, dry summers in Mediterranean countries such as Greece, Spain, Italy and southern France have made them popular destinations for tourists from cooler climates searching for summer sunshine. This has meant that tourism has become an important part of the economies of these countries. Resorts tend to be developed in strips along the coast, where closeness to the sea and pleasant beaches are also major attractions for people.

Farming

Those places with Mediterranean climates are home to some of the world's most important wine producers. Grape vines are particularly well adapted to the climate, as they have long roots and tough bark.

A vineyard in the Douro Valley, Portugal. The grapes are being hand-picked to make wine.

The Mediterranean climate is also good for growing citrus fruits, such as oranges and lemons. These have thick skins which help them to retain moisture and the hot summers help the fruit to ripen quickly.

Internet links

To find out where Mediterranean climates are located around the world, and the types of plants that thrive in this climate, follow the links at **www.usborne.com/quicklinks**

*Ocean currents, 97; temperate climates, 126

TEMPERATE CLIMATES

The areas of the globe between the Arctic and Antarctic Circles and the tropics have a temperate climate. As the term temperate suggests, temperatures there are never very extreme. This vast area contains a wide range of landscapes.

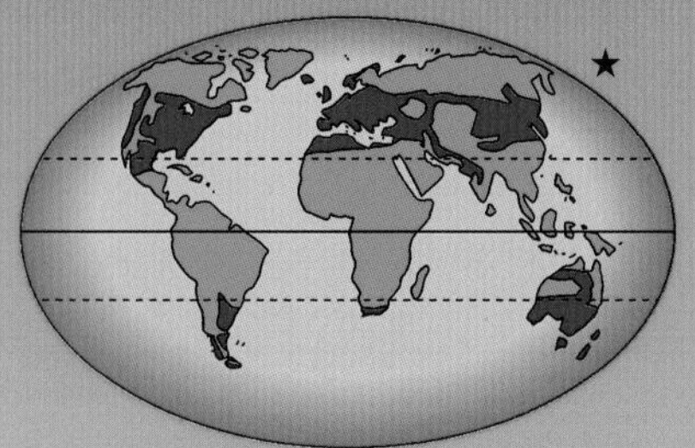

The dark blue areas of this map show the parts of the world with temperate climates.

Varied climates

The vegetation in temperate regions ranges from forests to dry grasslands. However, all the different areas have four seasons*: spring, summer, autumn and winter. This is because of the Earth's tilt and the way that each hemisphere faces the Sun in one season and then faces away from it in another.

Green lands

The mid-latitudes (between 40° and 60° north and south of the Equator) have a rainy climate, which is usually described as cool temperate. The steady rain throughout the year is the result of cool air from the poles meeting warm air from the tropics. The warm air is forced upward, causing swirling patterns of clouds and rain known as depressions.

The moderate temperatures in cool temperate regions mean that vegetation has a long period of uninterrupted growth, so the landscape is very green. Most trees are deciduous, which means that they lose their leaves in winter.

This region, which includes most of Europe, contains the richest farmland areas. The fertile soil and rainfall throughout the year make it suitable for a wide variety of crops, including grains, green vegetables and deciduous fruits.

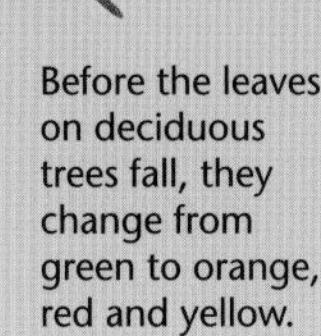

Before the leaves on deciduous trees fall, they change from green to orange, red and yellow.

*Seasons, 14

Grasslands

A view of the huge grasslands, or prairies, of North America

The prairies of North America and the steppes of Russia are huge temperate grasslands which lie in the middle of continents. Their summers are hot and sunny, but their winters can be quite harsh because they are away from the warming effects of the ocean*.

These areas receive too little rainfall for trees to grow, so the main vegetation is grasses. In the vast, treeless prairies of North America, winter frosts break up the rich soils, but summer days are long and warm. Wheat is suited to these conditions and is grown extensively.

Seasonal life

The lives of many animals and plants in temperate regions follow the cycle of the seasons. Annual plants complete their life's cycle in a year. They begin growing from seeds in spring and then flower in summer. In autumn, they produce their own seeds and fruit. At the end of the year the plants die.

Internet links

Find out more about places with temperate climates by following the links at **www.usborne.com/quicklinks**

Many animals prepare for the winter by storing up food. Some, such as the dormouse, cope with the lack of food by going into a deep sleep known as hibernation. During hibernation, an animal's breathing and heartbeat slow down and it does not need to eat. There are also animals that avoid the cold weather altogether by moving, or migrating, to warmer places.

A dormouse hibernating in its nest during the winter months

*Maritime climates, 101

POLAR REGIONS

The Arctic, the area around the North Pole, and the Antarctic, the area around the South Pole, are known as the polar regions. The temperatures there are usually below freezing and huge expanses of sea and land are covered in ice and snow.

Antarctic

In the middle of the Southern Ocean is a land mass, or continent, known as Antarctica, which is covered in a thick layer of ice. Temperatures there are so low that when snow falls it doesn't melt, but builds up with each snowfall. The weight of the snow on top presses down on the lower layers to form ice.

No land mammals live permanently in Antarctica because it is so cold, but some animals, such as seals, go there to breed. A number of seabirds, including penguins, live there permanently.

Penguins need to be well equipped to deal with the sub-zero temperatures of Antarctica. They have thick, warm feathers and a layer of fat under their skin for insulation.

Arctic

The Arctic is mainly made up of the Arctic Ocean, but several countries, including Canada, jut into it. The land there, called tundra, is warm enough for animals and plants to survive.

In summer, the ice on the tundra melts and the surface of the ground thaws. The ground often becomes boggy, because deeper down it is still frozen and the water can't seep through. The frozen layer is called permafrost.

Keeping warm

Some polar animals, such as penguins and seals, have adapted to living in the sea, away from icy winds. Other animals have different ways of coping with the cold. Polar bears have a thick layer of fat under their skin and musk oxen have thick, shaggy coats. Many polar animals have small ears, which help to reduce heat loss.

Blending in

Many polar animals have white coats, which enable them to blend in with the snowy landscape. This is called camouflage. It helps them to hide from predators or to stalk their prey without being seen. A few animals, such as arctic foxes and snowshoe hares, have different winter and summer coats. During the summer they have brown coats which blend in easily with rocks and plants. Then, as the snow falls in the winter, their coats change and become white, so they don't stand out.

Internet links

Discover more about Antarctica's wildlife and diverse landscape, and learn about the Canadian Arctic and the Inuit people by visiting the websites recommended at **www.usborne.com/quicklinks**

This polar bear's shaggy white coat blends in with the snow and protects it from the cold. It has fur all over its body except for on its nose and the pads on its feet.

Arctic shelters

Some animals that live in the Arctic build burrows or dens in the snow to protect themselves from the cold winds. For example, polar bears build dens with chambers in the snow for their cubs to take shelter.

This cutaway picture shows the inside of a polar bear's den.

MOUNTAINS

About 5% of the world's land surface is covered by high mountains and mountain ranges. Mountain areas have more than one type of climate because, as you go up a mountain, there are fewer particles in the air and the temperature falls.

The Great Basin Desert in Nevada, U.S.A., lies on the sheltered side, or rain shadow, of the Sierra Nevada mountains.

Mountain ranges

Most mountains are formed when the plates that make up the lithosphere* push together, forcing the land into fold mountains*. This is why mountains often occur in long lines, or ranges.

When air flows from the sea onto a mountain range, it is forced to rise. Clouds form as a result of condensation and rain or snow then falls on the mountainside. The sheltered land on the other side of the mountain, called the rain shadow, gets very little rain, and may become a desert.

Mountain levels

The higher up a mountain you go, the colder it gets. This is because the air higher up is thinner, so it can store less heat. There are different types of weather, vegetation and animal life at different heights up the mountain. Few species live on the windy peaks, but mountain goats and sheep graze on the grassy, rocky slopes below. Farther down, below a line called the treeline, it is warm enough for trees to grow. Animals such as cougars and hares live in mountain forests.

Mountain peaks in the Andes, on the border between Chile and Argentina

Internet links

Explore Everest, from base camp to the summit of the world's highest mountain, by following the links at **www.usborne.com/quicklinks**

The Alpine forget-me-not flower is adapted to mountain climates. It has shorter, thicker stems and deeper roots than the common forget-me-not.

This shepherd from the Basque region of France is holding two baby goats. Goats are suited to the mountain climate.

Mountain dwellers

Both animals and people living in high mountain areas have bigger lungs to help them breathe more easily in the thin air. Animals need thick fur and people need thick coats to keep them warm. Mountain people may be cut off from other cultures. For example, the Basque people, who have lived in the Pyrenees mountains between France and Spain for thousands of years, have a very unusual language which is unlike any other on Earth. This is because, for centuries, they rarely mixed with other peoples.

*Fold mountains, 21; lithosphere, 18

These tourists riding on dromedaries in Rajasthan, India, cast huge shadows on the desert sand.

PEOPLE AND THE WORLD

FARMING

Farming means growing plants or raising animals to meet human needs. It is the biggest industry in the world and produces much of what you eat, wear and use.

Crop farming

Livestock farming

Forests

Other land, such as cities, roads, national parks and wilderness

This pie chart shows how the world's land is used. Livestock farming uses more space than crop farming, but produces less food.

Types of farming

Growing plants is called crop farming or arable farming, and keeping animals is called livestock farming or pastoral farming. A mixture of both is called mixed farming. Farmers choose what to farm according to the type of land they have, the soil and the climate.

Yaks are adapted to surviving in high mountain areas. Farmers in the Himalayas keep them for milk and wool.

World industry

Around 45% of the world's workforce are farmers. Instead of just growing their own food, many farmers grow cash crops – crops grown specially to be sold and exported around the world. This is why, in some countries, you can buy different kinds of foods from all over the world in one supermarket.

Internet links

You can learn more about different kinds of farms and compare the jobs of people who live and work there by following the links at **www.usborne.com/quicklinks**

Wet soil and a warm climate are ideal for growing rice. In hilly areas, farmers build steps of land, or terraces, to hold the water and soil in place. This picture shows rice terraces in China.

Growing crops

Combine harvesters are used to gather all kinds of crops. It is much easier and quicker than harvesting fields of crop by hand.

Crop farming uses up around 11% of the world's land. It is the best way of producing as much food as possible from the soil, so poor countries usually grow a greater proportion of crops than rich countries do. Planting, protecting and harvesting (collecting) crops is hard work, but many farmers use machinery to do these tasks.

Animal care

Like crops, livestock has to be looked after carefully. The animals need food, water, shelter and protection from predators and diseases. Animal products also have to be "harvested", which means collecting the animals' milk, wool or eggs, or killing them for their meat.

Farm animals often have more than one use. We may use their wool or skins as well as meat. In many countries they also work, pulling carts or farm machinery.

★

Ostriches are farmed for meat, eggs and leather, and their feathers are used in fashion accessories.

FARMING METHODS

Farmers want to get as much as they can from their land. There are various ways of improving the yield, or amount of produce that comes from the land.

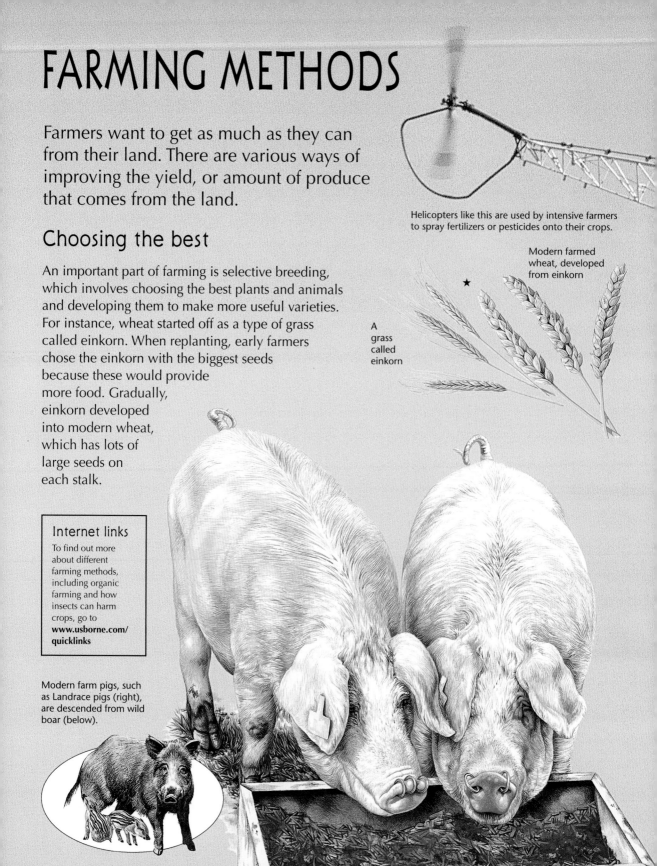

Choosing the best

An important part of farming is selective breeding, which involves choosing the best plants and animals and developing them to make more useful varieties. For instance, wheat started off as a type of grass called einkorn. When replanting, early farmers chose the einkorn with the biggest seeds because these would provide more food. Gradually, einkorn developed into modern wheat, which has lots of large seeds on each stalk.

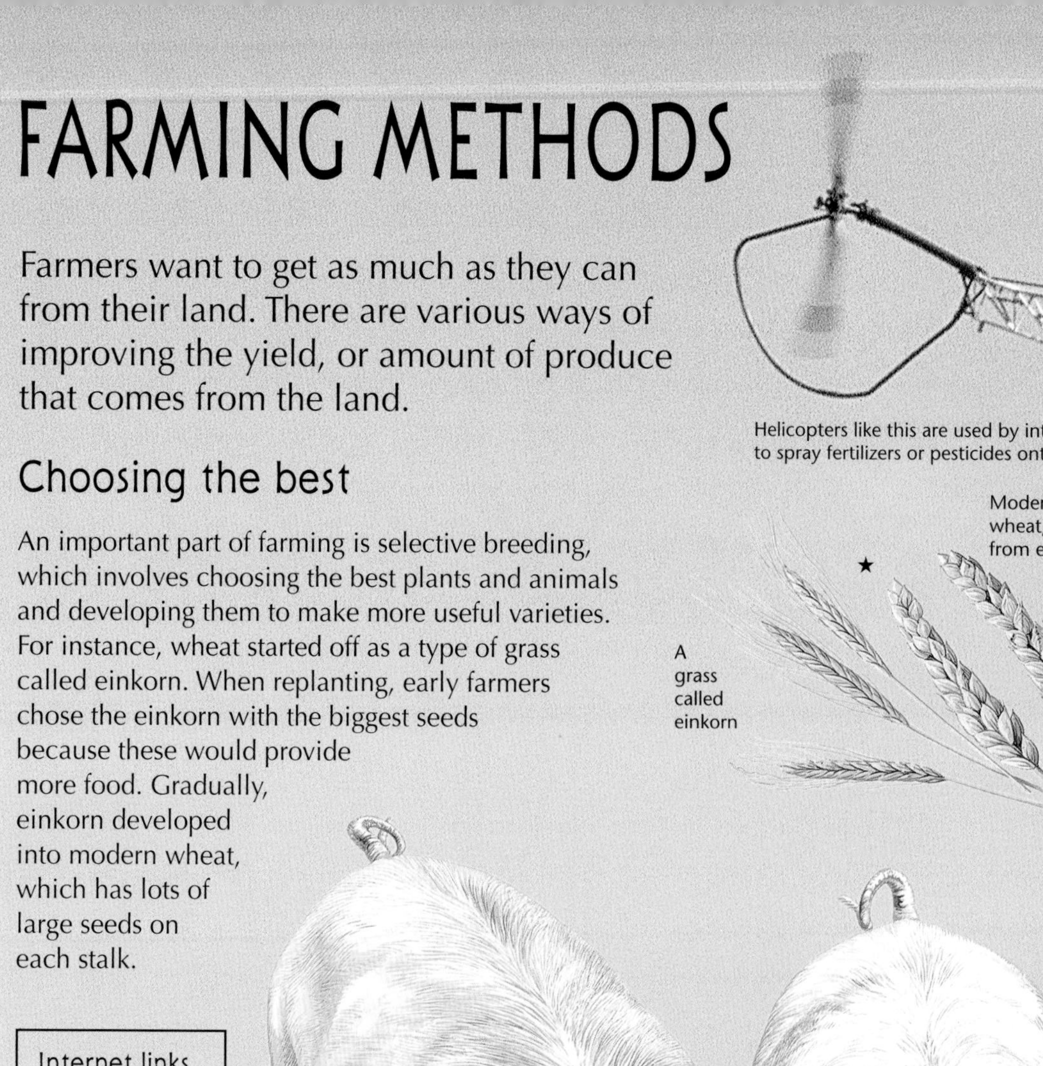

Helicopters like this are used by intensive farmers to spray fertilizers or pesticides onto their crops.

A grass called einkorn

Modern farmed wheat, developed from einkorn

> **Internet links**
> To find out more about different farming methods, including organic farming and how insects can harm crops, go to **www.usborne.com/quicklinks**

Modern farm pigs, such as Landrace pigs (right), are descended from wild boar (below).

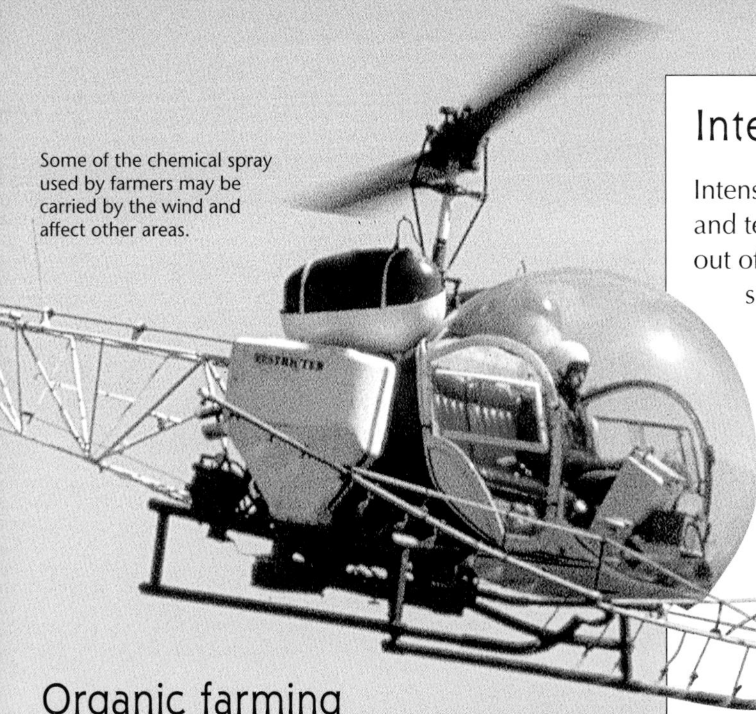

Some of the chemical spray used by farmers may be carried by the wind and affect other areas.

Chemical spray units attached to a helicopter

Intensive farming

Intensive farming means using chemicals and technology to get as much as possible out of the land. Intensively farmed animals, such as pigs or hens, are kept in small stalls or cages to save space. They are fed by automatic water and food dispensers and may be given drugs to make them grow faster. Intensive farming can increase yields, but the chemicals used can also cause pollution.

Some people think intensive farming is cruel, because the animals are kept in unnatural conditions. "Free range" animals live in more natural conditions and are allowed to move around, or range freely.

Intensively farmed battery hens live in small cages and are usually fed by machines. The eggs they lay roll into a tray and are carried away on a conveyor belt.

Organic farming

Organic farming means farming without using artificial chemicals or processes. Organic farmers use animal dung or compost instead of artificial fertilizer, and don't give animals drugs to make them grow faster. Organic food is expensive, because without drugs and artificial chemicals, diseases are harder to control and yields fall. However, there is a demand for organic products from people who are worried about their health, pollution and animal welfare.

Bug warfare

Insects and other bugs that eat farm crops can be a big problem. Intensive farmers (see right) often spray crops to kill insects, but organic farmers do not use chemical sprays. Instead, they sometimes try biological pest control. They change the ecosystem* in their fields by introducing another species to feed on the pest species.

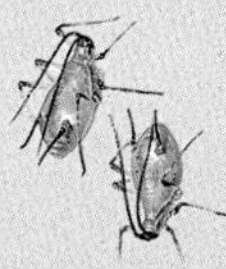

These tiny aphids damage many crops. Instead of spraying, some farmers release ladybirds (ladybugs) to eat them.

*Ecosystems, 112

SCIENCE AND FARMING

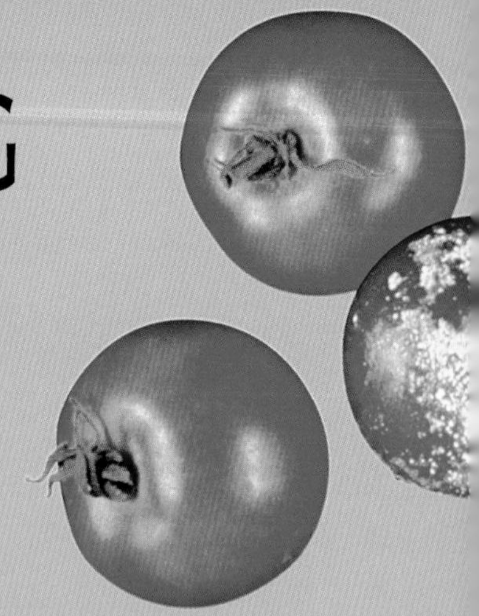

Farming has always made use of science and technology, in the form of machinery and selective breeding. But today, more complex science is being used. Computers can make farms more efficient, while genetic engineering is being used to create new crop species.

Big fields

Some modern farm machines, such as combine harvesters, are hard to use in small fields. So, in the last 100 years, fields in many parts of the world have been made bigger and bigger. They are more efficient than small fields because less space is taken up with walls and paths. However, large fields can also be harder to manage, as one field can contain several types of farmland and soil can be eroded more easily*.

The picture below shows a huge wheat field on a modern farm in Sweden.

Precision farming

Precision farming is a new way of using science and technology to manage farms, especially those with very large fields.

For example, some combine harvesters have recording systems that measure how much yield is being collected. At the same time, the farmer uses a Global Positioning System, linked to a satellite* in space, to record where the harvester is in the field. This information is used to make a yield map.

Computer power

Computer maps are used to compare the yield with other factors, such as the acidity or the dampness of the soil. The computer then calculates how much fertilizer or water is needed. This saves time and money, and helps farmers avoid using unnecessary fertilizer or water.

This computerized map shows which parts of a field are the most fertile. Darker areas show the highest yield, and pale areas show the lowest yield.

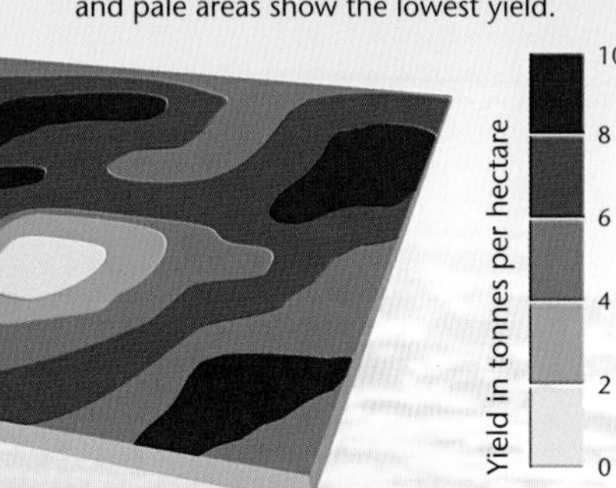

*Satellites, 252; soil erosion, 31

The tomatoes above are covered in a type of fungus, but the plant that produced the ones on the left was genetically engineered so that its tomatoes would be resistant to the fungus.

Instead of being grown from seeds, the plant shoots in this tub have been "cloned" from fragments of a parent plant to make sure they have exactly the same DNA.

Genetic engineering

Scientists have recently learned how to make changes to DNA, the code inside cells that tells living things how to grow. This is called genetic engineering and it is very important for farming. By altering DNA, we can now change plant species to make them work better as crops.

For example, cotton plants have been genetically engineered to resist a type of weedkiller called Roundup®, which kills all other plants. When the farmer applies the weedkiller, all the weeds die, but the crop stays alive.

Genetically modified foods

Many food crops are being genetically changed, or modified, to make them grow faster or resist pests. GM (genetically modified) foods are tested before they can be sold, but some people worry that they may be bad for us. Nobody yet knows what long-term problems they may cause. GM crops may also damage the environment, for example, by encouraging farmers to use more weedkiller which could harm animals. On the other hand, GM crops could be good news for farmers and consumers in places where crops often fail.

Internet links

Read debates about GM foods and find out why people disagree by visiting the websites suggested at **www.usborne.com/quicklinks**

POPULATION

Population is the number of people who live in a particular area. The population of the world has been rising for thousands of years, and is now going up faster than ever. In very crowded areas, it can sometimes be hard for people to get enough work, food or housing.

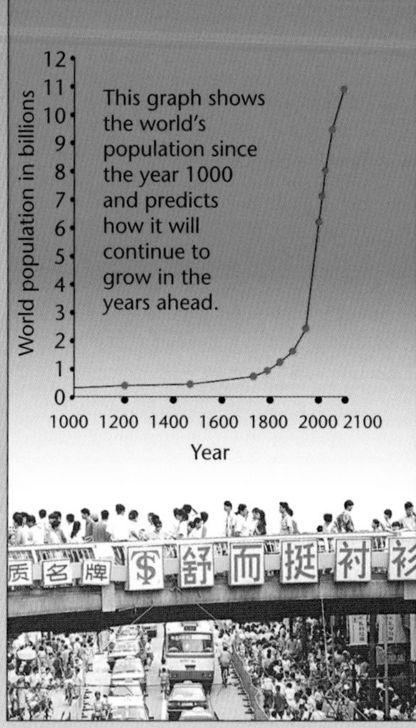

Counting people

With thousands of people being born and dying every day, it can be hard to measure population. Many countries hold a census, or population count, every ten years. Each household fills in a questionnaire, saying how many people live there. Experts use the results to estimate the population of a country at any one time, and to calculate the total population of the world.

Rising numbers

The world's population began to rise quickly in the 17th century, when there were about 500 million people on Earth. There are now over seven billion. Population is shooting up because the birth rate (the number of people being born in every 1,000) is higher than the death rate (the number of people dying in every 1,000). The death rate has dropped dramatically with advances in medicine and technology.

Finding a level

Population scientists, called demographers, predict that attempts to control population will eventually have an effect. They suggest the world's population total will reach 11 billion people by around 2100, then perhaps begin to level off.

Over and under

The world's population is not spread out evenly. Some areas are overpopulated, with not enough food, water or work for everyone. Other areas, such as the French countryside, are underpopulated, as young people leave the towns and villages for the big cities.

Population density

Population density is the number of people living in a given amount of space. It is measured in people per sq km or sq mile. For example, Mongolia (a big country with a small population) has a low population density of less than two people per sq km (five people per sq mile).

Internet links

To find out what the world's population was at the time of your birth and to explore how population growth affects the Earth, go to **www.usborne.com/quicklinks**

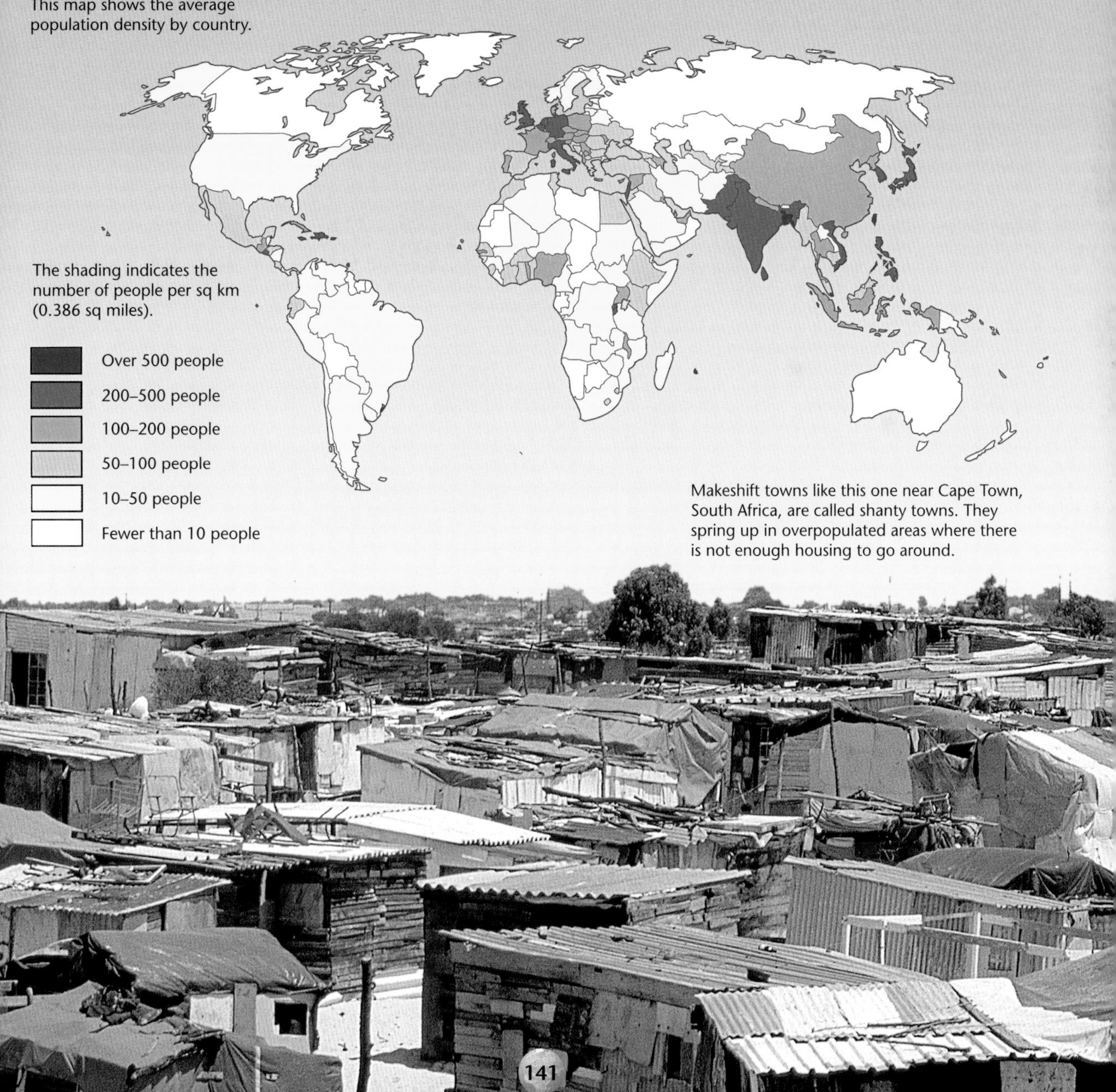

This map shows the average population density by country.

The shading indicates the number of people per sq km (0.386 sq miles).

- Over 500 people
- 200–500 people
- 100–200 people
- 50–100 people
- 10–50 people
- Fewer than 10 people

Makeshift towns like this one near Cape Town, South Africa, are called shanty towns. They spring up in overpopulated areas where there is not enough housing to go around.

MOVING AROUND

People have been moving from one part of the world to another for thousands of years. We travel for relaxation, to find food or better jobs, to escape from danger and poverty, and to transport goods around the globe.

This picture shows Haitian refugees sailing on a rickety boat to the U.S.A. They are fleeing Haiti for economic and political reasons, and hope that the U.S.A. will let them in.

Migration

A large number of people moving from one place to another is called a migration. The word migration is usually used to describe a permanent change of home, but it can also refer to seasonal and daily journeys. People may move within a city or country, or between countries. Many people migrate to places that have better jobs and opportunities, better schools for their children, or a better climate. Advantages like these are known as pull factors.

Forced to move

Sometimes people leave their homes because of negative factors, or push factors, such as war or low wages. People may be forced out because they are being attacked for their ethnic origin or political views. People who have been forced to find a new place to live are often called refugees (because they are seeking refuge, or safety).

Nomads

Some groups of people have a lifestyle which involves constantly moving around. This is called a nomadic lifestyle. Traditional nomads make their living from hunting and gathering or herding. For example, the !Kung San* people of southern Africa move around to find food and water, while the Sami* people of Lapland follow the seasonal migrations of the reindeer. There are also commercial nomads who make a living from trade and entertainment.

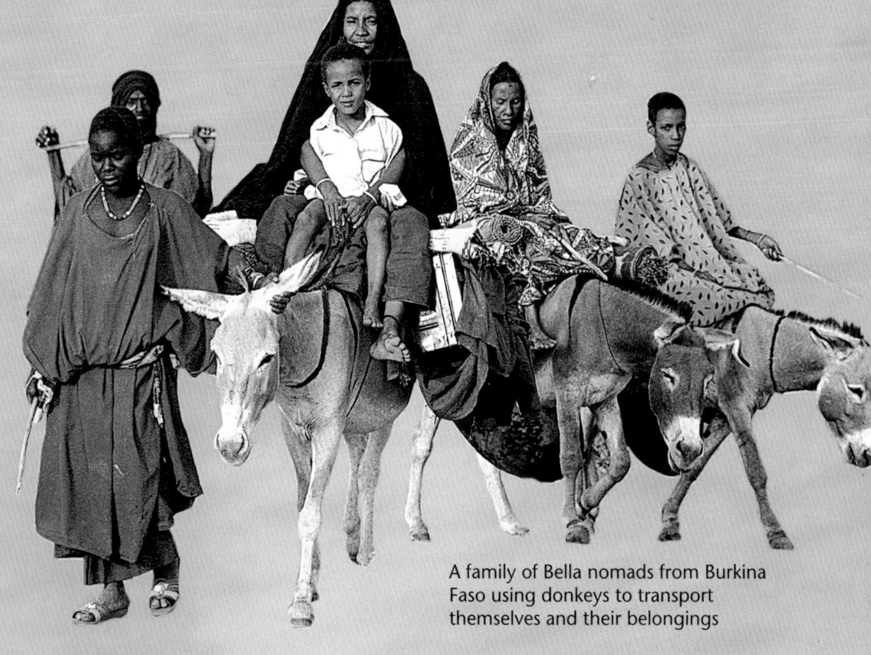

A family of Bella nomads from Burkina Faso using donkeys to transport themselves and their belongings

Right to enter

Most people have an identity card or passport showing which country they belong to. A passport allows you to travel out of and back into your country. Some countries will only let you cross their border if you also have a visa, which shows you have been given permission to be there for a certain period of time.

Internet links

For links to websites where you can find out why people have left their homes in search of a new life in another country and learn more about nomadic people who make their living from hunting and gathering or herding, go to **www.usborne.com/quicklinks**

These children are descendents of American soldiers in Vietnam. They are waiting for visas so that they can travel to the U.S.A.

*!Kung San, 243; Sami, 225

SETTLEMENTS

Most people in the world live in groups of houses, apartments, huts or tents. These groups are known as settlements. There are two main kinds of settlements: rural settlements, such as farms, hamlets and villages, and urban settlements, which are towns and cities.

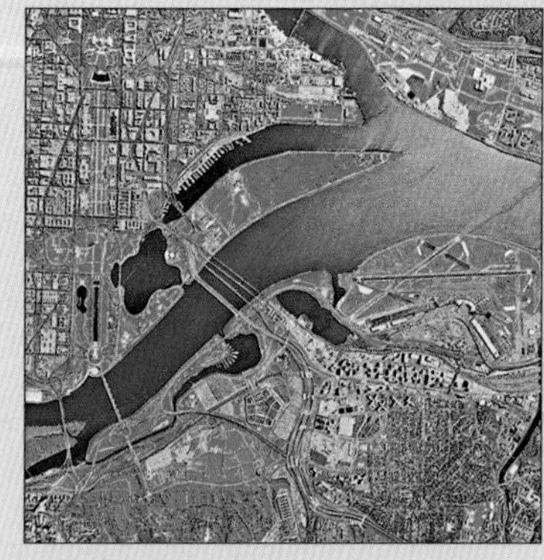

A satellite view of Washington D.C., capital of the U.S.A., which began as a small settlement by the Potomac River

Choosing a site

When people first looked for permanent places to settle, it was very important to choose a site that had nearby water and fuel supplies, fertile land and shelter from strong winds. Today, people also choose sites for political, social or economic reasons.

Good situations

Whether or not a settlement grows can depend on its situation in the surrounding area. Good situations for growth have tended to be near river mouths, in gaps in ranges of hills and at crossroads. In these areas it is easy for people to meet and trade with one another, so settlements in such places usually do well.

Fulfilling functions

Every settlement fulfils certain functions for the people who live there, and for those who live in the surrounding area. A settlement's functions can include providing housing, employment and services such as hospitals, schools and public transportation.

The site of this village in Sudan, East Africa, may have been chosen because it has nearby wood supplies for cooking and building.

Rural and urban

Rural settlements usually have smaller populations than urban settlements and cover smaller areas. Most of the people who live in rural settlements are employed in rural activities, such as farming or forestry, whereas people in urban settlements have a wider variety of jobs. Urban settlements are also more likely to be on good transportation routes.

Services

Urban settlements usually provide more goods and services than rural settlements. A village is likely to have only very basic services and will probably only serve the few hundred people living there. Geographers call small settlements with few services low-order settlements.

A town usually has many stores, businesses and special services such as banks and hospitals. As well as serving the thousands of people living there, it may serve people in surrounding rural areas. Large settlements with lots of services are known as high-order settlements.

Many urban settlements have shops and markets which offer a wide range of goods. This food market is in Hong Kong.

Internet links

Find information about different kinds of settlements by visiting the websites suggested online at **www.usborne.com/quicklinks**

TOWNS AND CITIES

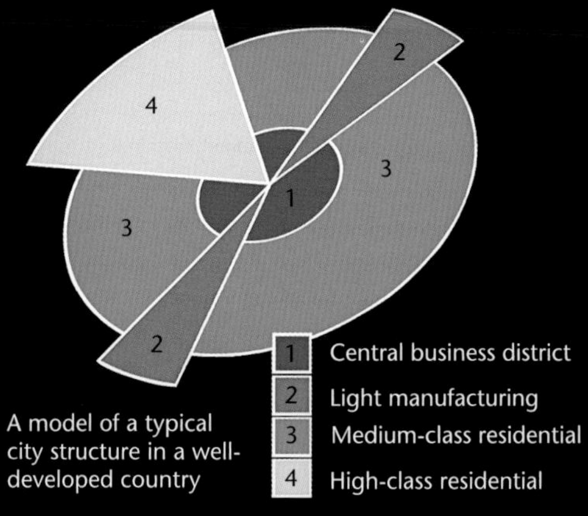

A model of a typical city structure in a well-developed country

Today, more people live in towns and cities than in the countryside and the numbers are increasing all the time as people move in search of jobs. This process of city growth is called urbanization.

Megacities

Some cities have so many people living in them that they are known as megacities. Megacities have populations of more than ten million people. They are formed when people from rural areas move to one or two urban areas in their country.

Geographers predict that these megacities will continue to grow. Mexico City, for example, has an estimated population of over 20 million people, although it's difficult to get accurate figures and the population changes rapidly. Most of the world's biggest cities are in less developed countries*.

Growing cities

As the population of a city grows, so does the size of the city itself. Eventually, towns and cities may merge and become one huge urban area, called a conurbation.

*Less developed countries, 152

City structure

Different parts of towns and cities usually have different functions. For example, in one part of a town you may find shopping areas, offices and banks. This is called the central business district (CBD), and is generally found in the middle of a city.

Another part of town may be mainly made up of housing, and yet another may be industrial. Many cities have industrial areas lining the major roads that lead out of the city.

This view of Atlanta, U.S.A., shows the busy roads leading in and out of the city.

Problems in cities

As urban populations continue to grow, towns and cities are faced with problems such as overcrowding, homelessness and pollution from industry and traffic. Housing shortages are a particular problem in poorer countries. Many people who move from the countryside to cities cannot find anywhere to live. They build huts from whatever they can find, usually on the outskirts of cities. Whole makeshift towns, called shanty towns, have grown up in this way. Some governments have tried to improve shanty towns by adding electricity, running water and sewage systems.

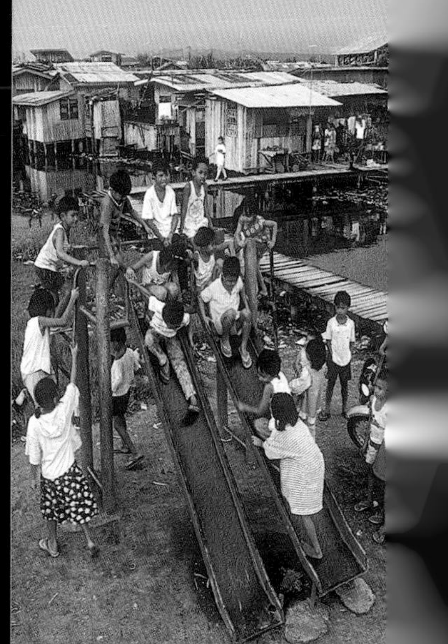

This shanty town in the Philippines has been improved by building a children's playground.

Internet links

Visit the websites recommended at **www.usborne.com/quicklinks** to find out about the inhabitants, histories and customs of some of the world's most famous cities. You can also find information about how modern megacities developed during different periods of history.

EARNING A LIVING

Most of the people in the world have to work to survive and support their families. As well as providing an income for their own families, the jobs most people do create wealth for their countries through taxes.

Working the land

Billions of people live by growing crops or raising animals. Some have small farms, while others move around with their herds of animals. They usually keep some of their produce for themselves, and sell the rest to make money to buy other things.

Working for wages

As the world becomes more industrialized and modern technology develops, more and more people are employed in paid jobs on big farms, in factories and mines, or in service industries* such as banking. Others are self-employed, which means they have their own businesses selling goods or services to other people.

Internet links

You can find out about the problems facing children around the world who work for a living, and read about some possible solutions, by following the links at **www.usborne.com/quicklinks**

A worker in a steel factory in Germany. Steel is important in industry because it is used to make tools, machinery and vehicles. Jobs like this that involve processing steel or other materials are called secondary jobs.

*Service industries, 151

In small factories, like this glass factory in Bangladesh, people still do many tasks by hand that would be done by machines in larger factories. This woman is inspecting glass containers.

Working conditions

Most countries have laws to protect workers. For example, they make sure workplaces are safe and make it illegal for young children to work. Some places have a minimum wage and maximum working hours. However, millions of people are very poor because they are paid too little for their work. In some parts of the world, children still work in factories and down mines to make enough money for their families to survive.

This mechanic is checking the engine of a jet plane to ensure that it is in good working order. Jobs like this that involve servicing products, transporting them or helping other people are called tertiary jobs.

Types of jobs

Geographers divide jobs into four main types:
Primary jobs involve obtaining raw materials from the Earth, e.g. mining, farming, fishing.
Secondary jobs involve making things out of raw materials, e.g. building, making cloth in a factory.
Tertiary jobs provide services for people, business and industry, e.g. hotel management, transporting goods.
Quaternary jobs provide information resources, e.g. accountancy, computing, property-development.

MANUFACTURING AND SERVICES

Making new products is called manufacturing. There are many different kinds of manufacturing industries, such as making clothes and making cars. People who work in service industries are doing or supplying something for other people, such as teaching and providing banking services.

Energy production is an example of a manufacturing industry. This power plant produces energy for homes and factories.

Heavy and light industries

The materials that are used to make new products are called raw materials. If an industry uses a large amount of heavy raw materials, such as coal and iron ore, it is known as a heavy industry. For example, ship-building is a heavy industry. Light industries use fewer raw materials and make products that are easy to transport.

This machine is being used to mine lignite, which will be used as fuel by industries close to the mining site.

Choosing a location

Today, most manufacturing companies make goods in factories. When a company builds a new factory, it has to choose its location carefully. Most factories are built near transportation links, so that they are accessible for workers and goods, and raw materials can be moved easily. Heavy industries tend to have factories near ports, as it is cheaper to transport heavy goods by ship. Heavy industries also need to be close to the source of their bulky raw materials, to reduce transport costs.

Footloose industries

Light industries, such as electronics companies, are often located near airports or major roads, so that they can transport their goods easily.

However, unlike heavy industries, they do not have to be close to their raw materials. Because light industries are more flexible about where they locate, they are also sometimes known as footloose industries.

Services

There are many different kinds of services, such as healthcare, transportation, tourism and retail. Many of these services are located in the central zones of towns and cities, where they are easily accessible to their customers and workers. However, if the land in a town becomes too expensive, people may build out-of-town shopping areas.

This is the sign for a motel in the U.S.A. Many of the people who work in the service industry have jobs in hotels, motels and restaurants.

Service jobs

In richer countries, many more people work in services than in manufacturing. This is because most of the work in manufacturing is now done by machines. However, service industries still need huge numbers of people. In poorer countries there are often only a few basic services available, so people have to do most things for themselves.

Computers at work

Many service jobs are now being done with the help of computers. For example, more and more train tickets are sold by computerized machines instead of by people. Computers speed things up and make people's jobs easier to do.

Internet links

Visit **www.usborne.com/quicklinks** for links to websites where you can learn more about industry and manufacturing in different countries around the world.

RICH AND POOR

Standards of living vary greatly around the world. Over 80% of the world's wealth is owned by 10% of its people. Most of this wealth is concentrated in Europe and North America. By contrast, many people in southern African countries live in total poverty.

There is poverty in wealthy countries as well as poorer ones. These people are homeless. They are sheltering under a bridge in Hamburg, Germany.

A Vietnamese businessman talking on a mobile phone and standing beside an expensive car. Ownership of cars and phones is often used as a measure of wealth.

Development

Development is about improving the conditions in a country or region. Poorer countries are known as less developed countries and richer countries as more developed countries. The less developed countries are mostly in the tropics and southern hemisphere.

Some poorer countries, such as Brazil, Mexico and Argentina, have recently increased wealth and improved standards of living through the development of modern industries. These are called newly industrialized countries.

Living in poverty

Poverty isn't just about having little money. In some countries many people lack basic resources such as food and safe drinking water. They may not be able to get a job or an education and may only have access to the most basic healthcare, so life expectancy is low. Many richer countries have some people living in poverty too.

Measuring development

Development can be measured in different ways. Sometimes a country's GNP, or gross national product, is used. This is the value of goods and services produced by a country. However, this only gives an indication of a country's wealth. An organization called the United Nations has studied the standard of living in different countries and has devised a system called the Human Development Index which considers other factors, such as life expectancy and education. These give us an idea of people's quality of life.

Internet links

Visit **www.usborne.com/quicklinks** to find out about the United Nations (U.N.), an international organization working for peace and development. Read about current food crises and international aid efforts to alleviate poverty and hunger.

Causes of poverty

Regions can be poor for many reasons. One main cause of poverty is the exploitation of certain countries by more powerful countries. Wars can also increase poverty. As well as killing and injuring people, they lead to the destruction of buildings and resources and interrupt food production and distribution.

Some countries have problems transporting people, food and goods, because of the long distances to remote places. Others suffer from natural hazards like floods and droughts. All these things can increase poverty.

This porter, in India, is carrying a tourist up a mountain. In some countries, jobs in tourism pay better than other jobs, but many people are still not paid fair wages or fees for their work.

A SMALL WORLD

With the invention of new, fast forms of transportation and communication, people often say that the world is getting smaller. This is because getting from place to place and sending messages is quicker and easier than ever before.

Satellites in space have greatly improved communication speed. This is the DIRECTV 1-R satellite. It picks up radio, TV and telephone signals from one part of the Earth and relays them to other parts of the globe.

Like many forms of transportation, trains are becoming faster. This is a magnetic suspension train developed in Germany. It uses magnetic forces to travel at high speeds.

Transportation and trade

Moving people and things from place to place is now one of the world's biggest industries. Millions of people have jobs building cars, planes, trains, trucks and ships, and transporting goods from one country to another.

If people want to transport things over long distances, the quickest way is usually by plane. However, heavy or bulky goods are generally carried by truck, train or boat. This takes longer but is much cheaper.

Globalization

People are now able to organize industry on a worldwide scale. This is called globalization. It means that companies in one part of the world can get materials or employ workers in another part of the world, often because they are cheaper or there are specialist skills or facilities there.

This may enable poorer countries to attract investment. But it can lead to exploitation, with companies profiting from the workforces and resources of poorer countries without paying a fair price.

Hong Kong's port, shown here with the Central Island district in the background, is very important to the city's success in international trade.

Communication

With satellite communication and the internet, information can be relayed quickly to a huge number of people. People can work from home via online computers and have video conferences with people on the other side of the world. Some people argue that a negative effect of this is that certain cultures become dominant and that local traditions are lost as people follow similar lifestyles.

Global tourism

Tourism is one of the world's fastest-growing industries. Over 600 million trips abroad are made by tourists each year. The sudden growth of tourism can damage the environment and culture of an area, and benefits may not be spread evenly. However, in some places people are developing sustainable tourism which addresses these problems.

Isolated areas

People around the world are not affected equally by improvements in transportation and communication. Africa has about 1% of the world's online computers, while North America has over 40%. In poorer countries, the roads are often in bad repair and few people have cars. Physical isolation often causes poverty because it makes trade and development difficult.

Internet links

To find out more about communication today, including how the internet and satellites work, and how goods are transported around the world, follow the links at **www.usborne.com/quicklinks**

In many parts of the world people use animals to transport heavy loads. This is a bullock cart in Thailand.

GLOBAL CITIZENSHIP

Global citizenship is about being interested in the wider world and thinking about the ways that different countries affect one another. It involves people everywhere becoming aware of global issues, such as poverty, the environment and human rights.

This boy is collecting safe water from a pump funded by a charity called Wateraid.

Giving aid

An important part of being a global citizen is wanting to help people in other countries. People in richer countries sometimes try to help poorer countries to develop by giving aid. This may be money, food, equipment or expert help from engineers and teachers.

However, it is not only richer countries that give aid. Poorer countries often help other countries in times of emergency, such as after a flood or an earthquake.

Kinds of aid

There are two main kinds of aid. Short-term aid may involve sending supplies to help a country after an emergency. Long-term aid aims to improve the quality of life of people in poorer countries, for example, through building and healthcare projects.

There can be problems with giving aid, such as countries becoming dependent on aid, or money not reaching the people who need help. Sometimes, in return for aid, rich countries make poorer countries promise to buy goods from them, even if they could buy them more cheaply elsewhere.

These children are protesting against the killing of whales. They are part of an international action group called "Kids for Whales", organized by Greenpeace.

Internet links

Go to **www.usborne.com/quicklinks** and follow the links to find out about the lives of children around the world. You can also learn about some of the latest global aid issues, too.

Human rights

A vital part of being a global citizen is believing that everyone has the same right to food, water, education, health, security and justice. People may choose to work for human rights by campaigning about a particular issue. However, it's important that they are well informed about the complexities of the situation and the effects of their actions.

The environment

Environmental problems not only affect the country which causes them, they can affect the whole world. For example, burning fossil fuels or chopping down trees in one country can lead to global warming*.

Being a global citizen is about learning how to take care of the world. Many people do this by joining environmental organizations, or by changing their lifestyles to help the environment, for example by using trains or buses instead of cars, or by recycling household waste.

This boy is protesting against French nuclear tests on Cook Island, in the Pacific.

*Global warming, 102

American football fans wave pom-poms at the Rose Bowl stadium, Los Angeles, California

PEOPLES OF
NORTH AMERICA

NORTH AMERICA

The name "North America" can be used to mean several different things. In this book, the northern part of the American continent begins with Panama in the south and stretches up to Canada and Greenland in the north. It includes the U.S.A., Mexico, Central America and the Caribbean.

This carved, painted pillar is part of a totem pole. Some Native American groups used these as community symbols or in memory of someone who had died.

Native Americans

Native Americans are the people who lived in North America before European explorers arrived. Each Native American group had its own lifestyles and customs and was governed by a chief.

In the 19th century, the European settlers forced Native Americans to live on areas of land called reservations and tried to force them to adopt European lifestyles. Many Native American traditions were forgotten. Now languages are being revived and Native Americans make and sell traditional pottery, baskets or textiles. However, people also lead modern lifestyles – for example some groups run casinos.

Internet links

Visit the websites recommended at **www.usborne.com/quicklinks** to explore more about the traditions, culture and music of Native Americans. You can also learn about different Native American languages.

This modern Native American is wearing traditional clothes, reflecting the interest in reviving traditional culture. But the Christian monument he is leaning against is a sign of the influence of European culture.

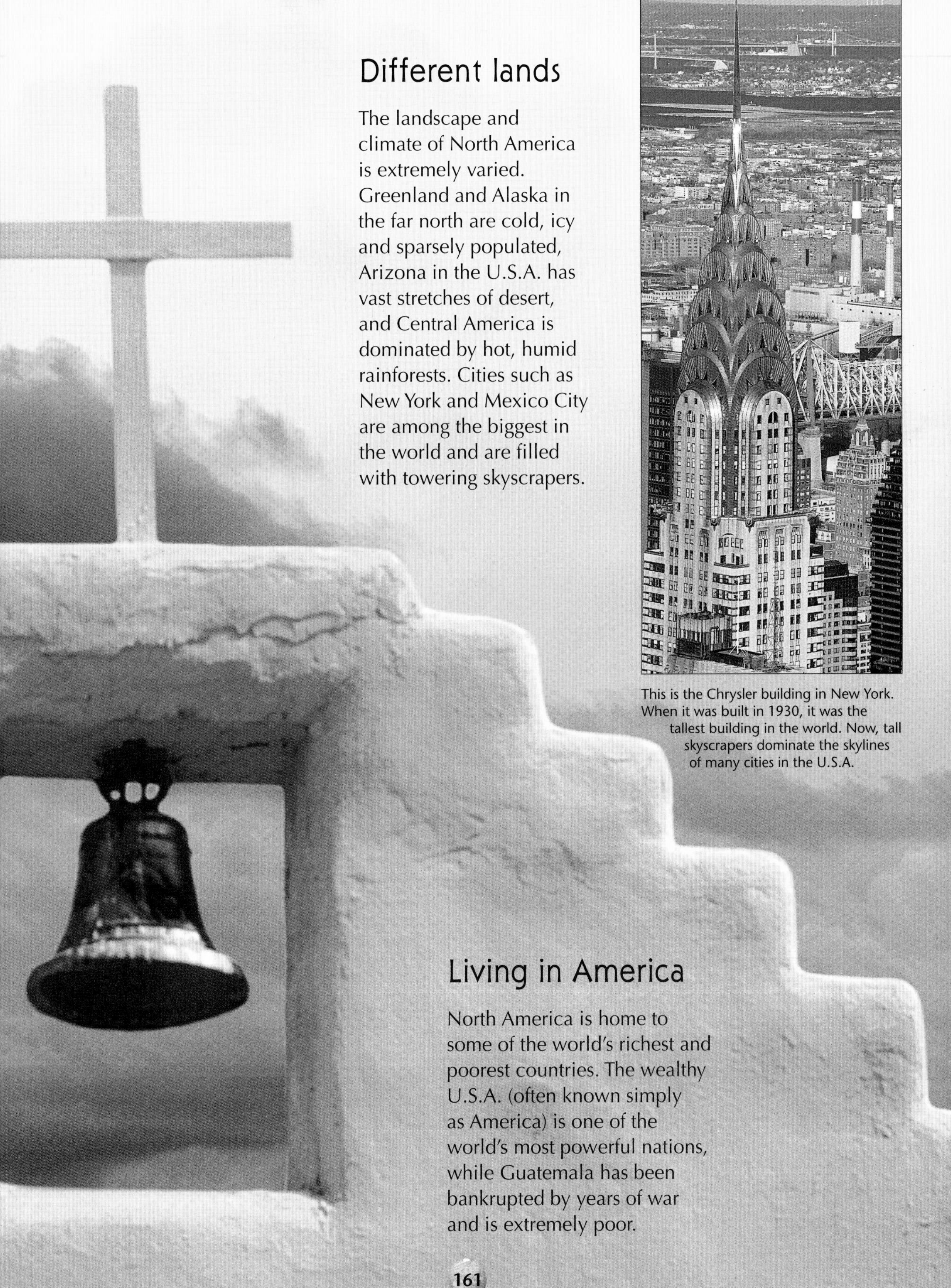

Different lands

The landscape and climate of North America is extremely varied. Greenland and Alaska in the far north are cold, icy and sparsely populated, Arizona in the U.S.A. has vast stretches of desert, and Central America is dominated by hot, humid rainforests. Cities such as New York and Mexico City are among the biggest in the world and are filled with towering skyscrapers.

This is the Chrysler building in New York. When it was built in 1930, it was the tallest building in the world. Now, tall skyscrapers dominate the skylines of many cities in the U.S.A.

Living in America

North America is home to some of the world's richest and poorest countries. The wealthy U.S.A. (often known simply as America) is one of the world's most powerful nations, while Guatemala has been bankrupted by years of war and is extremely poor.

THE U.S.A.

The United States of America, also known as the U.S.A. or America, is a huge country, although it's not much more than half the size of Russia, the biggest country in the world. The U.S.A. is very rich and has immense political and cultural influence worldwide.

The U.S.A. has hundreds of large theme parks with huge rides like this roller coaster.

Land and law

The U.S.A. is divided into 50 states. Power is shared between state governments and a central federal government based in the capital, Washington D.C. The southern states are warm, green and rich in oil, while the main farming areas are in the western states. The northeast is the main business region. Manufacturing has moved more to the southern states in recent years. Many computer companies are located in Silicon Valley in California.

The 'American Dream'

People from all over the world have moved to the U.S.A., and a million new immigrants arrive each year. Many are following the 'American Dream': the belief that, in America, anyone can become rich and successful. However, many Americans are still very poor.

The mixture of peoples gives the U.S.A. a rich, diverse culture. Jazz and blues music, for instance, developed out of rhythms brought to the U.S.A. from Africa, while cheesecake and bagels were originally Jewish foods.

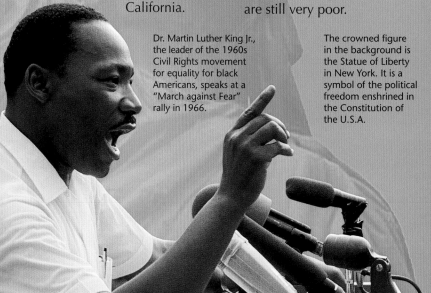

Dr. Martin Luther King Jr., the leader of the 1960s Civil Rights movement for equality for black Americans, speaks at a "March against Fear" rally in 1966.

The crowned figure in the background is the Statue of Liberty in New York. It is a symbol of the political freedom enshrined in the Constitution of the U.S.A.

Internet links

Visit **www.usborne.com/quicklinks** for links to websites where you can learn about America's history, listen to songs and explore different states. Read about historical events in the U.S.A. and about the structure of the U.S. government, too.

Science and power

The U.S.A. is the leading political world power, and science and technology have played an important part in its success. Nuclear science, which can be used to make powerful bombs, has helped give the U.S.A. political strength. As a result, the U.S.A. now plays a big part in making wars and keeping peace around the world. The nation's wealth and success also owe a lot to computer science, and the U.S.A. dominates internet technology. American English is the main language of the internet.

Entertainment

Entertainment is big business in the U.S.A. The country's main movie-making area, Hollywood, in California, produces films that can cost many millions of dollars to make, but which earn even more. Theme parks are also very popular.

Minnie Mouse posing for a photo with a young boy in Disney World, a theme park based on famous characters from the cartoons of Walt Disney

The reusable Space Shuttle spacecraft is part of America's world-famous multi-billion dollar space exploration industry.

THE FAR NORTH

In Canada, people ski in resorts where there are ski lifts and other facilities, but people also ski cross country just to get from place to place.

The far north of North America is taken up by Greenland, Canada and Alaska (part of the U.S.A.). This is a vast area: Canada is the second largest country in the world, and Greenland is the world's biggest island.

Many cultures

Canada is divided into ten provinces and three territories: the Yukon, Nunavut and the Northwest Territories.

Many Canadians have British, French or Native American ancestors and the offical languages are French and English. French culture is strong in the province of Quebec where cafes and shops reflect its influence.

Skiers swoop down a slope in Banff National Park, Alberta, Canada. Many tourists visit Canada for its natural beauty and outdoor activities.

Natural resources

Most Canadians live in large cities along the border with the U.S.A. The rest of the country has a varied landscape, including lakes, mountains, forests and grasslands, or prairies. These provide rich natural resources such as timber, water power, gas, oil and minerals. Outside the cities, many people's jobs are based around mining and forestry.

Winter sports

Outdoor sports and activities such as canoeing, riding horses and rafting are popular in Canada. But the country is particularly known for its winter sports, especially ice hockey which can be played on frozen ponds and lakes.

Snowmobiling at a winter sports festival in Canada

Greenland

Although Greenland is the world's largest island, its population is very small because conditions there are so harsh. Most of Greenland lies within the Arctic Circle, and its central region is covered by a layer of ice that never melts.

The island has a small road network, but planes and dog sleds provide a flexible and reliable way of getting around. The majority of Greenlanders live along the coast, where the climate is mildest, making a living from catching fish, shrimps and seals.

Villages in Greenland are small. This one has about 500 human residents and 2,000 sled dogs, which are used for hunting and transportation.

Internet links

Visit **www.usborne.com/quicklinks** for links to websites where you can take virtual trips around the Far North, and look at photographs of the region's landscape and wildlife. You can also explore Inuit culture and legends.

These Inuit people are wearing heavy animal-skin coats to keep warm.

Inuit people

The Inuit are the native people of northern Canada. In 1999, the Canadian government made part of the Northwest Territories into a new Inuit territory, giving back land which the Inuit had lost to settlers. The new territory is called Nunavut, which means "our land" in Inukitut, the Inuit language.

The Inuit keep their traditions alive by speaking Inukitut, hunting for food, and making wood and bone carvings. They also take advantage of modern technology, using snowmobiles, telephones and computers.

MEXICO

Mexico is a big country between the U.S.A. and Central America. It is very mountainous, but most Mexicans live in towns and cities in the middle of the country, where the land is flat.

A reconstruction of the Aztec calendar, on display in the National Museum of Anthropology in Mexico City

The Aztecs

From the early-14th century, Mexico was ruled by the Aztecs, a Native American people. They built an empire with a capital city called Tenochtitlan and ruled over many Native American peoples. The empire ended when the Spanish conquered Mexico in 1521. Today's Mexicans are mainly **mestizos**, of mixed Spanish and Native American descent.

Hot and spicy

Mexican food is popular all over the world. *Guacamole* (mashed avocados), *tortillas* (flat bread), and meat and beans cooked in tomato sauce with hot chillies* are typical Mexican dishes. Over 60 different kinds of chillies are grown in Mexico. In some areas, people eat salads made out of cactus plants.

Corn tortilla chips are eaten with Mexican-style dips around the world.

Mexico City

Mexico City, the capital of Mexico, was built directly over the ruins of the Aztec capital. Today, it is one of the world's biggest cities, with over 20 million people. The majority of the country's business is there, and the city is extremely busy, with lots of noise and traffic. It lies in a valley overlooked by volcanoes, and is regularly affected by earthquakes. The soil beneath it is so soft and swampy that the city sinks a little each year.

Tomatoes, chillies* and beans are key ingredients in many Mexican dishes.

*Chilies (U.S.A.)

Day of the Dead

The Day of the Dead is a joyous celebration that takes place on November 2 each year. All over Mexico, markets and shops sell skeletons and skulls made out of sugar or bread. People also dress up as skeletons and dance in huge parades. At home, families make small altars which they use to pray for and remember their dead friends and relatives. They decorate the altars with flowers, candles, food and photographs of those they want to remember.

Internet links

Go to **www.usborne.com/quicklinks** for links to websites where you can find out about the history of the Day of the Dead festival and see what items traditionally make up the altars. There are also links to websites where you can discover more about the religion, culture and everyday life of the ancient Aztecs.

This skeleton model has been made from papier-mâché for a Day of the Dead parade.

CENTRAL AMERICA

These girls are dressed as angels to take part in a religious procession in El Salvador. Religious festivals are common in Central America.

Central America is the narrow strip of land, or isthmus, connecting North and South America. The landscape of Central America is mainly made up of mountains and volcanoes and people's lives are affected by frequent earthquakes and volcanic eruptions.

Takeover

The Spanish arrived in Central America 500 years ago, and many people living there today are of mixed Spanish and Native American descent. But each country has its own mix of peoples. As well as Native Americans and people of European descent, there are people of African descent along the Caribbean coast.

Land of the Maya

The Maya had a powerful empire around AD200–900, when they built great cities. The empire covered most of Guatemala, and parts of Belize, Mexico, Honduras and El Salvador. Ruined cities can still be found in the jungles of Guatemala. The Maya are no longer powerful, but they still make up nearly half of Guatemala's population.

This Mayan girl in Guatemala is carrying a younger child on her back, wrapped in a traditional Mayan shawl.

Internet links

For links to websites where you can find out more about Central America today, the ancient empire of the Mayans and the Panama Canal, go to **www.usborne.com/quicklinks**

The Soccer War

Central America has suffered from decades of civil wars and conflict between countries. One war broke out between El Salvador and Honduras in 1969, after they had played soccer against each other in the World Cup. The real reasons, however, were disagreements over land, trade, and Salvadorean refugees in Honduras.

These tiny dolls are worry dolls. Their clothes are made by wrapping thread around the bodies.

Worry dolls

Children in Central America sometimes make tiny, bright dolls called worry dolls. There is a legend that if they tell the dolls their worries at night and then place them under their pillows, by morning all their worries will have disappeared.

The Panama Canal

The Panama Canal is one of the most important waterways in the world. It is a channel of water around 65km (40 miles) long that cuts through Panama, linking the Atlantic Ocean with the Pacific Ocean. Each vessel that uses the canal must pay a fee according to its weight. This means that while ships pay thousands of dollars, Richard Halliburton, who swam through the canal in 1928, only paid 36 cents.

Rainforest life

A large area of Central America is covered by rainforest, which is home to a huge variety of plants and animals. But the rainforest is being devastated and many plants and animals may die out as trees are cut down to make timber for export, and to clear land for farming.

A thatched bohio, or hut, in a rainforest clearing in Panama. Huts like these are the homes of the Guaymi people, who live on the border between Panama and Costa Rica.

THE CARIBBEAN

The Caribbean is the name given to the chain of hundreds of tropical islands stretching from North America to South America across the Caribbean Sea.

Slavery

From around 1500, Europeans fought with each other over possession of the Caribbean islands. They brought slaves from Africa, the Middle East, the Far East and India to work on sugar, tobacco and cocoa plantations. Many of today's inhabitants are descendants of these slaves. Languages from around the world have combined to form unique regional dialects known as *creoles*.

Tourism

The Caribbean islands are known for their white sandy beaches, clear blue sea and tropical sunshine. Their beauty and isolation has given them a reputation of being a "paradise on earth". As a result, tourism is one of the Caribbean's most important industries.

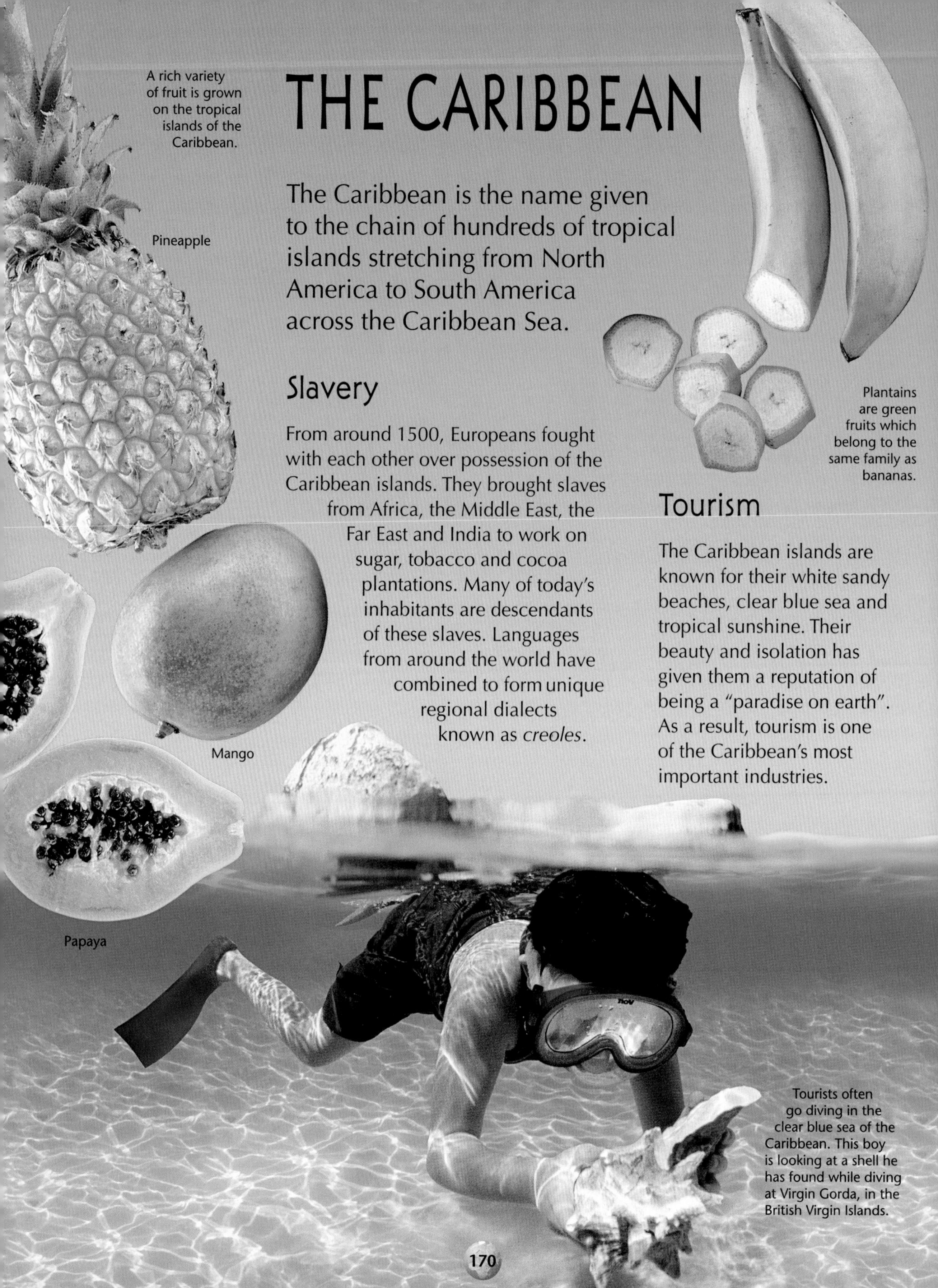

A rich variety of fruit is grown on the tropical islands of the Caribbean.

Pineapple

Mango

Papaya

Plantains are green fruits which belong to the same family as bananas.

Tourists often go diving in the clear blue sea of the Caribbean. This boy is looking at a shell he has found while diving at Virgin Gorda, in the British Virgin Islands.

Hard work

Although the Caribbean may be seen as a paradise by people who go there as tourists, life is not always easy for its inhabitants. Many of those who do not work in the tourist industry make a living growing sugar cane, the Caribbean's main export, and other crops such as bananas, coffee and tobacco. Some of the poorest countries, such as Haiti, suffer from severe unemployment. Many Haitians have to cross the border into the wealthier Dominican Republic to find work.

Music

Africa has had an important influence on the music of the Caribbean. Many Caribbean musical styles, such as reggae, conga, cha-cha-cha, plena and calypso, have African roots. Calypso, which originated in Trinidad, is the music style most associated with the Caribbean. Calypso songs are often improvised and tend to focus on social and political subjects.

Street parties

Carnivals held to mark religious festivals are an important part of island life. The main carnival season takes place before Lent (the period of 40 days leading up to Easter in the Christian calendar). The streets are filled with parades, loud music, and people singing and dancing in bright costumes.

Junkanoo is a huge festival in the Bahamas. People make flamboyant costumes like this to take part in parades.

Internet links

To explore the different Caribbean islands and read some accounts of their history, geography, climate and people, follow the links at **www.usborne.com/quicklinks**

A busy outdoor market in Zumbahua, Ecuador

PEOPLES OF SOUTH AMERICA

SOUTH AMERICA

The people of South America have a huge range of origins. Over the centuries, settlers have arrived from Europe, Africa and Asia to join the Native Americans who have lived there for thousands of years.

A pair of condors flying high in the Andes, the mountain range that runs most of the length of South America

Empty and crowded

Much of South America is covered in rainforest, mountains and deserts where it can be hard to survive. Many people live in small villages and work as farmers. Yet along the coast are some of the world's biggest cities, with towering skyscrapers and crowded shanty towns.

Internet links

Visit the websites recommended at **www.usborne.com/quicklinks** to find out about the lifestyles of modern South American people. You can read about life in the heart of the Peruvian Andes and learn about the ancient cultures of South America, too.

The Inca people had a powerful empire in South America around 500 years ago. This watchtower is part of Inca ruins at Machu Picchu, in the Andes mountains.

Native Americans

Experts think the first South Americans came from Asia. They probably walked across a strip of land in the north that once joined what are now Russia and Alaska. Their descendants now live mostly in South America's mountainous countries, such as Colombia, Bolivia, Ecuador and Peru.

Religions

Over 90% of the people in South America are Roman Catholics. This form of Christianity was introduced by Spanish and Portuguese invaders who took control of the continent in the 1500s.

Many South Americans also worship traditional Native American or African gods and spirits. Some traditional religions have priests called shamans, who are believed to have magical powers.

Latin languages

South America is sometimes called Latin America, because most South Americans speak the Latin-based languages Spanish and Portuguese. These were brought by the European invaders. However, many people speak Native American languages, such as Quechua and Aymara.

Christian festivals are important to many South Americans. This Brazilian pilgrim is carrying a cross in an Easter procession in Jerusalem.

IN THE MOUNTAINS

The vast Andes mountain range snakes down the western side of South America, through Colombia, Ecuador, Peru, Bolivia, Chile and Argentina. Despite dangers from volcanoes and earthquakes, the Andes are home to millions of miners, farmers, craftspeople and city-dwellers.

This young boy from Ecuador is harnessing a llama to lead it to market.

Fertile farms

The peaks of the Andes are covered in snow, but the lower slopes are good for growing crops. Mountain farmers grow corn, coffee and other crops on small plots of land, sometimes with terraces to stop the soil from being washed away. If the land is not good enough for crops, they keep herds of mountain animals, such as llamas and alpacas, which provide milk and wool, and which may also be used to transport goods.

Craft work

Many Native Americans live in villages in the Andes. Some earn a living from traditional crafts. They weave brightly striped shawls, blankets and hats. These are used by local people as well as being sold to tourists and exported around the world.

A traditional mountain folk band playing for tourists in Machu Picchu, Peru

Cities

The Andes has some large cities, including Colombia's capital, Bogota, and La Paz, one of Bolivia's two capitals (the other is Sucre). Most city-dwellers work in factories or mines. In the mountains there are huge deposits of gold, copper, tin, coal and jewels, especially emeralds. The biggest emerald mines are in Muzo, Colombia. While mine workers use modern machinery to extract the emeralds, poor *Guaqueros* (or "treasure hunters") sift through the dust and rubble, hoping to find leftover gems.

Inca influence

The Tahuantinsuyo, also known as the Incas, once ruled a large area of western South America. Their reign ended 400 years ago, but they still influence the Andean countries today.

Quechua, the Inca language, is spoken by about 13 million people. Mountain farmers use terraces that were built by the Incas, and ruined Inca cities, such as Machu Picchu in Peru, are tourist attractions.

This Peruvian girl in traditional costume is one of the Quechua people, who are descended from the Incas.

Internet links

Follow the website links at **www.usborne.com/quicklinks** to learn about the Inca trail and the fascinating ruins of Machu Picchu. You can also take a tour of the majestic Andes.

This is a view over La Paz, Bolivia. At over 3,650m (12,000ft), it is the world's highest capital city.

RAINFOREST PEOPLES

South America's huge Amazon valley is covered in millions of square miles of thick, humid rainforest. The Amazon rainforest is so big that it contains over a third of the world's trees. For thousands of years, it has also been the home of Native American peoples.

Leaders of the Kayapo people of Brazil sometimes wear lip-plates like this which emphasize their roles as public speakers.

Traditional lives

The rainforest is so vast that groups of people living in it have been cut off from the rest of the world for centuries. Some have only recently been discovered by outsiders. There may be others who have never had contact with the outside world. Rainforest peoples such as the Jivaro, Txikao and Kayapo have their own languages and customs. But many of them share similar lifestyles, surviving by hunting animals, gathering fruits and nuts, and growing crops in forest clearings.

Losing lifestyles

As new roads are built into the rainforest, the people who live there have more contact with outsiders. They may even lose their homes when parts of the rainforest are cut down. To make a living, they may have to learn more widely spoken languages or move away from the forest into towns and cities, leaving their old traditions and lifestyles behind.

Internet links

Visit the websites suggested at **www.usborne.com/quicklinks** to discover the unique lifestyles and cultures of some of the peoples of the Amazon. You can also explore the Amazon rainforest and river.

This man playing a wooden flute is one of the Jivaro people of the Amazon.

Clearing the forest

Rainforest trees provide all kinds of useful products, such as brazil nuts, cashew nuts, wax and rubber. At one time these things were simply collected from the forest, but now they are mostly farmed on plantations.

Traditionally, rainforest peoples cleared small areas of land to grow crops, and moved on after a few years. Because the cleared areas were tiny, this method, called shifting agriculture, did not harm much of the forest, and the trees eventually grew back. But since the 1960s, more rainforest has been cut down, for timber and to make space for farms, mines and factories. So the amount of rainforest is decreasing.

These are rainforest plants in Ecuador. Many rainforest plants can be used to make medicines.

Forest food

Although most rainforest peoples grow crops, they can also find food in the rainforest. Hunting and fishing provide them with a wide range of meat, including monkeys, toucans and caimans, which are reptiles similar to alligators. The Piaroa people of Venezuela sometimes eat tarantulas (a type of spider), cooking them by squeezing their insides onto a leaf and baking it over a fire.

Many rainforest peoples grow just enough food to supply their village. This woman is processing locally-grown manioc (a plant a little like a potato) to make flour.

COMBINED CULTURES

South American culture is influenced by the traditions of the different types of people who live there. For example, many South Americans love soccer, which came from Europe; samba music from Africa; and foods that combine Spanish, African and Native American influences.

This Peruvian woman is preparing guinea pigs for roasting.

Party!

Carnivals and costume parades take place frequently all over South America. Most of them celebrate Christian festivals, such as Lent, Easter and Christmas. They are lively occasions, with plenty of loud music, dancing, dressing up, eating and drinking. Many cities, towns and villages also hold their own local religious or historical celebrations.

Delicious dishes

All kinds of foods are eaten in South America. Argentinians and Uruguayans eat lots of meat, and Bolivians have dozens of varieties of potatoes. A typical meal in the Andes consists of fried beef, beans, a fried egg, rice and a slice of avocado. This type of dish is called *churrasco* in Ecuador and *bandeja paisa* in Colombia. Local delicacies include *cuy* (guinea pig) and *hormiga culona* (fried ants) in Colombia, and iguana (a type of lizard) in Guyana.

These costumed dancers are taking part in a parade in Venezuela, held to mark the Catholic feast of Corpus Christi.

Soccer fever

Soccer is the biggest sport in South America, and national team members are heroes. Uruguay hosted and won the first ever soccer World Cup in 1930 and Argentina and Brazil have since won it several times each. Children play soccer in the streets all over South America. Most towns and villages have local teams, and even rainforest-dwellers have a patch of land set aside for soccer games.

> **Internet links**
> To find out more about South American culture, carnivals, music, foods and soccer, visit the links at **www.usborne.com/quicklinks**

These children are playing informal games of soccer by an old fort at Sacsahuaman, near Cusco in Peru.

African influence

Culture along the east coast of South America has a strong African element. People from West Africa arrived as slaves hundreds of years ago, to work in mines and on sugar plantations for the area's European rulers. Their beliefs, music and culture had an important influence, which is still present today. African rhythms blended with Spanish, Portuguese and Native American sounds to produce musical styles such as samba and salsa. Many Brazilians follow a spiritual religion called Candomblé, which is based on African traditions.

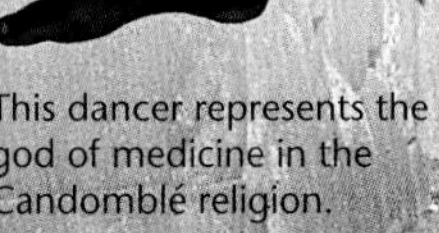

This dancer represents the god of medicine in the Candomblé religion.

BRAZIL

Brazil is the biggest country in South America. It contains most of the Amazon rainforest and also has some of the world's largest cities. In many ways it is a very modern country, with futuristic buildings and high-tech industries, but a lot of its people are still poor.

This 30m (100ft) high statue of Christ stands on Corcovado Hill above Rio de Janeiro. Its shape can be seen from far out at sea.

Portugal and Brazil

Unlike the rest of South America, Brazil was once ruled by Portugal, and its main language is Portuguese. This happened because just before 1500, news reached Europe that the Spanish had discovered lands not previously known to Europeans, which they called the "New World". Portugal wanted some of the land for itself, so the two countries agreed that Portugal could take over the eastern side of the continent. Brazil has been independent from Portugal since 1822.

Carnaval

Brazil is famous for its festivals, music and nightclubs. The most famous event is Carnaval (the Brazilian spelling of "carnival"). Carnaval celebrations are held all over Brazil every February or March, to mark the start of Lent.

The celebrations go on for five days, with feasting, dancing, a huge costume parade and samba competitions. Samba is a type of percussion music popular in Brazil. There are special samba schools where people can learn samba music and dancing.

A samba dancer twirls at Rio's famous Carnaval.

A new capital

In 1956 the Brazilian government began to build a new capital city, Brasilia. Brasilia was planned as a modern, hi-tech city and it is still known for its space-age buildings. It was designed to be fast and easy to drive around, so it had no traffic lights. But when people moved in, they complained that it was too hard to cross the roads, so the design was changed.

> **Internet links**
> To find out more about the history, culture and geography of Brazil, and see some famous Brazilian sites, visit the websites suggested at **www.usborne.com/quicklinks**

This is the Metropolitan Cathedral in Brasilia. It is a good example of the city's modern architecture.

Cities out of control

The populations of many of Brazil's cities, such as Sao Paulo and Rio de Janeiro, are rising fast as more and more people from rural areas arrive, looking for jobs and homes.

Often there is not enough housing for the new arrivals, and so shanty towns develop on the outskirts of cities. These are made up of makeshift houses built out of scrap metal and junk. The shanty towns are nicknamed *favelas* after a type of hillside flower.

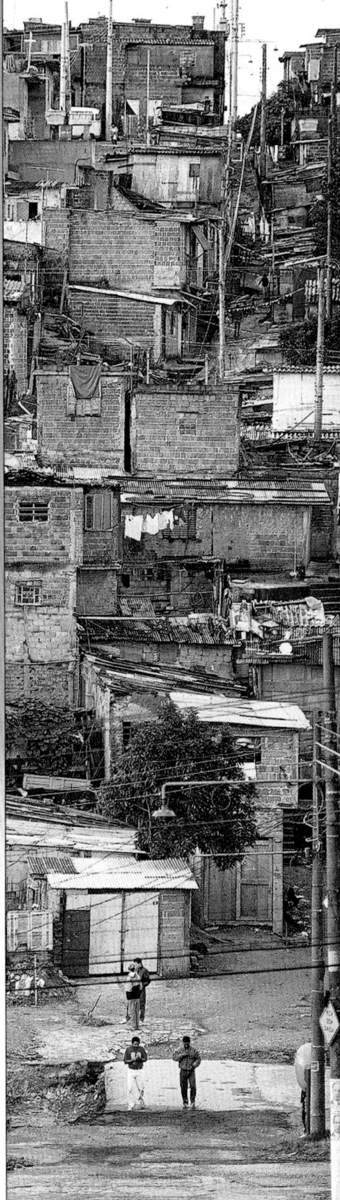

Shanty towns, like this one in Sao Paulo, often develop on hillsides, where the land is too steep to build bigger houses.

ARGENTINA

Argentina is the second biggest country in South America. It ranges from lakes and glaciers in the south, across flat grasslands, known as the Pampas, to mountains in the west and rainforest in the north. However, more than a third of the population lives in or around the capital city, Buenos Aires.

This is the Avenida 9 de Julio, Buenos Aires. It is the widest street in the world.

Invaders

The first people to live in Argentina were Native American groups who farmed the land. But then in 1516 a Spanish explorer named Juan de Solis arrived and claimed the land for the Spanish. The Spanish named the country Argentina, which means "Land of Silver", and ruled there until 1810.

This is La Boca, a district in Buenos Aires made up of brightly painted metal houses.

Buenos Aires

Around 12 million people live in Buenos Aires, making it one of the largest cities in the world. It is also Argentina's main port, and its inhabitants are known as *porteños*, or port people.

Buenos Aires is sometimes called the "Paris of South America", as its architecture is very European. In the 19th and 20th centuries people from all over Europe moved to Argentina, and most settled in Buenos Aires. Many of the immigrants lived together in districts called *barrios*. Today, you can still see these districts and each one has its own individual style and character.

Gauchos

Gauchos are Argentinian cowboys. The first gauchos lived in the 18th century and worked on the Pampas, taming wild horses and using them to catch cattle. Then, in the 1800s, Argentina's cattle industry began to develop. The Pampas were fenced into huge cattle ranches called *estancias* and gauchos became farmhands.

Internet links

You can learn about Argentinian history, and the wildlife and mountains of Patagonia, by following the links at **www.usborne.com/quicklinks**

The tango

Argentina is famous for the dance and music known as the tango. It began in the mid-19th century in the poor immigrant areas of Buenos Aires, as a mixture of Italian, Spanish and African music. At first, people found the tango shocking because the dancers' bodies were very close together, but by the 1900s it had become a craze in fashionable European circles. The tango is still danced today in many parts of the world. Finland has more than 2,000 tango clubs.

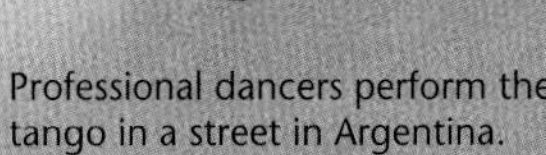

Professional dancers perform the tango in a street in Argentina.

Patagonia

With 90% of Argentinians living in cities, much of the country is wilderness. Patagonia, in the south, is one of the least populated regions in the world. It is home to many kinds of animals, such as elephant seals and some of the world's rarest birds.

Two girls in front of their thatched house in Samoa

PEOPLES OF AUSTRALASIA AND OCEANIA

AUSTRALASIA AND OCEANIA

The definitions of what makes up Australasia and Oceania vary, but Australasia usually refers to Australia and New Zealand and Oceania to the three main groups of Pacific Islands: Melanesia, Micronesia and Polynesia.

Small populations

Australasia and Oceania are not very heavily populated. The Pacific islands, including Papua New Guinea, are home to around six million people, 21 million people live in Australia and four million in New Zealand.

Land masses

Australia is more than three times the size of Greenland, the world's largest island. It is too large to be called an island, so it is usually described as a continent, or land mass. It is home to many unusual animals, such as kangaroos, wombats and koalas. There are thousands of tiny islands in the Pacific. Many have been formed by erupting volcanoes under the sea*.

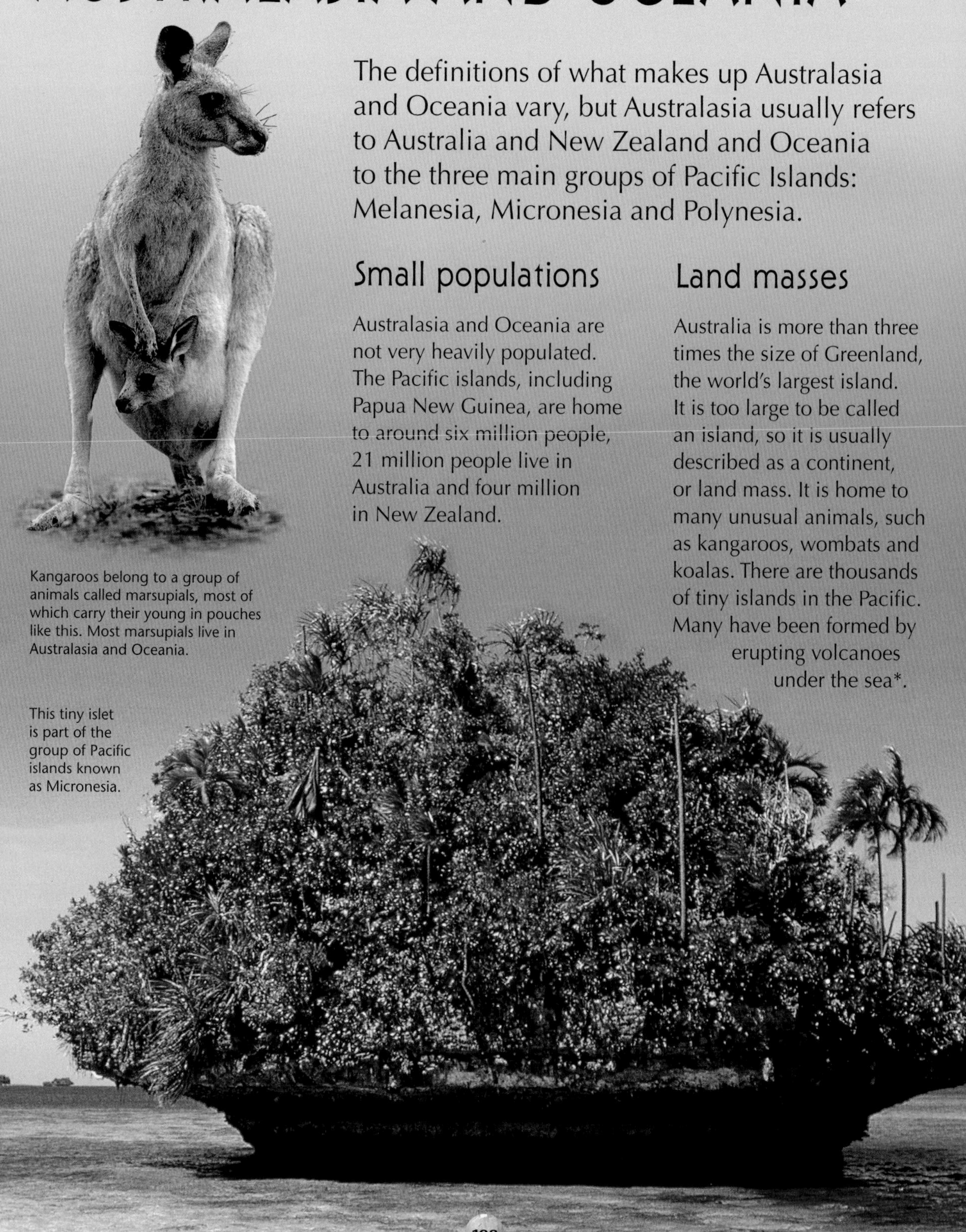

Kangaroos belong to a group of animals called marsupials, most of which carry their young in pouches like this. Most marsupials live in Australasia and Oceania.

This tiny islet is part of the group of Pacific islands known as Micronesia.

*Volcanic islands, 44

This is part of a wooden pillar of Maori carvings. Traditionally, the Maoris often used carvings to record details of real events.

Europeans arrive

In 1606, a Dutchman named Willem Jantszoon became the first European in Australia. In 1642, his countryman Abel Tasman was the first European to see New Zealand.

An English explorer, James Cook, landed at Botany Bay, on the east coast of Australia in 1770. Eighteen years later the British established a colony there for prisoners. During the 19th century, many parts of the Pacific were colonized by European countries. Today, most Pacific nations have gained independence.

Internet links

Delve into facts, maps and stories about the culture and exploration of Australia and the Pacific Islands by following the links at **www.usborne.com/quicklinks**

Early explorers

The first people to explore and inhabit Australasia and Oceania came originally from Southeast Asia. They include the Aborigines, who arrived in Australia between 40,000 and 60,000 years ago, the peoples who arrived on the Pacific islands about 7,000 years ago, and the Maoris, who arrived in New Zealand a little over 1,000 years ago.

This man from Papua New Guinea is holding the paddle of a traditional wooden canoe.

AUSTRALIA

Australia is bordered by the Pacific Ocean on one side and the Indian Ocean on the other. It is almost as big as Europe, yet has less than 3% of the population Europe has. Most Australians live on the country's eastern and southeastern coasts.

Australia's people

For many thousands of years the Aborigines and Torres Strait islanders were the only inhabitants of Australia. British colonists arrived in Australia in the 18th century, and in the 1850s gold was discovered. This brought a rush of people from Europe, China and the U.S.A., all hoping to make their fortunes by mining. In 1901 Australia ceased to be a set of colonies and became a federation.

City life

Over 80% of Australia's population lives in cities and towns along the coast, as this is where jobs are to be found. Canberra is the capital, but Sydney is the biggest city. Around four million people, a fifth of Australia's total population, live there. The other major Australian cities are Melbourne, Perth, Brisbane, Adelaide, Hobart and Darwin.

Many people in the outback live a long way from a hospital, so a medical service known as the Flying Doctors rescues sick people by plane.

The outback

The vast desert area in the middle of Australia, known as the outback, is one of the hottest, driest places in the world. The soil is too dry for crops, but farmers keep sheep and cattle on enormous farms called stations, which can have 15,000 sq km (5,800 sq miles) or more of land. With farms and towns so far apart, people living in the outback can lead isolated lives. Children often live so far from the nearest school that lessons have to be held via the internet, or transmitted by TV or radio.

Sydney's opera house sits on the edge of Sydney Harbour. Its roof mirrors the shape of the boats that sail past.

The coral reefs that make up the Great Barrier Reef support a huge variety of underwater life.

The first Australians

When the Aboriginal peoples came to Australia, they spread gradually across the country in large, nomadic groups, hunting animals and gathering plants. Sometimes they settled for quite long periods in some places. They believed that the land and its wildlife were sacred. When Europeans arrived, they seized much of the land for themselves, destroying many Aboriginal sacred places.

Today, less than 2% of the Australian population is Aboriginal, and many no longer have a traditional lifestyle. They are just as likely to live in cities and have modern jobs. However, most Aboriginal peoples want to preserve their culture and, after years of campaigning, some traditional lands are now being returned to their original owners.

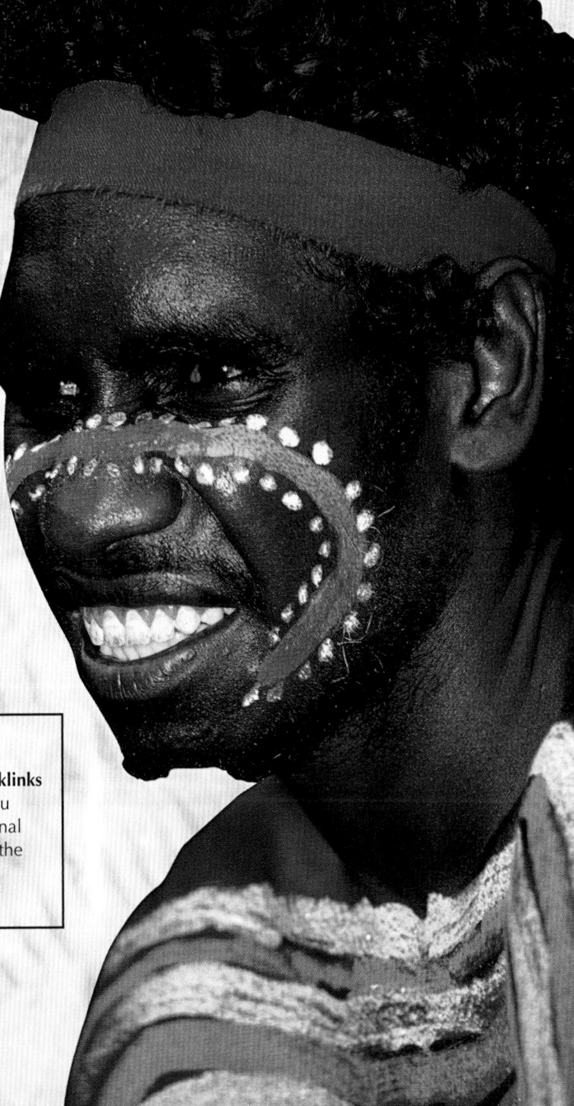

This Aboriginal man has painted his body and face as Aboriginal peoples have done for thousands of years. Body painting is a group activity and is usually done for special ceremonies.

Sun, sea and sports

Australians enjoy their warm, sunny climate and spend a lot of time outdoors, playing sports, swimming, surfing and sailing. The climate and range of outdoor activities available also make Australia attractive as a tourist destination. Swimming and diving at Australia's Great Barrier Reef are especially popular, although scientists are concerned that too much tourism will damage the wildlife living around the reef.

Internet links

Visit **www.usborne.com/quicklinks** for links to websites where you can learn more about Aboriginal culture. You can also explore the Great Barrier Reef and learn some Australian slang.

NEW ZEALAND

New Zealand lies in the South Pacific, about 1,500km (1,000 miles) southeast of Australia. The country is made up of two main islands, known as the North Island and the South Island, and several smaller ones. Much of New Zealand is wild and mountainous, and the country is sparsely populated, with fewer than four million people.

A young nation

New Zealand was one of the last places in the world to be inhabited. The first settlers, the Maoris, arrived just over 1,000 years ago, migrating from islands farther north. Europeans started to arrive in the late 18th century, and in 1840 New Zealand came under British rule. Today, it is an independent state. The majority of New Zealanders are still of British descent. The rest are mostly Maoris and South Sea islanders.

An experienced shearer can shear a sheep in just a few minutes. Wool is one of New Zealand's most important exports.

Important industries

Many New Zealanders make their living from farming. Over half the land is used for sheep farming and this is the country's biggest industry. Wool and lamb are major exports. Other exports include dairy products, wine, vegetables and fruit, such as oranges, lemons, grapefruits and kiwi fruit. New Zealand used to trade mainly with Britain, but today much of its trade is with Australia and Asian countries. Non-agricultural exports include wood and paper products, textiles and machinery.

This is a typical New Zealand sheep farm, stretching over a vast area.

These tourists are photographing a geyser spouting hot water in Waiotapua Thermal Park.

Clean and green

New Zealand does not use nuclear power, and has little heavy industry and relatively small towns and cities. As a result, it is one of the world's least polluted countries. Its beautiful scenery attracts many tourists. In the North Island, active volcanoes and spouting geysers can be seen, and in the South Island, there are spectacular mountains with huge glaciers.

Internet links

Follow the website links at **www.usborne.com/quicklinks** to explore the landscape of New Zealand and to learn more about Maori beliefs and lifestyle.

The Maoris

When they first arrived in New Zealand, the Maoris lived a traditional lifestyle. They hunted, fished and grew crops, and lived in small ethnic groups ruled by chiefs. Then in the 18th century, British colonists arrived. Battles raged over who owned the land and many Maoris were killed. Most of those that were left were forced to move to the new towns and cities.

This Maori man has tattoos known as *Ta Moko* on his face. He is carrying a club called a wahaika, to take part in a traditional dance.

Modern Maoris

Today, Maoris make up about 10% of the population of New Zealand and their culture is being re-established. The Maori language is taught in schools and traditional arts such as tattooing (*Ta Moko*) have been revived. But many Maoris are still campaigning for the return of lands they lost. Their name for New Zealand is *Aotearoa*, which means "land of the long white clouds".

PAPUA NEW GUINEA

New Guinea, the world's second largest island after Greenland, lies in the Pacific Ocean, to the north of Australia. Its western half, called Irian Jaya, is part of Indonesia*. Its eastern half, together with around 600 small islands, makes up the country of Papua New Guinea.

Internet links
For links to websites where you can browse photo galleries of Papua New Guinea and its peoples, follow the links at **www.usborne.com/quicklinks**

Peoples of Papua

Most Papua New Guineans are of Papuan or Melanesian* origin, although there are also people of European, Polynesian* and Chinese origin. The first inhabitants migrated from Southeast Asia over 40,000 years ago. They lived in small groups and found food by hunting and gathering.

The country is dominated by mountains and thick rainforests. This has meant that groups often became isolated. Today, there are still hundreds of different ethnic groups living in Papua New Guinea.

Languages

Because there are so many separate groups, many different languages have developed in Papua New Guinea. There are more than 700 in total, a huge number of languages for a population of about six million. The different groups communicate with each other in a language called Hiri Motu, or in pidgin English, which is a mixture of English and local languages. The official language is English, but in fact only 2% of the population can speak it.

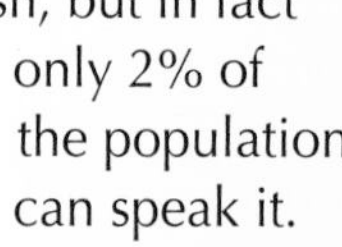

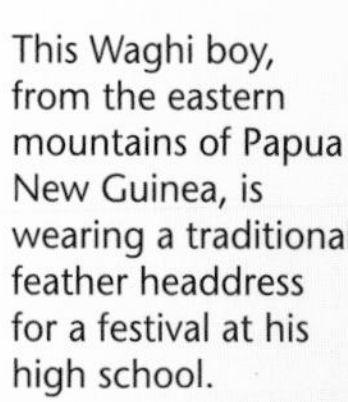

This Waghi boy, from the eastern mountains of Papua New Guinea, is wearing a traditional feather headdress for a festival at his high school.

*Indonesia, 213; Melanesia, 196; Polynesia, 196

Village life

About a fifth of Papua New Guinea's people live in towns, where many have moved to find work. The rest still have a traditional lifestyle, similar to that of their ancestors. They live in villages, grow fruit and vegetables, catch fish and keep pigs and poultry. Some farmers sell their produce at local markets. Villagers eat a diet based on starchy crops such as sweet potatoes in the highland areas, and sago in the lowlands.

A father and son display their catch of fish for sale to passers-by.

These are men from a village called Asaro. They are wearing mud masks and their bodies are covered in mud too. Warriors of Asaro are said to have once dressed like this in order to win a battle, and villagers still sometimes dress like this today for tourists.

Art and life

The art of Papua New Guinea is a key part of local life, history and culture. Traditions vary from region to region and most forms of art have a practical or religious function.

In Malangan culture, people make wooden masks to commemorate a death. The people of Kambot carve wooden story boards showing incidents from village life. Around the Gulf Province, shield-like objects called gope boards are hung outside houses. They are said to contain protective spirits which ward off sickness and evil. Many Papuan peoples also carve elaborate prows for canoes.

OCEANIA

Scattered over the vast Pacific Ocean are more than 20,000 islands, which are collectively known as Oceania. Some, such as New Guinea, are huge, but many are little more than specks in the ocean. Only a few thousand of the islands are inhabited.

This brightly-painted building is a Hindu temple in Nadi, Fiji.

Pacific peoples

The original inhabitants of the Pacific islands migrated from Southeast Asia about 7,000 years ago. They made long sea journeys and, over many generations, settled one group of islands after another. Later, in the 16th century, European explorers started to discover the Pacific islands. Colonists began to arrive, and by the 1800s many islands were under the control of other countries. Today, some Pacific islands are independent and others are still ruled by states such as the U.S.A., France and New Zealand.

Island groups

There are three main Pacific island groups: Melanesia, Polynesia and Micronesia. Polynesia means "many islands" and Micronesia means "small islands". Melanesia means "black islands"; it got its name because the people there tend to have darker skin than elsewhere in the Pacific.

These French Polynesian girls are wearing traditional flower garlands, known as leis.

Tourism

Some of the Pacific islands, such as those that make up Fiji, Tonga and Samoa, are among the most beautiful in the world. This, together with their tropical climate, makes them popular tourist destinations. Tourism brings money to the islands but too many tourists can also damage the environment.

Internet links

Visit the websites suggested at **www.usborne.com/quicklinks** to find out more about the history, culture and lifestyles of the different peoples of Oceania. You can also read about their art and craftwork, and explore Easter Island and its dramatic statues.

Huts cluster along the beach on Mana Island, one of the many islands that make up Fiji.

Island life

On more developed Pacific islands, many people live in urban areas and work in mining and tourism. However, traditional village life is still strong. Fishing is common, crops such as cassava, yams and sweet potatoes are grown and families often keep livestock – for example, chickens and pigs. On some islands, people live in large, extended families, and community and religious life is often important.

Testing weapons

Because of their remote locations, the Pacific islands have been used by a number of countries, including the U.K. and the U.S.A., for testing nuclear weapons. For example, in 1946, an atom bomb was detonated on Bikini, one of the Marshall Islands in Micronesia. Nuclear testing has damaged coral reefs, forced some islanders to move home and caused concern about the effects of radiation on local people's health.

This man is fishing by standing on a ledge jutting out just over the water and stabbing at fish with his spear.

Children carry balloons and flowers at the opening ceremony of a school in Hanoi, Vietnam

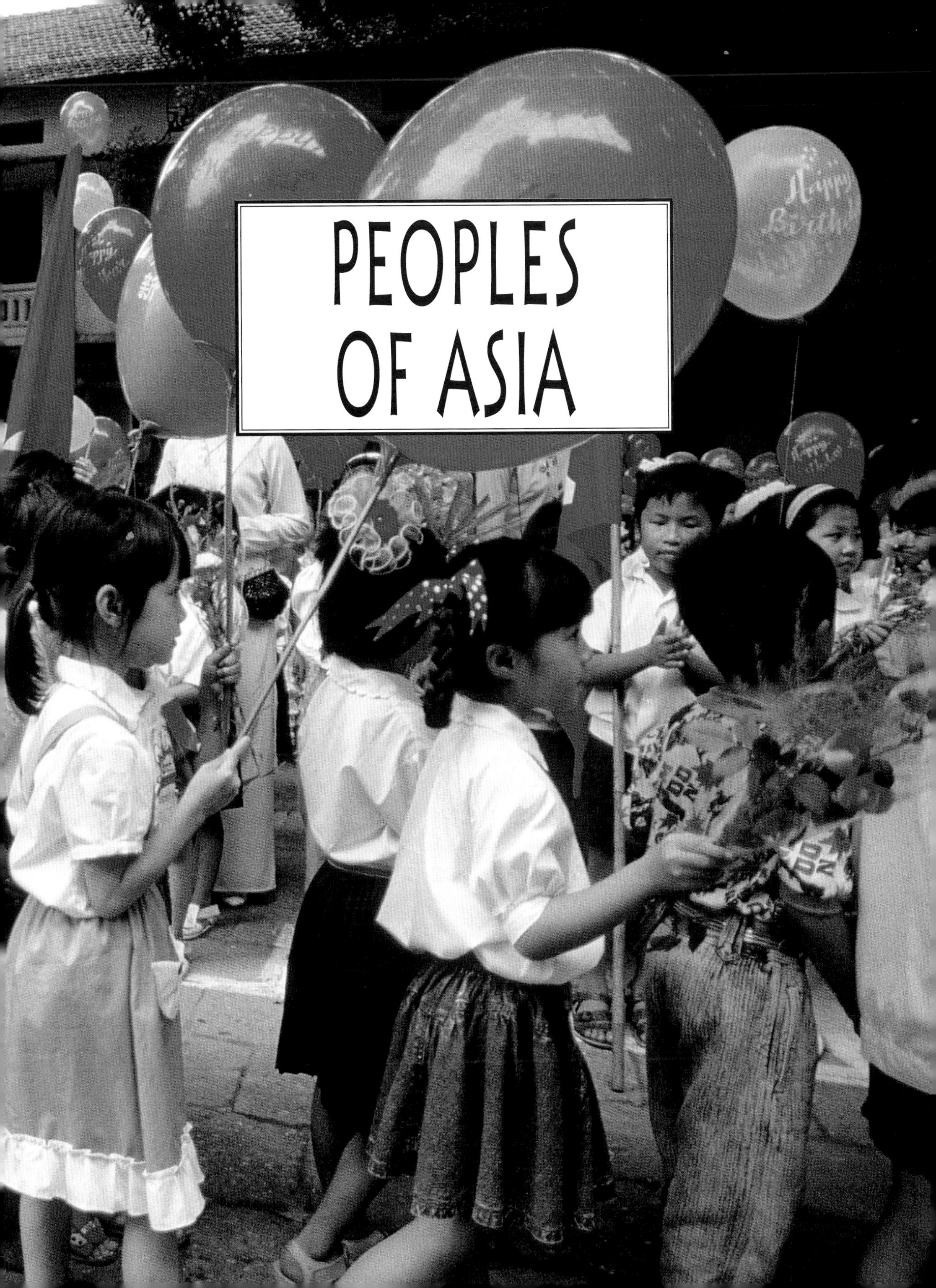

PEOPLES OF ASIA

ASIA

Asia is the world's biggest continent. It covers almost a third of the Earth's land surface, and 60% of the world's people live there. Asian peoples are very diverse, with many different cultures, lifestyles, religions and political systems.

A farm worker picking tea leaves in Malaysia. Tea is an important crop in Asia.

New states

Since 1991, Asia has gained several new states, including Tajikistan, Kyrgyzstan and Kazakhstan. These were once part of the U.S.S.R. (Union of Soviet Socialist Republics), a huge country governed from Moscow. In 1991 the U.S.S.R. dissolved into a number of independent states, including Russia.

Fishing and farming

Asia has thousands and thousands of miles of coastline, especially in the southeast, where there are over 15,000 islands. Because of this, fishing is a vital source of food and work for millions of Asians.

The continent also has vast areas of fertile farmland, with millions of tiny farms where poor families grow food for their own use. But Asia also has large farms that export crops such as rice, rubber, tea and coffee.

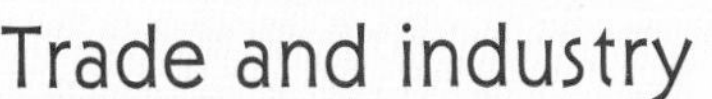

Trade and industry

Asia is also home to some of the world's biggest banking, manufacturing and trading nations. Wealthy cities such as Hong Kong, Singapore, Tokyo and Dubai tower with gleaming skyscrapers.

Many of the things you own, especially clothes, computers, toys, phones and CDs, have probably been made in Asia. Millions of factory workers in countries such as China, Taiwan and Japan make goods to be exported and sold all over the world.

Trade is important for many Asian nations. Here you can see people trading in the stock exchange in Malaysia.

Internet links

For links to websites where you can read about some of the diverse countries of Asia, learn about tea and rice production and discover more about different kinds of Asian lifestyles, go to **www.usborne.com/quicklinks**

The Buddhist religion plays a central role in the lives of many people throughout Southeast Asia and boys are encouraged to spend some time as monks. These boys are young Buddhist monks.

A RANGE OF RELIGIONS

All the world's major religions started in Asia. The continent still has a wide range of religions and many of them, such as Christianity, Islam and Judaism, have also spread around the world. For billions of Asians, religious rituals are an essential everyday activity.

Holy places

Important holy sites are found all over Asia. They include places where prophets were born or died, places where religions began, and cities, mountains and rivers that are believed to be sacred. Millions of people from all over the world make religious journeys, or pilgrimages, to these sites every year.

Holy water

The Ganges River in northern India is sacred to Hindus, who make up more than 80% of India's population. Pilgrims visit the Ganges to purify themselves by bathing in its waters, and religious ceremonies are held on its banks.

These women are bathing at dawn in the Ganges River at Varanasi, India. Steps have been built there so pilgrims can get in and out of the water safely.

A trip to Mecca

All Muslims are expected to make a pilgrimage (or *Hajj*) to the holy city of Mecca, in Saudi Arabia, at least once in their lives. It is the birthplace of Mohammed, the prophet of Islam. When they arrive, the pilgrims walk around a shrine called the Ka'bah, which is said to have been built by the prophet Ibrahim.

Jerusalem

Jerusalem, which is now the capital of Israel, is a holy city for Jews, Christians and Muslims. It contains the Western Wall, the remains of a Jewish temple, and the Dome of the Rock, a Muslim shrine marking the spot where the prophet Mohammed is said to have risen into heaven. Also, Jesus Christ, the central figure of Christianity, was crucified just outside the ancient city walls.

Internet links

Learn about the *Hajj* (pilgrimage) to Mecca, the religious sites of Jerusalem and the customs and rituals of the world's major religions by following the links at **www.usborne.com/quicklinks**

The silhouette in the background is part of the huge Borobudur Buddhist temple in Java, Indonesia.

Jewish pilgrims visit the Western Wall to mourn the destruction of their temple, and to insert prayers into cracks in the wall. In the background is the Dome of the Rock, part of a Muslim shrine.

Beautiful buildings

There are beautiful religious buildings all over Asia: Muslim mosques, Sikh gurdwaras, Christian churches, Hindu temples, and Buddhist pagodas. Many of these holy buildings have been created by the very best craftspeople, using expensive and gorgeous materials. Their impressive shapes often dominate cities' skylines.

Spiritual sounds

In Asia, many people take part in regular religious chanting, praying or singing. For example, Muslims are called to prayer five times a day, many Buddhists chant verses every day, and dancing and singing are an important part of Hindu ceremonies.

This man is calling Muslims to prayer. An official who does this is called a muezzin.

RUSSIA

These are matryoshka dolls, which open up into halves so that several dolls can fit one inside the other. The word matryoshka means mother in Russian.

Russia is the world's biggest country. It covers 11% of the Earth's land surface, is divided into 11 time zones and straddles two continents: Europe and Asia. It takes over a week to travel by train from St. Petersburg in the west to Vladivostok in the east.

Big changes

The independent country of Russia, officially known as the Russian Federation, has only existed since 1991. Before that, it belonged to the U.S.S.R. This was an even bigger country, created in 1917 when a Communist revolution overthrew the Russian czar, or king. For most of the 20th century, Communists ran the U.S.S.R.

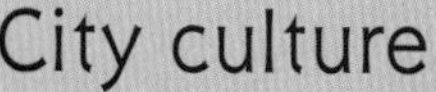

City culture

Russia's cities are famous across the world for their art and culture. Moscow and St. Petersburg (which are both in European Russia) have dozens of beautiful museums and palaces. Russia is also home to world-famous orchestras and ballet companies such as Moscow's Bolshoi Ballet.

Communism

Communism is a way of running a country. Under Communism, the state owns everything, including railways, roads, factories and houses, and it distributes things like food, money and medicine among the people. It is the opposite of Capitalism, in which people can own their own houses and run their own businesses. The government which ruled the U.S.S.R. from 1917 to 1991 was the world's best-known Communist system.

This is St. Basil's Cathedral, Moscow. The beautiful onion-shaped domes are characteristic of Russian church architecture.

This girl is playing outside the tent where her family lives, in Chukchi, in the far northeast of Russia.

Size matters

Russia stretches 7,700km (4,800 miles) along the Arctic Circle. When it's bedtime in the west, people in the east are just waking up. People in different parts of the country have very different lifestyles, depending on the climate and landscape where they live, and the influence of nearby countries. In the north, Russia extends beyond the Arctic Circle, but few people live there because it's too cold. There is a central government in Moscow, but many regions have their own laws, parliaments and languages.

New freedoms

Under Communism there were strict rules. Books and newspapers were tightly regulated, religion was suppressed and it was hard to leave the country. In 1991, the Communists were ousted and the U.S.S.R. broke up into 15 new countries. Many of the old rules were relaxed. However, the new freedoms also meant that crime increased. Many people are poorer than they were under Communism, because the state no longer looks after everyone.

Varied literature

Russian literature is well-known around the world. Russia's most famous writers include Dostoevsky, Tolstoy and Pushkin; they wrote realist novels. However Russia also has a rich tradition of magical folk tales and fairy tales, which have been passed down orally for centuries.

In some parts of Russia it can be extremely cold. These children live in the Kamchatka region where the average temperature is -40°C (-40°F).

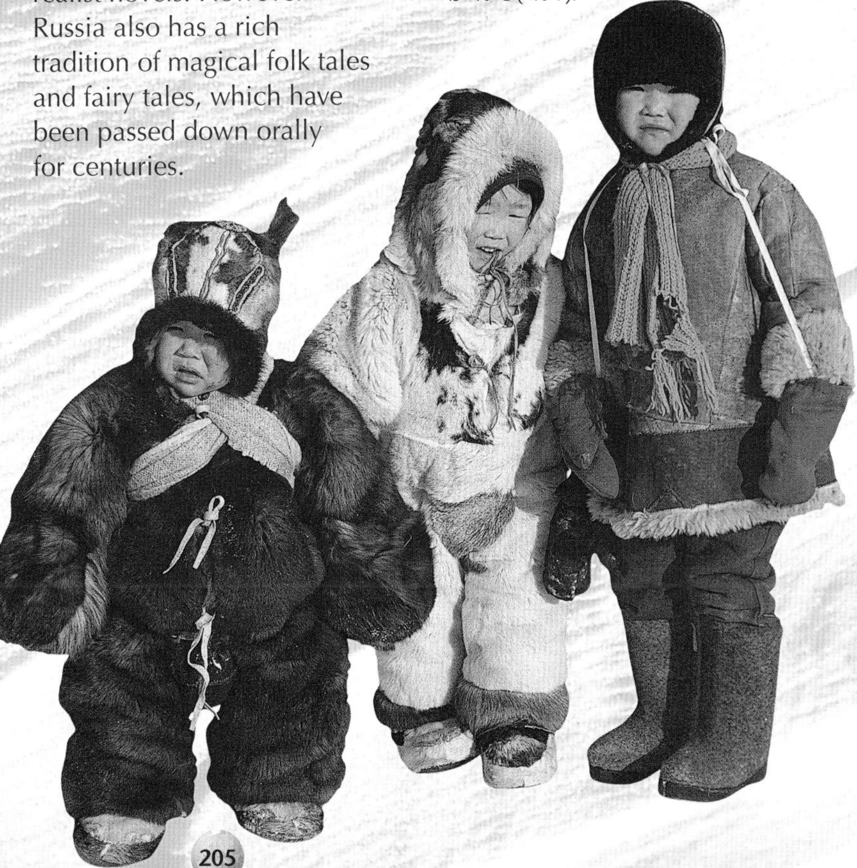

Internet links

Visit the websites suggested at **www.usborne.com/quicklinks** to discover more about Russia with facts about Russia's government and peoples, photo galleries of Moscow's famous buildings and a timeline of key leaders and events.

THE MIDDLE EAST

The Middle East is famous for its beautiful old buildings and wealthy modern cities, and the hospitality of its peoples. It was where Sumer, the home of the first civilization, was; and it is the nucleus of the world's oil industry. It is sometimes seen as a trouble spot, because of the many wars and revolutions that have taken place there.

These are Marsh Arabs, a people from Iraq who live in houses built on floating platforms of reeds. They are loading mats made from reeds onto a truck.

This woman in Oman is wearing a mask to cover her face. Some Islamic women cover their faces in public to protect their modesty.

What is the Middle East?

The Middle East is usually said to include the area between the Red Sea and the Persian Gulf, as well as Israel, Jordan, Syria, Lebanon, Iran and Iraq. It was named the Middle East by Europeans, because it is east of Europe, but not as far away as other Asian countries such as China and Japan (often referred to as the Far East).

Different peoples

The peoples of the Middle East belong to four main groups: Arabs, Persians, Turks and Jews. The area's Arabic countries (Bahrain, Saudi Arabia, Yemen, Oman, Qatar, Kuwait and United Arab Emirates) lie in and around the peninsula of Arabia. Their people are Muslims and speak Arabic languages. But Iran, once known as Persia, is not Arabic, and nor is Turkey, although they too are mainly Muslim. Israel is a Jewish state which was created in 1948. Many Arabs claim that Israel's land belongs to an Arabic people, the Palestinians.

Desert life

Stretching across the Middle East are vast deserts which contain important oil reserves. Few people live in these areas. However, some Bedouin herders still travel across the desert from one oasis to the next with their animals. They use either camels or four-wheel-drive vehicles to carry their tents and possessions.

Bedouin people are nomads who traditionally live in the desert. These Bedouins are leading a train of camels.

Ancient and modern

When oil was discovered in the Middle East, it made many nations rich. They were able to rebuild their cities with new apartments and skyscrapers, and to provide for new banks and businesses. But most cities still have old areas with narrow streets and traditional markets, called souks.

These huge towers in Kuwait are for water storage. Kuwait is a desert nation with no rivers or lakes, so sea water has to be processed to make it safe to drink, then stored.

Coffee and small talk

Coffee probably first came from Yemen, in southern Arabia, and it is still an important part of life in the Middle East. When Middle Eastern people have visitors, they usually offer them coffee, along with dates or pieces of cake called baklava. Then, even if there is something important to discuss, it is polite to make small talk over coffee before getting down to business.

This is the traditional Middle Eastern way of pouring coffee, holding the pot up high to create a long, fine flow.

Internet links

To find out more about the histories and cultures of Middle Eastern peoples follow the website links at **www.usborne.com/quicklinks**

CHINA

Nearly a quarter of the people on Earth are Chinese, and China is one of the world's oldest nations. It has existed for about 2,000 years, and had one of the earliest civilizations. The ancient Chinese invented paper, silk, gunpowder and seismology, the science of predicting earthquakes.

In Chinese cities people often use pedal power to get around. These children are riding in a wooden trailer on the back of a tricycle.

Ancient arts

China has a lot of traditional art and culture, including opera, pottery (known as china), kite making and jade carving. A type of beautiful writing known as calligraphy is also considered a form of art. It usually consists of black letters painted using a brush.

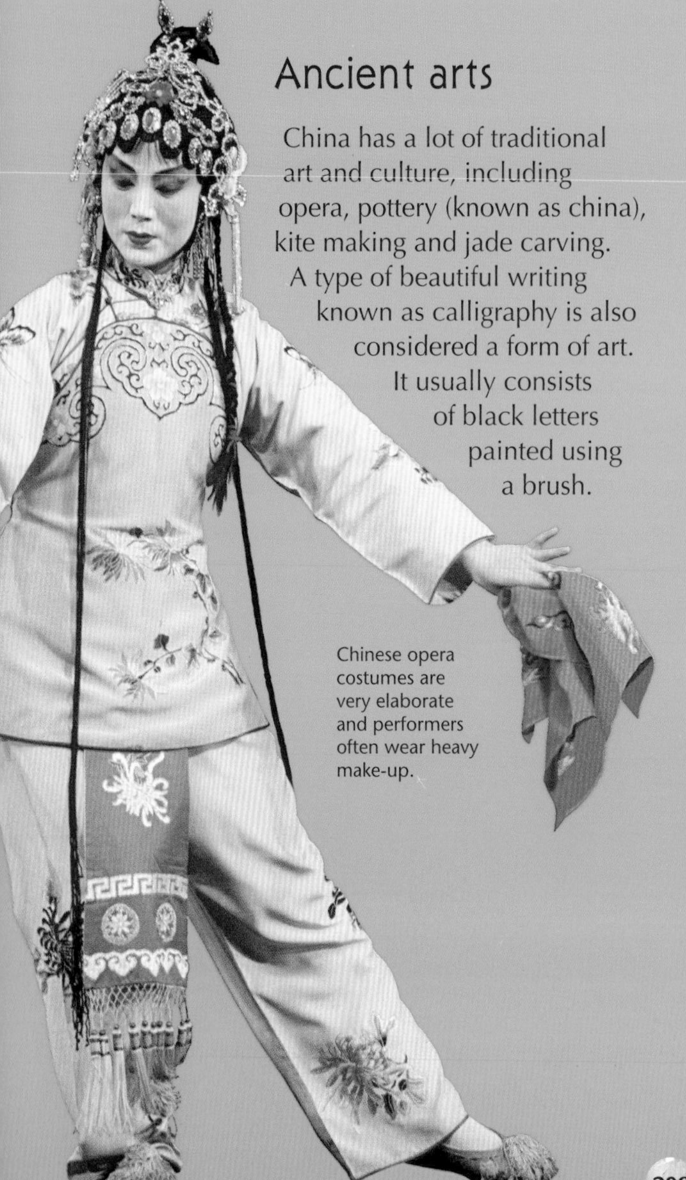

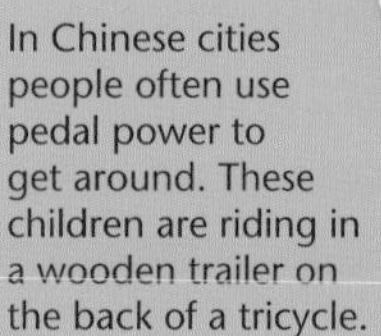

Chinese opera costumes are very elaborate and performers often wear heavy make-up.

Population explosion

In 1982, China became the first country to have over a billion people. It now has around 1.3 billion. It is hard for China to provide enough food, schools and doctors for all its people. Since the 1950s, the government has tried to slow down the population increase. Couples are encouraged to get married later in life, and to have only one child.

Farming nation

Even though China has a lot of big cities, nearly three-quarters of its people live in the countryside and survive by farming. Their main crops are rice, wheat and millet.

China is mountainous, and only about 10% of its land is fertile, so all the soil has to be used carefully. Terraces built into hillsides allow farmers to grow crops on steep slopes. Throughout China, farmland is irrigated, or watered, using systems of canals and streams.

Chinese beliefs

Many people in China follow Confucianism, a way of behaving based on the ideas of Confucius, who lived in the area 2,500 years ago. He taught that people should be polite and considerate and obey their elders.

The ancient Chinese worshipped their ancestors and various gods. These old beliefs are remembered at certain times of the year. For example, many families keep a picture of the kitchen god next to the kitchen stove. Just before the New Year, they take it down and smear honey and wine on the god's lips to keep him happy. When the New Year arrives, a new picture is put up.

This is a holder for burning incense sticks. Incense gives off a scent which is said to attract the attention of the gods.

New Year

The start of the Chinese year, which is usually in February, is marked with celebrations, including fireworks, parades and feasts. People decorate their homes with symbols of good fortune and unmarried people receive red envelopes containing money for good luck.

Internet links

For links to websites where you can discover more about China's ancient arts, the Chinese New Year and how to write Chinese characters, go to **www.usborne.com/quicklinks**

Spellings

Chinese writing uses symbols, or characters, to represent words. In other languages, Chinese words have to be written down as they sound. Recently these spellings have been changed to make them more consistent, so you might see different spellings in different books.

The Chinese characters on the right spell out the phrase "Peoples of the World".

世界各民族

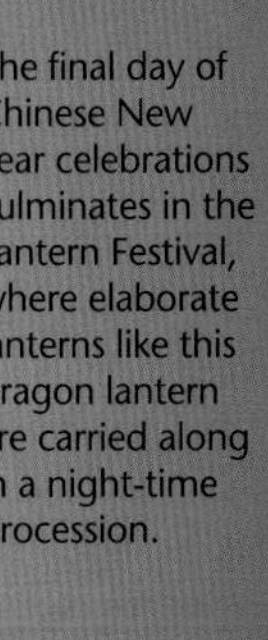

The final day of Chinese New Year celebrations culminates in the Lantern Festival, where elaborate lanterns like this dragon lantern are carried along in a night-time procession.

INDIA AND PAKISTAN

India and Pakistan straddle the area where, around 4,500 years ago, a complex ancient society began in and around the Indus Valley. The two countries are now both modern states, but many of their people also follow ancient traditions and beliefs.

Pakistani truck, van and bus drivers are proud of their hand-decorated vehicles, like this truck covered in patterns and symbols.

Dividing into states

India and Pakistan used to be one country, which was ruled by Britain in the 19th century. Britain agreed to grant India its independence in 1947, but Hindus and Muslims wanted their own separate states. So the country was divided into two parts: Pakistan for the Muslims, and India for the more numerous Hindus. At first, Bangladesh was part of Pakistan, but it too became independent in 1971.

East and West

Britain's influence can be seen all over India and Pakistan. European-style buildings from the time of British rule stand among mosques and temples. Cricket, originally an English game, is an important sport in both India and Pakistan.

Indians and Pakistanis wear a mixture of European-style clothes and traditional dress, such as the *shalwar kameez* (baggy shirt and trousers) in Pakistan and the sari, a wrap-around gown, in India.

Women from Rajasthan, in India, carrying heavy loads on their heads

The building in the background is the Taj Mahal, near the city of Agra. It is an elaborate tomb built by a 17th-century Indian emperor, Shah Jahan, for his wife, Mumtaz Mahal.

Film fanatics

India has the world's biggest film industry, based in Mumbai (Bombay) and known as "Bollywood". Bollywood films are usually love stories or historical dramas, with lots of songs and dance routines. The top film stars and singers are incredibly rich and famous.

Getting around

In crowded cities such as Lahore and Calcutta, the streets are full of buses, trams, taxis, rickshaws and bikes jostling for space with pedestrians and market stalls. In India, cows wander the streets as well. Hindus regard cows as sacred animals and no one is allowed to harm them, so they slow down the traffic as everyone tries to keep out of their way.

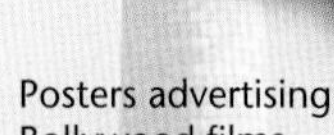

Posters advertising Bollywood films.

> **Internet links**
> To discover more about the people, cities, foods and famous sites of India and Pakistan, go to **www.usborne.com/quicklinks**

A rickshaw is a kind of open-air taxi. Rickshaws can be motorized or driven by pedal power. When a pedal rickshaw comes to a hill, the passengers get out and push it.

Caste

In Indian tradition, most people are born with a *Jati,* or caste, an inherited status. In ancient India, it determined the job you did, and you could only marry someone from the same group. *Jati* is still important to many people and people of the same *Jati* support each other. But some of the old laws have been abolished, so that Indians from all levels of society can hold positions of power.

Curry craze

Spicy food from Pakistan and India is popular across the globe. Its name "curry" comes from *kari*, from the Tamil language of southern India. Curry is usually vegetables or meat with a sauce, eaten with rice or bread. Hindus avoid eating meat, so Indian food is often vegetarian.

SOUTHEAST ASIA

Southeast Asia stretches out into the sea to the south of China and Japan. The countries there, including Thailand, Vietnam, Laos, Malaysia and Indonesia, are spread out over a long peninsula and a series of hilly, forested islands.

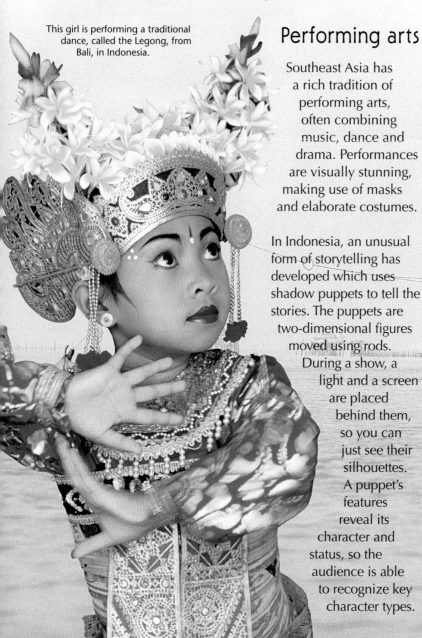

This girl is performing a traditional dance, called the Legong, from Bali, in Indonesia.

Performing arts

Southeast Asia has a rich tradition of performing arts, often combining music, dance and drama. Performances are visually stunning, making use of masks and elaborate costumes.

In Indonesia, an unusual form of storytelling has developed which uses shadow puppets to tell the stories. The puppets are two-dimensional figures moved using rods. During a show, a light and a screen are placed behind them, so you can just see their silhouettes. A puppet's features reveal its character and status, so the audience is able to recognize key character types.

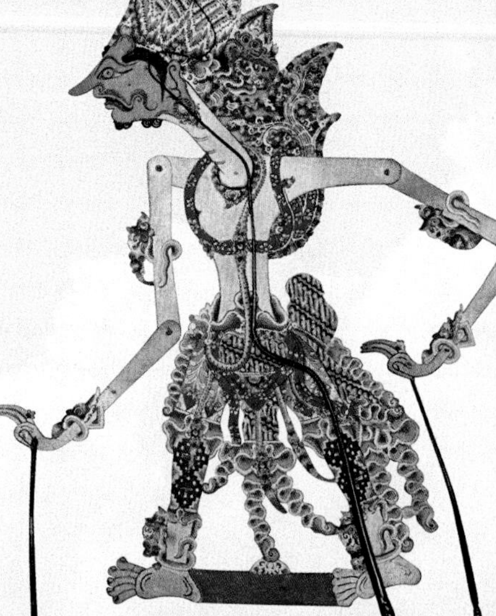

This is an Indonesian shadow puppet. It is moved using the rods attached to its arms and head.

Temples and mosques

In Southeast Asia, many different religions exist side by side, usually peacefully. Some countries, such as Burma, are mainly Buddhist; others, such as Indonesia, are mainly Muslim; but other religions such as Christianity and Hinduism are also common. Temples, mosques and churches are found everywhere. There are also many ruined temples which have now been abandoned.

Internet links

For links to websites with more information about shadow puppet plays and some virtual tours through different South East Asian countries, go to **www.usborne.com/quicklinks**

Nations in pieces

Malaysia, Indonesia and the Philippines stretch across a vast archipelago (a network of islands) southeast of the Asian mainland. Even within the same country, different islands can be very unlike each other.

For example, Bali, one of Indonesia's most populated islands, is small and crowded, with farms, towns and a big tourist industry. Its main religion is a type of Hinduism, and it has thousands of temples.

Irian Jaya, part of the much bigger island of New Guinea, is very remote, with thick forests. Most of its peoples live by farming, fishing and hunting. Some have converted to Christianity, while others worship the spirits of their ancestors.

On the marshy eastern coast of Sumatra in Indonesia, men and boys spend part of the year fishing from huts on tall stilts built up to 10km (6 miles) out at sea.

Elephant work

On the Southeast Asian mainland, elephants are used to transport people and for moving heavy loads, such as logs. Sometimes they are also dressed up in glittery costumes for parades and special occasions.

In Laos (which was once known as the Land of a Million Elephants) and Thailand, each working elephant has its own trainer, or mahout. One mahout may spend his whole life caring for the same animal.

A mahout starts working with an elephant while it is still young. Over the years they build up a close relationship. These baby elephants are just starting to be trained.

Rice and spice

Although Southeast Asia has some big cities, most of its people are farmers and live in the countryside. Rice is their main crop and it forms a part of almost every meal.

Thailand and Indonesia are famous for their spicy food. Spices are not a major crop now, but hundreds of years ago they made this part of the world rich. Merchants came from India, Arabia, Europe and China to buy cloves, mace and nutmeg, which were more valuable than gold.

BIG BUSINESS

Although many Asians are poor and live by farming, Asia is also home to some of the world's biggest banking, trading and manufacturing nations.

A farm worker in India gathers crocuses to collect saffron from them. Saffron is added to food and can be used as a yellow dye.

Trading history

Some of the reasons for the success of Asian cities are historical. Hong Kong, Singapore and Dubai are ancient ports on trading routes that have been used for centuries. The Chinese, in particular, have a long history of trading. They invented paper money in the 9th century.

These are banknotes from Singapore. Singapore is one of Asia's "Four Tigers" – countries which became known for their fast-growing economies.

New resources

As the population of Asia has risen, some countries have been unable to make enough money from traditional industries such as farming, so they have turned to business and services instead. For example, Japan has very little fertile land, but banking and manufacturing have allowed it to become rich without relying on its natural resources.

Money from oil

In some parts of Asia, especially the Middle East, a lot of wealth comes from selling oil. The money can then be lent to other businesses and used to build hotels, restaurants and new apartments. This type of financial service is provided by banks called merchant banks, which can become very rich in the process. In this way, these countries provide for when the oil runs out.

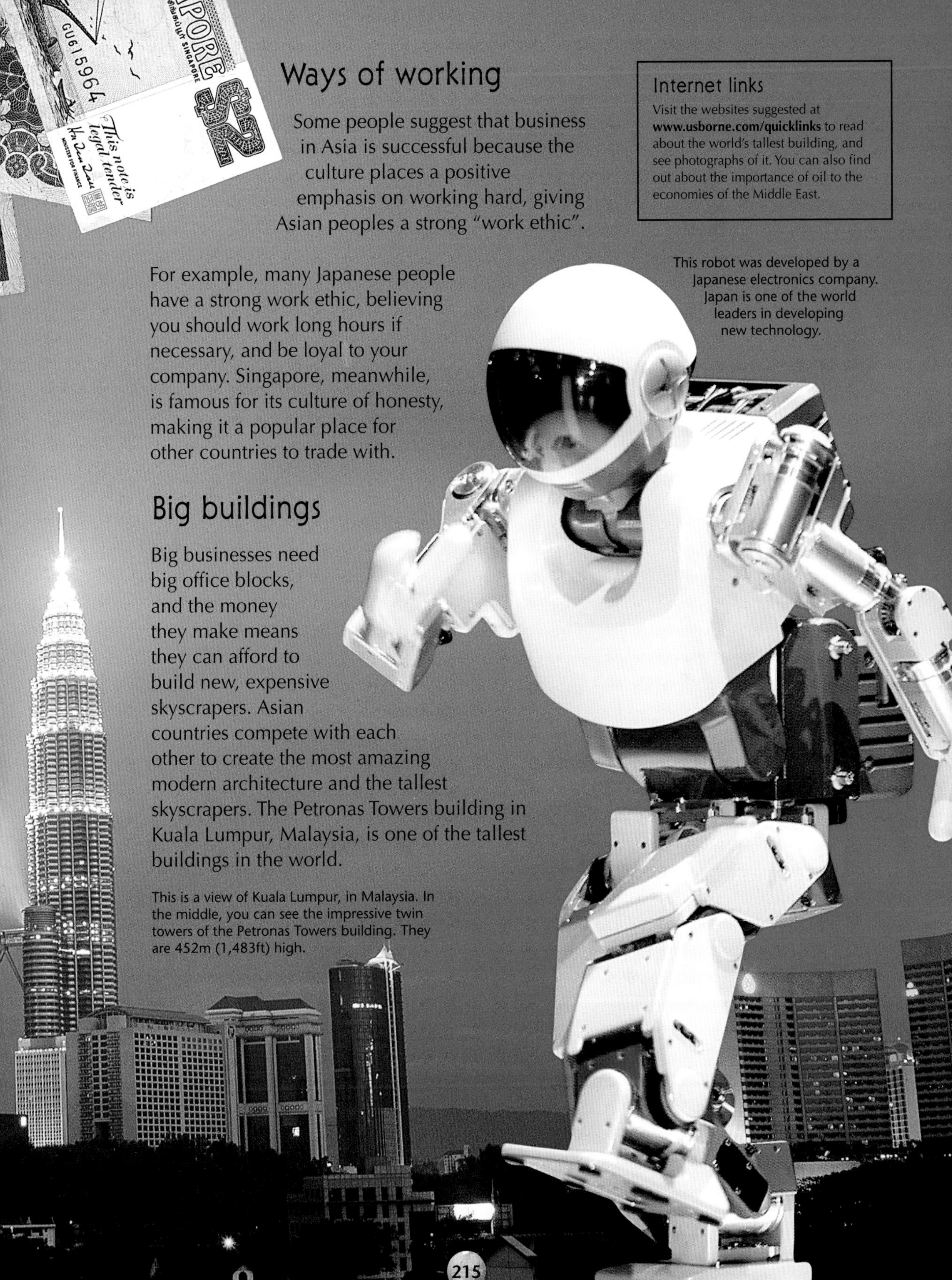

Ways of working

Some people suggest that business in Asia is successful because the culture places a positive emphasis on working hard, giving Asian peoples a strong "work ethic".

For example, many Japanese people have a strong work ethic, believing you should work long hours if necessary, and be loyal to your company. Singapore, meanwhile, is famous for its culture of honesty, making it a popular place for other countries to trade with.

Internet links

Visit the websites suggested at **www.usborne.com/quicklinks** to read about the world's tallest building, and see photographs of it. You can also find out about the importance of oil to the economies of the Middle East.

This robot was developed by a Japanese electronics company. Japan is one of the world leaders in developing new technology.

Big buildings

Big businesses need big office blocks, and the money they make means they can afford to build new, expensive skyscrapers. Asian countries compete with each other to create the most amazing modern architecture and the tallest skyscrapers. The Petronas Towers building in Kuala Lumpur, Malaysia, is one of the tallest buildings in the world.

This is a view of Kuala Lumpur, in Malaysia. In the middle, you can see the impressive twin towers of the Petronas Towers building. They are 452m (1,483ft) high.

Masked partygoers at the Venice Carnival in Italy

PEOPLES OF EUROPE

EUROPE

This is a picture of St. John from a 12th century Christian manuscript.

Although Europe is the second smallest continent in the world, it contains 50 countries, and its peoples speak over 50 different languages. Throughout history there have been many migrations* within, to and from Europe.

Ancient Europe

For nearly six centuries, until around 1,500 years ago, the Romans ruled much of Europe. Today, there are similarities in law, language, architecture and education across the continent that date back to the Romans. You can still see the ruins of Roman towns throughout Europe. The Romans took many of their ideas from the Greeks, who had their own powerful empire and culture.

Christianity

Christianity has been the main religion in Europe since the days of the Roman Empire. Today, many Europeans do not go to church regularly, and many others follow different religions. Yet the influence of Christianity on art, architecture and culture can be seen all over Europe.

Internet links

For links to websites where you can learn more about the peoples and geography of Europe, the history of the Roman Empire and much more, go to **www.usborne.com/quicklinks**

*Migrations, 142; U.S.S.R., 204

People climbing on the Berlin Wall in 1989

Europe divided

After the Second World War, much of eastern Europe was under the control of the Communist U.S.S.R.* Political differences between the U.S.S.R. and the non-Communist west increased until Europe split in two. In 1961, East German authorities built a wall in the German city of Berlin to prevent people fleeing from east to west. The wall was guarded by armed soldiers. In 1989, protests against the lack of freedom led to the destruction of the Berlin Wall.

European arts

Europe has produced many great artists, composers and writers. The ancient Greek poet Homer and the English playwright Shakespeare, composers like Bach, Mozart and Beethoven, and artists such as Michelangelo and Picasso are famous around the world. Europe also attracts millions of tourists every year to see its ancient ruins, beautiful architecture and fine art galleries.

As well as having a great history of art, Europe still produces a wide range of art today. This is a modern sculpture, known as the "Angel of the North", by artist Antony Gormley. It was erected in the north of England in 1998. Its huge steel structure is 22m (72ft) tall.

WESTERN EUROPE

In western Europe, most people live in cities or towns. City life can be fast and exciting and most western European cities have lots of stores, restaurants, cinemas, concert halls and museums. But many cities are also crowded and polluted.

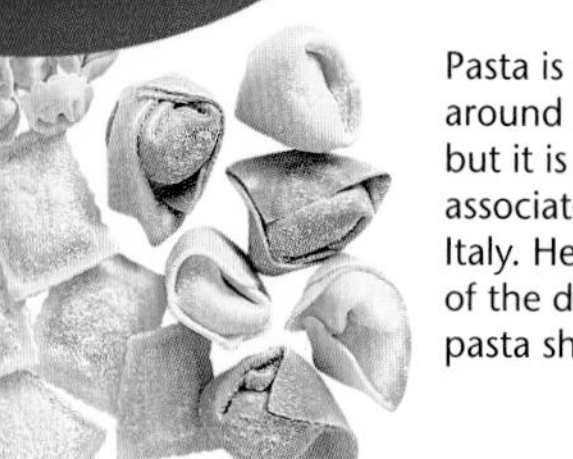

Pasta is popular around the world, but it is particularly associated with Italy. Here are some of the different pasta shapes.

Food culture

The food of western Europe is extremely varied and many countries are known for particular foods or ways of eating. For example, Italy is known for pizzas and pasta, Germany for sausages, Greece for kebabs and France for breads and cheeses. Many Spanish bars serve small snacks called tapas with drinks. These foods are popular in other countries around the world, too.

Work in industry

Many western Europeans have jobs in manufacturing industries, designing and making products such as cars and clothes. However, as more factories use machines and computers to make their products, more people are getting jobs in service industries. These are jobs which involve doing things for other people. Hotel staff, bank managers and TV presenters are examples of service jobs.

Rural life

In a few parts of western Europe, farmers still use oxen to pull farm machinery, and harvest their crops by hand. But in most areas, only large, industrialized modern farms can survive, so smaller farms are disappearing.

The Mediterranean

The northern coast of the Mediterranean Sea forms the southern border of Europe. People who live there enjoy long, hot, dry summers, which make the Mediterranean area a popular tourist destination. Many of the people living around the coast work in the tourist industry.

Internet links

For links to websites where you can take virtual tours of Western European countries including England, France and Spain, float through the canals of Venice and find out about unusual festivals celebrated by Western Europeans, go to **www.usborne.com/quicklinks**

These are small ornamental masks sold as souvenirs in Venice. Full-size masks like these are worn by "masqueraders" at Venice's annual carnival.

A watery city

Western Europe has many impressive historical cities, but one of the most unusual is Venice in Italy, which is divided into more than a hundred tiny islands by a network of canals. No cars are allowed in Venice's old town, so people get around on foot or by boat. There are special boats that provide public transportation and long, narrow boats called gondolas which tourists take rides in.

Unusual festivals

Western Europeans celebrate many festivals including religious and national holidays, but there are also many unusual regional celebrations. For example, near Gloucester, England, there is a competition where people chase cheeses down a steep hill.

At the Sylvesterchlausen New Year celebration in Urnasch, Switzerland, people wearing masks go from house to house ringing bells and dancing. Spain has lots of local festivals. In Bunol, there is a huge annual tomato fight, and in Catalonia people make human castles by standing on one another's shoulders. Pamplona has a festival where people run through the streets ahead of bulls.

This dancer is performing a traditional Spanish flamenco dance, involving dramatic stamping and twirling movements.

The Arc de Triomphe in Paris, France's capital, is a war monument which was commissioned by Napoleon in 1806. Today it is surrounded by huge, traffic-filled roads.

EASTERN EUROPE

Until the 1990s much of eastern Europe was ruled by the former Communist power the U.S.S.R.* But in the late 1980s and the 1990s, people rebelled against their Communist leaders, and today the area is a patchwork of independent states.

This is a corridor in a school near Chernobyl which was evacuated after a nuclear disaster.

Peoples at war

Over the centuries, eastern Europe has seen many wars. Most recently, fighting broke out when ethnic groups demanded more freedom from the people who ruled them. For example, Yugoslavia was once a large country containing many peoples: Serbs, Bosnians, Albanians, Croats, Slovenes, Montenegrins, Kosovars and Macedonians. After the Communist system collapsed in 1990, wars raged here as ethnic groups fought to have their own states. It has now been replaced by Serbia, Bosnia and Herzegovina, Albania, Croatia, Slovenia, Montenegro, Kosovo and Macedonia.

Pollution

Pollution is a big problem in eastern Europe. Many factories, set up under Communism, still use old-fashioned fuels and methods which allow toxic gases to escape. In 1986, an accident at a nuclear power station in Chernobyl, Ukraine, sent radioactive dust into the air, polluting large areas of Europe. Hundreds of people had to leave their villages and the radiation made many people ill.

Trade links

The collapse of the U.S.S.R. and Communism has led to an explosion of trade between eastern Europe and the rest of the world. As well as selling products such as wine and factory goods, eastern European countries have become major buyers of new technology such as computing systems and mobile phones.

This is a statue from Statue Park, in Hungary. The park contains Communist statues that once stood in public places.

*Communism, U.S.S.R., 204

Spa towns

Spas are springs containing minerals. During the 19th century, it became fashionable throughout Europe to drink and bathe in spa waters. Many resorts were developed to cater for visitors. There are numerous spas throughout eastern Europe which remain popular today, such as those in Budapest in Hungary, and Karlovy Vary and Marianske Lazne in the Czech Republic. People can still go to these places to drink the waters.

Architecture

Many cities of eastern Europe, such as Prague, Krakow and Budapest, have well-preserved old towns. These have winding cobbled streets and a wide variety of architecture, including impressive churches and castles. Some houses are made from wood and many larger houses have distinctive painted facades, or fronts. However, some cities, such as Warsaw in Poland, which had to be heavily rebuilt after the Second World War, are dominated by modern apartment buildings.

This modern building in Prague was designed by an architect named Frank Gehry. It is nicknamed "Ginger and Fred" after the dancers Ginger Rogers and Fred Astaire, because its shape looks a little like a dancing couple.

Internet links

For links to websites where you can find out about the collapse of Communism, discover what happened at Chernobyl, Ukraine, and browse photo galleries of Prague, Budapest and other cities of eastern Europe, go to **www.usborne.com/quicklinks**.

Old age record

Georgia has more people who live to be over 100 than any other country. Many Georgians suggest this is due to their outdoor lifestyle, gentle climate and fertile farmland. According to Georgian legend, when God created the Georgians, he didn't have any land left for them to live on. So he had to give them the piece of land he had saved for himself, which was the best in the world.

NORTHERN EUROPE

Denmark, Sweden, Norway and Finland form the area known as Scandinavia. Together with the volcanic island of Iceland, they make up northern Europe. There is very little poverty in Scandinavia and Iceland, and their clean cities and countryside are envied by many.

People bathing in the Blue Lagoon, a warm spring near Keflavik in Iceland

Land of the Midnight Sun

The northern part of Scandinavia juts far into the Arctic, the area around the North Pole. In midwinter, for about a month, the people who live there see no daylight at all, while from the end of May until the end of July the Sun never sets. Because of this, it is sometimes known as the Land of the Midnight Sun.

This hotel in Sweden is made entirely of ice. Every summer it melts and has to be rebuilt the following winter. Even the glasses people drink from are made of ice.

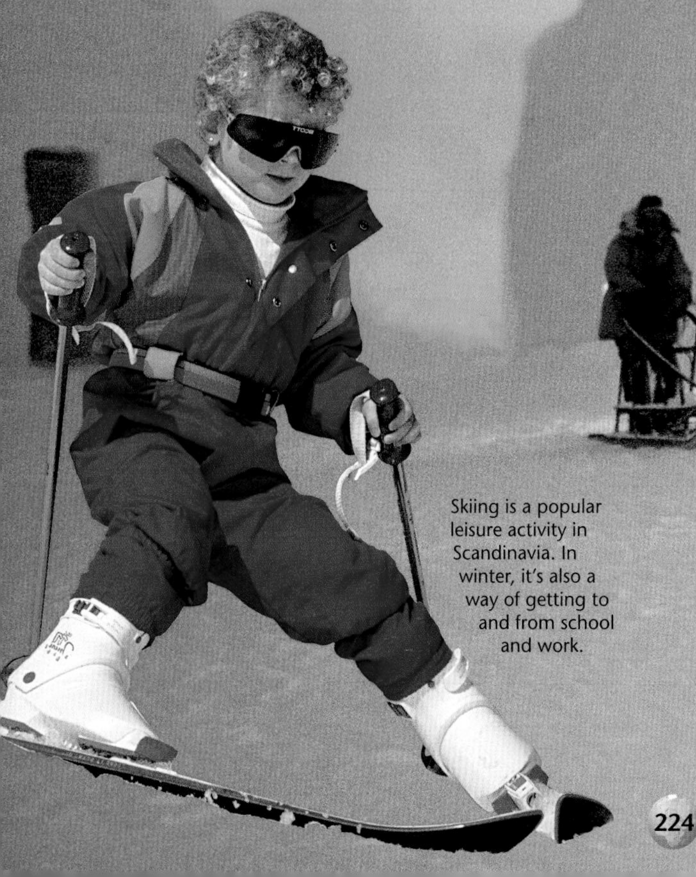

Skiing is a popular leisure activity in Scandinavia. In winter, it's also a way of getting to and from school and work.

Winter months

During the winter, much of northern Europe is covered in snow. In many places, skiing becomes the easiest way of getting around. Children often learn to ski as soon as they can walk, and some ski to school every morning. Many places hold annual ski competitions.

The environment

Many children and adults in Scandinavia belong to "green" groups that try to protect the environment by looking after the countryside and preventing pollution. Governments run recycling projects to collect reusable products from people's homes, and Scandinavia leads the way in building eco-friendly homes which use solar panels and insulation to save energy.

Lapland

Lapland, in the far north of Scandinavia, is one of the last areas of wilderness in Europe. It stretches from northern Russia across the north of Finland, and through parts of Sweden and Norway. It is home to the Sami, a people with their own language and culture. Some of the Sami still live a traditional lifestyle and herd reindeer. Their traditional homes are conical tents called *kota*. But these days most Sami live in houses, grouped together in small villages.

Internet links

Follow the website links at **www.usborne.com/quicklinks** to explore Iceland and Scandinavia, see inside Sweden's amazing Ice Hotel and find out about the Sami people who herd reindeer.

A Sami reindeer herder in northern Norway tends a newborn reindeer calf.

Daring design

Scandinavia is famous for its exciting design styles. Scandinavian companies are renowned for making everyday objects, like chairs, tables and cars, that are simple to use yet beautiful to look at. The Scandinavian style is now copied all over the world.

A UNITING EUROPE

Most of Europe's countries belong to organizations such as the European Union and the Council of Europe, in which several states band together to support each other. Many Europeans feel this has major advantages, although others worry that countries may lose their individuality.

Representatives of E.U. states meet in Strasbourg, France.

What is the E.U.?

The E.U., or European Union, is the most important European organization. It dates from 1957, when Belgium, France, Italy, Germany, Luxembourg and the Netherlands formed the E.E.C. (European Economic Community) to improve trade and cooperation between their countries. The group changed over the years, and in 1993 it became known as the European Union. By the year 2013 it had 28 members, with more applying to join.

Internet links

To find out about the European Union (E.U.), its member countries and Euro currency, visit the recommended websites at **www.usborne.com/quicklinks**

The E.U. flag (at the top) and the flags of some of its member states.

Free trade

The E.U. has set up laws to allow its member states to trade with each other easily. The E.U. also has laws to regulate measuring systems and safety standards for its workers, and workers from any E.U. state can work in any other without a visa or work permit.

These are 50-cent coins, part of the Euro currency. There are 100 cents in one Euro.

Single currency

In the 1990s, the European Union began to introduce a single currency called the Euro. Eventually it is intended to replace the national currencies of all the member states. However, some countries did not join the single currency immediately. It was launched on January 1, 1999, with 11 member states taking part.

The Council of Europe

The Council of Europe is not part of the E.U. It is a European organization that exists to protect human rights in Europe. It has 47 members, many more than the E.U. The citizens of any of its member states can appeal to the European Court, run by the Council of Europe, if they feel they are not being treated fairly by the legal system in their own country.

The E.U. flag has 12 stars representing the 12 states which were members when the E.U. was named in 1993.

Euro-skeptics

Although belonging to European organizations brings benefits, it may also have disadvantages. Some people in Europe are worried that the increasing power of European organizations could threaten the unique culture of individual countries. In several countries, political activists, sometimes called Euro-skeptics, campaign to stop their governments from signing up to European laws and joining the single currency.

These are farmers from all over Europe protesting in Strasbourg against some of the European Union's agricultural policies.

EUROPE AND THE WORLD

Over the centuries, European countries have explored and dominated many other lands, imposing their languages, customs and cultures. Europe itself has also been greatly influenced by the cultures it has come into contact with.

Internet links

For links to websites about European exploration and colonization, and facts, maps and video clips of the First and Second World Wars, go to **www.usborne.com/quicklinks**

This cloud was produced by the atomic bomb that was dropped on Nagasaki, in Japan, on August 9, 1945. Five days later Japan surrendered, ending the Second World War.

Two world wars

The First and Second World Wars of the 20th century both began in Europe. They grew larger as nations around the world became involved. Both wars spread as far as Africa and the Far East.

The Second World War in particular had a huge impact on the world. It began in 1939 after German troops, under the leadership of Adolf Hitler, began invading other European countries. Nations worldwide took sides in the conflict, and the war only ended in 1945, after the U.S.A. used newly invented nuclear weapons against two Japanese cities, Hiroshima and Nagasaki.

Science

Europe's inventors and scientists have changed the world. The idea that the world was round and not flat began in ancient Greece. When it was finally proved in the 15th century, it spurred European explorers to discover and colonize other continents.

Europeans also invented machines such as the steam engine, which led to the Industrial Revolution in the 18th century. This meant goods began to be mass-produced in factories instead of being made by individual craftspeople. Colonization ensured that European-style factories soon spread around the world.

Cultural exchanges

In the past, many Europeans saw it as their right to spread European culture in the places they colonized. For example, Spanish missionaries spread Catholicism in South America, and British educational and political systems were put in place in India. Most former European colonies are now independent, but some aspects of European culture, such as religions and clothes styles, remain behind. These former colonies have also had an influence on European culture and some people from them have moved to Europe.

This is the Royal Pavilion in Brighton, in the south of England. The design of the building was influenced by architecture in India, a former British colony.

These young Indian boys are learning to play cricket, which was brought to India from Britain.

Colonization

Like other peoples around the world, Europeans have been exploring for thousands of years. On many expeditions, European explorers also attempted to colonize the places they found, and bring them under European control.

From the 1500s onwards, Spain and Portugal ruled much of South America, Britain colonized India, and several European nations claimed parts of Africa. During the 18th and 19th centuries, European countries ruled over more than half the people in the world.

Zulu men wearing traditional headdresses for a celebration in Durban, South Africa

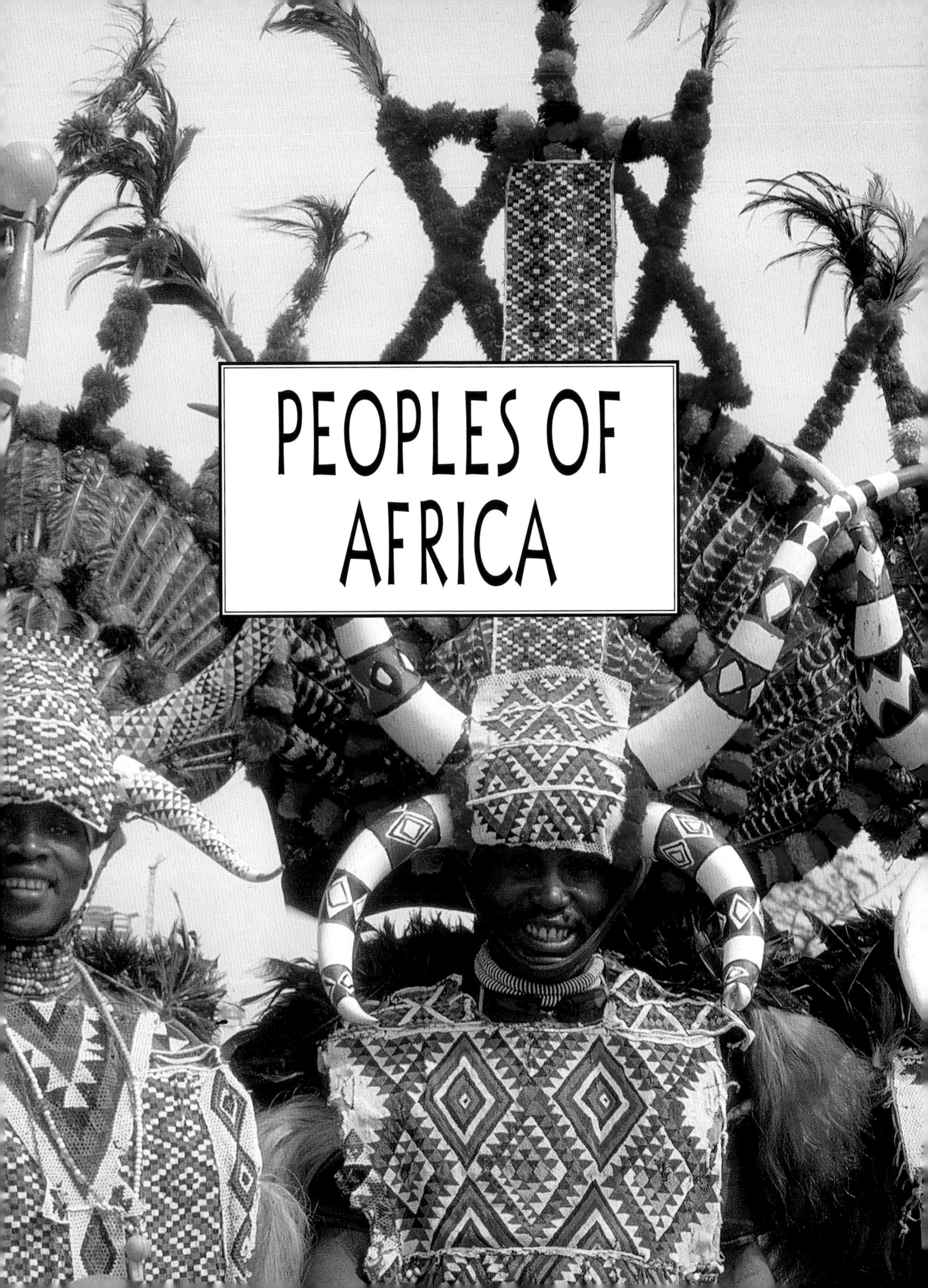

PEOPLES OF AFRICA

AFRICA

Africa is a huge continent, the second biggest in the world. It contains more than 50 countries, many hundreds of peoples and many different religions and ways of life. Yet many Africans also have a sense of belonging together as one big group, especially in the part of the continent south of the Sahara Desert.

These women are collecting water from a village well in Burkina Faso.

Freedom

In the 15th century, Europeans began to transport people from West Africa to Europe and North and South America to work as slaves.

Slavery was abolished in the 19th century, but European countries then began to take over Africa for themselves. Most of the continent was divided into colonies ruled by Portugal, Belgium, Italy, France, Britain and Germany. The African peoples resisted foreign rule, and most African countries became independent in the 1960s and 1970s.

1,000 languages

Over 1,000 languages are spoken in Africa. Countries with lots of languages usually have an official language as well, so that everyone can communicate with each other easily.

Most people learn the official language for use at work and at school, but may speak other languages at home and with their friends.

> **Internet links**
>
> Go to **www.usborne.com/quicklinks** for links to websites where you can journey through the history of Africa and learn about the horrors of the slave trade. You can take a virtual tour of the continent, too.

Two Masai* women, wearing traditional dress, talk together. The language they speak is also called Masai. The Masai people live in Kenya and Tanzania.

Africa's peoples

Africa's largest populations are mainly in its capital cities, but Africa as a whole is sparsely populated and many of its people lead rural lives. Around three thousand different ethnic groups have been classified. One country can contain many different peoples, while a single ethnic group can spread across several countries.

A Herero woman milks a cow in her village in Botswana. Herero women wear bright dresses with full skirts, and skilfully arranged headscarves called *taku* or distinctive hats.

*Masai, 241

PEOPLES AND POWER

Africa was once made up of ethnic kingdoms, each with its own language and culture. But when European powers split Africa into countries, the new borders ran across the kingdoms of peoples such as the Tuareg and the Masai, dividing up their homelands.

This woman is one of the Berber people of northern Africa. She is spinning wool in the traditional way.

Ethnic emphasis

Africans often feel that their ethnic group is just as important as their nationality. Instead of just being Ghanaian or Kenyan, for example, Africans may introduce themselves as Yoruba, Bantu, Mundani, !Kung San, Berber, or one of hundreds of other groups.

Wars and civil wars

After countries such as Chad, Nigeria and Angola gained independence from Europe, different ethnic groups began to fight for power. Many of the wars still going on in Africa are based on ethnic disagreements. Often, as in the conflict between Hutu and Tutsi peoples in Rwanda and Burundi in the 1990s, people on the losing side are forced to flee across borders to nearby countries for safety. These people are called refugees*. When there are large numbers of refugees they may have to live in temporary refugee camps.

This is a refugee camp in Rwanda. It provided a temporary shelter for thousands of people who were forced to leave home by the war there in 1994.

*Refugees, 142

Local leaders

Although African countries are ruled by their governments, many villages and ethnic groups also have their own local leaders, or chiefs. A chief has the power to settle disputes, and presides over ceremonies and official celebrations. The role of chief is usually passed from father to son.

This is a leader of the Anlo-Ewe people of Ghana, dressed in ceremonial clothing.

Internet links

For links to websites where you can find out about everyday life in Africa today, learn about education and farming in Africa and see some examples of traditional, tribal clothing, go to **www.usborne.com/quicklinks**

The Nanas Benz of Togo

Women rarely gain political power in African governments. But some African peoples have matriarchal societies. This means that power is passed from mother to daughter. In parts of Togo, for example, rich female cloth traders called "Nanas Benz" are the most powerful people in their communities. They pass on their businesses and their wealth to their daughters. If they only have sons, they pass everything to their nieces instead.

DESERT LANDS

The Sahara, the world's biggest desert, divides northern Africa from the rest of the continent. The Mediterranean countries (Morocco, Algeria, Tunisia, Libya and Egypt) are Muslim nations. They tend to have more in common with the Middle East than with the rest of Africa.

These pendants represent the Hand of Fatima, the daughter of Mohammed who is the main prophet of Islam.

Life in the desert

The Sahara takes up most of northern Africa, though only a few people live there. These include the Tuareg, a nomadic people who looked after trade routes in the desert in ancient times. Because of severe droughts in the last few decades, many desert people have had to abandon their old lifestyles and move to the cities.

Fatima's hand

In Northern Africa, the Muslim religion is very important. Most people pray several times each day. They also protect themselves from bad luck with images of a patterned hand, called the Hand of Fatima. It is said to ward off the "evil eye", which means a curse caused by a jealous glance.

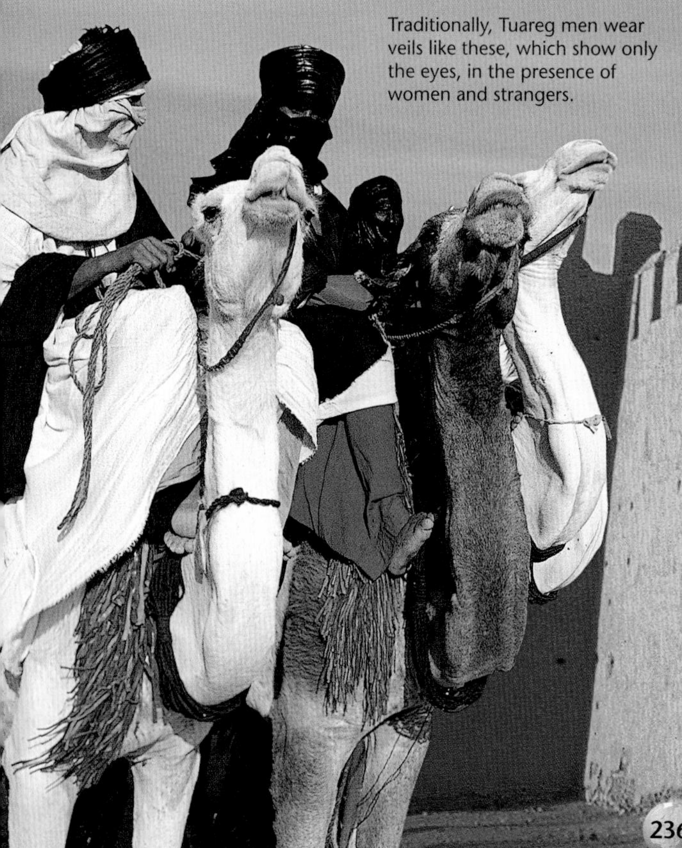

Traditionally, Tuareg men wear veils like these, which show only the eyes, in the presence of women and strangers.

Walled cities

In some modern northern African cities, such as Marrakesh in Morocco and Tunis in Tunisia, there are still old medieval towns, or *medinas*. Surrounded by tall, thick walls, these old towns are crammed with tiny winding streets, along which markets, or *souks*, are held. Different kinds of goods are sold or made in different areas of the town. For example, noisy or smelly trades such as leather-making take place near the edge of the town, while crafts such as bookbinding are close to the main mosque.

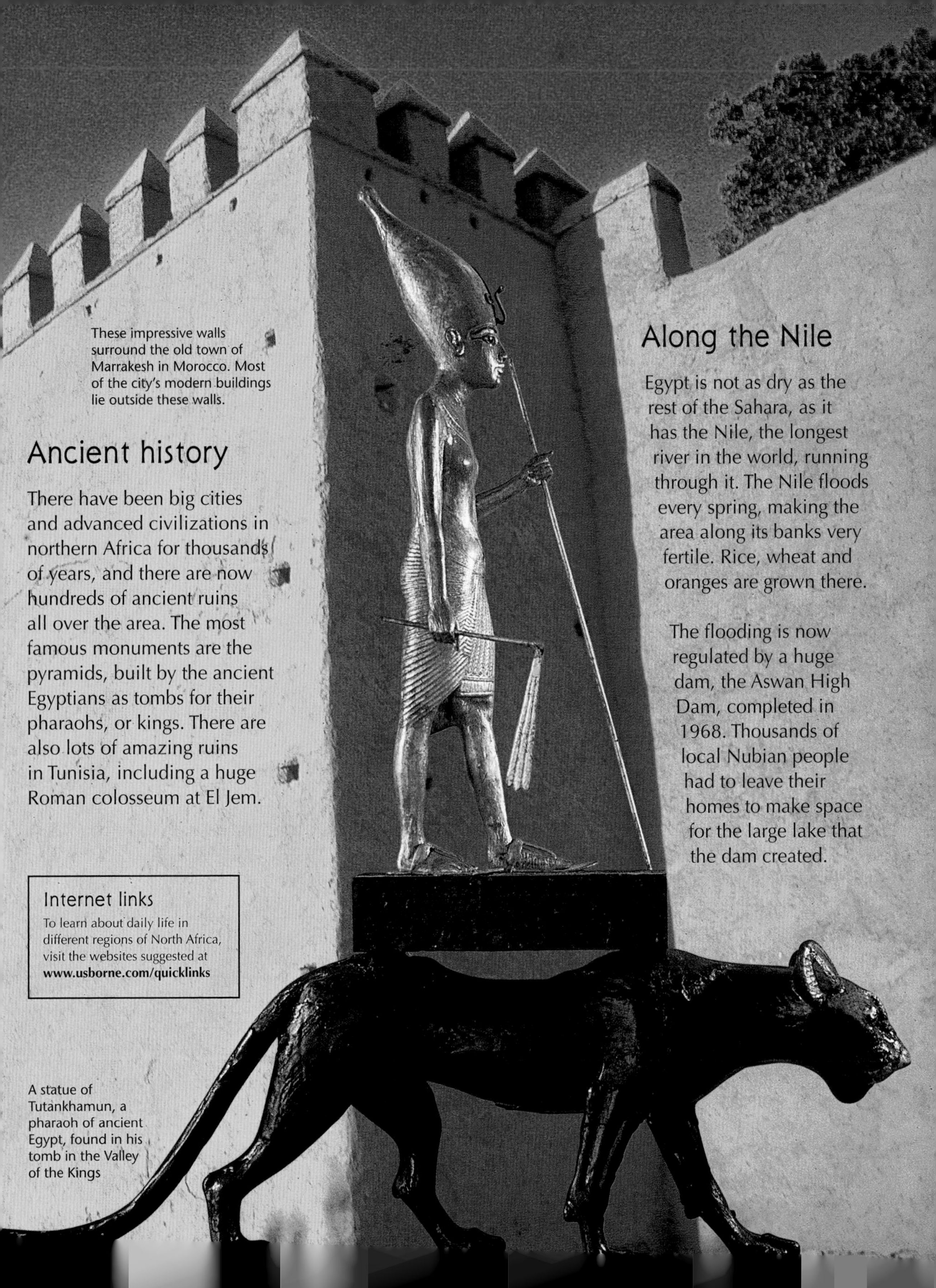

These impressive walls surround the old town of Marrakesh in Morocco. Most of the city's modern buildings lie outside these walls.

Ancient history

There have been big cities and advanced civilizations in northern Africa for thousands of years, and there are now hundreds of ancient ruins all over the area. The most famous monuments are the pyramids, built by the ancient Egyptians as tombs for their pharaohs, or kings. There are also lots of amazing ruins in Tunisia, including a huge Roman colosseum at El Jem.

Along the Nile

Egypt is not as dry as the rest of the Sahara, as it has the Nile, the longest river in the world, running through it. The Nile floods every spring, making the area along its banks very fertile. Rice, wheat and oranges are grown there.

The flooding is now regulated by a huge dam, the Aswan High Dam, completed in 1968. Thousands of local Nubian people had to leave their homes to make space for the large lake that the dam created.

Internet links

To learn about daily life in different regions of North Africa, visit the websites suggested at **www.usborne.com/quicklinks**

A statue of Tutankhamun, a pharaoh of ancient Egypt, found in his tomb in the Valley of the Kings

WEST AND CENTRAL AFRICA

The countries of West and Central Africa are tightly packed around a huge bay known as the Gulf of Guinea. Nigeria, right in the middle of this region, is Africa's most populous country. This part of the world is characterized by its diversity of peoples, cultures and religions, and its thriving art and music scene.

The Sahel

The Sahel is a strip of dry land south of the Sahara Desert. Countries there, such as Chad, Niger and Mali, are cut off from the coast and have little fertile land. Bad droughts happen every few years. Nomadic herders, such as the Tuareg, live in the north of the Sahel. In the south, the land is greener and people live by farming and fishing.

Left: Dogon people dance on stilts at a traditional celebration in the village of Sangha, Mali.

Along the coast

The small countries along the western African coast, such as Ghana and Senegal, are among Africa's wealthier nations. As well as farming and fishing, many of them mine valuable deposits of iron ore, diamonds and gold. Having been ruled by Europe, these countries gained their independence in the mid-20th century. But some, such as Sierra Leone, have been damaged by wars between groups battling for power.

Nigeria

Nigeria is a land of huge diversity, from the high-rise coastal city of Lagos to tropical forests in the east, and dusty plains and mud-walled villages in the central regions. Nigeria also has many different peoples, belonging to over 250 ethnic groups. The biggest groups are the mainly-Muslim Hausa and Fulani peoples of the north, the Christian Igbo of the south, and the southwestern Yoruba people, most of whom follow traditional local religions.

This statue is part of a Yoruba shrine in Oshogbo, southwestern Nigeria, dedicated to a river goddess called Oshun.

Internet links

Follow the website links at **www.usborne.com/quicklinks** to explore websites where you can take tours of West and Central African countries. You can view photographs, try out recipes, listen to music and find out about the sports, arts and daily life of their peoples, too.

Diverse religions

Across Africa, many ancient, local belief systems are still strong. They often involve animism, a belief in spirits belonging to plants or animals. The spirit world is believed to exist alongside the physical world and to be able to affect it in various ways.

A street in Lagos, Nigeria's biggest city, crammed with cars, buses, pedestrians and busy markets

These Buduma people are fishing from a papyrus reed boat. The Buduma live on a series of islands in Lake Chad, which is bordered by Chad, Niger, Nigeria and Cameroon.

LANDSCAPES OF THE EAST

Africa's most famous landscapes are found along its eastern side, where deserts in the north give way to grasslands, lakes and wildlife reserves in the Great Rift Valley. This region has been influenced by many peoples, including Indians, Arabs, and local ethnic groups such as the Masai.

Eastern Africa has huge expanses of open grasslands which are home to many large animals, such as lions.

The Horn of Africa

The Horn of Africa is a hook-shaped piece of land sticking out into the sea just south of Arabia. The countries there, such as Ethiopia, Djibouti and Somalia, are hot and dry, and most people live by herding cattle from place to place.

Recently Ethiopia and Somalia have suffered from famines, triggered by droughts which have killed crops and farm animals. Money has often been spent on wars instead of food, and areas have become so dangerous that aid workers are unable to reach them.

Ecotourism

In Kenya and Tanzania, the Great Rift Valley's grassy plains teem with leopards, lions, antelopes and other wildlife. These countries have set aside huge national parks and reserves, which not only protect the animals, but also make money from tourism. In the past, people paid to hunt these animals, but now tourists go on safaris to spot and photograph them.

The round, thatched huts in this farming village near Belet Weyne, Somalia, are typical traditional East African homes. There is also a pen for the cattle.

Losing a lake

The peoples who live around Lake Victoria, which straddles Uganda, Tanzania and Kenya, have fished in the lake and used it as a way to get around for centuries. But recently Lake Victoria has been polluted by fertilizers running into it from coffee and tea fields, and the amount of fish in it has fallen.

Great Rift Valley

The Great Rift Valley is made up of a huge series of valleys and lakes which stretch all the way down East Africa. The lakes and fertile hillsides make this a good area for fishing and farming. Archaeologists searching there have found skulls and tools which suggest that East Africa was the home of the first ever human beings.

The Masai

East Africa is home to many local ethnic groups. The Masai, who live in Tanzania and Kenya, are proud of their nomadic cattle-herding lifestyle. They rarely slaughter their cattle for food. Instead, they get protein by drinking milk and blood drawn from the cattle.

Today, Masai people also visit towns to sell their cattle and buy goods. Some also make money by selling their famous beadwork and posing in traditional dress for tourists.

Internet links

Visit the websites recommended at **www.usborne.com/quicklinks** to see lions, elephants and other wildlife of the grasslands, and meet the Masai people to learn about their traditions and lifestyle.

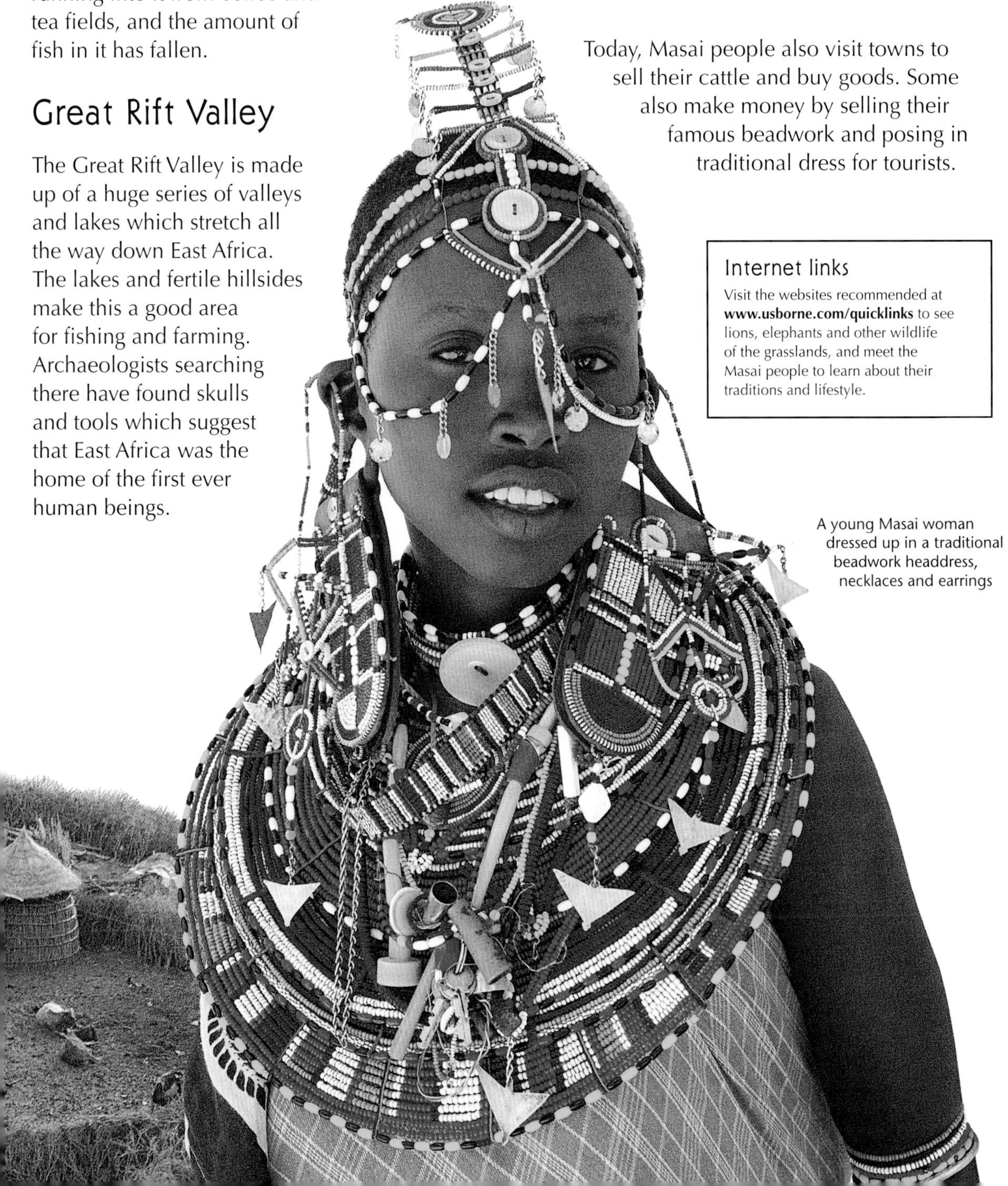

A young Masai woman dressed up in a traditional beadwork headdress, necklaces and earrings

SOUTHERN AFRICA

Southern Africa is a region of rich farmland, dusty deserts, beautiful coasts and steamy swamps. It is dominated by South Africa, Africa's richest country. South Africa's mines, farms and factories provide work for many people from other southern African countries. Yet South Africa itself is in the midst of huge changes.

The mining of precious stones such as diamonds creates jobs for many people in South Africa.

Divisions and inequality

In 1994, South Africa held its first free election after more than 40 years of a regime known as apartheid. Under apartheid (which means "apartness"), only white people could vote. They ruled the country, and the main ethnic groups were forced to live separately from each other.

At the election, a party called the African National Congress was voted into power and things began to change. People of all ethnic groups can now live and work together. But there are big inequalities, and many South Africans still struggle with poverty, violence and a high crime rate.

Nelson Mandela was a leading member of South Africa's anti-apartheid movement. He was the country's president from 1994 to 1999.

Diamonds and gold

A lot of southern Africa's wealth comes from its rich deposits of valuable minerals. The world's biggest goldfield is in Witwatersrand, near Johannesburg in South Africa, and thousands of people across southern Africa work in mines extracting precious stones and metals.

Internet links

For links to websites where you can find out about Nelson Mandela and South Africa's anti-apartheid movement, and learn more about tribal peoples of this region, go to **www.usborne.com/quicklinks**

!Kung San

The Kalahari is a stony desert which occupies parts of Botswana, South Africa and Namibia. It has been home to the !Kung San people for several thousand years. Many have moved to the cities, but a few still live as hunter-gatherers. The men hunt wild animals, while the women and children collect nuts, fruit and honey.

The !Kung San, along with many other southern African peoples, speak a language belonging to a group called Khoisan languages. As well as vowels and consonants, these languages include clicking noises made with the tongue. The ! sign stands for just one of many different types of click.

Hunter-gatherers, like these !Kung San picking berries in the Kalahari, have one of the world's oldest lifestyles.

Island life

These young boys from Madagascar are carrying a fishing net. Fishing is an important part of island life.

To the east of southern Africa lie the islands of Madagascar, Mauritius, Comoros and the Seychelles. The first people to live there came from Southeast Asia, over 4,000km (2,500 miles) away across the Indian Ocean. Today, the people are a mix of African, south Asian and Arabic ethnic groups. They make a living from fishing and tourism, and from growing spices.

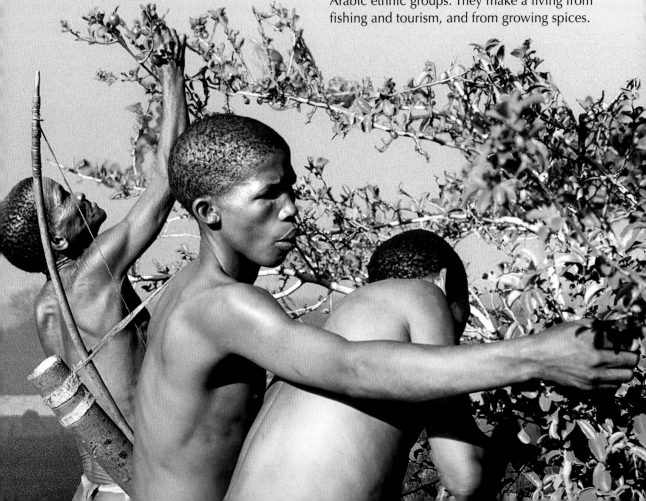

AFRICAN ART

Africa is famous for its arts and crafts of all kinds: sculpture and mask-making, painting, beadwork, pottery and carving. Traditionally, African artworks were used in religious ceremonies or worn on special occasions. Today, they are also sold to tourists, exported, or shown in art galleries.

Prehistoric pictures

8,000-year-old rock paintings and engravings found in the Sahara Desert are the earliest examples of African art. The hunting scenes in these pictures suggest that the Sahara was once much greener than it is today, with more people and wildlife living in it.

A prehistoric rock painting found in Tassili, Algeria, showing people with a herd of cattle

Masks and statues

Masks and statues are much more common in African art than pictures of landscapes or objects. This is because African art is often designed for use in ceremonies. Masks and statues can show gods, spirits, or images of perfect beauty, and can also be used for good luck. Some Ashanti women in Ghana, for example, carry a figure of a baby as a charm to help them have healthy children.

This mask is from Zimbabwe. It is part of a ceremonial dancing costume.

Symbolic coffins

In Accra, Ghana's capital city, an unusual art form has developed. Those who can afford it can be buried in special coffins built to represent their lifestyles. For example, a businessman might have a car-shaped coffin or a fisherman could have a fish or boat-shaped coffin.

This chicken-shaped coffin was probably built for a farmer.

Internet links

Follow the links at **www.usborne.com/quicklinks** to see different examples of traditional African art, including masks, statues, fabrics and other objects. You can also learn about ancient African art, such as Egyptian tomb paintings and hieroglyphics, too.

Body art

Earrings and nose rings, face painting and elaborate hairstyles are vital elements of many traditional ceremonies. Some peoples also use tattooing and scarification (marking the skin with scars) to create a kind of body art.

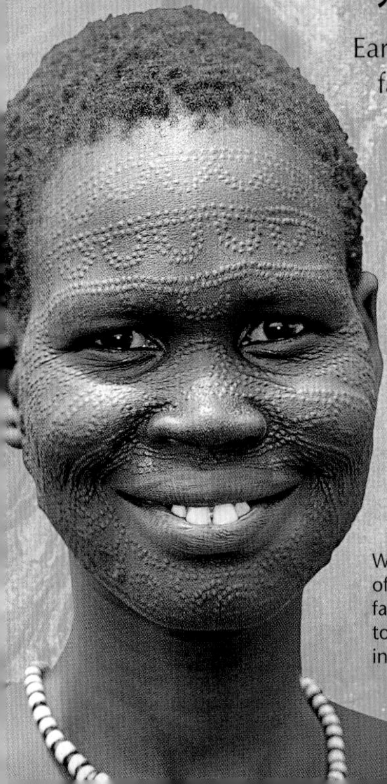

Women of the Nuer people of South Sudan have their faces patterned with scars to mark their passage into adulthood.

Ancient Egyptian artworks, like this carving in Saqqara, attract many tourists to Africa every year.

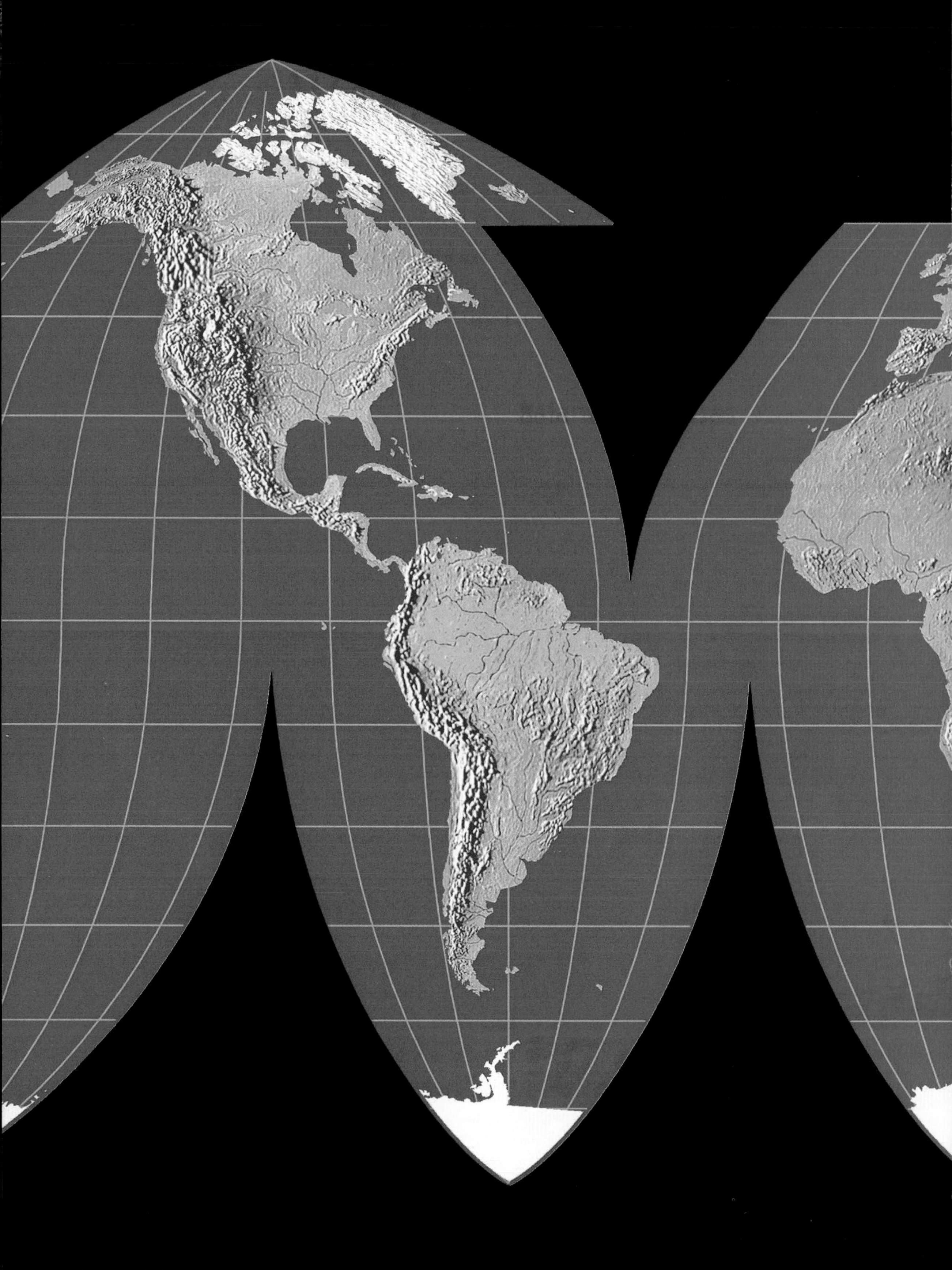

This map projection is called Boggs Eumorphic. It is a modified cylindrical projection. This type of map reduces the distortion of land areas.

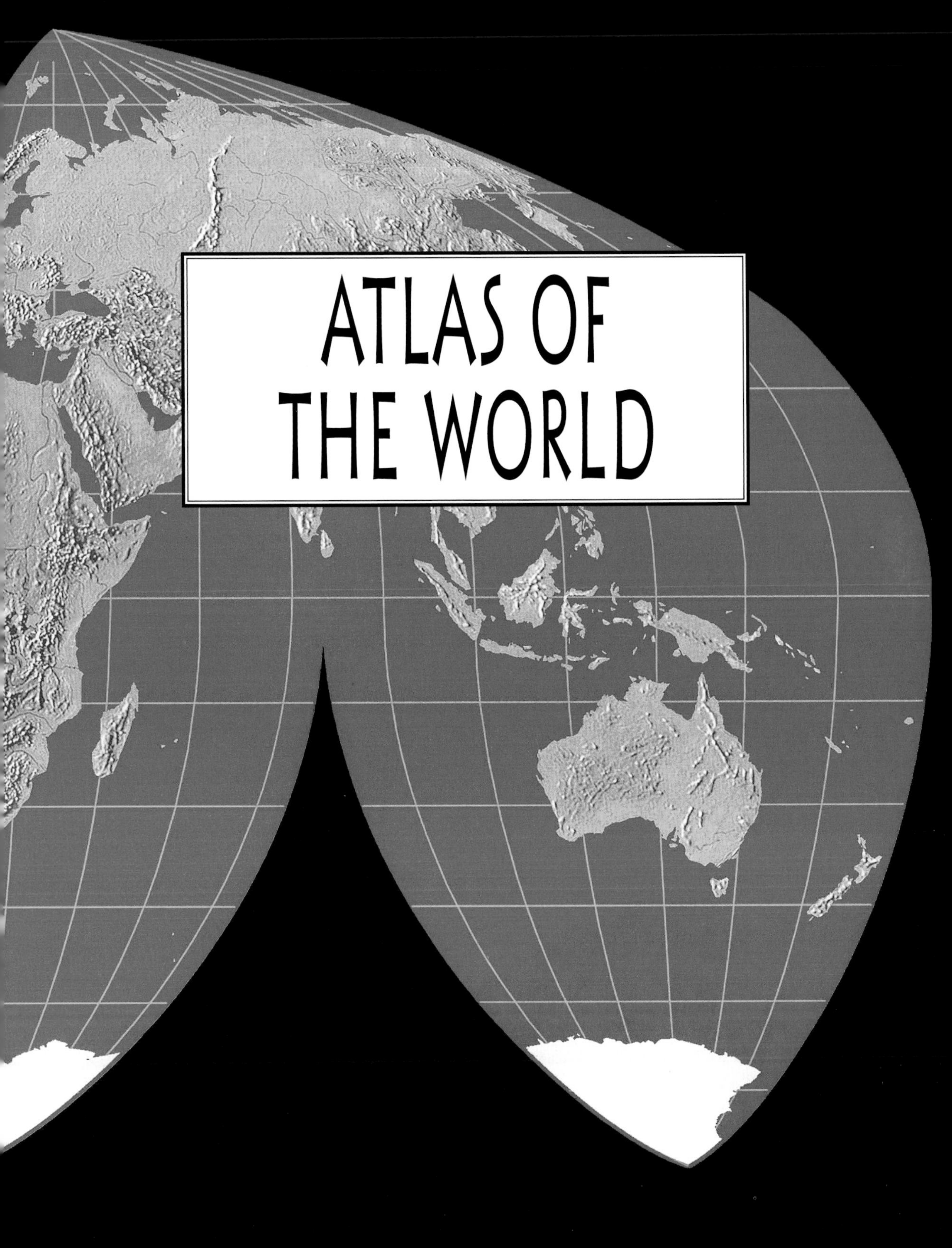

ATLAS OF THE WORLD

WHAT IS A MAP?

A map is an image that represents a particular area of the Earth's surface, usually from above and at a reduced size. A map can show the whole world or just a street. There can be many kinds of maps of the same place, each giving different types of information.

This map was drawn in 1584. Although people at this time knew much less about the shapes and locations of countries, they still created many maps of the world.

What maps show

Unlike an aerial photograph, which shows exactly what an area looks like from above, a map can show features of the area in a clearer, simplified way. It can also give different kinds of information about the area, such as the names of places, the position of borders between countries, or the types of crops that grow there.

On the left is a simple map of Baltimore Harbor, U.S.A. It just shows the area's main streets.

On this aerial photograph of the same area it's difficult to see the streets.

Internet links

Follow the website links at **www.usborne.com/quicklinks** to look at physical and political maps of different countries. Find street maps of towns and cities around the world, too.

Map features

Maps are designed to be clear, so most of them use conventions to help us recognize certain features. Land is often shown as green, and seas, rivers and lakes are usually shown as blue. Symbols can also be used to represent features. The meanings of the symbols are usually explained in a key.

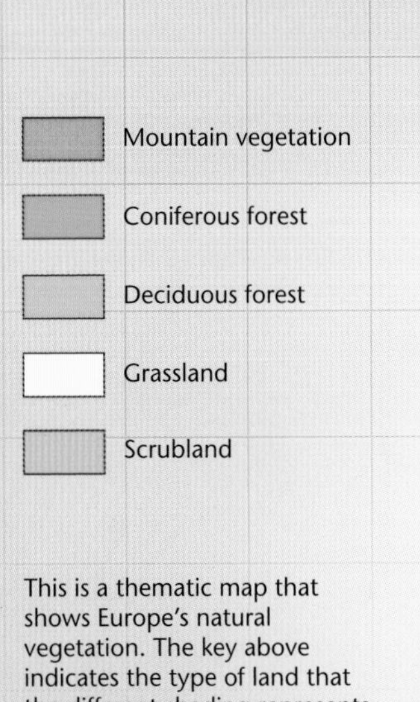

This is a thematic map that shows Europe's natural vegetation. The key above indicates the type of land that the different shading represents.

Kinds of maps

There are many different kinds of maps. Physical maps focus on natural features such as mountains, rivers and lakes. Political maps focus on the division of the Earth's surface into separate states*. Some maps are thematic. This means that only certain information, such as climate types or population, is represented. Thematic maps can help us make comparisons between the features of different areas.

Which way is up?

Although the Earth doesn't have a top and a bottom, north is usually at the top of maps. But it is sometimes more convenient to reposition a map, so north might not necessarily be at the top. Some maps have a compass symbol that indicates where north lies.

Scale

The size of a map in relation to the area it shows is called its scale. Some maps have a scale bar, which is a rule with measurements. It tells you how many miles or km are represented by a certain distance on the map. Other maps show this ratio in numbers. The figure 1:100 may mean, for example, that 1cm on the map represents 100cm on the Earth's surface. The scale of a map depends on its purpose. A map showing the whole world is on a very small scale, but a town plan is on a much larger scale so that features, such as roads and buildings, can be shown clearly.

1:80,000,000

0 1,000 2,000 3,000km

0 1,000 2,000 miles

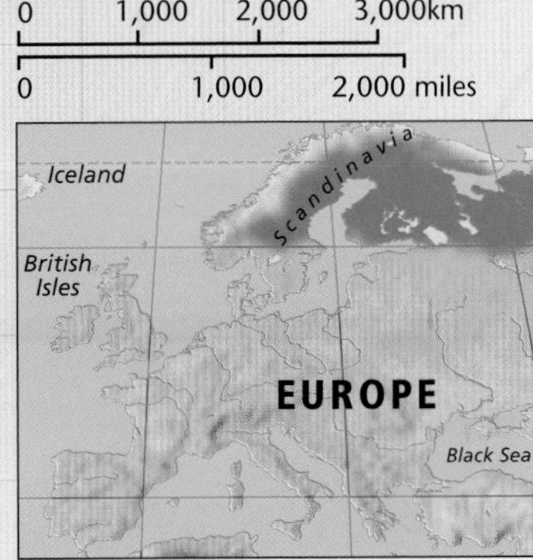

This map of Europe is on a small scale so that it all fits onto one small map.

1:7,000,000

0 100 200 300km

0 100 200 miles

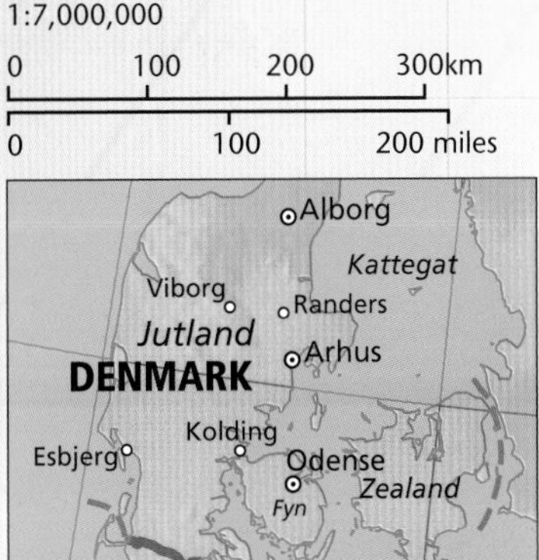

This map of Denmark is on a larger scale to show more detail.

*States, 256

DIVIDING LINES

We divide up the Earth with imaginary lines to help us measure distances and find where places are. There are two sets of lines, called latitude and longitude.

Latitude lines

Lines of latitude run around the globe. They are parallel to each other and get shorter the closer they are to the two poles. The latitude line that runs around the middle of the Earth is called the Equator. It is the most important line of latitude as all other lines are measured north or south of it.

Longitude lines

Lines of longitude run from the North Pole to the South Pole. All the lines are the same length, and they all meet at the North and South Poles.

The most important line of longitude is the Prime Meridian Line, which runs through Greenwich, in England. All other lines of longitude are measured east or west of this line.

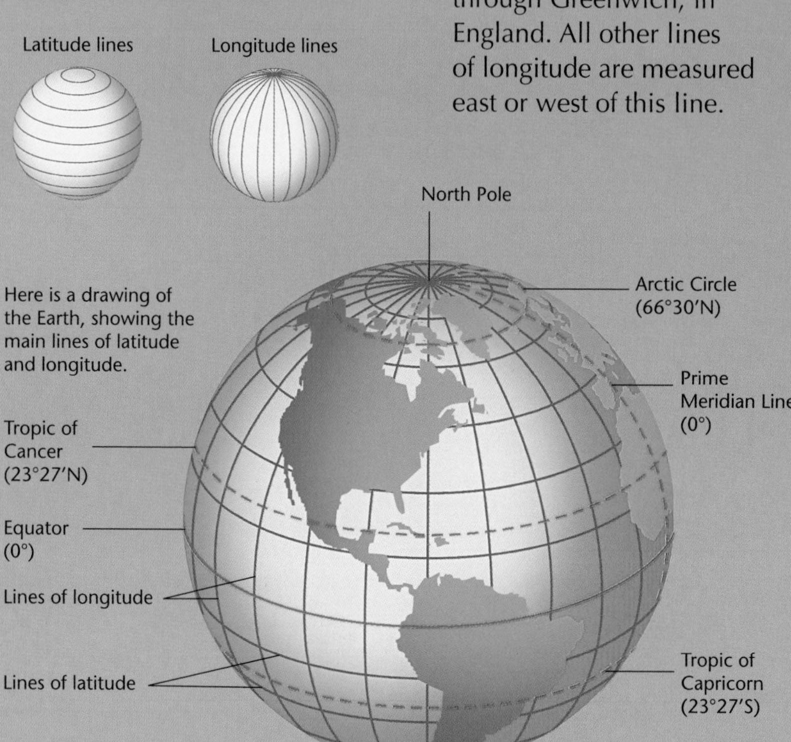

Here is a drawing of the Earth, showing the main lines of latitude and longitude.

This arctic fox lives in northern Canada, very near the Arctic Circle line of latitude.

Other lines

The Equator is not the only named latitude line. The Tropic of Cancer is a line north of the Equator. The Tropic of Capricorn is at the same distance south of the Equator. Between these lines is the hottest, stormiest part of the world. It is called the tropics.

The Arctic Circle is a latitude line far north of the Equator. The area north of this includes the North Pole and is called the Arctic. On the other side of the globe is the Antarctic Circle. The area south of this includes the South Pole and is known as the Antarctic.

Internet links

To find out more about lines of latitude and longitude, then see if you can work out the latitude and longitude of where you live, follow the links at **www.usborne.com/quicklinks**

Using the lines

Lines of latitude and longitude are measured in degrees (°). We describe the positions of places according to which lines of latitude and longitude are nearest to them. For example, a place with a location of 50°S and 100°E has a latitude 50 degrees south of the Equator, and a longitude 100 degrees east of the Prime Meridian Line.

Exact locations

The distance between degrees is divided up to give even more precise measurements. Each degree is divided into 60 minutes (′), and each minute is divided into 60 seconds (″). The subdivisions allow us to locate any place on Earth. For example, the city of New York, U.S.A., is at 40°42′51″N and 74°00′23″W.

The steamy rainforests of Malaysia lie near the Equator. Many orangutans, like the one shown here, live in these rainforests.

This is a map of New Zealand, with a grid formed by lines of latitude and longitude.

Using a grid

Lines of latitude and longitude form grids on maps. The maps in this book look similar to the one on the left. The vertical columns formed by lines of longitude are marked with letters, and the horizontal rows formed by lines of latitude are numbered.

All the places listed in the map index on page 376 have a letter and a number reference that tell you where to find them on a particular page. For example, on the map on the left, the city of Christchurch would have a grid reference of C3.

LOOKING AT THE EARTH

Modern technology has enabled scientists to make more accurate maps of the world than ever before. Even remote places, such as deserts, ocean floors and mountain ranges, have been mapped in detail using information from satellites that observe the Earth from space.

What is a satellite?

Artificial satellites are machines that orbit, or travel around, the Earth. They observe the Earth using a technique called remote sensing. Instruments on the satellite monitor the Earth without touching it, and send back pictures of its surface. Satellites also monitor moons and other planets.

This satellite monitors the Earth 24 hours a day. It uses powerful radar that pierces through clouds. This means that the satellite can provide images of the Earth in all weather conditions.

Satellite movement

Some satellites orbit the Earth at a height of between 5km (3 miles) and 1,500km (930 miles), providing views of different parts of the planet. Others stay above the same place all the time, moving at the same speed as the Earth rotates to give a constant view of a particular area. These are called geostationary satellites. They travel at a height of around 36,000km (22,370 miles).

Internet links

To zoom in on satellite images of the Earth and find out about the different uses of satellites and how they work, follow the links at **www.usborne.com/quicklinks**

This satellite image of Sicily was taken in July 2001. It shows the volcano Mount Etna erupting. You can see smoke from the volcano on the right of the picture.

Satellite uses

The information provided by satellites helps scientists to produce accurate maps. Satellite pictures can also be used to help predict and monitor natural hazards such as volcanic eruptions or earthquakes. Some satellites monitor the weather*. Satellite images can also show the effects that people have on their environment, for example the destruction of rainforests in South America.

Remote sensing

Satellites use a range of remote sensing techniques. One type is radar, which can provide images of the Earth even when it is dark or cloudy. Radar works by reflecting radio waves off a target object. The time it takes for a wave to bounce back indicates how far away the object is.

Powerful cameras provide pictures of the Earth's surface. Often, infrared cameras are used. Different surfaces reflect the infrared rays differently, so infrared images of the Earth are able to show its various types of land surfaces, such as deserts, grasslands and forests.

This satellite image of the Earth shows different types of land. Deserts and other dry regions are red, and areas with lots of vegetation are orange and yellow.

*Weather satellites, 90

HOW MAPS ARE MADE

The process of making maps is called cartography. Map-makers, or cartographers, compile each map by gathering information about the area and then representing it as an image as accurately as possible.

Internet links

To view different map projections, watch video clips about how maps are made and explore more global maps, follow the website links at **www.usborne.com/quicklinks**

Creating maps

Many sources are used to create maps. These include satellite images and aerial photographs. Cartographers often visit the area to be mapped, where they take many extra measurements.

In addition, cartographers use statistics, such as population figures, from censuses* and other documents. As the maps are being made, many people check them to make sure they are accurate and up-to-date.

Map projections

Cartographers can't draw maps that show the world exactly as it is, because it is impossible to show a curved surface on a flat map without distorting (stretching or squashing) some areas. A representation of the Earth on a map is called a projection. Projections are worked out using complex mathematics.

There are three basic types of projections – cylindrical, conical and azimuthal, but there are also variations on these. They all distort the Earth's surface in some way, either by altering the shapes or sizes of areas of land or the distance between places.

A cartographer uses an electronic distance measurer to check the measurements of an area of land.

*Censuses, 140

Cylindrical projections

A cylindrical projection is similar to what you would get if you wrapped a piece of paper around a globe to form a cylinder and then shone a light inside the globe. The shapes of countries would be projected onto the paper. Near the middle they would be accurate, but farther away they would be distorted.

Cartographers often alter the basic cylindrical projection to make the distortion less obvious in certain areas, but they can never make a map that is completely accurate.

This picture of a piece of paper wrapped around a globe illustrates how a cylindrical projection is made.

Below is a type of cylindrical projection called the Mercator projection, which was invented in 1596 by a cartographer called Gerardus Mercator. It makes countries the right shape, but makes those near the poles too big.

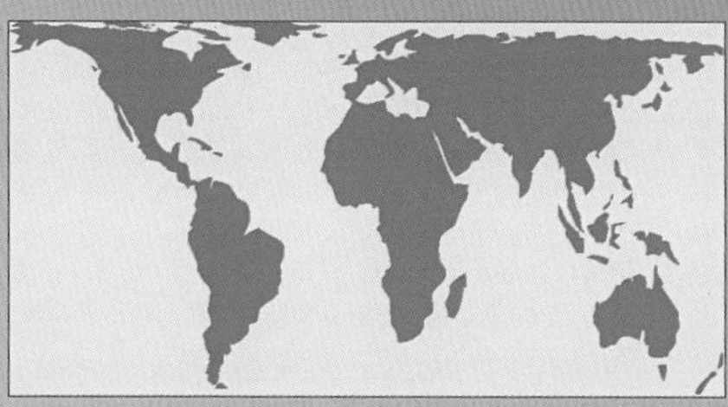

This cylindrical projection makes countries the right size in relation to each other, but some parts are too long. The projection was created in 1973 by Arno Peters. It is called the Peters Projection.

Conical projections

A conical projection is similar to the image you would get if you wrapped a cone of paper around part of a globe, then shone a light inside the globe. Where the cone touches the globe, the projection will be most accurate.

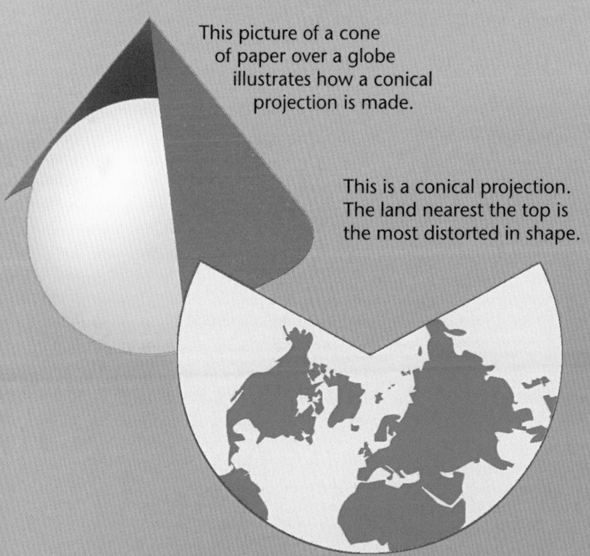

This picture of a cone of paper over a globe illustrates how a conical projection is made.

This is a conical projection. The land nearest the top is the most distorted in shape.

Azimuthal projections

An azimuthal projection is like an image made by holding paper in front of a globe, and shining a light through it. Land projected onto the middle of the paper would be accurate, but areas farther away would be distorted.

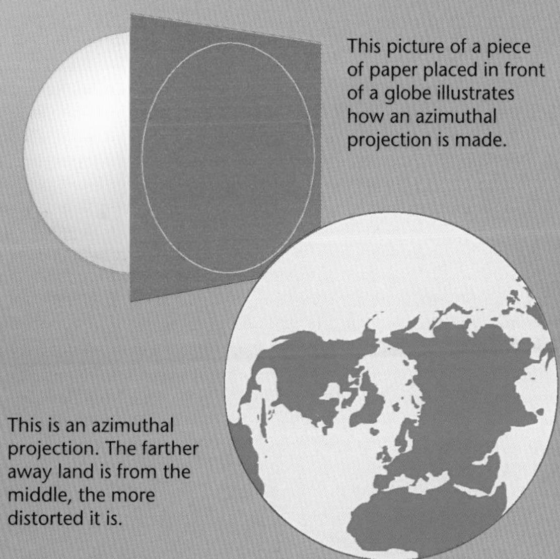

This picture of a piece of paper placed in front of a globe illustrates how an azimuthal projection is made.

This is an azimuthal projection. The farther away land is from the middle, the more distorted it is.

STATES AND BORDERS

The world's main land masses, which are called continents, are divided into independent states and dependent territories. The different areas are separated by borders.

What is a state?

A state is an area of land that has its own government* and is fully independent. Independent states are also known as countries.

Some large countries, such as the U.S.A., are split into several regions. Each region has its own government, which is responsible for the affairs of that region. In the U.S.A. these regions are also known as states.

Changing states

States don't always stay the same. They can divide or merge. For example, Germany was split into two states after the Second World War, and was then reunited as one state in 1990. Sometimes an area becomes independent and a new state is formed. For example, Croatia and Slovenia were once part of Yugoslavia, but are now separate states.

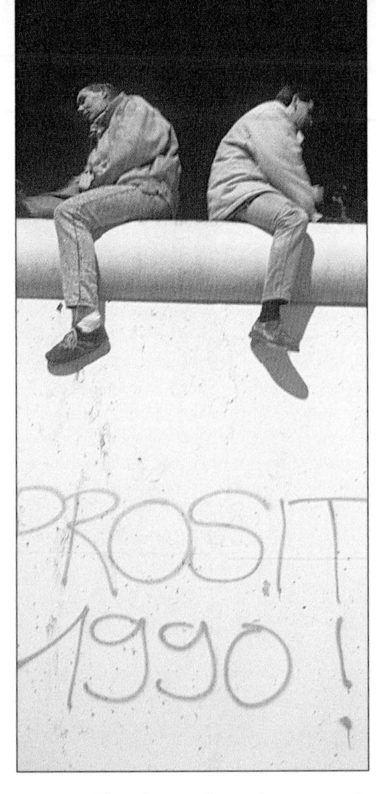

The picture above shows people sitting on the Berlin Wall. The wall formed a border between East and West Berlin when East and West Germany were separate states. It has now been pulled down.

What is a territory?

A dependent territory is an area of land that has a very limited government or no government at all. Instead, the land is owned and governed by a separate, independent state. For example, French Guiana in South America is a dependent territory of France.

*Governments, 353

Border disputes

Sometimes states disagree about where the border between them should be. This can lead to long conflicts, such as the war between Eritrea and Ethiopia. Eritrea was once part of Ethiopia but became an independent state in 1993. The two countries are still disputing the position of the border between them. Thousands of people have been killed in the conflict.

Borders often follow natural features such as rivers or mountain ranges. The Danube River separates several countries. Above, it is shown separating Serbia (left) and Romania (right).

Internet links

Try quizzes to test your knowledge of different countries around the world by visiting the websites suggested at **www.usborne.com/quicklinks**

Some borders are marked by barriers. Guards check that anyone crossing from one state to another is permitted to do so. This barrier marks the border between Belarus and Poland.

HOW TO USE THE MAPS

The maps in this book are divided up by continent. At the beginning of each section there is a political map showing the whole continent. The rest of the maps are larger scale maps showing more detailed views of the region.

Political maps

The shading on the political maps in this book is there to help you see clearly the different states, or countries, that make up each continent. The main purpose of these maps is to show country borders and capital cities. Alongside them there are facts and figures about the continents and their features.

This is a section of the political map of South America. You can see the whole map on pages 276–7.

Environmental maps

The majority of the maps in this book are environmental maps, like the one on the right. The shading on these maps shows different types of land, or environments, such as desert, mountain or wetland.

The main key on the opposite page shows what the different shading means. It also shows the symbols used to represent towns, cities and other features. There is a smaller key on each environmental map repeating the most important information from this key.

Finding places

To find a particular place or feature on the environmental maps, look up its name in the index on pages 376–389. Its page number and grid reference is given next to the name. You can find out how to use the grid on page 251.

The map on the right is part of the environmental map of the U.S.A. The numbered labels at the top explain some important features of these maps.

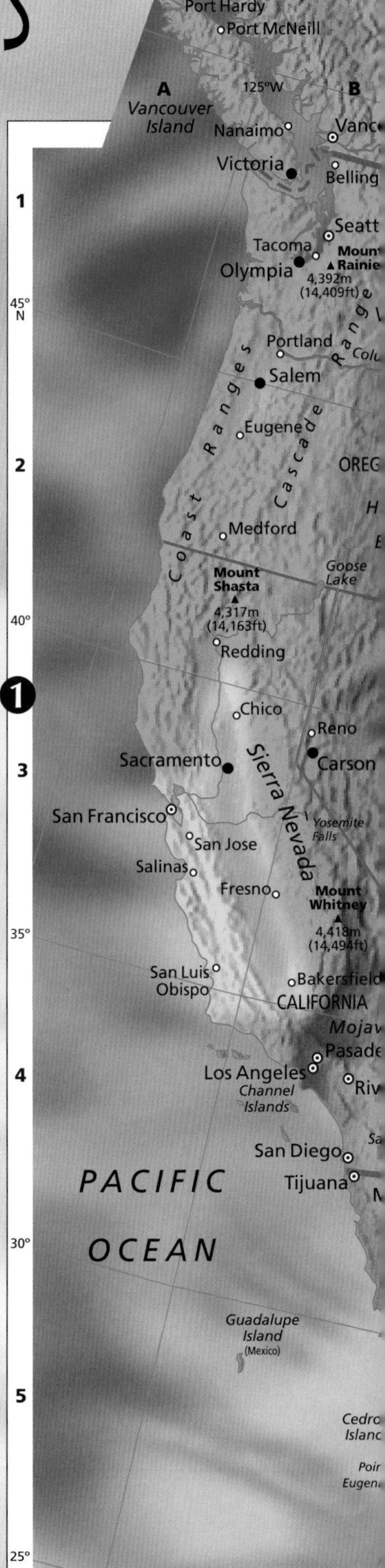

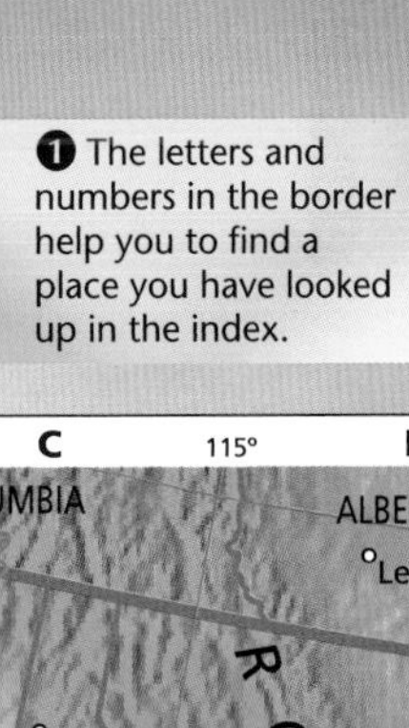

❶ The letters and numbers in the border help you to find a place you have looked up in the index.

❷ Lines of latitude and longitude are shown as thin blue lines.

❸ The names of countries are shown in large, bold type with capital letters.

❹ The thick purple lines are country boundaries.
❺ The thinner purple lines are boundaries of internal regions within a country.

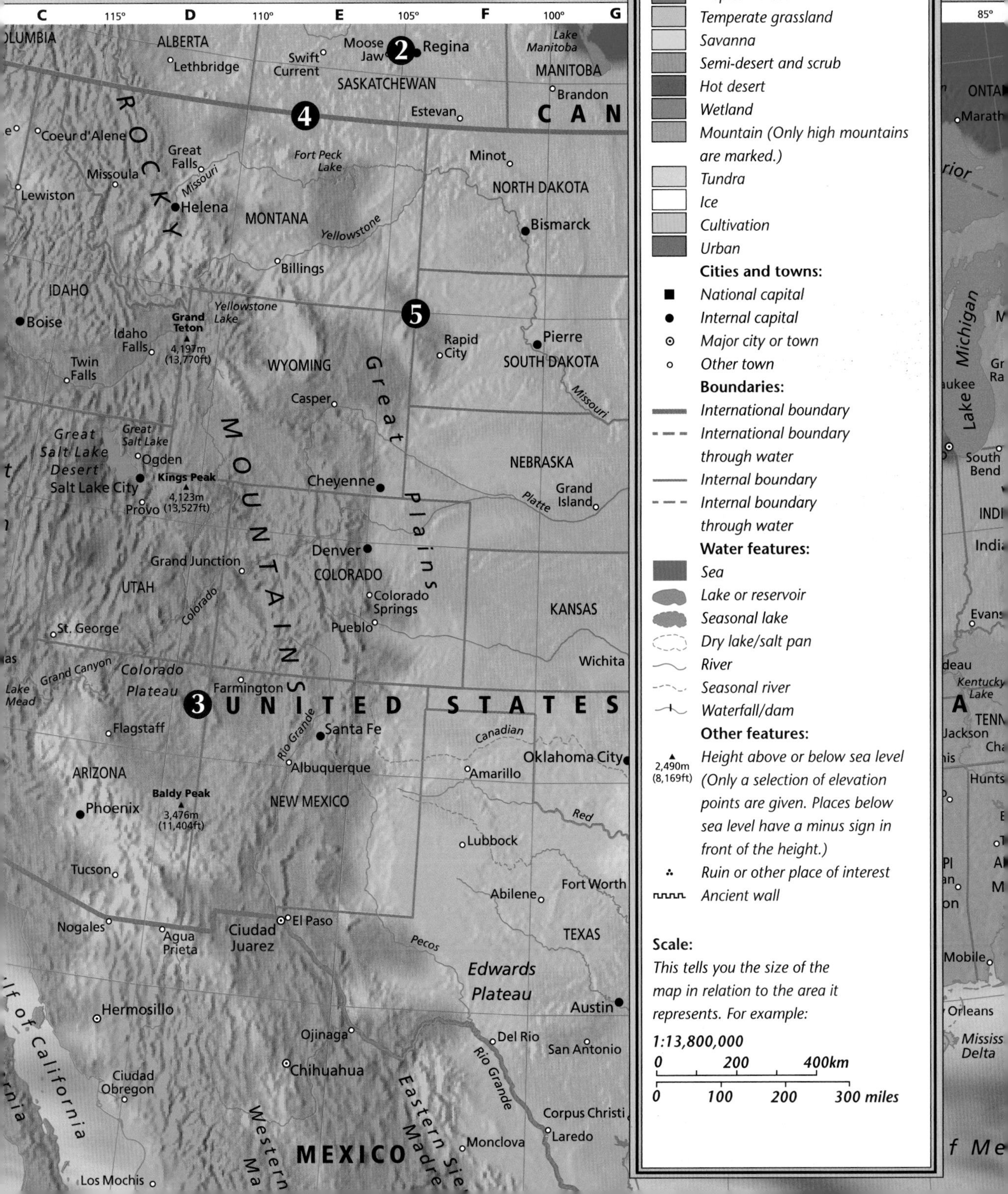

Main key

Land cover:

- *Boreal forest*
- *Temperate forest*
- *Tropical forest*
- *Temperate grassland*
- *Savanna*
- *Semi-desert and scrub*
- *Hot desert*
- *Wetland*
- *Mountain (Only high mountains are marked.)*
- *Tundra*
- *Ice*
- *Cultivation*
- *Urban*

Cities and towns:

- *National capital*
- *Internal capital*
- *Major city or town*
- *Other town*

Boundaries:

- *International boundary*
- *International boundary through water*
- *Internal boundary*
- *Internal boundary through water*

Water features:

- *Sea*
- *Lake or reservoir*
- *Seasonal lake*
- *Dry lake/salt pan*
- *River*
- *Seasonal river*
- *Waterfall/dam*

Other features:

- 2,490m (8,169ft) *Height above or below sea level (Only a selection of elevation points are given. Places below sea level have a minus sign in front of the height.)*
- *Ruin or other place of interest*
- *Ancient wall*

Scale:

This tells you the size of the map in relation to the area it represents. For example:

1:13,800,000

0 200 400km

0 100 200 300 miles

GREENLAND
(Denmark)
ICELAND
Arctic Circle
ALASKA
(U.S.A.)
CANADA
IRELAND
UNITED KINGDOM
UNITED STATES OF AMERICA
SPAIN
PORTUGAL
Azores
(Portugal)
MOROCCO
Canary Islands
(Spain)
WESTERN SAHARA
(Morocco)
Tropic of Cancer
THE BAHAMAS
MEXICO
CUBA
DOMINICAN REPUBLIC
HAITI
JAMAICA
Hawaiian Islands
(U.S.A.)
BELIZE
GUATEMALA
HONDURAS
EL SALVADOR
NICARAGUA
Caribbean Sea
DOMINICA
CAPE VERDE
MAURITANIA
MALI
SENEGAL
THE GAMBIA
GUINEA-BISSAU
GUINEA
BURKINA FASO
TOGO
SIERRA LEONE
LIBERIA
IVORY COAST
GHANA
TRINIDAD AND TOBAGO
COSTA RICA
PANAMA
VENEZUELA
GUYANA
SURINAME
FRENCH GUIANA
(France)
PACIFIC OCEAN
COLOMBIA
Equator
Galapagos Islands
(Ecuador)
ECUADOR
SAO TOME AND PRINCIPE
KIRIBATI
ATLANTIC OCEAN
PERU
BRAZIL
Cook Islands
(New Zealand)
French Polynesia
(France)
BOLIVIA
Tropic of Capricorn
Pitcairn Islands
(U.K.)
PARAGUAY
CHILE
URUGUAY
ARGENTINA
1:92,000,000
0 1,000 2,000 3,000 4,000 5,000km
0 1,000 2,000 3,000 miles
Falkland Islands
(U.K.)
South Georgia
(U.K.)
Antarctic Circle
Weddell Sea
160° 140° 120° 100° 80° 60° 40° 20° W
80° 60° 40° 20° N 20° S

Abbreviations used on map:
ALB. ALBANIA
ARM. ARMENIA
AUST. AUSTRIA
AZER. AZERBAIJAN
BELG. BELGIUM
B.H. BOSNIA AND HERZEGOVINA
CRO. CROATIA
CZECH REP. CZECH REPUBLIC
KOS. KOSOVO
LEB. LEBANON
LUX. LUXEMBOURG
MAC. MACEDONIA
MONT. MONTENEGRO
NETH. NETHERLANDS
SERB. SERBIA
SLOV. SLOVENIA
SWITZ. SWITZERLAND
U.A.E. UNITED ARAB EMIRATES
RUSSIA
FINLAND
ESTONIA
LATVIA
LITHUANIA
BELARUS
UKRAINE
MOLDOVA
ROMANIA
BULGARIA
Black Sea
GEORGIA
ARM.
AZER.
Caspian Sea
KAZAKHSTAN
UZBEKISTAN
KYRGYZSTAN
TURKMENISTAN
TAJIKISTAN
MONGOLIA
GREECE
TURKEY
CYPRUS
SYRIA
LEB.
ISRAEL
JORDAN
IRAQ
IRAN
AFGHANISTAN
PAKISTAN
KUWAIT
BAHRAIN
QATAR
U.A.E.
SAUDI ARABIA
OMAN
EGYPT
NEPAL
BHUTAN
BANGLADESH
INDIA
CHINA
NORTH KOREA
SOUTH KOREA
JAPAN
Taiwan (China)
BURMA (MYANMAR)
LAOS
THAILAND
VIETNAM
CAMBODIA
PHILIPPINES
SUDAN
ERITREA
YEMEN
DJIBOUTI
ETHIOPIA
SOUTH SUDAN
CENTRAL AFRICAN REPUBLIC
SOMALIA
UGANDA
KENYA
CONGO (DEMOCRATIC REPUBLIC)
RWANDA
BURUNDI
TANZANIA
SEYCHELLES
MALDIVES
SRI LANKA
BRUNEI
MALAYSIA
SINGAPORE
INDONESIA
EAST TIMOR
COMOROS
ZAMBIA
MALAWI
ZIMBABWE
MADAGASCAR
MAURITIUS
BOTSWANA
MOZAMBIQUE
Reunion (France)
SWAZILAND
LESOTHO
SOUTH AFRICA
INDIAN OCEAN
PACIFIC OCEAN
Northern Mariana Islands (U.S.A.)
MARSHALL ISLANDS
PALAU
FEDERATED STATES OF MICRONESIA
NAURU
KIRIBATI
PAPUA NEW GUINEA
SOLOMON ISLANDS
TUVALU
SAMOA
Coral Sea Islands Territory (Australia)
VANUATU
FIJI
TONGA
New Caledonia (France)
AUSTRALIA
NEW ZEALAND
Kerguelen Islands (France)
SOUTHERN OCEAN
ANTARCTICA
Arctic Circle
Tropic of Cancer
Equator
Tropic of Capricorn
Antarctic Circle
The shading on this map is there to help you see the different countries clearly.

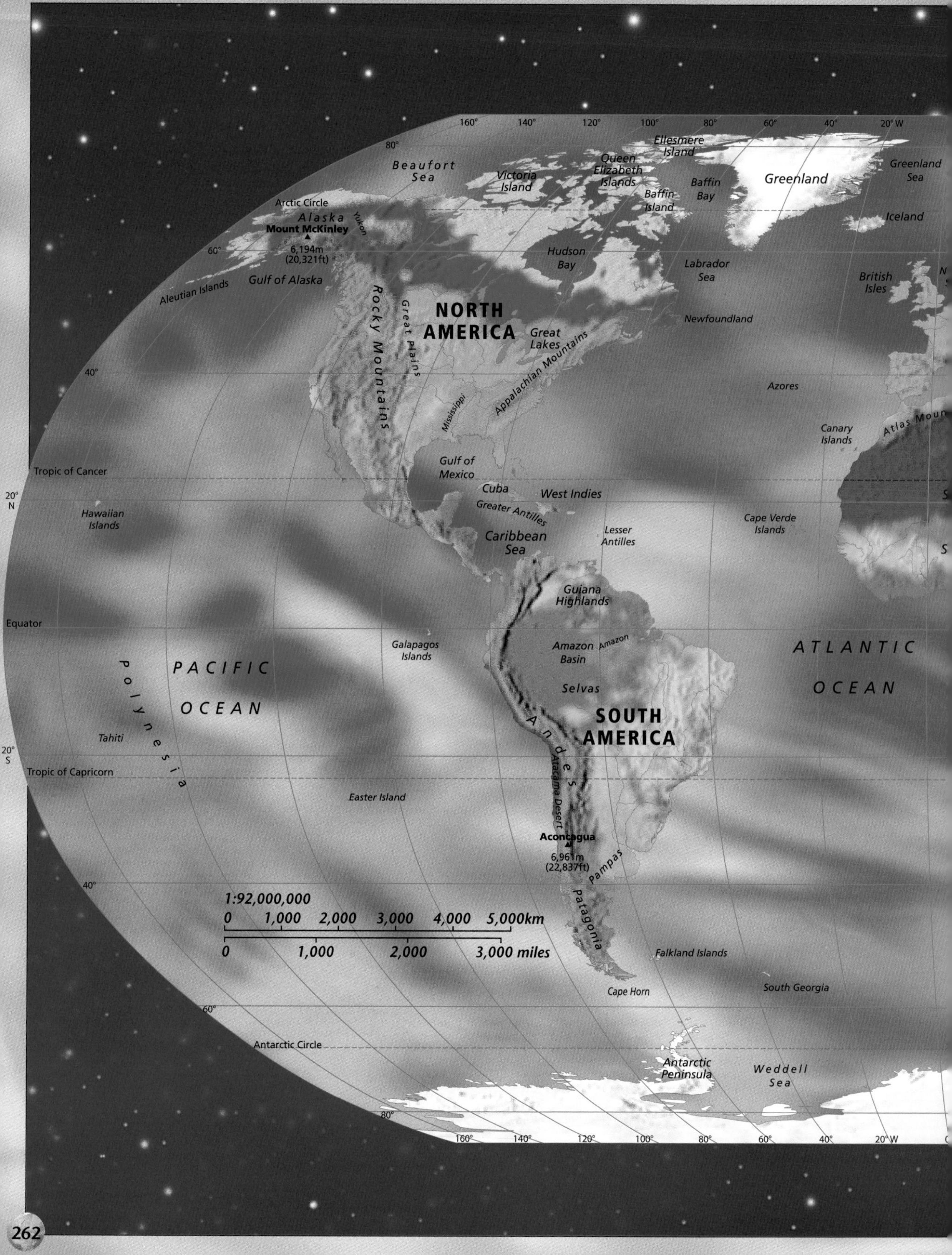
160°
140°
120°
100°
80°
60°
40°
20° W
80°
Ellesmere Island
Beaufort Sea
Queen Elizabeth Islands
Victoria Island
Baffin Bay
Greenland
Greenland Sea
Baffin Island
Arctic Circle
Alaska
Yukon
Mount McKinley
6,194m (20,321ft)
Iceland
60°
Hudson Bay
Labrador Sea
British Isles
Aleutian Islands
Gulf of Alaska
Rocky Mountains
Great Plains
NORTH AMERICA
Newfoundland
Great Lakes
Appalachian Mountains
40°
Azores
Mississippi
Canary Islands
Atlas Moun
Gulf of Mexico
Tropic of Cancer
20° N
Cuba
West Indies
Hawaiian Islands
Greater Antilles
Lesser Antilles
Cape Verde Islands
Caribbean Sea
Guiana Highlands
Equator
Galapagos Islands
Amazon Basin
Amazon
ATLANTIC OCEAN
PACIFIC OCEAN
Polynesia
Selvas
SOUTH AMERICA
Andes
Tahiti
20° S
Atacama Desert
Tropic of Capricorn
Easter Island
Aconcagua
6,961m (22,837ft)
Pampas
40°
1:92,000,000
0 1,000 2,000 3,000 4,000 5,000km
0 1,000 2,000 3,000 miles
Patagonia
Falkland Islands
Cape Horn
South Georgia
60°
Antarctic Circle
Antarctic Peninsula
Weddell Sea
80°
160°
140°
120°
100°
80°
60°
40°
20° W

RCTIC OCEAN
Severnaya Zemlya
Novaya Zemlya
Kara Sea
Laptev Sea
New Siberia Islands
East Siberian Sea
albard
Cape
Barents Sea
navia
Arctic Circle
Verkhoyansk Range
Yenisey
Ob
Siberia
European Plain
Ural Mountains
Volga
ASIA
Lake Baikal
Sea of Okhotsk
Kamchatka Peninsula
ROPE
Danube
Mount Elbrus
5,642m (18,510ft)
Black Sea
Caspian Sea
Aral Sea
Altai Mountains
Gobi Desert
Hokkaido
Huang He (Yellow)
Yellow Sea
Honshu
erranean Sea
Zagros Mountains
Himalayas
Chang Jiang (Yangtze)
East China Sea
Mount Everest
8,848m (29,029ft)
Ganges
Nile
Chang Jiang
Tropic of Cancer
Arabian Peninsula
Taiwan
Red Sea
Deccan Plateau
Bay of Bengal
Arabian Sea
Mekong
South China Sea
Philippine Islands
Micronesia
PACIFIC OCEAN
RICA
Ethiopian Highlands
Sri Lanka
Celebes Sea
Lake Victoria
Borneo
Equator
Congo Basin
Kilimanjaro
5,895m (19,341ft)
Seychelles
Sumatra
New Guinea
Mount Wilhelm
4,509m (14,793ft)
Melanesia
INDIAN OCEAN
Greater Sunda Islands
Java
Solomon Islands
Comoro Islands
Rift Valley
Arafura Sea
Lesser Sunda Islands
Coral Sea
Great Barrier Reef
Madagascar
Mauritius
Reunion
New Caledonia
Fiji Islands
Great Sandy Desert
Great Dividing Range
Tropic of Capricorn
Kalahari Desert
Drakensberg
AUSTRALASIA AND OCEANIA
Great Victoria Desert
f Good Hope
Tasman Sea
North Island
Tasmania
South Island
Kerguelen Islands
OUTHERN OCEAN
Antarctic Circle
See key on page 259
ANTARCTICA

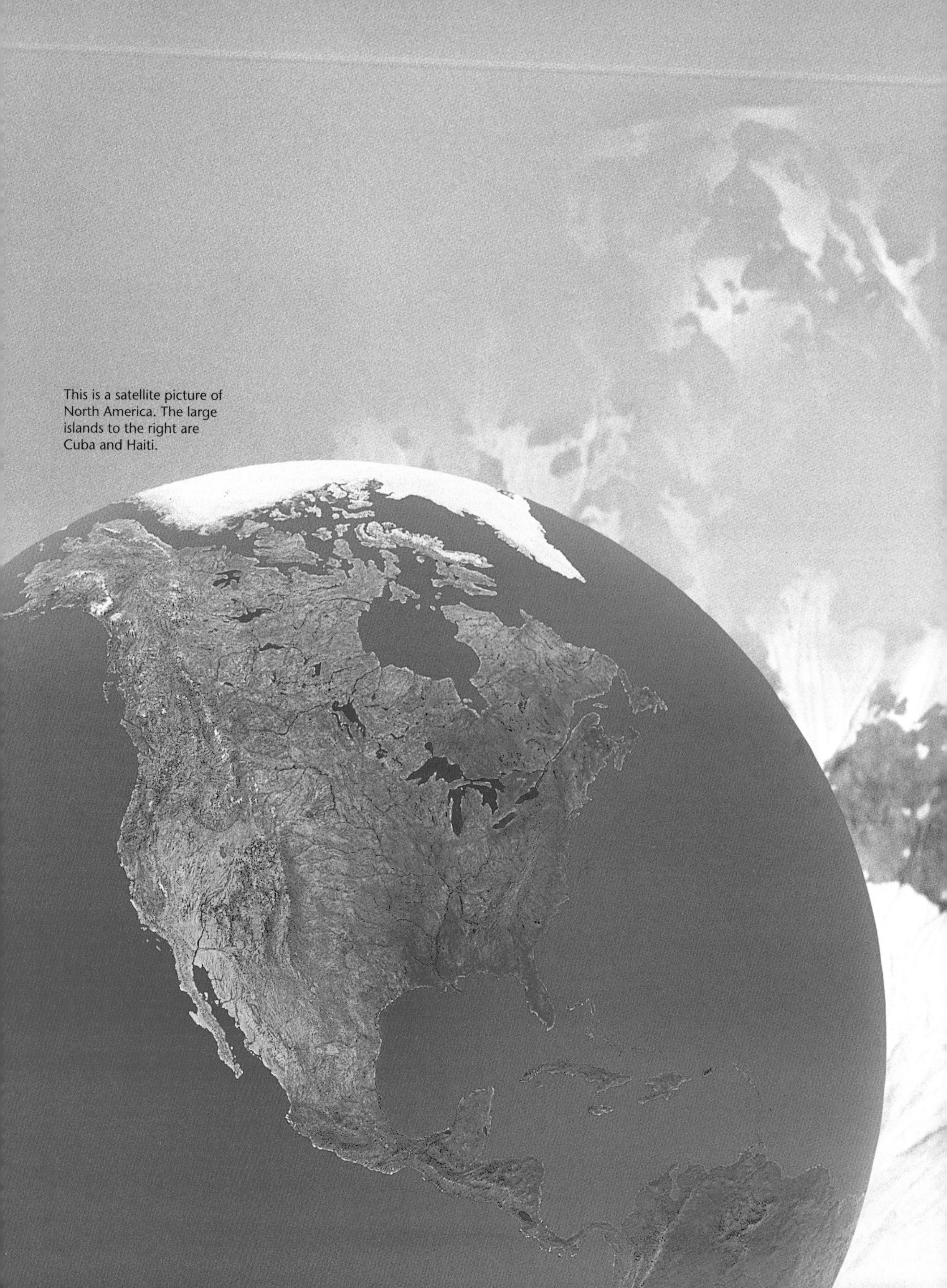

This is a satellite picture of North America. The large islands to the right are Cuba and Haiti.

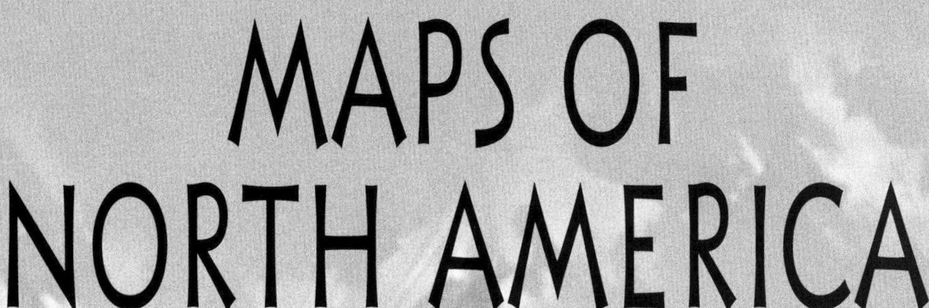

MAPS OF NORTH AMERICA

A bald eagle flying over the glaciers of Alaska, U.S.A.

In this atlas, North America includes Canada, the U.S.A., the Caribbean, and the countries of Central America, which run along the narrow strip of land between the U.S.A. and South America. This large continent contains over 20 countries, ranging from Canada, the world's second largest state, to tiny islands such as Grenada and Saint Lucia.

These are columns of rock called hoodoos in Bryce Canyon National Park, U.S.A.

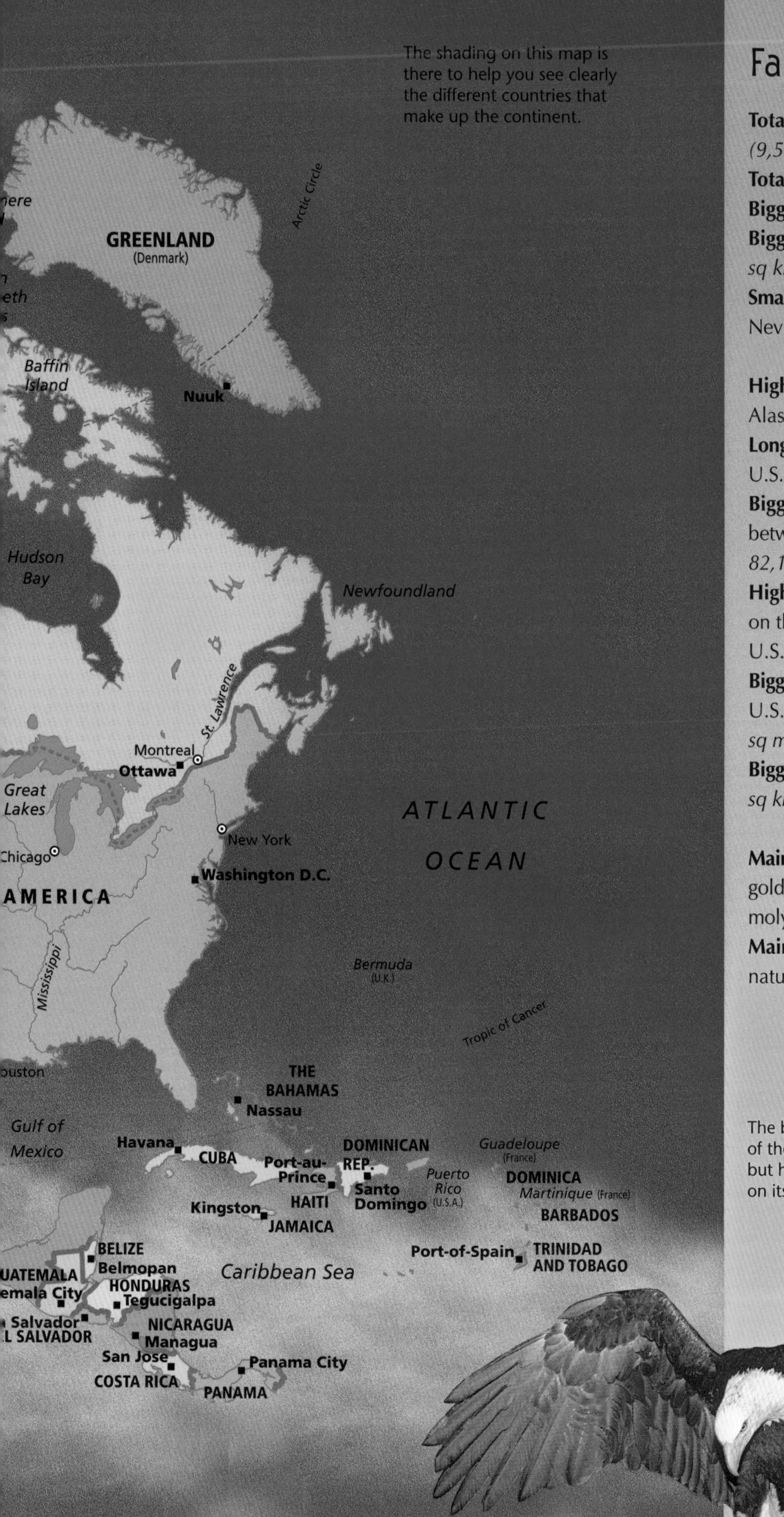

Facts

Total land area *24,709,000 sq km (9,540,198 sq miles)*
Total population 565 million
Biggest city New York City, U.S.A.
Biggest country Canada *9,984,670 sq km (3,855,103 sq miles)*
Smallest country Saint Kitts and Nevis *261 sq km (101 sq miles)*

Highest mountain Mount McKinley, Alaska, U.S.A. *6,194m (20,321ft)*
Longest river Mississippi/Missouri, U.S.A. *6,019km (3,740 miles)*
Biggest lake Lake Superior, between the U.S.A. and Canada *82,100 sq km (31,700 sq miles)*
Highest waterfall Yosemite Falls, on the Yosemite Creek, California, U.S.A. *739m (2,425ft)*
Biggest desert Great Basin Desert, U.S.A. *492,000 sq km (189,962 sq miles)*
Biggest island Greenland *2,166,086 sq km (836,330 sq miles)*

Main mineral deposits Silver, gold, copper, lead, zinc, graphite, molybdenum, nickel
Main fuel deposits Oil, coal, natural gas, uranium

The bald eagle is the national bird of the U.S.A. It is not really bald, but has white feathers on its head.

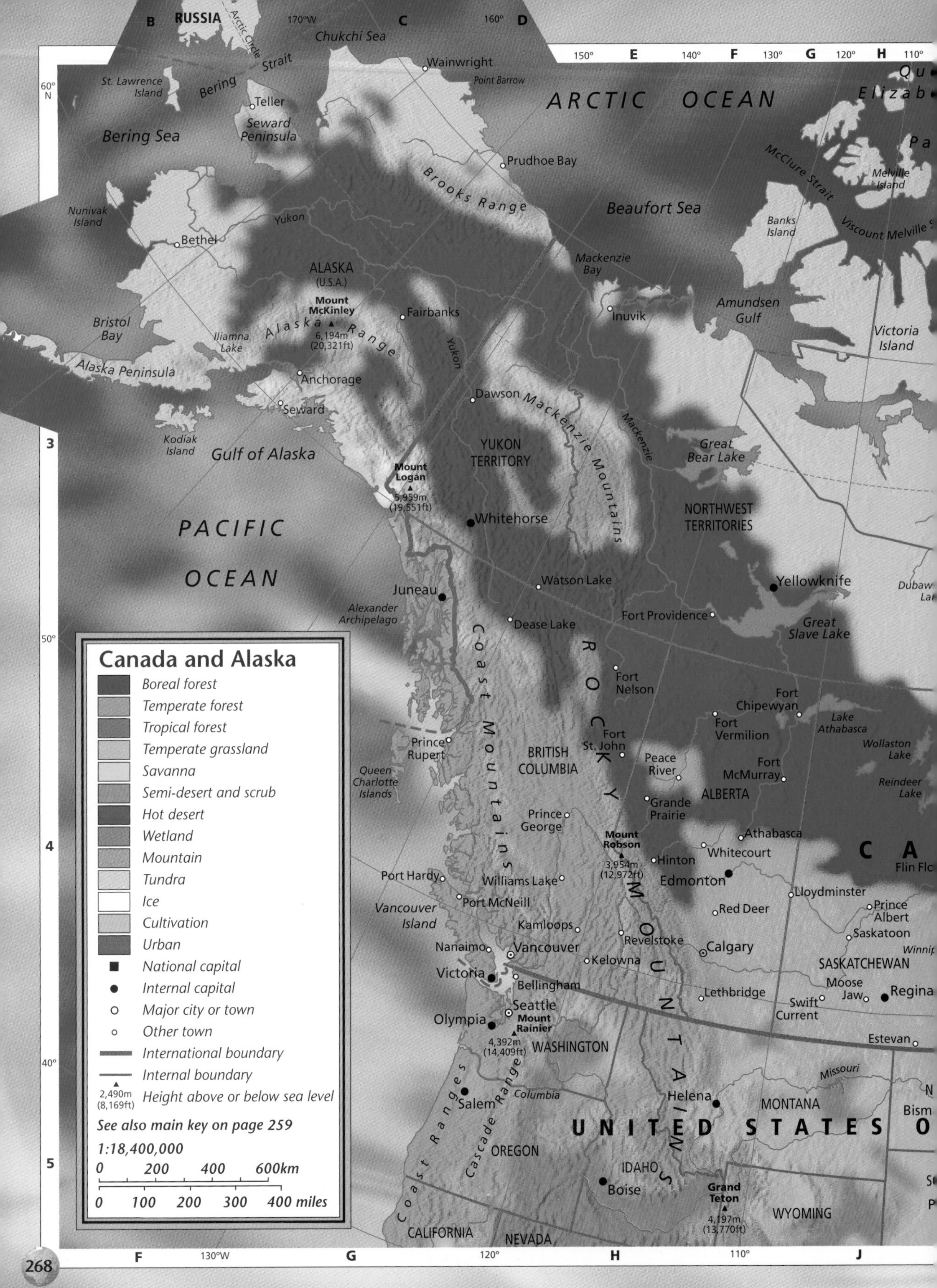

Canada and Alaska
Boreal forest
Temperate forest
Tropical forest
Temperate grassland
Savanna
Semi-desert and scrub
Hot desert
Wetland
Mountain
Tundra
Ice
Cultivation
Urban
National capital
Internal capital
Major city or town
Other town
International boundary
Internal boundary
2,490m (8,169ft) Height above or below sea level
See also main key on page 259
1:18,400,000
0 200 400 600km
0 100 200 300 400 miles
RUSSIA
Arctic Circle
Bering Strait
Chukchi Sea
St. Lawrence Island
Bering Sea
Teller
Seward Peninsula
Wainwright
Point Barrow
ARCTIC OCEAN
Prudhoe Bay
Brooks Range
Beaufort Sea
McClure Strait
Melville Island
Banks Island
Viscount Melville
Nunivak Island
Yukon
Bethel
ALASKA (U.S.A.)
Mount McKinley 6,194m (20,321ft)
Alaska Range
Fairbanks
Mackenzie Bay
Inuvik
Amundsen Gulf
Victoria Island
Bristol Bay
Iliamna Lake
Alaska Peninsula
Anchorage
Seward
Dawson
Mackenzie Mountains
Mackenzie
Great Bear Lake
Kodiak Island
Gulf of Alaska
YUKON TERRITORY
Mount Logan 5,959m (19,551ft)
Whitehorse
NORTHWEST TERRITORIES
PACIFIC OCEAN
Watson Lake
Yellowknife
Juneau
Alexander Archipelago
Dease Lake
Fort Providence
Great Slave Lake
Coast Mountains
ROCKY MOUNTAINS
Fort Nelson
Fort Chipewyan
Fort Vermilion
Lake Athabasca
Wollaston Lake
Prince Rupert
Fort St. John
BRITISH COLUMBIA
Peace River
Fort McMurray
Reindeer Lake
Queen Charlotte Islands
Grande Prairie
ALBERTA
Prince George
Mount Robson 3,954m (12,972ft)
Athabasca
Whitecourt
Hinton
Edmonton
Port Hardy
Williams Lake
Lloydminster
Vancouver Island
Port McNeill
Red Deer
Prince Albert
Kamloops
Revelstoke
Saskatoon
Nanaimo
Vancouver
Calgary
SASKATCHEWAN
Kelowna
Victoria
Bellingham
Lethbridge
Moose Jaw
Regina
Swift Current
Seattle
Olympia
Mount Rainier 4,392m (14,409ft)
WASHINGTON
Estevan
Missouri
Columbia
Salem
Cascade Range
Coast Ranges
Helena
MONTANA
UNITED STATES
OREGON
IDAHO
Boise
Grand Teton 4,197m (13,770ft)
WYOMING
CALIFORNIA
NEVADA
170°W 160° 150° 140° 130° 120° 110°
60° N
50°
40°
130°W 120° 110°

Bering Sea
Aleutian Islands
Shishaldin Volcano
2,857m (9,372ft)
Unimak Island
Attu Island
Near Islands
Fox Islands
Unalaska Island
Umnak Island
Rat Islands
Andreanof Islands
Atka Island
Same scale as main map
Ellesmere Island
Baffin Bay
Devon Island
Lancaster Sound
Somerset Island
Gulf of Boothia
Boothia Peninsula
Baffin Island
Cumberland Peninsula
GREENLAND (Denmark)
Cape Farewell
Davis Strait
Labrador Sea
Melville Peninsula
Foxe Basin
Nettilling Lake
Iqaluit
Amadjuak Lake
Foxe Peninsula
ATLANTIC OCEAN
NUNAVUT
Southampton Island
Hudson Strait
Cape Chidley
Ivujivik
Ungava Peninsula
Ungava Bay
Nain
Makkovik
Cartwright
Kuujjuaq
All islands within Hudson Bay, James Bay and Ungava Bay lie within Nunavut.
NEWFOUNDLAND
Inukjuak
Happy Valley-Goose Bay
Smallwood Reservoir
Churchill Falls
Hudson Bay
Churchill
Gander
St. John's
Labrador City
Newfoundland
Belcher Islands
Corner Brook
La Grande Reservoir
Fort Severn
QUEBEC
Manicouagan Reservoir
Anticosti Island
St. Pierre and Miquelon (France)
James Bay
Radisson
Gulf of St. Lawrence
Baie-Comeau
Gaspe
Sydney
Lake Mistassini
PRINCE EDWARD ISLAND
Fort Albany
Bathurst
Charlottetown
Waskaganish
Lake Winnipeg
Chicoutimi
Edmundston
NEW BRUNSWICK
Moncton
Halifax
Fredericton
ONTARIO
Quebec
Saint John
NOVA SCOTIA
Val-d'Or
Trois-Rivieres
St. Lawrence
MAINE
Lake Nipigon
Kirkland Lake
Dryden
Lake of the Woods
Kenora
Marathon
Yarmouth
Augusta
Thunder Bay
Montreal
Ottawa
Montpelier
Lake Superior
Sudbury
North Bay
VERMONT
NEW HAMPSHIRE
Sault Ste. Marie
Huntsville
Concord
MINNESOTA
Kingston
Boston
Lake Huron
Owen Sound
Lake Ontario
MASSACHUSETTS
Albany
Providence
MICHIGAN
Toronto
RHODE ISLAND
NEW YORK
Hartford
St. Paul
Niagara Falls
Minneapolis
Mississippi
WISCONSIN
Lake Michigan
Hamilton
Buffalo
CONNECTICUT
London
New York
Lansing
Detroit
Lake Erie
Trenton
Madison
Erie
PENNSYLVANIA
NEW JERSEY
Windsor
Cleveland
Philadelphia
Harrisburg
Chicago
ILLINOIS
INDIANA
Pittsburgh
Dover
OHIO
Annapolis
DELAWARE
Washington D.C.
Columbus

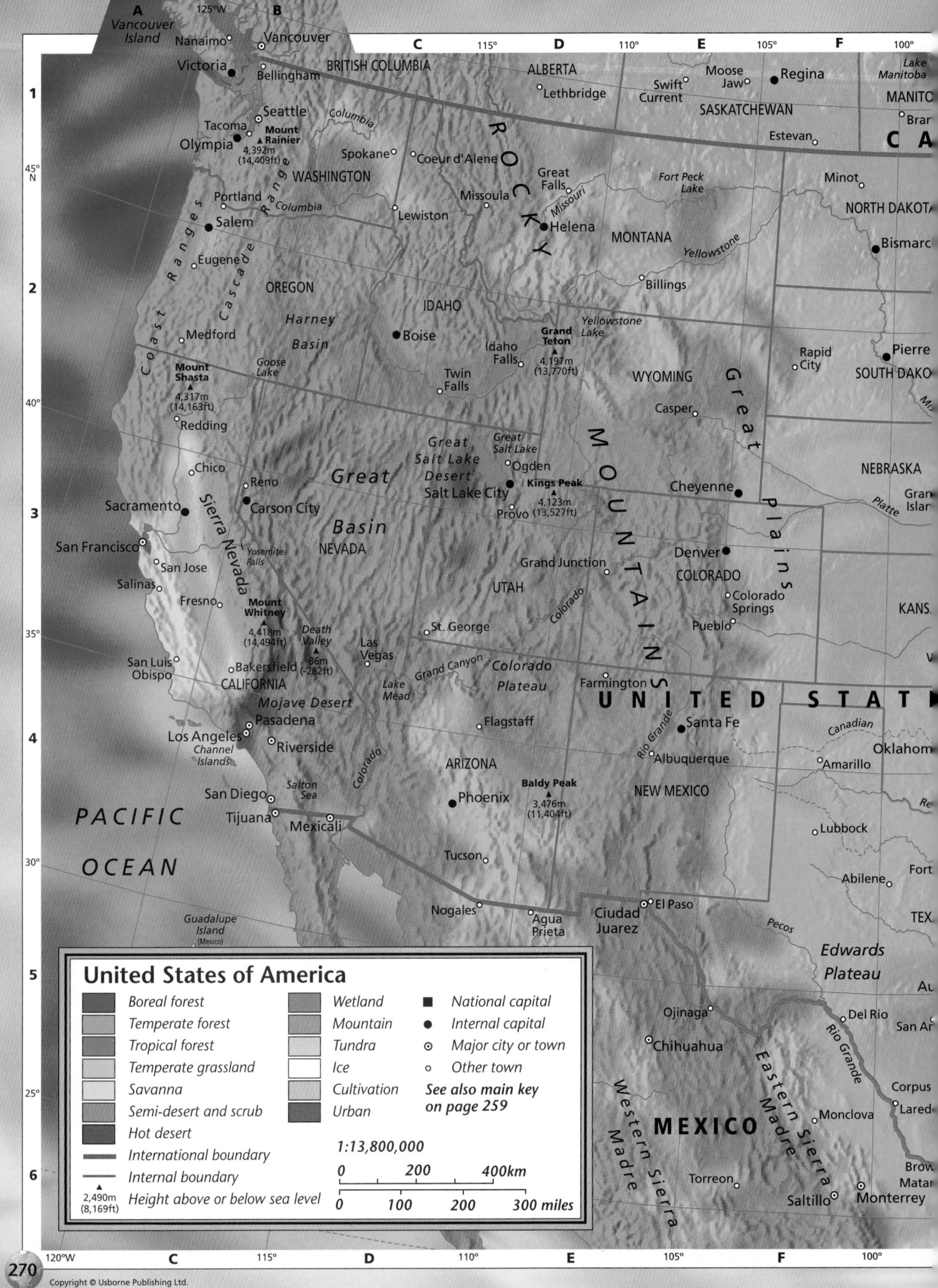

United States of America
Boreal forest
Temperate forest
Tropical forest
Temperate grassland
Savanna
Semi-desert and scrub
Hot desert
International boundary
Internal boundary
Height above or below sea level
Wetland
Mountain
Tundra
Ice
Cultivation
Urban
National capital
Internal capital
Major city or town
Other town
See also main key on page 259
1:13,800,000
0 200 400km
0 100 200 300 miles
PACIFIC OCEAN
ROCKY MOUNTAINS
UNITED STATES
MEXICO
BRITISH COLUMBIA
ALBERTA
SASKATCHEWAN
WASHINGTON
OREGON
IDAHO
MONTANA
WYOMING
NORTH DAKOTA
SOUTH DAKOTA
NEBRASKA
NEVADA
UTAH
COLORADO
CALIFORNIA
ARIZONA
NEW MEXICO
Great Basin
Great Plains
Colorado Plateau
Mojave Desert
Great Salt Lake Desert
Harney Basin
Edwards Plateau
Coast Ranges
Cascade Range
Sierra Nevada
Eastern Sierra Madre
Western Sierra Madre
Vancouver Island
Vancouver
Victoria
Nanaimo
Bellingham
Seattle
Tacoma
Olympia
Mount Rainier 4,392m (14,409ft)
Spokane
Coeur d'Alene
Lethbridge
Swift Current
Moose Jaw
Regina
Estevan
Lake Manitoba
Minot
Bismarck
Portland
Salem
Eugene
Lewiston
Missoula
Helena
Great Falls
Fort Peck Lake
Billings
Medford
Boise
Idaho Falls
Twin Falls
Grand Teton 4,197m (13,770ft)
Yellowstone Lake
Mount Shasta 4,317m (14,163ft)
Goose Lake
Redding
Chico
Reno
Carson City
Sacramento
San Francisco
San Jose
Salinas
Fresno
Yosemite Falls
Mount Whitney 4,418m (14,494ft)
Death Valley -86m (-282ft)
Great Salt Lake
Ogden
Salt Lake City
Provo
Kings Peak 4,123m (13,527ft)
Casper
Cheyenne
Rapid City
Pierre
Denver
Grand Junction
Colorado Springs
Pueblo
St. George
Las Vegas
Lake Mead
Grand Canyon
Farmington
Santa Fe
Albuquerque
Amarillo
Lubbock
Abilene
San Luis Obispo
Bakersfield
Pasadena
Los Angeles
Channel Islands
Riverside
Salton Sea
San Diego
Tijuana
Mexicali
Flagstaff
Phoenix
Baldy Peak 3,476m (11,404ft)
Tucson
Nogales
Agua Prieta
Ciudad Juarez
El Paso
Guadalupe Island (Mexico)
Ojinaga
Chihuahua
Del Rio
Corpus
Monclova
Torreon
Saltillo
Monterrey
Columbia
Missouri
Yellowstone
Colorado
Rio Grande
Pecos
Canadian
Platte

95° H 90° J 85° K 80° L 75° M 70° N 65°

Chicoutimi
Bathurst
Edmundston
Gouin Reservoir
Lake Nipigon
ONTARIO
QUEBEC
NEW BRUNSWICK
Kenora
Dryden
Lake of the Woods
Marathon
Val-d'Or
Quebec
St. Lawrence
Fredericton
Kirkland Lake
Thunder Bay
Cabonga Reservoir
Trois-Rivieres
MAINE
Saint John
St. Stephen
Forks
Lake Superior
Bangor
Sault Ste. Marie
Sudbury
North Bay
Montreal
Augusta
Duluth
Ottawa
VERMONT
Huntsville
MINNESOTA
Montpelier
Portland
Kingston
NEW HAMPSHIRE
Gulf of Maine
Lake Huron
NEW YORK
Concord
Owen Sound
St. Paul
Minneapolis
MICHIGAN
Lake Michigan
Toronto
Lake Ontario
Albany
Boston
Green Bay
MASSACHUSETTS
Cape Cod
Syracuse
WISCONSIN
Hamilton
Niagara Falls
Rochester
Springfield
Providence
Mississippi
Grand Rapids
London
Buffalo
Hartford
RHODE ISLAND
Falls
Milwaukee
Lansing
Lake Erie
Jamestown
CONNECTICUT
Madison
Detroit
Erie
Windsor
Newark
New York
Sioux City
Rockford
PENNSYLVANIA
Trenton
Cedar Rapids
Toledo
Cleveland
IOWA
Chicago
South Bend
Harrisburg
Philadelphia
Fort Wayne
Pittsburgh
NEW JERSEY
Omaha
Des Moines
OHIO
Atlantic City
Peoria
Baltimore
Dover
Lincoln
INDIANA
MARYLAND
DELAWARE
ILLINOIS
Columbus
Annapolis
Quincy
Indianapolis
WEST VIRGINIA
Washington D.C.
Springfield
Cincinnati
Charleston
Charlottesville
Kansas City
Topeka
Jefferson City
Ohio
Frankfort
VIRGINIA
Richmond
St. Louis
Evansville
Lexington
Roanoke
Virginia Beach
MISSOURI
KENTUCKY
Cape Girardeau
Appalachian Mountains
Springfield
Kentucky Lake
Greensboro
Raleigh
Cape Hatteras
Ozark Plateau
OF AMERICA
Nashville
Knoxville
NORTH CAROLINA
Tulsa
TENNESSEE
Tennessee
Charlotte
ATLANTIC OCEAN
Jonesboro
Jackson
Chattanooga
Memphis
Clark Hill Lake
Columbia
Little Rock
Huntsville
SOUTH CAROLINA
OKLAHOMA
Tupelo
ARKANSAS
Mississippi
Birmingham
Atlanta
Charleston
Greenville
Tuscaloosa
Macon
Texarkana
MISSISSIPPI
ALABAMA
GEORGIA
Savannah
Shreveport
Meridian
Columbus
Dallas
Vicksburg
Jackson
Montgomery
Albany
LOUISIANA
Valdosta
Hattiesburg
Jacksonville
Toledo Bend Reservoir
Sam Rayburn Reservoir
Mobile
Tallahassee
Baton Rouge
Pensacola
Daytona Beach
Beaumont
New Orleans
Apalachee Bay
Houston
Orlando
Cape Canaveral
FLORIDA
Galveston
Mississippi Delta
Tampa
St. Petersburg
Grand Bahama
Lake Okeechobee
Abaco
Freeport City
THE BAHAMAS
Fort Lauderdale
Eleuthera
Gulf of Mexico
The Everglades
Miami
Nassau
Cat Island
Florida Keys
Andros
Key West
Straits of Florida
Tropic of Cancer
Long Island
Acklins Island
Matanzas
Havana
CUBA
Santa Clara
Cienfuegos
Ciego de Avila
Pinar del Rio
Camaguey

160°W
Same scale as main map
Hawaiian Islands
Kauai
Oahu
Molokai
Honolulu
Kahului
Maui
HAWAII (U.S.A.)
20°N
4,205m (13,796ft)
Hilo
PACIFIC OCEAN
Hawaii
P
160°W 155°

1 2 3 4 5 6 7 8
45° N 40° 35° 30° 25°
95° H 90° J 85° 80° 75°

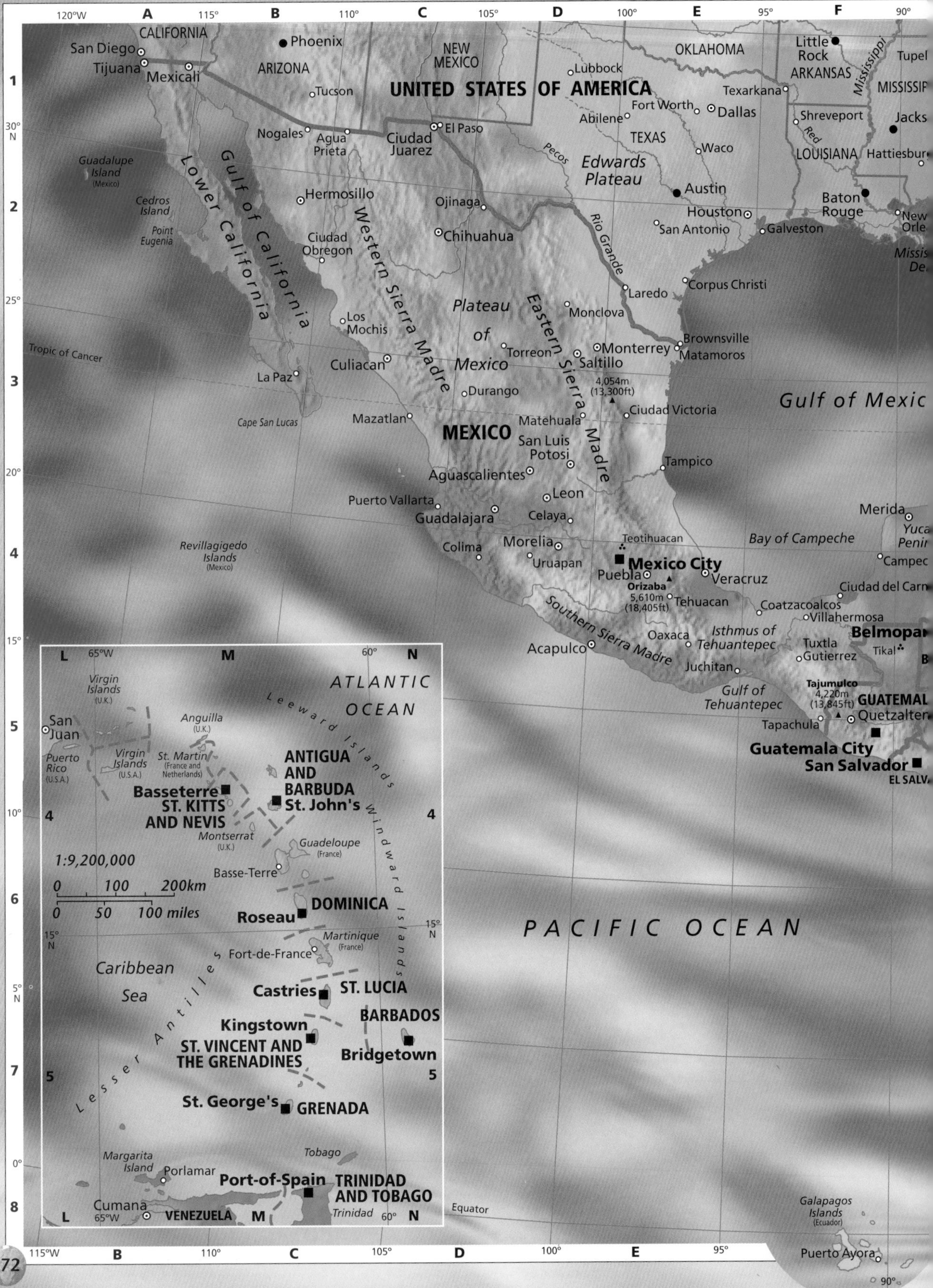
120°W
A
115°
B
110°
C
105°
D
100°
E
95°
F
90°
1
2
3
4
5
6
7
8
30° N
25°
20°
15°
10°
5° N
0°
CALIFORNIA
San Diego
Tijuana
Mexicali
Phoenix
ARIZONA
Tucson
NEW MEXICO
UNITED STATES OF AMERICA
OKLAHOMA
Little Rock
ARKANSAS
Mississippi
Tupel
MISSISSIP
Lubbock
Texarkana
Fort Worth
Dallas
Abilene
Shreveport
Jacks
Nogales
Agua Prieta
Ciudad Juarez
El Paso
TEXAS
Red
Pecos
Waco
LOUISIANA
Hattiesbur
Guadalupe Island
(Mexico)
Lower California
Gulf of California
Edwards Plateau
Austin
Baton Rouge
Hermosillo
Ojinaga
Rio Grande
Houston
New Orle
Cedros Island
Point Eugenia
Western Sierra Madre
Chihuahua
San Antonio
Galveston
Ciudad Obregon
Missis De
Corpus Christi
Laredo
Plateau of Mexico
Eastern Sierra Madre
Monclova
Los Mochis
Brownsville
Matamoros
Tropic of Cancer
Torreon
Monterrey
Saltillo
Culiacan
La Paz
4,054m (13,300ft)
Durango
Gulf of Mexic
Cape San Lucas
Mazatlan
Matehuala
Ciudad Victoria
MEXICO
San Luis Potosi
Tampico
Aguascalientes
Leon
Puerto Vallarta
Guadalajara
Celaya
Merida
Yuca Penir
Teotihuacan
Bay of Campeche
Revillagigedo Islands
(Mexico)
Colima
Morelia
Uruapan
Mexico City
Campec
Puebla
Veracruz
Orizaba
5,610m (18,405ft)
Tehuacan
Ciudad del Carm
Coatzacoalcos
Villahermosa
Southern Sierra Madre
Oaxaca
Isthmus of Tehuantepec
Belmopa
Acapulco
Tuxtla Gutierrez
Tikal
Juchitan
Gulf of Tehuantepec
Tajumulco
4,220m (13,845ft)
GUATEMAL
Quetzalter
Tapachula
Guatemala City
San Salvador
EL SALV
PACIFIC OCEAN
Equator
Galapagos Islands
(Ecuador)
Puerto Ayora
90°
115°W
B
110°
C
105°
D
100°
E
95°
L
65°W
M
60°
N
ATLANTIC OCEAN
Virgin Islands
(U.K.)
Anguilla
(U.K.)
Leeward Islands
San Juan
Puerto Rico
(U.S.A.)
Virgin Islands
(U.S.A.)
St. Martin
(France and Netherlands)
ANTIGUA AND BARBUDA
St. John's
Basseterre
ST. KITTS AND NEVIS
Montserrat
(U.K.)
Guadeloupe
(France)
Windward Islands
1:9,200,000
0 100 200km
0 50 100 miles
Basse-Terre
DOMINICA
Roseau
15° N
Martinique
(France)
Fort-de-France
Caribbean Sea
Castries
ST. LUCIA
BARBADOS
Lesser Antilles
Kingstown
ST. VINCENT AND THE GRENADINES
Bridgetown
St. George's
GRENADA
Tobago
Margarita Island
Porlamar
Port-of-Spain
TRINIDAD AND TOBAGO
Cumana
VENEZUELA
Trinidad

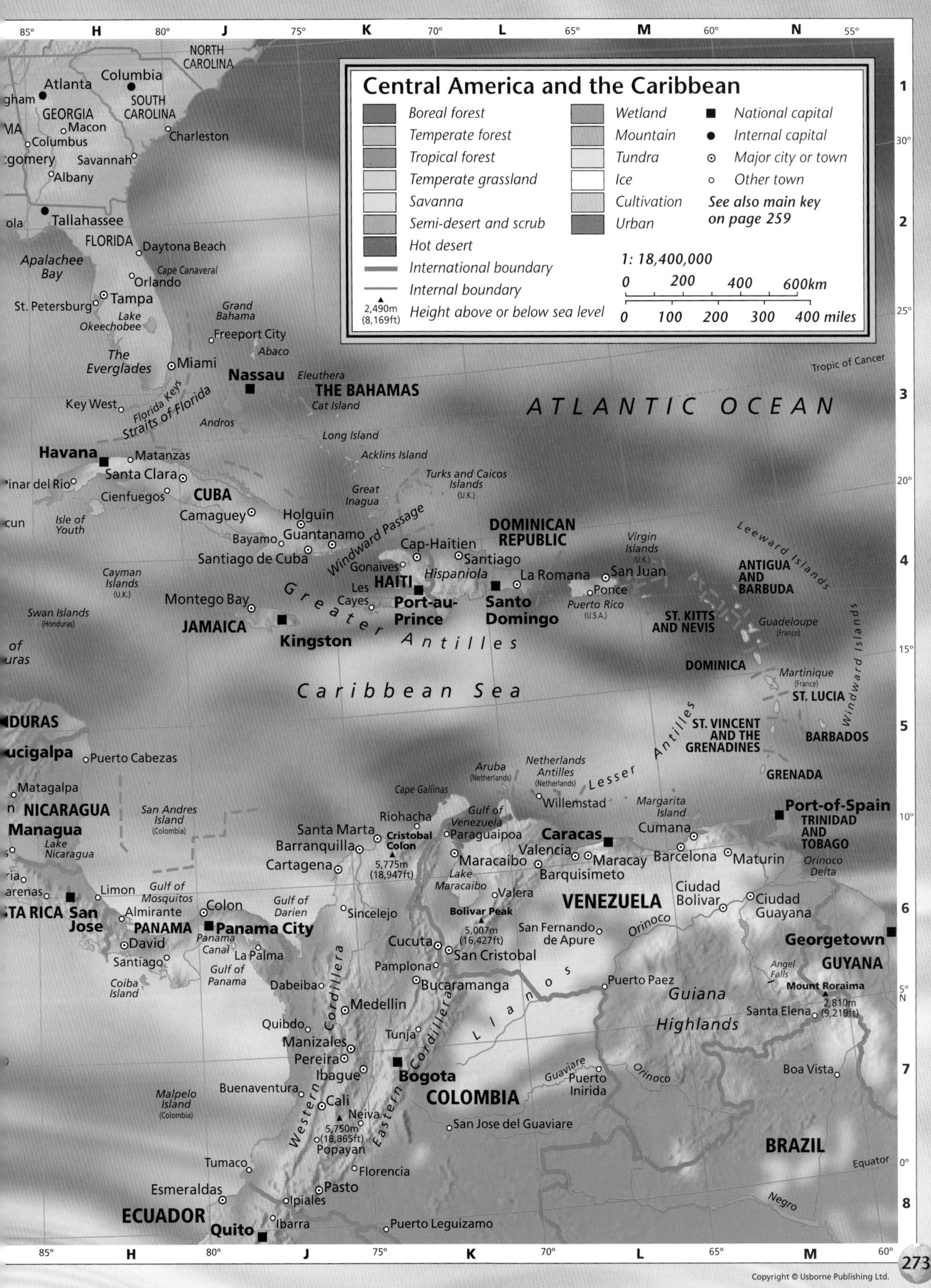
Central America and the Caribbean
Boreal forest
Temperate forest
Tropical forest
Temperate grassland
Savanna
Semi-desert and scrub
Hot desert
International boundary
Internal boundary
2,490m (8,169ft) Height above or below sea level
Wetland
Mountain
Tundra
Ice
Cultivation
Urban
National capital
Internal capital
Major city or town
Other town
See also main key on page 259
1: 18,400,000
0 200 400 600km
0 100 200 300 400 miles
ATLANTIC OCEAN
Caribbean Sea
Greater Antilles
Lesser Antilles
Leeward Islands
Windward Islands
Tropic of Cancer
Equator
NORTH CAROLINA
SOUTH CAROLINA
GEORGIA
FLORIDA
Atlanta
Columbia
Macon
Columbus
Charleston
Savannah
Albany
Tallahassee
Daytona Beach
Apalachee Bay
Cape Canaveral
Orlando
Tampa
St. Petersburg
Lake Okeechobee
The Everglades
Miami
Key West
Florida Keys
Straits of Florida
Grand Bahama
Freeport City
Abaco
Nassau
Eleuthera
THE BAHAMAS
Cat Island
Andros
Long Island
Acklins Island
Turks and Caicos Islands (U.K.)
Great Inagua
Havana
Matanzas
Santa Clara
Pinar del Rio
Cienfuegos
CUBA
Camaguey
Holguin
Isle of Youth
Bayamo
Guantanamo
Santiago de Cuba
Windward Passage
Cayman Islands (U.K.)
Montego Bay
JAMAICA
Kingston
Swan Islands (Honduras)
Cap-Haitien
Gonaives
HAITI
Les Cayes
Port-au-Prince
Hispaniola
DOMINICAN REPUBLIC
Santiago
Santo Domingo
La Romana
San Juan
Ponce
Puerto Rico (U.S.A.)
Virgin Islands (U.K.)
ANTIGUA AND BARBUDA
ST. KITTS AND NEVIS
Guadeloupe (France)
DOMINICA
Martinique (France)
ST. LUCIA
ST. VINCENT AND THE GRENADINES
BARBADOS
GRENADA
Port-of-Spain
TRINIDAD AND TOBAGO
Orinoco Delta
Aruba (Netherlands)
Netherlands Antilles (Netherlands)
Willemstad
Margarita Island
Cumana
Barcelona
Maturin
Cape Gallinas
Gulf of Venezuela
Riohacha
Santa Marta
Cristobal Colon
5,775m (18,947ft)
Barranquilla
Cartagena
Paraguaipoa
Maracaibo
Lake Maracaibo
Caracas
Valencia
Maracay
Barquisimeto
Valera
VENEZUELA
Ciudad Bolivar
Ciudad Guayana
Bolivar Peak
5,007m (16,427ft)
San Fernando de Apure
Orinoco
Georgetown
GUYANA
Angel Falls
Mount Roraima
2,810m (9,219ft)
Santa Elena
Guiana Highlands
Puerto Paez
Llanos
Boa Vista
Guaviare
Puerto Inirida
BRAZIL
Negro
HONDURAS
Tegucigalpa
Puerto Cabezas
Matagalpa
NICARAGUA
Managua
Lake Nicaragua
San Andres Island (Colombia)
Limon
Gulf of Mosquitos
COSTA RICA
San Jose
Almirante
PANAMA
Colon
Panama City
Panama Canal
David
Santiago
La Palma
Gulf of Panama
Gulf of Darien
Coiba Island
Sincelejo
Cucuta
San Cristobal
Pamplona
Bucaramanga
Dabeiba
Medellin
Quibdo
Manizales
Pereira
Ibague
Tunja
Bogota
COLOMBIA
Western Cordillera
Eastern Cordillera
Malpelo Island (Colombia)
Buenaventura
Cali
Neiva
5,750m (18,865ft)
Popayan
Florencia
San Jose del Guaviare
Tumaco
Esmeraldas
Pasto
Ipiales
Ibarra
ECUADOR
Quito
Puerto Leguizamo

A parrot snake

MAPS OF SOUTH AMERICA

This is a satellite image of South America. The brown, mottled streak along the west coast is the Andes mountain range.

Triangle-shaped South America is made up of only 12 independent countries, along with French Guiana, which belongs to France. A huge part of this continent is taken up with the Amazon rainforest, which covers the Amazon basin with over a third of the world's trees. South America also has dusty deserts, towering mountains and, in Venezuela, the world's highest waterfall – Angel Falls.

This is a guanaco. Guanacos are members of the camel family that live in South America. Guanaco hair is used to make textiles.

The shading on this map is there to help you see clearly the different countries that make up the continent.

This is a red-eyed tree frog. These frogs live in rainforests in South and Central America.

Facts

Total land area *17,840,000 sq km (6,888,062 sq miles)*
Total population 407 million
Biggest city Sao Paulo, Brazil
Biggest country Brazil *8,514,877 sq km (3,287,612 sq miles)*
Smallest country Suriname *163,820 sq km (63,251 sq miles)*

Highest mountain Aconcagua, Argentina *6,961m (22,837ft)*
Longest river Amazon, mainly in Brazil *6,437km (4,000 miles)*
Biggest lake Lake Maracaibo, Venezuela *13,210 sq km (5,100 sq miles)*
Highest waterfall Angel Falls, on the Churun River, Venezuela *979m (3,212ft)*
Biggest desert Patagonian Desert, Argentina *673,000 sq km (259,847 sq miles)*
Biggest island Tierra del Fuego *47,401 sq km (18,302 sq miles)*

Main mineral deposits Copper, tin, molybdenum, bauxite, emeralds
Main fuel deposits Oil, coal

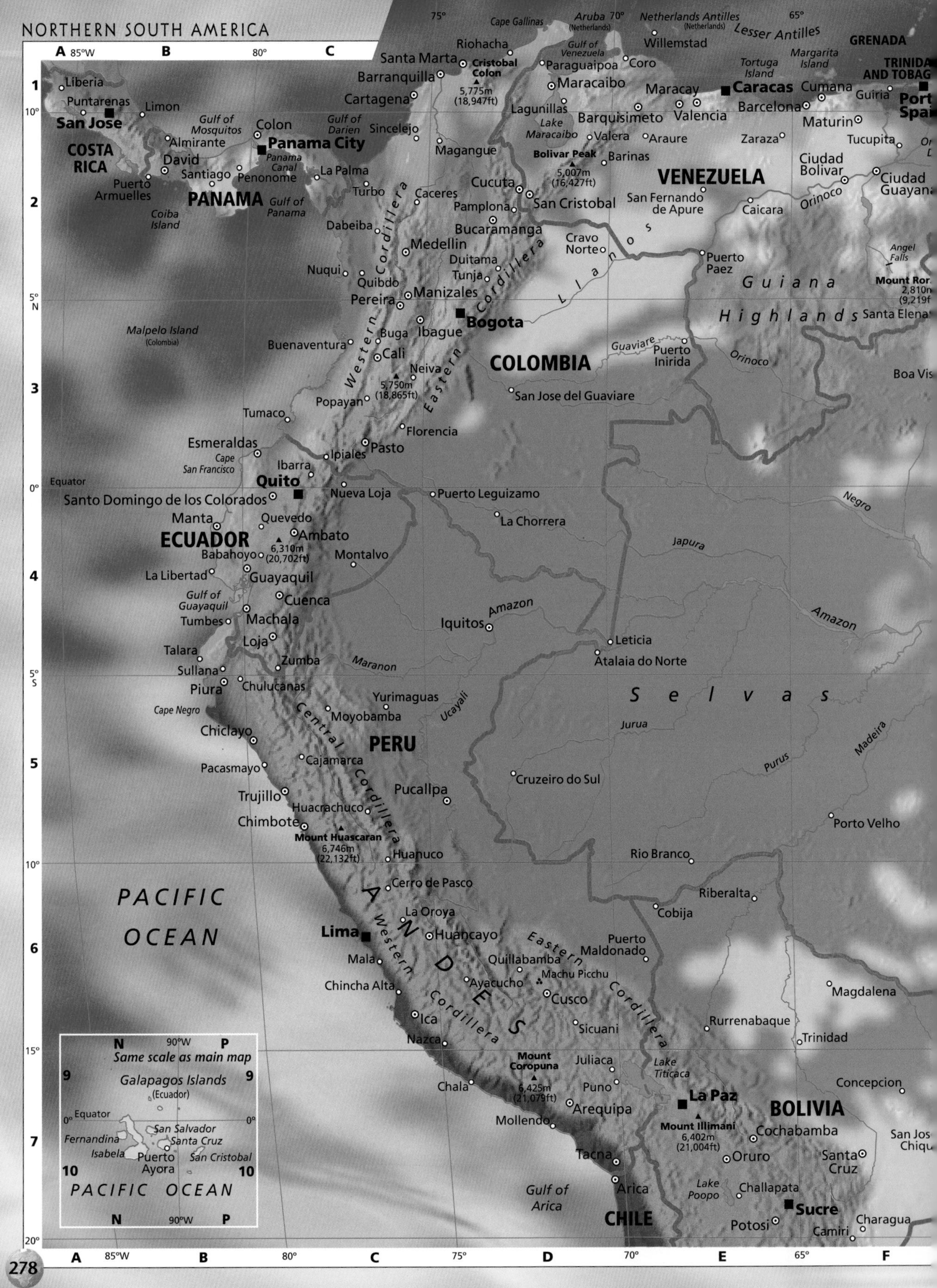

Cape Gallinas
Aruba (Netherlands)
Netherlands Antilles (Netherlands)
Lesser Antilles
GRENADA
Gulf of Venezuela
Willemstad
Riohacha
Santa Marta
Cristobal Colon
5,775m (18,947ft)
Paraguaipoa
Coro
Tortuga Island
Margarita Island
TRINIDAD AND TOBAGO
Barranquilla
Maracaibo
Maracay
Caracas
Cumana
Guiria
Port of Spain
Cartagena
Lagunillas
Lake Maracaibo
Barquisimeto
Valencia
Barcelona
Maturin
Liberia
Puntarenas
Limon
San Jose
Gulf of Mosquitos
Colon
Gulf of Darien
Sincelejo
Valera
Araure
Zaraza
Tucupita
COSTA RICA
Almirante
Panama City
Magangue
Bolivar Peak
5,007m (16,427ft)
Barinas
Ciudad Bolivar
David
Panama Canal
La Palma
Santiago
Penonome
Ciudad Guayana
Puerto Armuelles
Turbo
Caceres
Cucuta
VENEZUELA
PANAMA
Gulf of Panama
Pamplona
San Cristobal
San Fernando de Apure
Caicara
Orinoco
Coiba Island
Dabeiba
Bucaramanga
Cravo Norte
Llanos
Angel Falls
Medellin
Duitama
Puerto Paez
Nuqui
Tunja
Guiana
Quibdo
Mount Roraima
2,810m (9,219ft)
Manizales
Pereira
Western Cordillera
Eastern Cordillera
Bogota
Highlands
Santa Elena
Malpelo Island (Colombia)
Buga
Ibague
Guaviare
Puerto Inirida
Buenaventura
Cali
COLOMBIA
Orinoco
Neiva
5,750m (18,865ft)
Boa Vista
Popayan
San Jose del Guaviare
Tumaco
Florencia
Esmeraldas
Pasto
Ipiales
Cape San Francisco
Ibarra
Equator
Quito
Santo Domingo de los Colorados
Nueva Loja
Puerto Leguizamo
Negro
Manta
Quevedo
La Chorrera
ECUADOR
Ambato
6,310m (20,702ft)
Japura
Babahoyo
Montalvo
La Libertad
Guayaquil
Gulf of Guayaquil
Cuenca
Amazon
Tumbes
Machala
Iquitos
Amazon
Loja
Leticia
Talara
Atalaia do Norte
Zumba
Maranon
Sullana
Piura
Chulucanas
Selvas
Yurimaguas
Cape Negro
Moyobamba
Ucayali
Jurua
Central Cordillera
Chiclayo
PERU
Madeira
Pacasmayo
Cajamarca
Purus
Cruzeiro do Sul
Pucallpa
Trujillo
Huacrachuco
Porto Velho
Chimbote
Mount Huascaran
6,746m (22,132ft)
Huanuco
Rio Branco
PACIFIC OCEAN
Cerro de Pasco
ANDES
Riberalta
La Oroya
Cobija
Lima
Western Cordillera
Huancayo
Eastern Cordillera
Puerto Maldonado
Mala
Quillabamba
Machu Picchu
Ayacucho
Magdalena
Chincha Alta
Cusco
Ica
Rurrenabaque
Sicuani
Nazca
Trinidad
N
90°W
P
Same scale as main map
9
Galapagos Islands
(Ecuador)
Equator
San Salvador
Fernandina
Santa Cruz
Isabela
Puerto Ayora
San Cristobal
10
PACIFIC OCEAN
Mount Coropuna
Juliaca
Lake Titicaca
6,425m (21,079ft)
Puno
Concepcion
Chala
La Paz
BOLIVIA
Arequipa
Mount Illimani
6,402m (21,004ft)
Mollendo
Cochabamba
San Jose de Chiquitos
Oruro
Santa Cruz
Tacna
Arica
Gulf of Arica
Lake Poopo
Challapata
Sucre
CHILE
Potosi
Camiri
Charagua
A
B
C
D
E
F
85°W
80°
75°
70°
65°
10°
5° N
0°
5° S
15°
20°
1
2
3
4
5
6
7

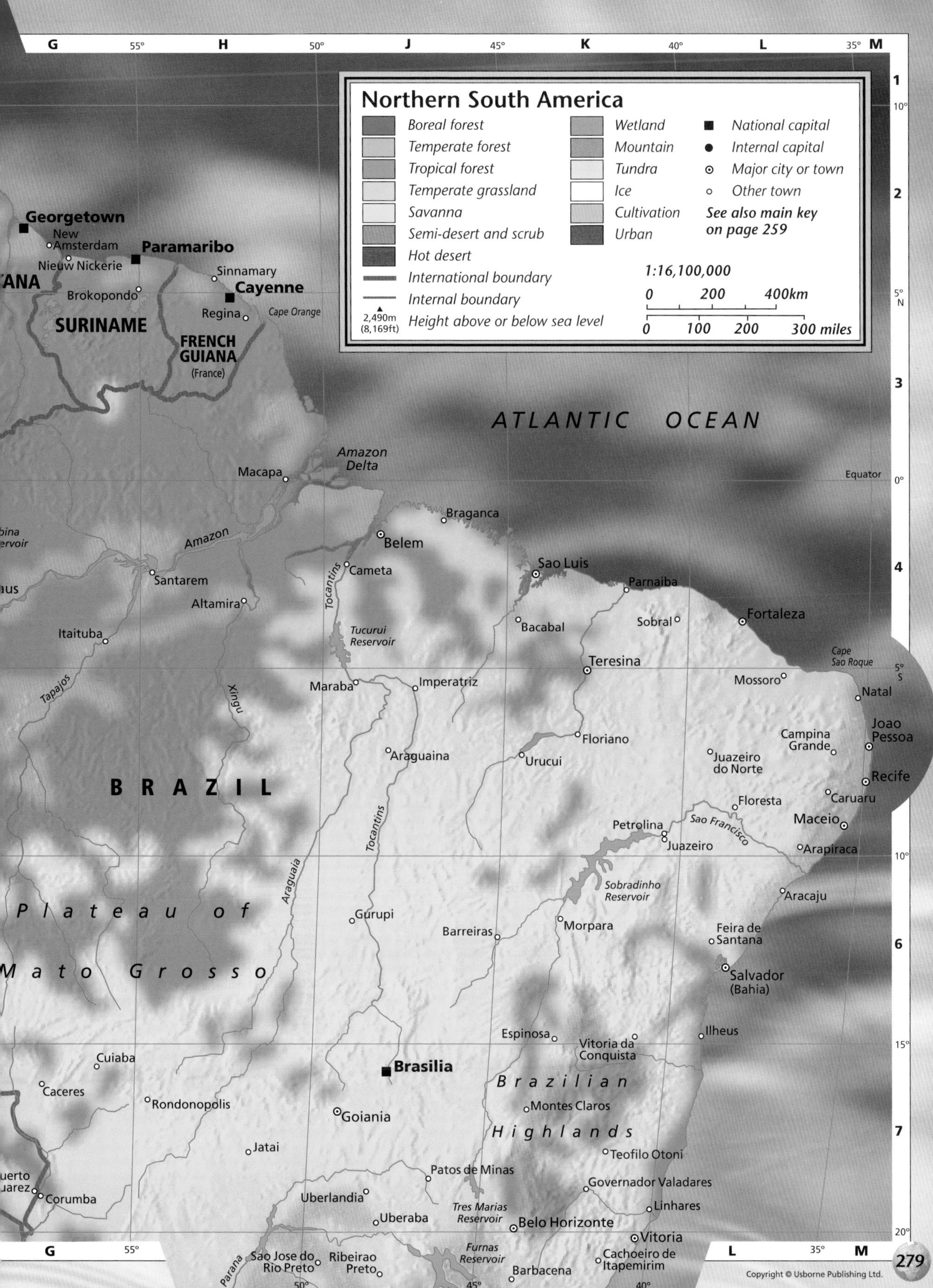
G
55°
H
50°
J
45°
K
40°
L
35°
M
Northern South America
Boreal forest
Temperate forest
Tropical forest
Temperate grassland
Savanna
Semi-desert and scrub
Hot desert
International boundary
Internal boundary
2,490m (8,169ft)
Height above or below sea level
Wetland
Mountain
Tundra
Ice
Cultivation
Urban
National capital
Internal capital
Major city or town
Other town
See also main key on page 259
1:16,100,000
0 200 400km
0 100 200 300 miles
1
2
3
4
5
6
7
10°
5° N
0°
5° S
10°
15°
20°
Equator
ATLANTIC OCEAN
Georgetown
New Amsterdam
Nieuw Nickerie
Paramaribo
Brokopondo
SURINAME
Sinnamary
Cayenne
Regina
Cape Orange
FRENCH GUIANA
(France)
Amazon Delta
Macapa
Amazon
Braganca
Belem
Santarem
Cameta
Tocantins
Altamira
Itaituba
Tucurui Reservoir
Tapajos
Xingu
Maraba
Imperatriz
Sao Luis
Parnaiba
Bacabal
Sobral
Fortaleza
Teresina
Cape Sao Roque
Mossoro
Natal
Joao Pessoa
Campina Grande
Floriano
Urucui
Araguaina
Juazeiro do Norte
Recife
Caruaru
Floresta
BRAZIL
Tocantins
Petrolina
Sao Francisco
Juazeiro
Maceio
Arapiraca
Araguaia
Sobradinho Reservoir
Aracaju
Plateau of Mato Grosso
Gurupi
Barreiras
Morpara
Feira de Santana
Salvador (Bahia)
Espinosa
Vitoria da Conquista
Ilheus
Cuiaba
Brasilia
Caceres
Rondonopolis
Goiania
Brazilian Highlands
Montes Claros
Jatai
Teofilo Otoni
Patos de Minas
Governador Valadares
Corumba
Uberlandia
Tres Marias Reservoir
Linhares
Uberaba
Belo Horizonte
Vitoria
Furnas Reservoir
Cachoeiro de Itapemirim
Sao Jose do Rio Preto
Ribeirao Preto
Parana
Barbacena
Copyright © Usborne Publishing Ltd.

Plateau of Mato Grosso
BRAZIL
Brazilian Highlands
PERU
BOLIVIA
PARAGUAY
URUGUAY
CHILE
ANDES
Gran Chaco
Atacama Desert
Tropic of Capricorn
Brasilia
La Paz
Sucre
Asuncion
Santiago
Mount Illimani 6,402m (21,004ft)
Mount Ojos del Salado 6,908m (22,664ft)
Aconcagua 6,961m (22,837ft)
Mount Agulhas Negras 2,787m (9,144ft)
Lake Titicaca
Lake Poopo
Sobradinho Reservoir
Tres Marias Reservoir
Furnas Reservoir
Iguacu Falls
Patos Lagoon
Mirim Lake
Araguaia
Tocantins
Parana
Paraguay
Pilcomayo
Salado
Rio Branco
Riberalta
Cobija
Puerto Maldonado
Magdalena
Rurrenabaque
Trinidad
Juliaca
Puno
Concepcion
Cochabamba
Santa Cruz
San Jose de Chiquitos
Tacna
Oruro
Arica
Challapata
Puerto Suarez
Corumba
Potosi
Charagua
Iquique
Pica
Uyuni
Camiri
Ollague
Tupiza
Tarija
Calama
Tartagal
San Pedro de Atacama
Antofagasta
San Salvador de Jujuy
Salta
Taltal
Chanaral
San Miguel de Tucuman
Copiapo
Santiago del Estero
Vallenar
Catamarca
La Rioja
Coquimbo
Ovalle
Illapel
San Juan
Valparaiso
Mendoza
Merlo
San Luis
Villa Mercedes
Cordoba
San Francisco
Villa Maria
Rio Cuarto
Rosario
Venado Tuerto
Santa Fe
San Nicolas de los Arroyos
Gualeguaychu
Concordia
Salto
Paysandu
Tacuarembo
Rivera
Durazno
Melo
Bage
Pelotas
Rio Grande
Reconquista
Corrientes
Formosa
Villarrica
Encarnacion
Posadas
Uruguaiana
Ciudad del Este
Foz do Iguacu
Eldorado
Cascavel
Guarapuava
Santa Maria
Passo Fundo
Porto Alegre
Caxias do Sul
Criciuma
Florianopolis
Itajai
Curitiba
Paranagua
Pedro Juan Caballero
Concepcion
Ponta Pora
Dourados
Campo Grande
Caceres
Cuiaba
Rondonopolis
Jatai
Goiania
Gurupi
Sao Jose do Rio Preto
Presidente Prudente
Londrina
Itapetininga
Marilia
Araraquara
Campinas
Sao Paulo
Ribeirao Preto
Pocos de Caldas
Uberlandia
Uberaba
Patos de Minas
Barreiras
Morpara
Feira de Santana
Espinosa
Ilheus
Vitoria da Conquista
Montes Claros
Teofilo Otoni
Governador Valadares
Linhares
Belo Horizonte
Vitoria
Cachoeiro de Itapemirim
Barbacena
Juiz de Fora
Campos
Macae
Nova Iguacu
Rio de Janeiro

Southern South America
Boreal forest
Temperate forest
Tropical forest
Temperate grassland
Savanna
Semi-desert and scrub
Hot desert
Wetland
Mountain
Tundra
Ice
Cultivation
Urban
National capital
Internal capital
Major city or town
Other town
International boundary
Internal boundary
2,490m (8,169ft) Height above or below sea level
See also main key on page 259
1:16,000,000
0 200 400km
0 100 200 300 miles
Chillan
Concepcion
Los Angeles
Victoria
Temuco
Valdivia
Osorno
Puerto Montt
Chiloe Island
Quellon
Chonos Archipelago
Coihaique
Mount San Valentin 4,058m (13,313ft)
Gulf of Penas
Wellington Island
A N D E
Zapala
Neuquen
General Roca
Esquel
Santa Rosa
Pampa
Patagonia
Dolores
Cape San Antonio
Olavarria
Tandil
Mar del Plata
Tres Arroyos
Necochea
Bahia Blanca
Colorado
Blanca Bay
San Antonio Oeste
Viedma
Gulf of San Matias
Valdes Peninsula
Rawson
Comodoro Rivadavia
Gulf of San Jorge
Lake Buenos Aires
Cape Tres Puntas
Puerto Deseado
San Julian
Lake Viedma
Lake Argentino
Grande Bay
Rio Gallegos
Puerto Natales
Strait of Magellan
Punta Arenas
Porvenir
Rio Grande
Tierra del Fuego
Ushuaia
Cape Horn
Drake Passage
PACIFIC OCEAN
ATLANTIC OCEAN
Falkland Islands (U.K.)
West Falkland
East Falkland
Stanley
South Georgia (U.K.)
Grytviken
South Sandwich Islands (U.K.)
South Shetland Islands (U.K.)
King George Island
Elephant Island
South Orkney Islands (U.K.)
SOUTHERN OCEAN
A 85°W B 80° C 75° D 70° E 65°
60° 55° 50° 45° 40° 35°
30° N 25° P
7 8 9 10 11
40° 45° 50° 55° 60°

MAPS OF AUSTRALASIA AND OCEANIA

A school of barracuda fish

This is a satellite image of Australasia, which includes Australia and New Zealand, and Oceania, which is the name given to the other islands in the Pacific Ocean.

Australasia and Oceania are made up of Australia, New Zealand, Papua New Guinea and thousands of other islands stretching out into the Pacific Ocean. This is one of the world's least populated areas. Some of its countries are made up of hundreds of islands.

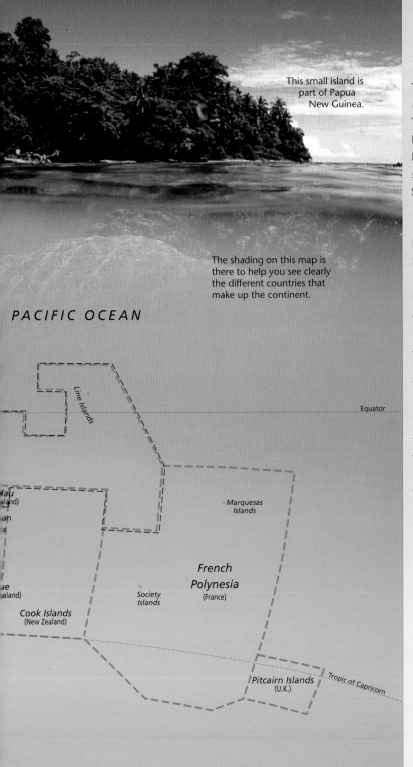

This small island is part of Papua New Guinea.

The shading on this map is there to help you see clearly the different countries that make up the continent.

PACIFIC OCEAN

Line Islands

Equator

Marquesas Islands

French Polynesia (France)

Society Islands

Cook Islands (New Zealand)

Pitcairn Islands (U.K.)

Tropic of Capricorn

Facts

Total land area *8,564,400 sq km (3,306,733 sq miles)*
Total population 38 million
Biggest city Sydney, Australia
Biggest country Australia *7,741,220 sq km (2,988,902 sq miles)*
Smallest country Nauru *21 sq km (8 sq miles)*

Highest mountain Mount Wilhelm, Papua New Guinea *4,509m (14,793ft)*
Longest river Murray/Darling River, Australia *3,718km (2,310 miles)*
Biggest lake Lake Eyre, Australia *9,500 sq km (3,668 sq miles)*
Highest waterfall Sutherland Falls, on the Arthur River, New Zealand *580m (1,903ft)*
Biggest desert Great Victoria Desert, Australia *348,750 sq km (134,653 sq miles)*
Biggest island New Guinea *786,000 sq km (303,476 sq miles)* (Australia is counted as a continental land mass and not as an island.)

Main mineral deposits Iron, nickel, precious stones, lead, bauxite
Main fuel deposits Oil, coal, uranium

The Moorish idol fish is found in shallow waters throughout the Pacific. It has a long, distinctive dorsal fin.

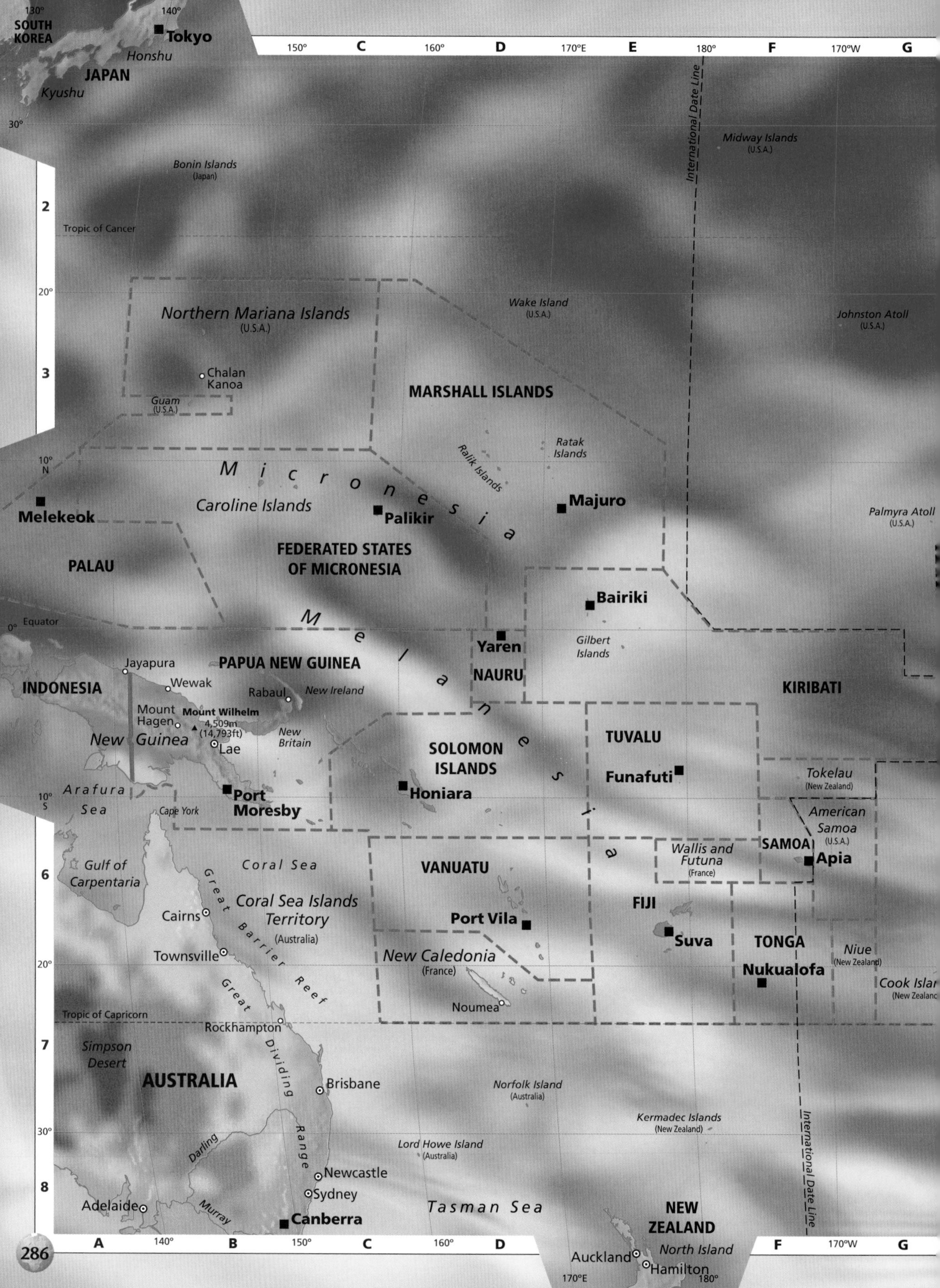
SOUTH KOREA
Tokyo
Honshu
JAPAN
Kyushu
International Date Line
Midway Islands
(U.S.A.)
Bonin Islands
(Japan)
Tropic of Cancer
Northern Mariana Islands
(U.S.A.)
Wake Island
(U.S.A.)
Johnston Atoll
(U.S.A.)
Chalan Kanoa
Guam
(U.S.A.)
MARSHALL ISLANDS
Ratak Islands
Ralik Islands
Micronesia
Caroline Islands
Melekeok
Palikir
Majuro
Palmyra Atoll
(U.S.A.)
PALAU
FEDERATED STATES OF MICRONESIA
Bairiki
Equator
Melanesia
Yaren
NAURU
Gilbert Islands
Jayapura
PAPUA NEW GUINEA
INDONESIA
Wewak
Rabaul
New Ireland
KIRIBATI
Mount Hagen
Mount Wilhelm
4,509m
(14,793ft)
New Guinea
Lae
New Britain
SOLOMON ISLANDS
TUVALU
Funafuti
Tokelau
(New Zealand)
Arafura Sea
Port Moresby
Honiara
Cape York
American Samoa
(U.S.A.)
SAMOA
Apia
Wallis and Futuna
(France)
Gulf of Carpentaria
Coral Sea
VANUATU
Coral Sea Islands Territory
(Australia)
Cairns
Great Barrier Reef
Port Vila
FIJI
Suva
TONGA
Niue
(New Zealand)
Townsville
New Caledonia
(France)
Nukualofa
Cook Islar
(New Zealanc
Noumea
Tropic of Capricorn
Rockhampton
Simpson Desert
Great Dividing Range
AUSTRALIA
Brisbane
Norfolk Island
(Australia)
Kermadec Islands
(New Zealand)
Darling
Lord Howe Island
(Australia)
Newcastle
Sydney
Adelaide
Murray
Canberra
Tasman Sea
NEW ZEALAND
North Island
Auckland
Hamilton

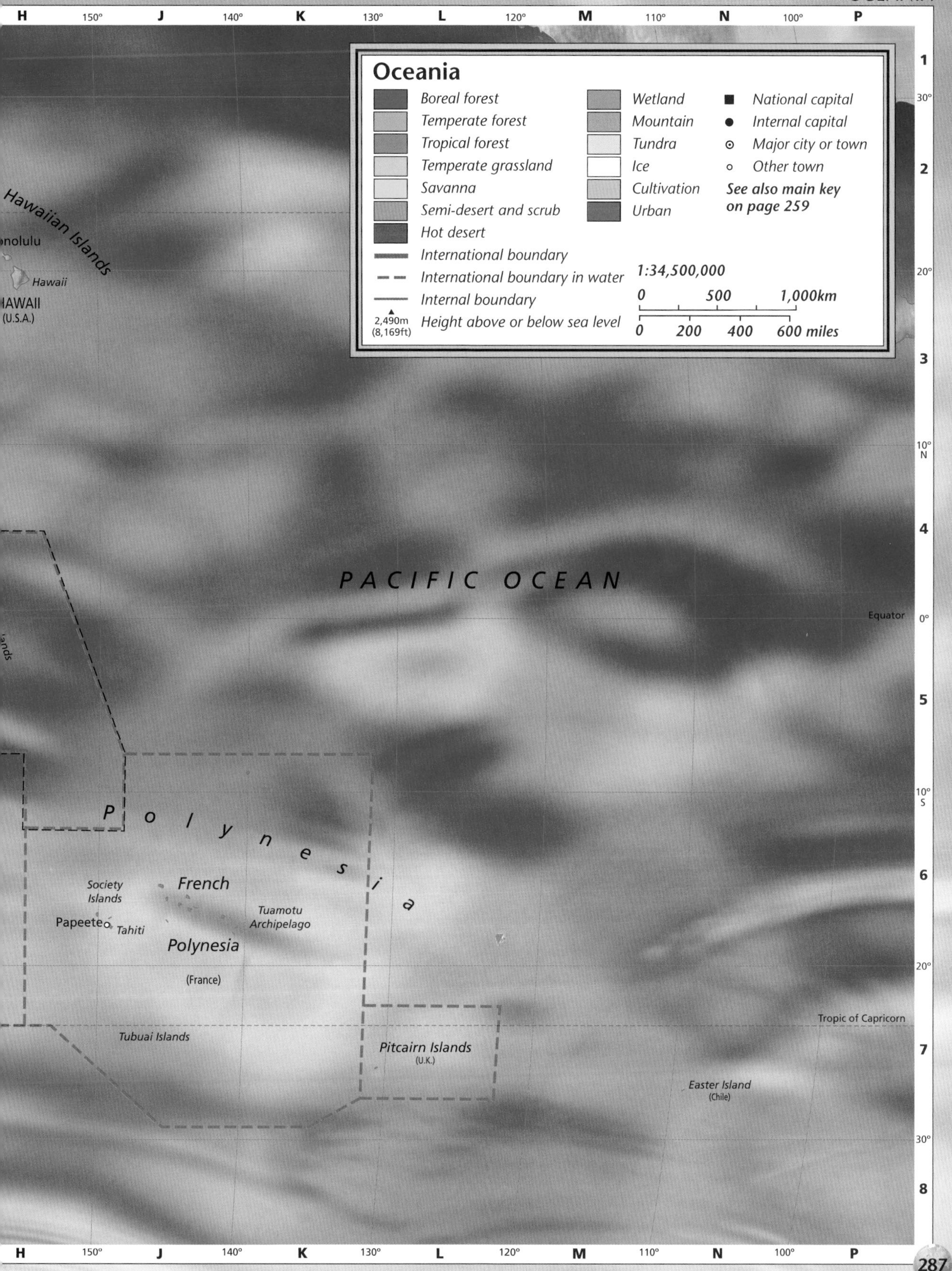
H
150°
J
140°
K
130°
L
120°
M
110°
N
100°
P
1
30°
2
20°
3
10° N
4
5
10° S
6
20°
7
30°
8
Oceania
Boreal forest
Temperate forest
Tropical forest
Temperate grassland
Savanna
Semi-desert and scrub
Hot desert
International boundary
International boundary in water
Internal boundary
2,490m (8,169ft)
Height above or below sea level
Wetland
Mountain
Tundra
Ice
Cultivation
Urban
National capital
Internal capital
Major city or town
Other town
See also main key on page 259
1:34,500,000
0 500 1,000km
0 200 400 600 miles
Hawaiian Islands
nolulu
Hawaii
IAWAII
(U.S.A.)
PACIFIC OCEAN
Equator
0°
Polynesia
Society Islands
French Polynesia
(France)
Papeete
Tahiti
Tuamotu Archipelago
Tubuai Islands
Pitcairn Islands
(U.K.)
Tropic of Capricorn
Easter Island
(Chile)

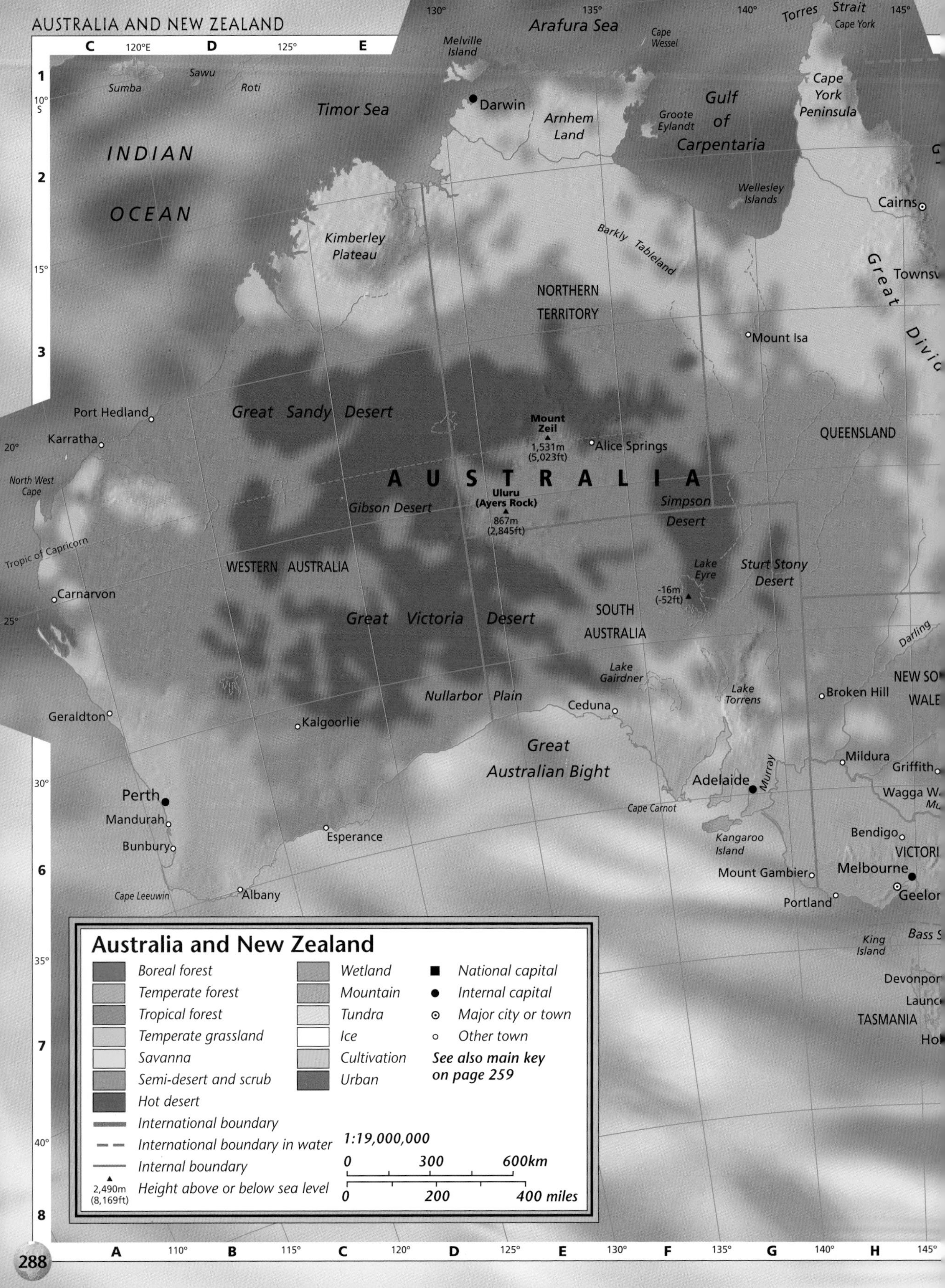

Arafura Sea
Torres Strait
Cape York
Melville Island
Cape Wessel
Sumba
Sawu
Roti
Timor Sea
Darwin
Arnhem Land
Groote Eylandt
Gulf of Carpentaria
Cape York Peninsula
INDIAN OCEAN
Wellesley Islands
Cairns
Kimberley Plateau
Barkly Tableland
Great Dividing
Townsv
NORTHERN TERRITORY
Mount Isa
Port Hedland
Great Sandy Desert
Mount Zeil 1,531m (5,023ft)
Alice Springs
QUEENSLAND
Karratha
North West Cape
AUSTRALIA
Uluru (Ayers Rock) 867m (2,845ft)
Gibson Desert
Simpson Desert
Tropic of Capricorn
WESTERN AUSTRALIA
Lake Eyre
-16m (-52ft)
Sturt Stony Desert
Carnarvon
Great Victoria Desert
SOUTH AUSTRALIA
Darling
Lake Gairdner
Lake Torrens
Broken Hill
NEW SO
WALE
Nullarbor Plain
Ceduna
Geraldton
Kalgoorlie
Great Australian Bight
Mildura
Griffith
Adelaide
Murray
Perth
Cape Carnot
Wagga W.
Mandurah
Esperance
Bendigo
Bunbury
Kangaroo Island
VICTORI
Mount Gambier
Melbourne
Cape Leeuwin
Albany
Portland
Geelor
King Island
Bass S
Devonpor
Launc
TASMANIA
Ho
Australia and New Zealand
Boreal forest
Temperate forest
Tropical forest
Temperate grassland
Savanna
Semi-desert and scrub
Hot desert
International boundary
International boundary in water
Internal boundary
2,490m (8,169ft) Height above or below sea level
Wetland
Mountain
Tundra
Ice
Cultivation
Urban
National capital
Internal capital
Major city or town
Other town
See also main key on page 259
1:19,000,000
0 300 600km
0 200 400 miles

SOLOMON ISLANDS
Rennell Island
Santa Cruz Islands
TUVALU
Coral Sea
Coral Sea Islands Territory
(Australia)
VANUATU
Banks Islands
Espiritu Santo
Luganville
Malakula
Efate
Port Vila
FIJI
Vanua Levu
Lautoka
Viti Levu
Suva
Chesterfield Islands
New Caledonia
(France)
Noumea
Loyalty Islands
Mackay
Bundaberg
Fraser Island
Gympie
Brisbane
Gold Coast
Grafton
Port Macquarie
Newcastle
Sydney
Wollongong
Canberra
AUSTRALIAN CAPITAL TERRITORY
Tropic of Capricorn
PACIFIC OCEAN
Norfolk Island
(Australia)
Lord Howe Island
(Australia)
Kermadec Islands
(New Zealand)
North Cape
Whangarei
Auckland
North Island
Hamilton
East Cape
Rotorua
New Plymouth
Lake Taupo
Cape Farewell
Napier
Nelson
Cook Strait
Wellington
Tasman Sea
South Island
Aoraki (Mount Cook)
3,754m (12,316ft)
Christchurch
NEW ZEALAND
Sutherland Falls
Cape Providence
Dunedin
Invercargill
Stewart Island
South West Cape
Chatham Islands
(New Zealand)

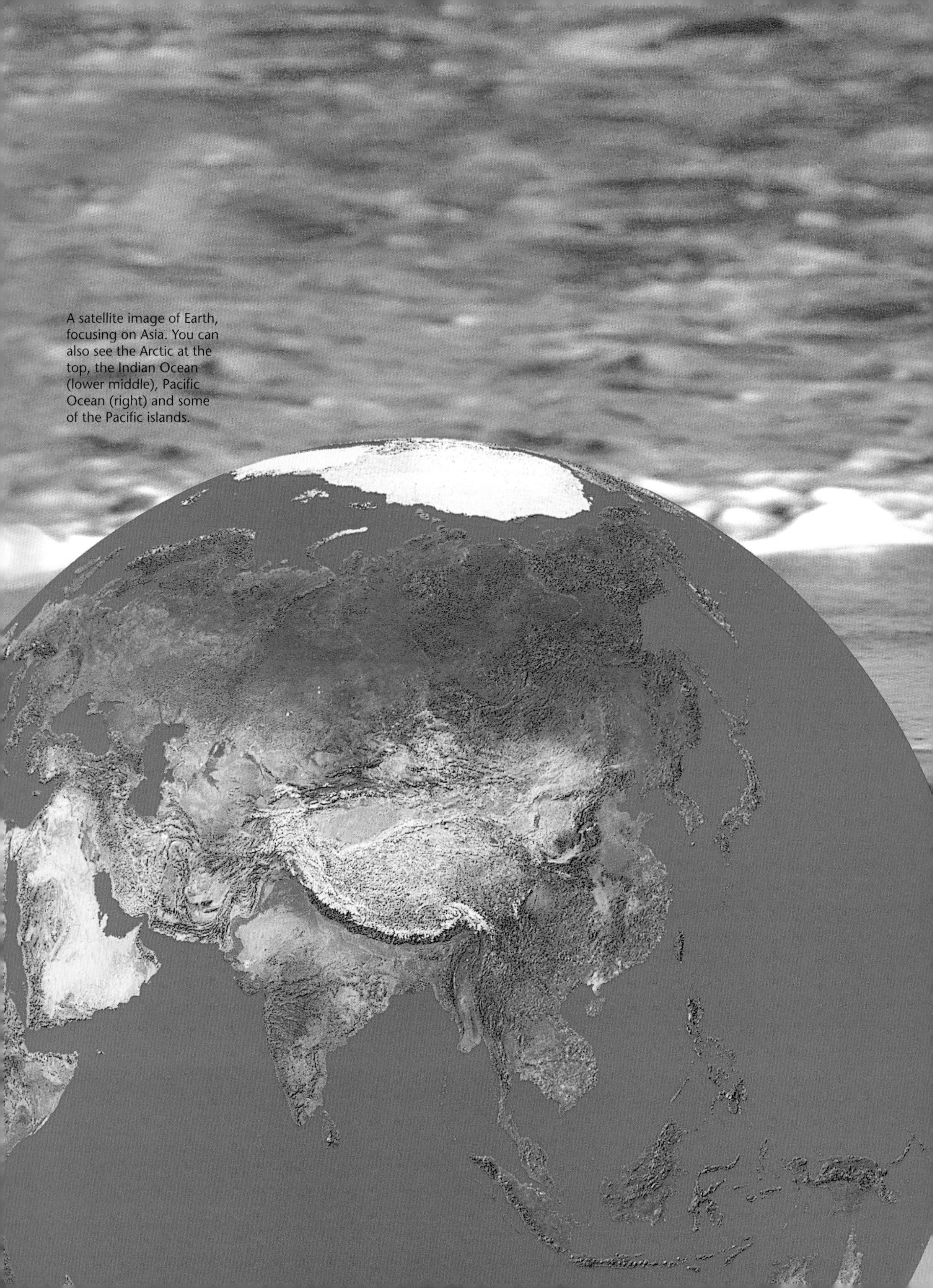

A satellite image of Earth, focusing on Asia. You can also see the Arctic at the top, the Indian Ocean (lower middle), Pacific Ocean (right) and some of the Pacific islands.

MAPS OF ASIA

A Bengal tiger

Asia is the world's largest continent and has 49 countries, including Russia, the biggest country in the world. As well as large land masses, it has thousands of islands and inlets, giving it over 160,000km (100,000 miles) of coastline. Asia also contains the Himalayas, the world's highest mountain range. Turkey and Russia are part in Europe and part in Asia, but both are shown in full on this map.

The shading on this map is there to help you see clearly the different countries that make up the continent.

A type of Chinese sailing boat called a junk in the port at Singapore

Wrangel Island
Bering Sea
East Siberian Sea
New Siberia Islands
ernaya mlya
Laptev Sea
Lena
Sea of Okhotsk
A
Lake Baikal
Hokkaido
Ulan Bator
MONGOLIA
NORTH KOREA
JAPAN
Tokyo
Pyongyang
Seoul
Beijing
Honshu
SOUTH KOREA
Huang He (Yellow)
East China Sea
Tropic of Cancer
C H I N A
Chang Jiang (Yangtze)
N
Irrawaddy
Taiwan
PACIFIC OCEAN
a
BURMA (MYANMAR)
Hanoi
LAOS
Vientiane
Pyi Taw
Mekong
South China Sea
PHILIPPINES
Manila
oon
THAILAND
VIETNAM
Philippine Sea
Bangkok
CAMBODIA
ndaman Islands (India)
Phnom Penh
Equator
Nicobar Islands (India)
BRUNEI
MALAYSIA
Kuala Lumpur
New Guinea
Putrajaya
SINGAPORE
Borneo
Celebes
Arafura Sea
Sumatra
INDONESIA
Dili
EAST TIMOR
Jakarta
Java

Facts

Total land area *44,537,920 sq km (17,196,187 sq miles)*

Total population 4.3 billion (including all of Russia)

Biggest city Tokyo, Japan

Biggest country Russia *Total area: 17,075,200 sq km (6,592,772 sq miles) Area of Asiatic Russia: 12,780,800 sq km (4,934,694 sq miles)*

Smallest country Maldives *300 sq km (116 sq miles)*

Highest mountain Mount Everest, Nepal/China border *8,848m (29,029ft)*

Longest river Chang Jiang (Yangtze), China *6,380km (3,964 miles)*

Biggest lake Caspian Sea, western Asia *386,400 sq km (149,190 sq miles)*

Highest waterfall Jog Falls, on the Sharavati River, India *253m (830ft)*

Biggest desert Arabian Desert, in and around Saudi Arabia *2,330,000 sq km (900,000 sq miles)*

Biggest island Borneo *748,168 sq km (288,869 sq miles)*

Main mineral deposits Zinc, mica, tin, chromium, iron, nickel

Main fuel deposits Oil, coal, uranium, natural gas

These are lotus flowers, Asian water lilies known for their beauty. In China they are associated with purity and for Buddhists they are sacred.

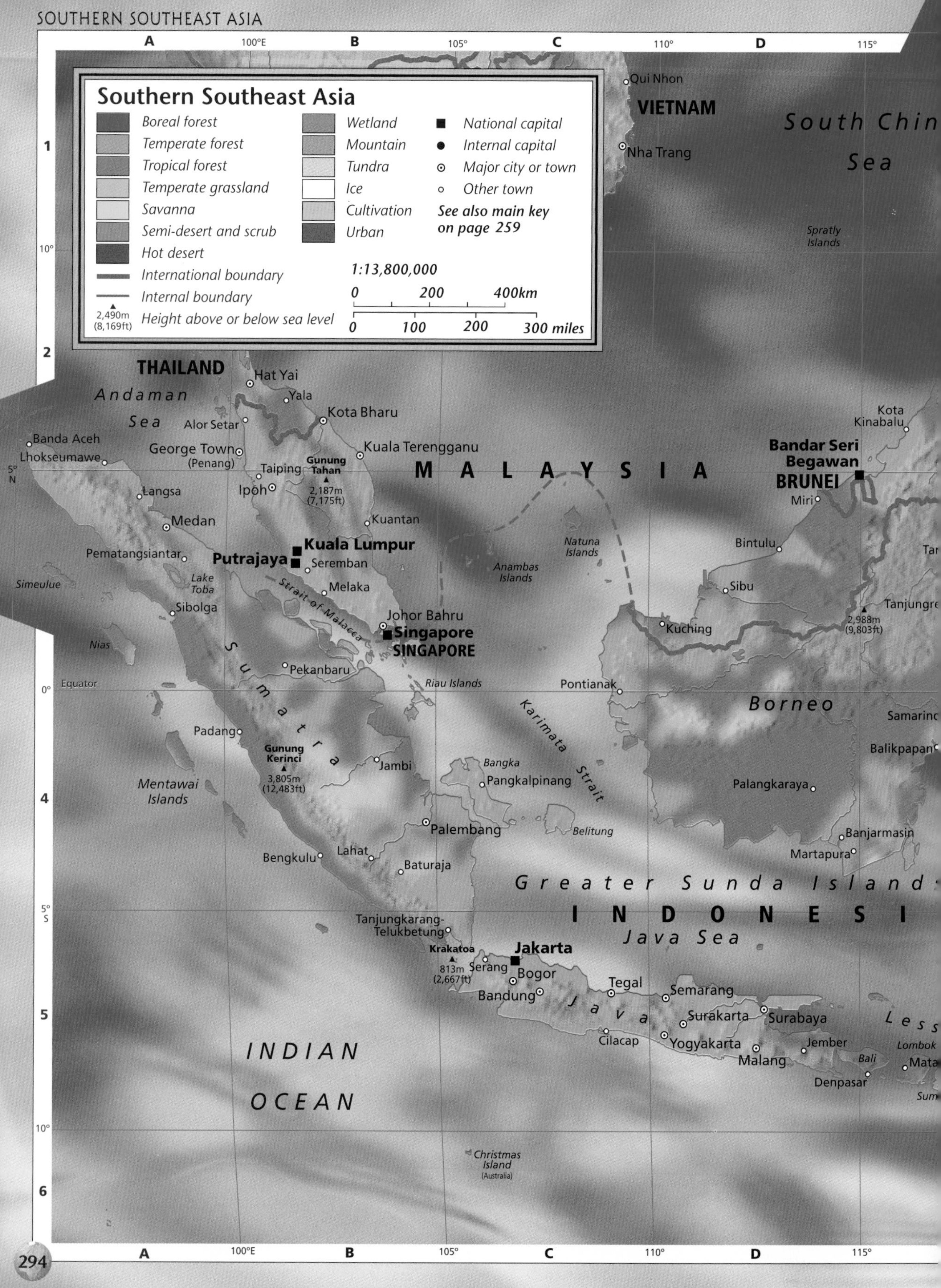

A
100°E
B
105°
C
110°
D
115°
1
2
4
5
6
10°
5° N
0°
5° S
10°
Southern Southeast Asia
Boreal forest
Temperate forest
Tropical forest
Temperate grassland
Savanna
Semi-desert and scrub
Hot desert
International boundary
Internal boundary
2,490m (8,169ft)
Height above or below sea level
Wetland
Mountain
Tundra
Ice
Cultivation
Urban
National capital
Internal capital
Major city or town
Other town
See also main key on page 259
1:13,800,000
0 200 400km
0 100 200 300 miles
Qui Nhon
VIETNAM
Nha Trang
South China Sea
Spratly Islands
THAILAND
Hat Yai
Yala
Andaman Sea
Alor Setar
Kota Bharu
Banda Aceh
Lhokseumawe
George Town (Penang)
Kuala Terengganu
Taiping
Gunung Tahan 2,187m (7,175ft)
Ipoh
Langsa
Medan
Kuantan
MALAYSIA
Kota Kinabalu
Bandar Seri Begawan
BRUNEI
Miri
Bintulu
Kuala Lumpur
Putrajaya
Pematangsiantar
Seremban
Simeulue
Lake Toba
Melaka
Strait of Malacca
Natuna Islands
Anambas Islands
Sibu
Sibolga
Johor Bahru
Singapore
SINGAPORE
Kuching
Tanjungre
2,988m (9,803ft)
Nias
Sumatra
Pekanbaru
Equator
Riau Islands
Pontianak
Borneo
Samarinc
Balikpapan
Karimata Strait
Padang
Gunung Kerinci 3,805m (12,483ft)
Jambi
Bangka
Pangkalpinang
Palangkaraya
Mentawai Islands
Palembang
Belitung
Banjarmasin
Martapura
Bengkulu
Lahat
Baturaja
Greater Sunda Islands
INDONESI
Tanjungkarang-Telukbetung
Java Sea
Krakatoa 813m (2,667ft)
Jakarta
Serang
Bogor
Bandung
Tegal
Semarang
Java
Surakarta
Surabaya
Cilacap
Yogyakarta
Malang
Jember
Bali
Denpasar
Lombok
Mata
Less
Sum
INDIAN OCEAN
Christmas Island (Australia)

PHILIPPINES
Manila
Quezon City
Luzon
Cabanatuan
Olongapo
Lucena
Naga
Legaspi
Calapan
Mindoro
Masbate
Calbayog
Samar
Roxas
Panay
Tacloban
Philippine Sea
Taytay
Iloilo
Bacolod
Cebu
Negros
Bohol
Surigao
Dumaguete
Butuan
Cagayan de Oro
Iligan
Pagadian
Mindanao
Davao
Zamboanga
General Santos
Jolo
Sulu Archipelago
Celebes Sea
Talaud Islands
Sangihe Islands
Morotai
PACIFIC OCEAN
PALAU
Manado
Ternate
Halmahera
Gorontalo
Molucca Sea
Equator
Palu
Peleng
Obi
Sorong
Biak
Misool
Yapen
Sula Islands
Celebes
Ceram Sea
Jayapura
Palopo
Ceram
Fakfak
Buru
Ambon
Maoke Range
Puncak Jaya
5,030m (16,502ft)
New Guinea
Kendari
Watampone
Buton
Ujung Pandang
Banda Sea
Aru Islands
Flores Sea
Wetar
Tanimbar Islands
Dolak
Flores
Ende
Dili
EAST TIMOR
Sumba
Sawu Sea
Timor
Arafura Sea
Torres Strait
Sawu
Kupang
Roti
Timor Sea
AUSTRALIA
Darwin
NORTHERN TERRITORY
Jayapura
Wewak
Bismarck Sea
Admiralty Islands
PACIFIC OCEAN
New Ireland
Rabaul
Mount Wilhelm 4,509m (14,793ft)
Madang
Mount Hagen
New Britain
New Guinea
Lae
PAPUA NEW GUINEA
Kerema
Solomon Sea
Gulf of Papua
D'Entrecasteaux Islands
Port Moresby
Torres Strait
Cape York
1:20,700,000
0 400km
0 200 miles
Cape York Peninsula
AUSTRALIA

A B C D E
90°E 95° 100° 105°
2 3 4 5 6 7
25° N 20° 15° 10° 5°
Himalayas
Mount Everest 8,848m (29,029ft)
NEPAL
Thimphu
BHUTAN
INDIA
Lhasa
Brahmaputra
Darjeeling
Biratnagar
Darbhanga
Bhagalpur
Rangpur
Guwahati
Shillong
Dibrugarh
Jorhat
Ganges
Rajshahi
Sylhet
BANGLADESH
Dhaka
Asansol
Jamshedpur
Kolkata (Calcutta)
Khulna
Chittagong
Imphal
Aizawl
Mouths of the Ganges
Bay of Bengal
INDIAN OCEAN
Andaman Islands (India)
Port Blair
Little Andaman
Ten Degree Channel
Nicobar Islands (India)
Andaman Sea
Monywa
Mandalay
Mount Victoria 3,053m (10,016ft)
BURMA (MYANMAR)
Meiktila
Taunggyi
Sittwe
Nay Pyi Taw
Pye
Sandoway
Irrawaddy
Henzada
Pegu
Pathein
Rangoon
Thaton
Moulmein
Mouths of the Irrawaddy
Tavoy
Mergui
Mergui Archipelago
Myitkyina
Lashio
Salween
Mekong
Chang Jiang (Yangtze)
Chengdu
Gongga Shan 7,556m (24,790ft)
Leshan
Neijiang
Chongqing
Wanxian
Luzhou
Yibin
Xichang
Zhaotong
Panzhihua
Zunyi
Guiyang
Anshun
CH
Dali
Baoshan
Kunming
Red
Kaiyuan
Gejiu
Simao
Ha Giang
Lao Cai
Phongsali
Thai Nguyen
Son La
Hanoi
Hai Phong
Qinzhou
Liuzh
Nar
Louangphrabang
Thanh Hoa
Gulf of Tonkin
Vinh
LAOS
Vientiane
Chiang Mai
Udon Thani
Phitsanulok
Savannakhet
Khon Kaen
Hue
Da N
Nakhon Sawan
THAILAND
Ubon Ratchathani
Pakxe
Nakhon Ratchasima
Attapu
Bangkok
VIETN
Stoeng Treng
Angkor
Tonle Sap
Pattaya
Batdambang
CAMBODIA
Qui Nho
Buon Thuot
Prachuap Khiri Khan
Kampong Chhnang
Kampong Cham
Da Lat
Krong Kaoh Kong
Phnom Penh
Bien Hoa
Chumphon
Kampong Saom
Mekong
Ho Chi Minh C (Saigon)
Long Xuyen
Can Tho
Gulf of Thailand
Bac Lieu
Con Son
Nakhon Si Thammarat
Hat Yai
Yala
Alor Setar
Kota Bharu
Banda Aceh
Lhokseumawe
George Town (Penang)
Kuala Terengganu
Sumatra
Gunung Tahan 2,187m (7,175ft)
Taiping
Ipoh
Langsa
INDONESIA
MALAYSIA
Natuna Islands (Indonesia)

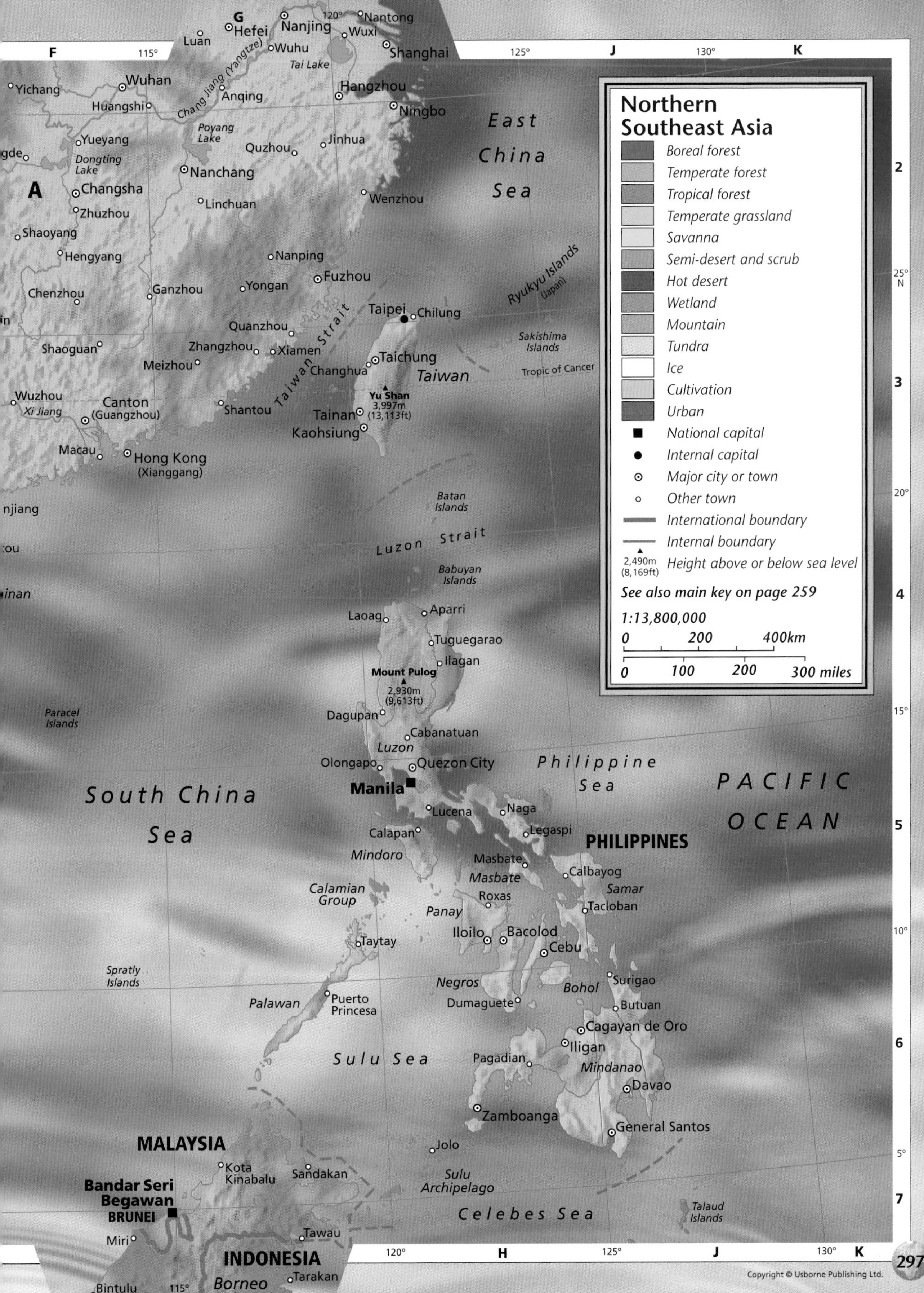

Northern Southeast Asia
Boreal forest
Temperate forest
Tropical forest
Temperate grassland
Savanna
Semi-desert and scrub
Hot desert
Wetland
Mountain
Tundra
Ice
Cultivation
Urban
National capital
Internal capital
Major city or town
Other town
International boundary
Internal boundary
2,490m (8,169ft) Height above or below sea level
See also main key on page 259
1:13,800,000
0 200 400km
0 100 200 300 miles
F
115°
G
120°
125°
J
130°
K
H
2
3
4
5
6
7
25° N
20°
15°
10°
5°
A
Luan
Hefei
Nanjing
Nantong
Wuxi
Wuhu
Shanghai
Tai Lake
Chang Jiang (Yangtze)
Yichang
Wuhan
Huangshi
Anqing
Hangzhou
Ningbo
Poyang Lake
Yueyang
Dongting Lake
Jinhua
Quzhou
Nanchang
Changsha
Zhuzhou
Linchuan
Wenzhou
Shaoyang
Hengyang
Nanping
Fuzhou
Yongan
Ganzhou
Chenzhou
Taipei
Chilung
Quanzhou
Shaoguan
Zhangzhou
Xiamen
Meizhou
Taiwan Strait
Taichung
Changhua
Taiwan
Yu Shan 3,997m (13,113ft)
Wuzhou
Xi Jiang
Canton (Guangzhou)
Shantou
Tainan
Kaohsiung
Macau
Hong Kong (Xianggang)
East China Sea
Ryukyu Islands (Japan)
Sakishima Islands
Tropic of Cancer
Batan Islands
Luzon Strait
Babuyan Islands
Laoag
Aparri
Tuguegarao
Ilagan
Mount Pulog 2,930m (9,613ft)
Dagupan
Cabanatuan
Luzon
Olongapo
Quezon City
Manila
Paracel Islands
South China Sea
Philippine Sea
PACIFIC OCEAN
Lucena
Naga
Legaspi
Calapan
PHILIPPINES
Mindoro
Masbate
Masbate
Calbayog
Samar
Calamian Group
Roxas
Tacloban
Panay
Iloilo
Bacolod
Cebu
Taytay
Spratly Islands
Negros
Bohol
Surigao
Palawan
Puerto Princesa
Dumaguete
Butuan
Cagayan de Oro
Iligan
Sulu Sea
Pagadian
Mindanao
Davao
Zamboanga
General Santos
MALAYSIA
Jolo
Kota Kinabalu
Sandakan
Sulu Archipelago
Bandar Seri Begawan
BRUNEI
Celebes Sea
Talaud Islands
Tawau
Miri
INDONESIA
Borneo
Tarakan
Bintulu

A
80°E
B
85°
C
90°
D
95°
E
100°
F
105°
G
110°
2
3
4
5
6
7
40° N
35°
30°
25°
20°
15°
KAZAKHSTAN
Almaty
Lake Issyk
KYRGYZSTAN
Pik Pobedy
7,439m
(24,406ft)
Aksu
Yining
Karamay
Kuytun
Shihezi
Urumqi
Dzungarian Basin
Tien Shan
Turpan
-154m
(-505ft)
Turpan Depression
Bosten Lake
Korla
Hami
Altai Mountains
Altay
Bulgan
Ulan Bator
MONGOLIA
Gobi Desert
Tarim Basin
Taklimakan Desert
Hotan
Lop Lake
Mogao Caves
Yumen
The Great Wall of China
5,547m
(18,199ft)
Altun Mountains
Kunlun Mountains
Qaidam Basin
Golmud
Qinghai Lake
Xining
Lanzhou
Huang He (Yellow)
Baotou
Hohh
Wuhai
Yinchuan
CHINA
Plateau of Tibet
Siling Lake
TIBET
Yushu
Baoji
Mount Li (Terracotta
Xian
Himalayas
Nam Lake
Brahmaputra
Salween
Mekong
Chang Jiang (Yangtze)
Lhasa
NEPAL
Kathmandu
Mount Everest
8,848m
(29,029ft)
Darjeeling
Darbhanga
Biratnagar
Patna
Thimphu
BHUTAN
Gongga Shan
7,556m
(24,790ft)
Chengdu
Leshan
Chongqing
Yichang
Shiyan
Xiang
Changd
Luzhou
Ganges
Bhagalpur
Rangpur
Dibrugarh
Guwahati
Shillong
INDIA
Ranchi
Asansol
Rajshahi
Sylhet
BANGLADESH
Tropic of Cancer
Dhaka
Imphal
Myitkyina
Irrawaddy
Xichang
Panzhihua
Zunyi
Guiyang
Huaihua
Heng
Dali
Kunming
Guilin
Aizawl
Kolkata
(Calcutta)
Khulna
Chittagong
Cuttack
Mouths of the Ganges
Lashio
Red
Liuzhou
Gejiu
Simao
Wuzhou
Monywa
Mandalay
Mount Victoria
3,053m
(10,016ft)
BURMA
(MYANMAR)
Bay of Bengal
Sittwe
Taunggyi
Lao Cai
Nanning
Yulin
Phongsali
Son La
Thai Nguyen
Hanoi
Nay Pyi Taw
INDIAN OCEAN
Sandoway
Pye
Mekong
Louangphrabang
Hai Phong
Gulf of Tonkin
Zhanjia
Haikou
Chiang Mai
Thanh Hoa
LAOS
VIETNAM
Henzada
Pegu
THAILAND
Haina
Pathein
Rangoon
Vientiane
Vinh
Udon Thani
Sanya
Mouths of the Irrawaddy
Moulmein
Ere
Tai
C
90°E
D
95°
100°
F
105°
G
110°

China, Korea and Japan
Boreal forest
Temperate forest
Tropical forest
Temperate grassland
Savanna
Semi-desert and scrub
Hot desert
Wetland
Mountain
Tundra
Ice
Cultivation
Urban
National capital
Internal capital
Major city or town
Other town
International boundary
Internal boundary
2,490m (8,169ft) Height above or below sea level
See also main key on page 259
1:16,100,000
0 200 400km
0 100 200 300 miles
RUSSIA
MANCHURIA
NNER NGOLIA
NORTH KOREA
SOUTH KOREA
JAPAN
PHILIPPINES
Hailar
Hulun Lake
Greater Khingan Range
Qiqihar
Daqing
Ulanhot
Yichun
Hegang
Amur
Jiamusi
Harbin
Jixi
Mudanjiang
Lake Khanka
Sikhote Alin Range
La Perouse Strait
Kuril Islands (Russia)
Asahikawa
Hokkaido
Kushiro
Sapporo
Tomakomai
Hakodate
Vladivostok
Nakhodka
Changchun
Jilin
Yanji
Xilinhot
Tongliao
Liaoyuan
Chongjin
Aomori
Akita
Chifeng
Fuxin
Fushun
Shenyang
Hyesan
Kanggye
Kimchaek
Jinzhou
Anshan
Sendai
Fukushima
Niigata
Honshu
Zhangjiakou
Dandong
Sinuiju
Hamhung
Wonsan
Pyongyang
Beijing
Qinhuangdao
Tangshan
Korea Bay
Nampo
Utsunomiya
Toyama
Tokyo
Kanazawa
Fukui
Mount Fuji 3,776m (12,388ft)
Shizuoka
Nagoya
Kyoto
Hamamatsu
Osaka
Wakayama
Okayama
Hiroshima
Tianjin
Gulf of Chihli
Dalian
Seoul
Inchon
Suwon
Chongju
Taejon
Taegu
Pusan
Kwangju
Shijiazhuang
Yantai
Handan
Zibo
Weifang
Qingdao
Yellow Sea
Taian
Huang He (Yellow)
Jining
Matsuyama
Shikoku
Kitakyushu
Fukuoka
Korea Strait
Lianyungang
Grand Canal
Zhengzhou
Xuzhou
Cheju
Nagasaki
Kumamoto
Kyushu
Kagoshima
Yancheng
Nanjing
Hefei
Wuxi
Tai Lake
Shanghai
Chang Jiang (Yangtze)
Wuhan
Anqing
Hangzhou
Ningbo
Poyang Lake
Jinhua
Nanchang
Wenzhou
Linchuan
East China Sea
Ryukyu Islands (Japan)
Amami
Okinawa
Nanping
Fuzhou
Ganzhou
Yongan
Chilung
Taipei
Quanzhou
Xiamen
Sakishima Islands
Tropic of Cancer
Taiwan Strait
Taichung
Changhua
Meizhou
Yu Shan 3,997m (13,113ft)
Canton
Shantou
Tainan
Kaohsiung
Taiwan
PACIFIC OCEAN
Hong Kong (Xianggang)
Batan Islands
South China Sea
Luzon Strait
Babuyan Islands
Aparri
Luzon
Laoag
Tuguegarao

KAZAKHSTAN
MONGOLIA
CHINA
UZBEKISTAN
TURKMENISTAN
TAJIKISTAN
KYRGYZSTAN
AFGHANISTAN
PAKISTAN
NEPAL
BHUTAN
TIBET
JAMMU AND KASHMIR
Aral Sea
Syr Darya
Amu Darya
Lake Balkhash
Lake Zaysan
Lake Issyk
Altai Mountains
Dzungarian Basin
Turpan Depression
Bosten Lake
Lop Lake
Mogao Caves
Altun Mountains
Qaidam Basin
Tarim Basin
Taklimakan Desert
Kunlun Mountains
Plateau of Tibet
Tien Shan
Karakorum Range
Hindu Kush
Himalayas
Salween
Nam Lake
Siling Lake
Brahmaputra
Indus
Ganges
Helmand
Thar Desert
Pik Pobedy 7,439m (24,406ft)
Kongur Shan 7,719m (25,325ft)
Pik Imeni Ismail Samani 7,495m (24,590ft)
K2 8,612m (28,253ft)
5,143m (16,873ft)
Mount Everest 8,848m (29,029ft)
-154m (-505ft)
Altay
Hami
Golmud
Turpan
Urumqi
Shihezi
Korla
Kuytun
Karamay
Yining
Aksu
Hotan
Kashi
Balqash
Taldyqorghan
Almaty
Karakol
Bishkek
Kara-Balta
Jalal-Abad
Osh
Taraz
Namangan
Fargona
Khujand
Angren
Tashkent
Turkistan
Shymkent
Shieli
Qyzylorda
Jizzax
Samarqand
Navoiy
Buxoro
Urgench
Turkmenabat
Mary
Dushanbe
Qurghonteppa
Kulob
Khorugh
Konduz
Mazar-e Sharif
Kabul
Jalalabad
Herat
Kandahar
Peshawar
Islamabad
Gilgit
Srinagar
Jammu
Sialkot
Gujranwala
Gujrat
Lahore
Amritsar
Sargodha
Faisalabad
Sahiwal
Multan
Bahawalpur
Dera Ghazi Khan
Quetta
Rahimyar Khan
Sukkur
Larkana
Nawabshah
Panjgur
Ludhiana
Chandigarh
Saharanpur
Meerut
Delhi
New Delhi
Aligarh
Agra
Taj Mahal
Gwalior
Jaipur
Ajmer
Bikaner
Bareilly
Lucknow
Kanpur
Gorakhpur
Pokhara
Kathmandu
Biratnagar
Darbhanga
Darjeeling
Thimphu
Lhasa
Guwahati
Dibrugarh
Jorhat
A
B
C
H
1
2
3
4
5
45° N
40°
35°
30°
65°E
70°
75°
80°
85°
90°
95°

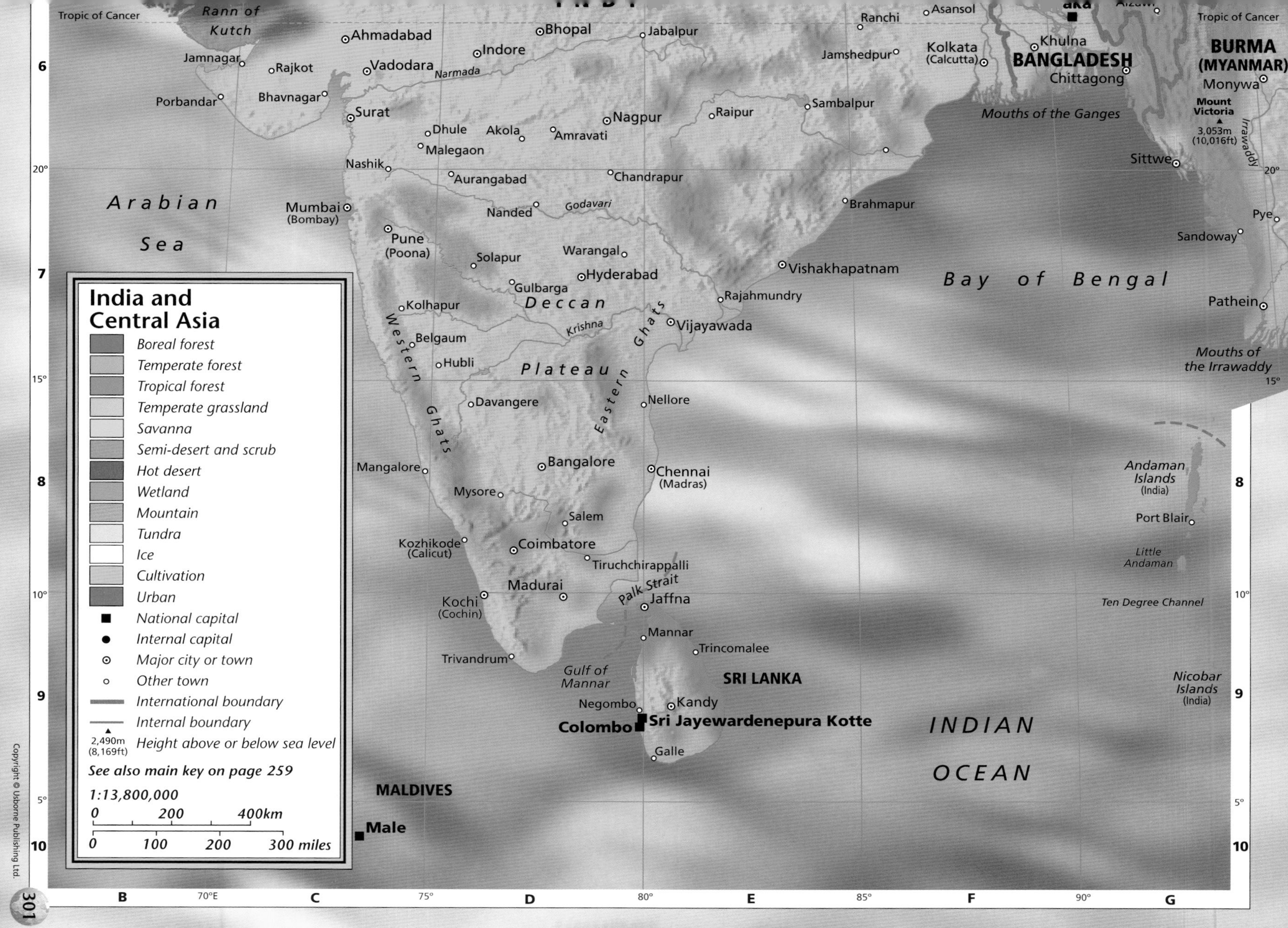
India and Central Asia
Boreal forest
Temperate forest
Tropical forest
Temperate grassland
Savanna
Semi-desert and scrub
Hot desert
Wetland
Mountain
Tundra
Ice
Cultivation
Urban
National capital
Internal capital
Major city or town
Other town
International boundary
Internal boundary
2,490m (8,169ft) Height above or below sea level
See also main key on page 259
1:13,800,000
0 200 400km
0 100 200 300 miles
Tropic of Cancer
Rann of Kutch
Ahmadabad
Bhopal
Jabalpur
Ranchi
Asansol
Jamnagar
Rajkot
Vadodara
Narmada
Indore
Jamshedpur
Kolkata (Calcutta)
Khulna
BANGLADESH
Chittagong
BURMA (MYANMAR)
Monywa
Mount Victoria 3,053m (10,016ft)
Irrawaddy
Porbandar
Bhavnagar
Surat
Dhule
Malegaon
Akola
Amravati
Nagpur
Raipur
Sambalpur
Mouths of the Ganges
Nashik
Aurangabad
Chandrapur
Sittwe
Arabian Sea
Mumbai (Bombay)
Nanded
Godavari
Brahmapur
Pye
Sandoway
Pune (Poona)
Solapur
Warangal
Hyderabad
Vishakhapatnam
Gulbarga
Deccan Plateau
Rajahmundry
Bay of Bengal
Pathein
Kolhapur
Krishna
Vijayawada
Belgaum
Hubli
Western Ghats
Eastern Ghats
Mouths of the Irrawaddy
Davangere
Nellore
Mangalore
Bangalore
Chennai (Madras)
Andaman Islands (India)
Mysore
Port Blair
Salem
Kozhikode (Calicut)
Coimbatore
Tiruchchirappalli
Little Andaman
Madurai
Palk Strait
Kochi (Cochin)
Jaffna
Ten Degree Channel
Mannar
Trincomalee
Trivandrum
Gulf of Mannar
SRI LANKA
Nicobar Islands (India)
Negombo
Kandy
Colombo
Sri Jayewardenepura Kotte
INDIAN OCEAN
Galle
MALDIVES
Male
B C D E F G
6 7 8 9 10
70°E 75° 80° 85° 90°
20° 15° 10° 5°

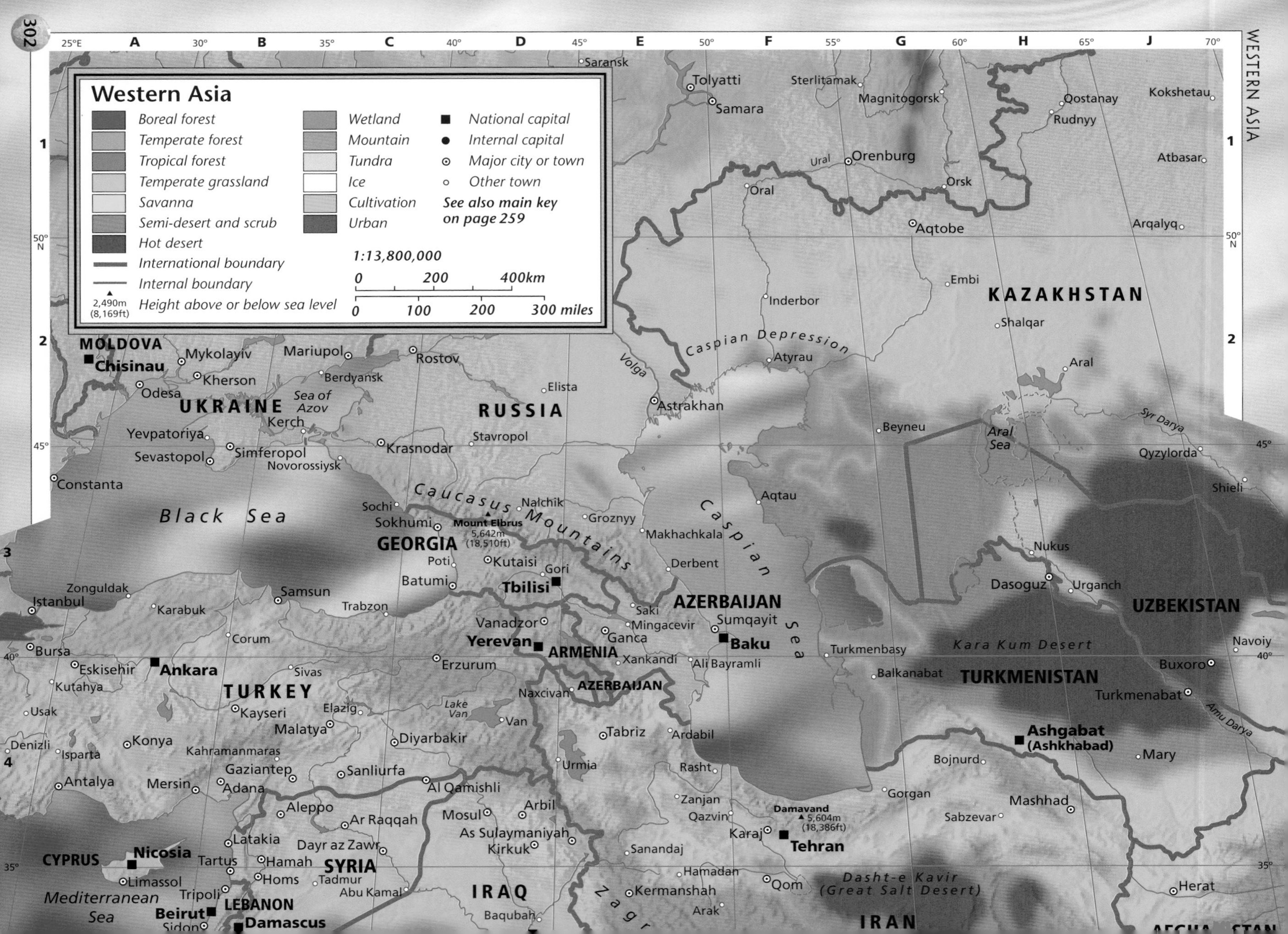
Western Asia
Boreal forest
Temperate forest
Tropical forest
Temperate grassland
Savanna
Semi-desert and scrub
Hot desert
International boundary
Internal boundary
2,490m (8,169ft)
Height above or below sea level
Wetland
Mountain
Tundra
Ice
Cultivation
Urban
National capital
Internal capital
Major city or town
Other town
See also main key on page 259
1:13,800,000
0 200 400km
0 100 200 300 miles
KAZAKHSTAN
RUSSIA
UKRAINE
MOLDOVA
GEORGIA
ARMENIA
AZERBAIJAN
UZBEKISTAN
TURKMENISTAN
TURKEY
SYRIA
LEBANON
CYPRUS
IRAQ
IRAN
Black Sea
Caspian Sea
Aral Sea
Sea of Azov
Mediterranean Sea
Caspian Depression
Caucasus Mountains
Kara Kum Desert
Dasht-e Kavir (Great Salt Desert)
Mount Elbrus 5,642m (18,510ft)
Damavand 5,604m (18,386ft)
Lake Van
Volga
Ural
Syr Darya
Amu Darya
Chisinau
Odesa
Mykolayiv
Kherson
Yevpatoriya
Simferopol
Sevastopol
Kerch
Novorossiysk
Mariupol
Berdyansk
Rostov
Krasnodar
Stavropol
Elista
Sochi
Sokhumi
Poti
Batumi
Kutaisi
Gori
Tbilisi
Yerevan
Vanadzor
Baku
Sumqayit
Ganca
Mingacevir
Saki
Xankandi
Naxcivan
Ali Bayramli
Nalchik
Groznyy
Makhachkala
Derbent
Astrakhan
Saransk
Tolyatti
Samara
Oral
Atyrau
Inderbor
Aqtau
Sterlitamak
Orenburg
Magnitogorsk
Orsk
Aqtobe
Embi
Beyneu
Shalqar
Aral
Qostanay
Rudnyy
Kokshetau
Atbasar
Arqalyq
Qyzylorda
Shieli
Nukus
Urganch
Dasoguz
Buxoro
Navoiy
Turkmenabat
Mary
Turkmenbasy
Balkanabat
Ashgabat (Ashkhabad)
Mashhad
Herat
Bojnurd
Sabzevar
Gorgan
Tehran
Karaj
Qazvin
Qom
Zanjan
Rasht
Ardabil
Tabriz
Urmia
Hamadan
Arak
Kermanshah
Sanandaj
Arbil
Mosul
Kirkuk
As Sulaymaniyah
Baqubah
Al Qamishli
Dayr az Zawr
Abu Kamal
Ar Raqqah
Aleppo
Hamah
Homs
Tadmur
Latakia
Tartus
Tripoli
Beirut
Sidon
Damascus
Nicosia
Limassol
Istanbul
Bursa
Eskisehir
Kutahya
Usak
Denizli
Isparta
Antalya
Konya
Mersin
Adana
Ankara
Karabuk
Zonguldak
Corum
Samsun
Trabzon
Kayseri
Sivas
Malatya
Elazig
Kahramanmaras
Gaziantep
Sanliurfa
Diyarbakir
Erzurum
Van
Constanta

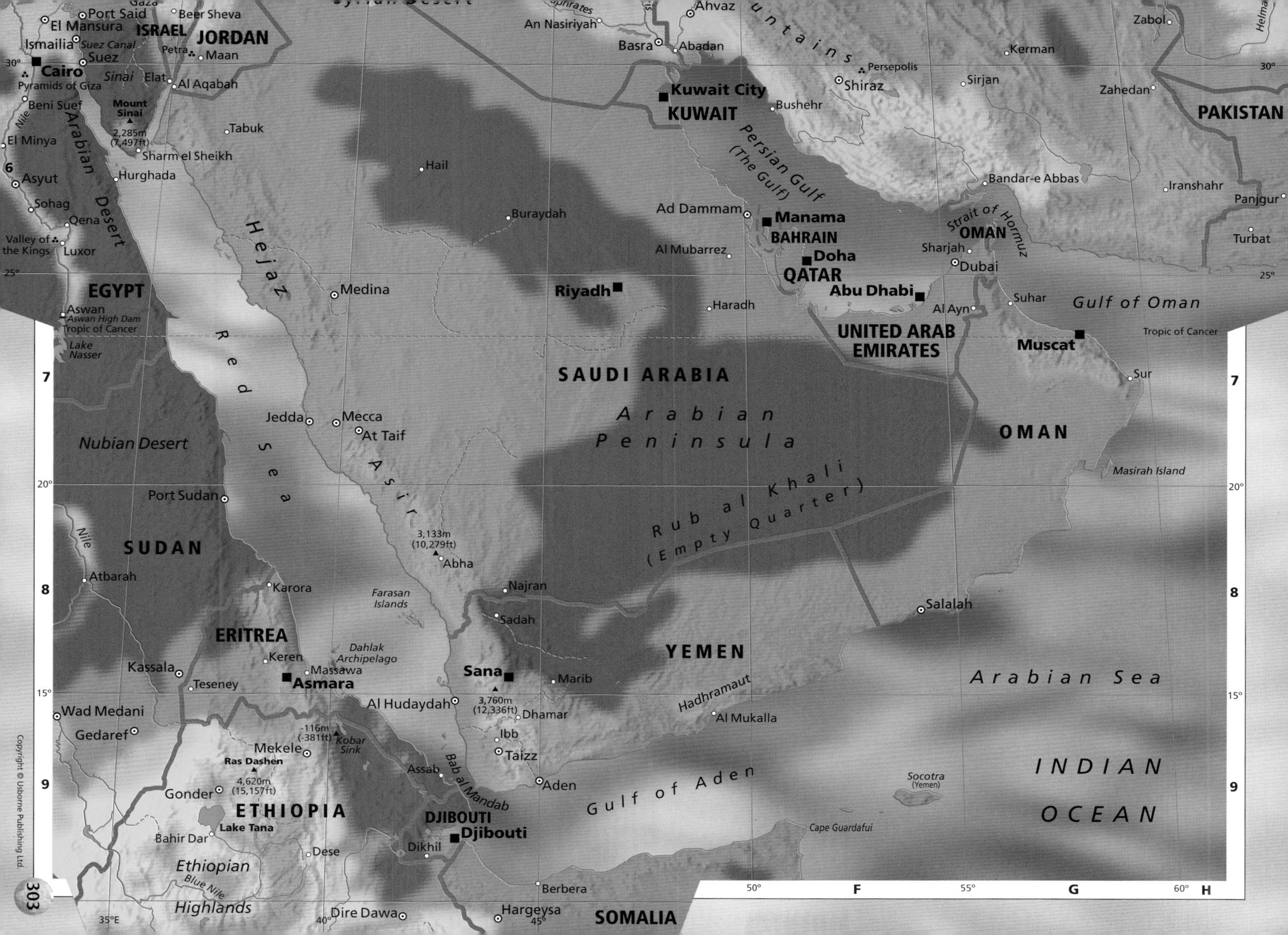

Port Said
El Mansura
Ismailia
Suez Canal
Suez
Cairo
Pyramids of Giza
Sinai
Beni Suef
Nile
El Minya
Asyut
Sohag
Qena
Valley of the Kings
Luxor
Arabian Desert
Mount Sinai
2,285m (7,497ft)
Sharm el Sheikh
Hurghada
Beer Sheva
ISRAEL
JORDAN
Petra
Maan
Elat
Al Aqabah
Tabuk
EGYPT
Aswan
Aswan High Dam
Tropic of Cancer
Lake Nasser
Nubian Desert
Port Sudan
SUDAN
Nile
Atbarah
Kassala
Teseney
Wad Medani
Gedaref
Hejaz
Red Sea
Medina
Jedda
Mecca
At Taif
Asir
3,133m (10,279ft)
Abha
Hail
Buraydah
An Nasiriyah
Basra
Abadan
Ahvaz
Kuwait City
KUWAIT
Persian Gulf (The Gulf)
Bushehr
Shiraz
Persepolis
Sirjan
Kerman
Zahedan
Zabol
PAKISTAN
Iranshahr
Panjgur
Turbat
Bandar-e Abbas
Strait of Hormuz
OMAN
Sharjah
Dubai
Ad Dammam
Manama
BAHRAIN
Al Mubarrez
Doha
QATAR
Abu Dhabi
Al Ayn
Suhar
Gulf of Oman
Tropic of Cancer
Muscat
Sur
Riyadh
Haradh
UNITED ARAB EMIRATES
SAUDI ARABIA
Arabian Peninsula
OMAN
Masirah Island
Rub al Khali (Empty Quarter)
Salalah
Najran
Sadah
Farasan Islands
ERITREA
Karora
Keren
Massawa
Asmara
Dahlak Archipelago
YEMEN
Sana
3,760m (12,336ft)
Marib
Al Hudaydah
Dhamar
Ibb
Taizz
Aden
Hadhramaut
Al Mukalla
Arabian Sea
-116m (-381ft)
Kobar Sink
Mekele
Ras Dashen
4,620m (15,157ft)
Gonder
ETHIOPIA
Lake Tana
Bahir Dar
Dese
Ethiopian Highlands
Blue Nile
Assab
Bab al Mandab
DJIBOUTI
Djibouti
Dikhil
Gulf of Aden
Socotra (Yemen)
Cape Guardafui
INDIAN OCEAN
Berbera
Hargeysa
Dire Dawa
SOMALIA
30°
25°
20°
15°
35°E
40°
45°
50°
55°
60°
F
G
H
6
7
8
9

60° 2 80° 1

Svalbard (Norway) A 20° B ARCT

UNITED KINGDOM London North Sea Norwegian Sea Arctic Circle

Paris NETHERLANDS NORWAY Oslo 40° Franz Josef Land C 60°

BELGIUM DENMARK SWEDEN North Cape D 80°

LUXEMBOURG FRANCE

GERMANY Berlin Stockholm Barents Sea Novaya Zemlya

3 Baltic Sea FINLAND Murmansk Kola Peninsula

CZECH REPUBLIC Helsinki Kara Sea

AUSTRIA POLAND LITHUANIA ESTONIA Lake Ladoga

SLOVAKIA Warsaw LATVIA Vilnius St. Petersburg Arkhangelsk

Budapest HUNGARY Minsk BELARUS Lake Onega

Lviv Cherepovets Vorkuta

Ukhta No

Moscow

ROMANIA Kiev Ural Mountains Novyy Urengoy

MOLDOVA Chisinau UKRAINE Ryazan Nizhniy Novgorod Ob West Siberian

Kharkiv Odesa Voronezh Volga Kazan Perm Plain

Dnipropetrovsk Surgut Yenisey

Simferopol Samara Yekaterinburg Ob

40° N Black Sea Rostov Irtysh R U

Volgograd Krasnodar Oral Chelyabinsk

Ankara Orenburg

TURKEY Volga Tomsk Krasnoy

Mount Elbrus 5,642m (18,510ft) Astrakhan Aqtobe Omsk

Adana Atyrau Novosibirsk

GEORGIA

Tbilisi KAZAKHSTAN Pavlodar Barnaul Ab

ARMENIA Yerevan Astana

Aleppo Aqtau Caspian Sea

SYRIA AZERBAIJAN Baku Aral Sea Qaraghandy K

Oskemen

Mosul Tabriz Nukus Qyzylorda Balqash

Dasoguz UZBEKISTAN Lake Balkhash Altay

Baghdad TURKMENISTAN A

IRAQ Damavand Shymkent

4 Tehran 5,604m (18,386ft) Ashgabat (Ashkhabad) Almaty

Tashkent Bishkek KYRGYZSTAN Urumqi

Ahvaz Esfahan Turkmenabat Samarqand Osh Tien Shan

Mashhad Dushanbe Aksu

Kuwait City KUWAIT IRAN TAJIKISTAN

SAUDI ARABIA Persian (The Gulf) Gulf Tarim Basin

Herat Mazar-e Sharif Taklimakan Desert

Shiraz AFGHANISTAN

Riyadh Hotan K2 8,612m (28,253ft)

Manama Kabul

QATAR Doha Bandar-e Abbas Zahedan Kandahar Islamabad Srinagar

Abu Dhabi Indus Plateau of Tibet

PAKISTAN Lahore INDIA

C 60°E D 80° E

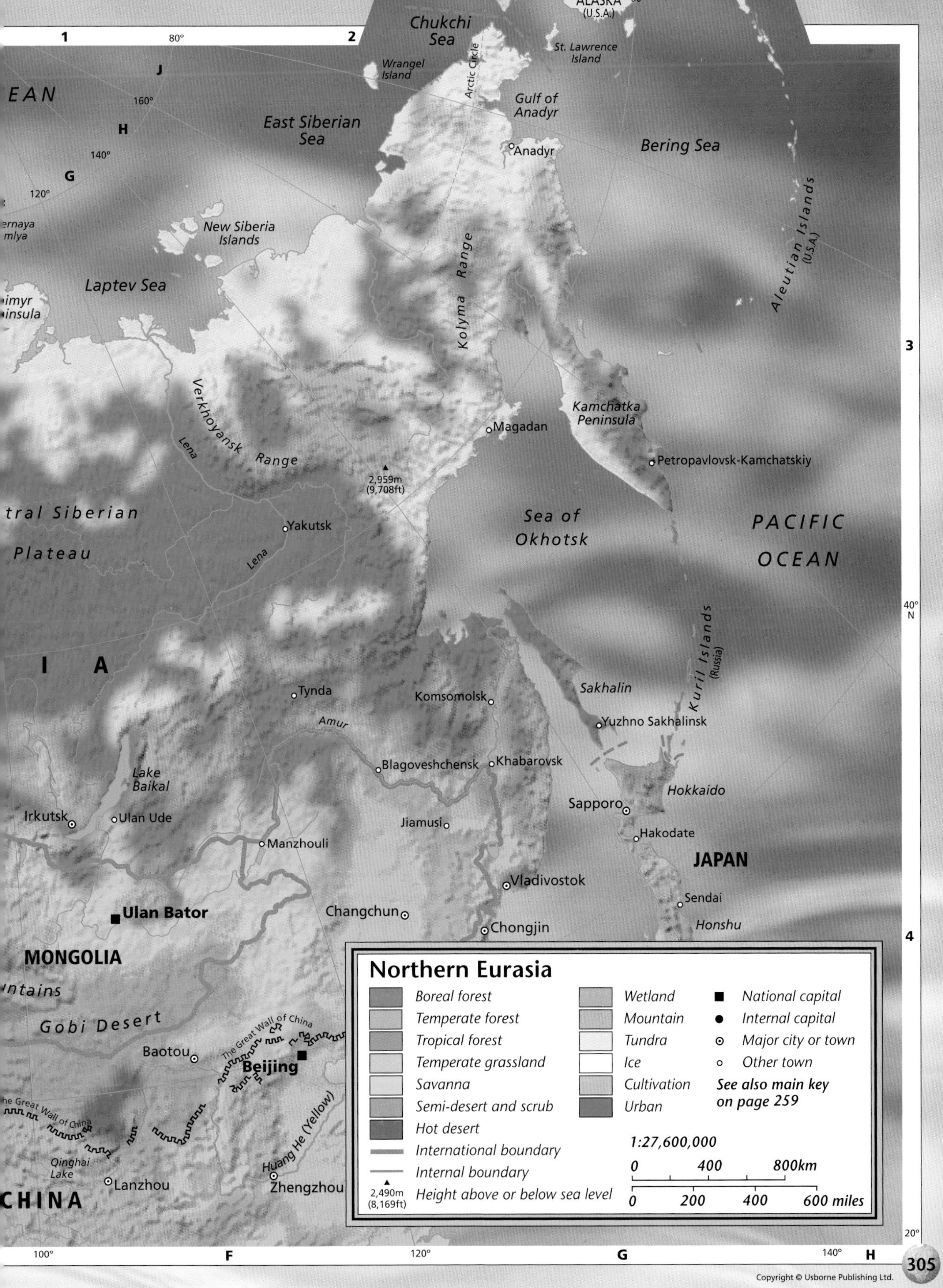

Northern Eurasia

	Boreal forest		Wetland	■	National capital
	Temperate forest		Mountain	●	Internal capital
	Tropical forest		Tundra	⊙	Major city or town
	Temperate grassland		Ice	○	Other town
	Savanna		Cultivation		See also main key on page 259
	Semi-desert and scrub		Urban		
	Hot desert				
	International boundary				
	Internal boundary				
▲ 2,490m (8,169ft)	Height above or below sea level				

1:27,600,000

0 400 800km

0 200 400 600 miles

MAPS OF EUROPE

This is a satellite image of Europe. You can see how the continent joins on to Asia to the east.

This is a red squirrel, a species which is widespread throughout Europe but declining in numbers in Britain.

Europe is a small continent, but it holds 50 countries and more than 700 million people. It has no deserts, but its geography ranges from high mountain ranges to icy tundra, rocky islands and lush farmland. With dozens of islands and peninsulas, many of Europe's countries are largely surrounded by sea.

The shading on this map is there to help you see clearly the different countries that make up the continent.

Barents Sea
Arctic Circle
Murmansk
Arkhangelsk
FINLAND
RUSSIA
St. Petersburg
Tallinn
ESTONIA
Nizhniy Novgorod
Kazan
LATVIA
Moscow
Vilnius
Minsk
BELARUS
Volga
Kiev
Volgograd
Dnieper
UKRAINE
MOLDOVA
Chisinau
ROMANIA
Bucharest
Danube
Black Sea
BULGARIA
Sofia
Skopje
TURKEY
Athens
Crete

Facts

Total land area *10,180,000 sq km (3,930,520 sq miles)* (including European Russia)
Total population 742 million (including all of Russia)
Biggest city Moscow, Russia
Biggest country Russia *Total area: 17,075,200 sq km (6,592,772 sq miles) Area of European Russia: 4,294,400 sq km (1,658,077 sq miles)*
Smallest country Vatican City *0.44 sq km (0.17 sq miles)*

Highest mountain Elbrus, Russia *5,642m (18,510ft)*
Longest river Volga *3,692km (2,294 miles)*
Biggest lake Lake Ladoga, Russia *17,700 sq km (6,834 sq miles)*
Highest waterfall Vinnufossen, Norway *865m (2,837ft)*
Biggest desert No deserts in Europe
Biggest island Great Britain *209,331 sq km (80,823 sq miles)*

Main mineral deposits Bauxite, zinc, iron, potash, fluorspar
Main fuel deposits Oil, coal, natural gas, peat, uranium

A dairy cow in Devon, in the south of England

FINLAND
Helsinki
Turku
Hameenlinna
Lahti
Kouvola
Lappeenranta
Kotka
Espoo
Mikkeli
Vyborg
Paijanne Lake
Pihlaja Lake
Saimaa Lake
Aland Islands
Baltic Sea
Gulf of Finland
Hiiumaa
Tallinn
ESTONIA
Haapsalu
Kohtla-Jarve
Narva
Kuressaare
Saaremaa
Parnu
Gulf of Riga
Tartu
Lake Peipus
Lake Pskov
Voru
Ventspils
Cesis
Jurmala
Riga
Jelgava
Aluksne
LATVIA
Jekabpils
Ludza
Daugavpils
Siauliai
Panevezys
LITHUANIA
Kaunas
Marijampole
Alytus
Vilnius
Lake Ladoga
Lake Onega
Zelenogorsk
St. Petersburg
Kingisepp
Gatchina
Pushkin
Volkhov
Tikhvin
Kirishi
Konosha
White Lake
North European Plain
Novgorod
Lake Ilmen
Borovichi
Cherepovets
Vologda
Rybinsk Reservoir
Rybinsk
Pskov
Opochka
Valdai Hills
343m (1,125ft)
Vyshniy Volochek
Volga
Yaroslavl
Kostroma
Kineshma
Gorki Reservoir
Ivanovo
Velikiye Luki
Tver
Rzhev
Sergiyev Posad
Zelenograd
Vladimir
Nizhn Novg
Moscow
Podolsk
Oka
Murom
Obninsk
Kolomna
Arzan
Serpukhov
Kaluga
Ryazan
Tula
Western Dvina
Navapolatsk
Polatsk
Vitsyebsk
Hrodna
Lida
Maladzyechna
Barysaw
Orsha
Dnieper
Smolensk
Minsk
Zhodzina
Baranavichy
BELARUS
Mahilyow
Roslavl
Slutsk
Babruysk
Salihorsk
Zhlobin
Pinsk
Pripet Marshes
Pripet
Svyetlahorsk
Homyel
Klintsy
Bryansk
Desna
Mazyr
Rechytsa
293m (961ft)
Orel
Central Russian Uplands
Yelets
Michurinsk
Lipetsk
Tambov
Kamenka
Penz
Sarar
Lutsk
Rivne
Korosten
Chernihiv
Shepetivka
Kievske Reservoir
Kursk
Voronezh
Staryy Oskol
Zhytomyr
Kiev
Sumy
417m (1,368ft)
Khmelnytskyy
Bila Tserkva
Lubny
Vinnytsya
Kamyanets-Podilskyy
Kharkiv
Cherkasy
Kremenchukske Reservoir
Poltava
Kamys
Dniester
Uman
UKRAINE
Kremenchuk
Botosani
Balti
Kirovohrad
Oleksandriya
Slovyansk
Kramatorsk
Lysychansk
Rabnita
Iasi
MOLDOVA
Yuzhnoukrayinsk
Dniprodzerzhynsk
Dnipropetrovsk
Donets
Horlivka
Luhansk
Volgograd
Kryvyy Rih
Chisinau
Tiraspol
Tighina
Zaporizhzhya
Nikopol
Donetsk
Tsimlyansk Reservoir
ROMANIA
Mykolayiv
Kakhovske Reservoir
Don
Novocherkassk
Volgodonsk
Bilhorod Dnistrovskyy
Odesa
Kherson
Melitopol
Mariupol
Rostov
Galati
Berdyansk
Braila
Tulcea
Mouths of the Danube
Black Sea
Sea of Azov
20°E
25°
30°
35°
40°
30°E
55° N
50°
45°
B
C
D
E
2
3
4

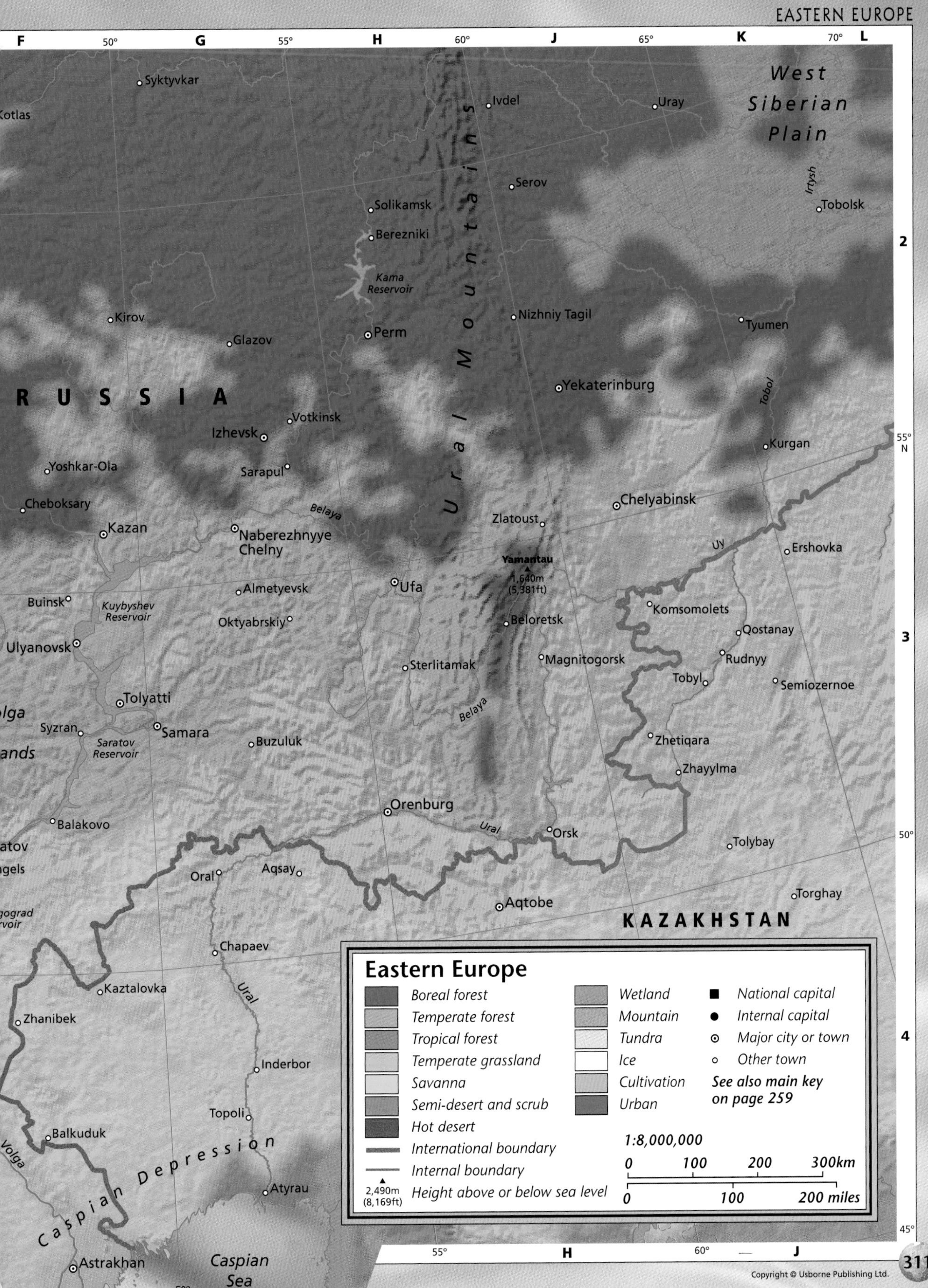

F
G
H
J
K
L
50°
55°
60°
65°
70°
West Siberian Plain
Syktyvkar
Kotlas
Ivdel
Uray
Irtysh
Tobolsk
Serov
Solikamsk
Berezniki
Kama Reservoir
Ural Mountains
Kirov
Glazov
Perm
Nizhniy Tagil
Tyumen
RUSSIA
Yekaterinburg
Tobol
Votkinsk
Izhevsk
Kurgan
Yoshkar-Ola
Sarapul
Cheboksary
Belaya
Chelyabinsk
Zlatoust
Kazan
Naberezhnyye Chelny
Uy
Ershovka
Yamantau
1,640m (5,381ft)
Ufa
Almetyevsk
Buinsk
Kuybyshev Reservoir
Komsomolets
Oktyabrskiy
Beloretsk
Qostanay
Ulyanovsk
Magnitogorsk
Rudnyy
Sterlitamak
Tobyl
Semiozernoe
Tolyatti
Belaya
Syzran
Samara
Buzuluk
Saratov Reservoir
Zhetiqara
Zhayylma
Orenburg
Balakovo
Ural
Orsk
Tolybay
Oral
Aqsay
Torghay
Aqtobe
KAZAKHSTAN
Chapaev
Kaztalovka
Ural
Zhanibek
Inderbor
Topoli
Balkuduk
Volga
Caspian Depression
Atyrau
Astrakhan
Caspian Sea
55° N
50°
45°
2
3
4
55°
H
60°
J
Eastern Europe
Boreal forest
Temperate forest
Tropical forest
Temperate grassland
Savanna
Semi-desert and scrub
Hot desert
International boundary
Internal boundary
2,490m (8,169ft) Height above or below sea level
Wetland
Mountain
Tundra
Ice
Cultivation
Urban
National capital
Internal capital
Major city or town
Other town
See also main key on page 259
1:8,000,000
0 100 200 300km
0 100 200 miles

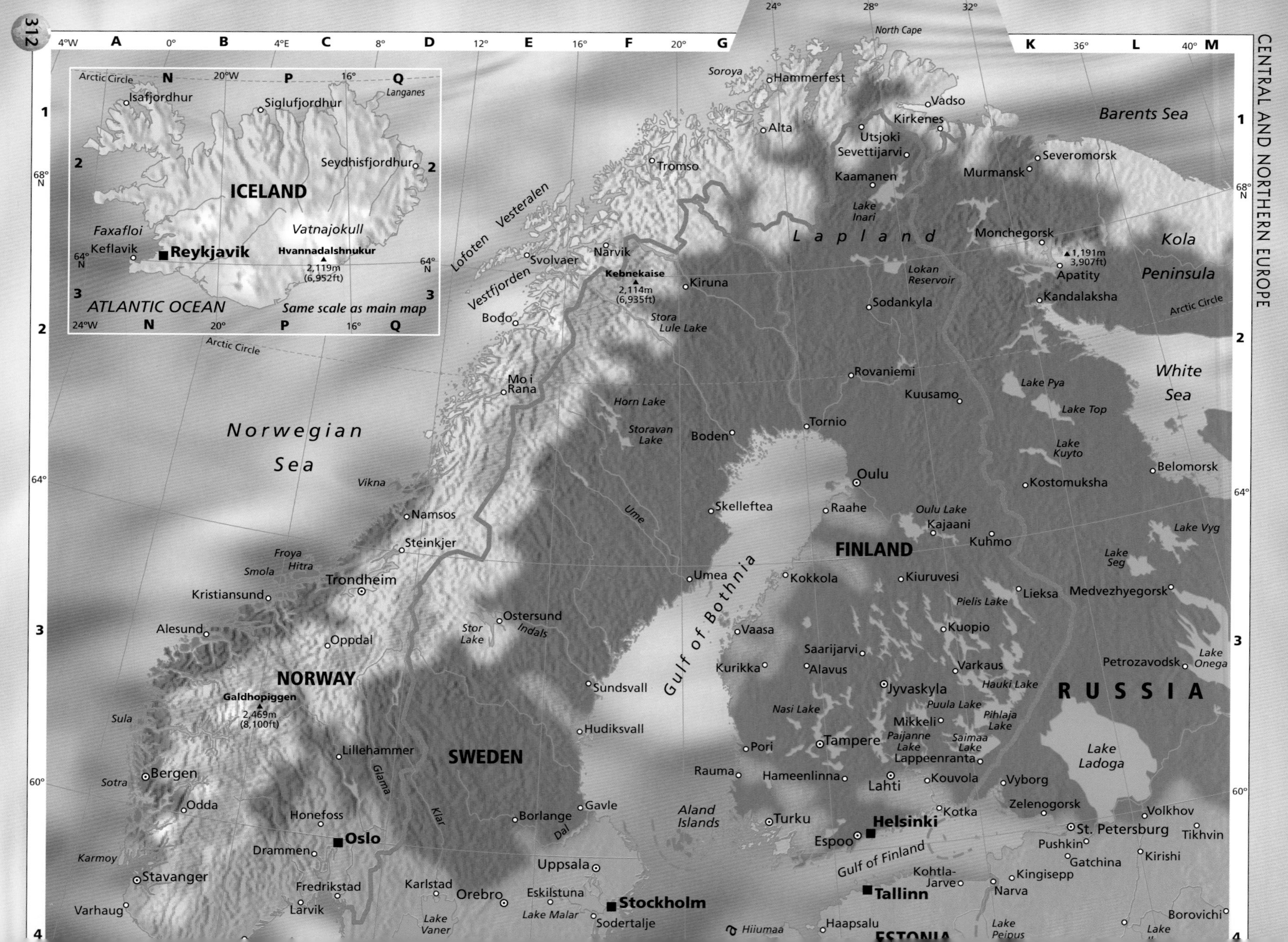

Barents Sea
Kola Peninsula
White Sea
Arctic Circle
North Cape
Lapland
Severomorsk
Murmansk
Monchegorsk
Apatity
1,191m 3,907ft
Kandalaksha
Belomorsk
Kostomuksha
Lake Vyg
Lake Seg
Lake Onega
Medvezhyegorsk
Petrozavodsk
Lake Pya
Lake Top
Lake Kuyto
Lake Ladoga
RUSSIA
Lieksa
Kuhmo
Vyborg
Zelenogorsk
St. Petersburg
Pushkin
Gatchina
Volkhov
Tikhvin
Kirishi
Borovichi
Kingisepp
Narva
Lake Peipus
Kohtla-Jarve
Tallinn
Haapsalu
Hiiumaa
Gulf of Finland
Helsinki
Espoo
Kotka
Kouvola
Lahti
Lappeenranta
Saimaa Lake
Pihlaja Lake
Hauki Lake
Varkaus
Kuopio
Pielis Lake
Mikkeli
Puula Lake
Paijanne Lake
Jyvaskyla
Kiuruvesi
Kajaani
Oulu Lake
Kuusamo
Rovaniemi
Sodankyla
Lokan Reservoir
Lake Inari
Kaamanen
Sevettijarvi
Utsjoki
Kirkenes
Vadso
Hammerfest
Alta
Soroya
Tornio
Oulu
Raahe
FINLAND
Kokkola
Saarijarvi
Alavus
Tampere
Nasi Lake
Hameenlinna
Turku
Pori
Rauma
Kurikka
Vaasa
Aland Islands
Gulf of Bothnia
Skelleftea
Umea
Boden
Kiruna
Stora Lule Lake
Tromso
Narvik
Kebnekaise
2,114m (6,935ft)
Horn Lake
Storavan Lake
Ume
Sundsvall
Hudiksvall
Gavle
Uppsala
Stockholm
Sodertalje
Eskilstuna
Lake Malar
Dal
Borlange
Orebro
Karlstad
Lake Vaner
Klar
SWEDEN
Ostersund
Indals
Stor Lake
Svolvaer
Vesteralen
Lofoten
Vestfjorden
Bodo
Mo i Rana
Namsos
Steinkjer
Trondheim
Vikna
Norwegian Sea
Froya
Hitra
Smola
Kristiansund
Oppdal
NORWAY
Lillehammer
Glama
Oslo
Honefoss
Drammen
Fredrikstad
Larvik
Galdhopiggen
2,469m (8,100ft)
Alesund
Bergen
Odda
Stavanger
Varhaug
Sula
Sotra
Karmoy
ICELAND
Isafjordhur
Siglufjordhur
Seydhisfjordhur
Langanes
Vatnajokull
Hvannadalshnukur
2,119m (6,952ft)
Reykjavik
Keflavik
Faxafloi
ATLANTIC OCEAN
Same scale as main map

Central and Northern Europe
Boreal forest
Temperate forest
Tropical forest
Temperate grassland
Savanna
Semi-desert and scrub
Hot desert
Wetland
Mountain
Tundra
Ice
Cultivation
Urban
National capital
Internal capital
Major city or town
Other town
International boundary
Internal boundary
2,490m (8,169ft) Height above or below sea level
See also main key on page 259
1:8,000,000
0 100 200 300km
0 100 200 miles
North Sea
DENMARK
Jutland
Alborg
Viborg
Randers
Arhus
Kattegat
Kolding
Esbjerg
Odense
Fyn
Zealand
Copenhagen
Malmo
Helsingborg
Varberg
Halmstad
Vaxjo
Karlshamn
Oskarshamn
Oland
Kalmar
Visby
Gotland
Baltic
North Frisian Islands
Flensburg
Lolland
Nykobing
Ronne
Bornholm (Denmark)
Kiel
Cuxhaven
GERMANY
Rostock
Berlin
Potsdam
Cottbus
Dresden
Chemnitz
Szczecin
Koszalin
Slupsk
Gdynia
Gulf of Gdansk
Gdansk
Kaliningrad
RUSSIA
Neman
Ventspils
Gulf of Riga
Riga
Jurmala
Jelgava
Cesis
Aluksne
LATVIA
Ludza
Jekabpils
Daugavpils
Liepaja
Klaipeda
Siauliai
Panevezys
LITHUANIA
Kaunas
Vilnius
Marijampole
Alytus
Opochka
Velikiye Luki
Western Dvina
Hills
Navapolatsk
Polatsk
Vitsyebsk
Smolensk
Orsha
Roslavl
Maladzyechna
Barysaw
Zhodzina
Mahilyow
Dnieper
Minsk
BELARUS
Lida
Hrodna
Babruysk
Klintsy
Zhlobin
Homyel
Baranavichy
Slutsk
Salihorsk
Svyetlahorsk
Rechytsa
Suwalki
Olsztyn
Bialystok
Grudziadz
Bydgoszcz
Vistula
Wloclawek
Plock
Gorzow Wielkopolski
Poznan
Warsaw
Brest
Pinsk
Pripet Marshes
Mazyr
Pripet
Chernihiv
Kievske Reservoir
Oder
Zielona Gora
Kalisz
Lodz
POLAND
Radom
Lublin
Kovel
Korosten
Kiev
Legnica
Wroclaw
Walbrzych
Opole
Czestochowa
Kielce
Zamosc
Lutsk
Rivne
Shepetivka
Zhytomyr
Bila Tserkva
Liberec
Most
Hradec Kralove
Prague
Pilsen
CZECH REPUBLIC
Katowice
Rybnik
Krakow
Tarnow
Rzeszow
Lviv
417m (1,368ft)
UKRAINE
Ternopil
Khmelnytskyy
Vinnytsya
Uman
Ostrava
Olomouc
Zlin
Brno
Ceske Budejovice
Zilina
Gerlachovsky stit
2,655m (8,711ft)
Presov
Kosice
Ivano-Frankivsk
Dniester
Kamyanets-Podilskyy
Banska Bystrica
SLOVAKIA
Uzhhorod
Chernivtsi
Linz
Wels
St. Polten
Vienna
Trnava
Nitra
Bratislava
Miskolc
Carpathian Mountains
Botosani
Suceava
Rabnita
Balti
AUSTRIA
Knittelfeld
Graz
Gyor
Szombathely
Budapest
Szekesfehervar
Debrecen
Satu Mare
Baia Mare
Iasi
Chisinau
Tighina
MOLDOVA
Tiraspol
Odesa
Lake Balaton
HUNGARY
Kecskemet
Oradea
Cluj-Napoca
Piatra Neamt
Bacau
Villach
Klagenfurt
Zalaegerszeg
Bekescsaba
Targu Mures
Bilhorod Dnistrovskyy
Maribor
Kranj
Ljubljana
Danube
Szeged
Arad
ROMANIA
Pecs
Subotica
Timisoara
Sibiu
Brasov
Focsani
Galati
Novo Mesto
Trieste
Zagreb
D
E
F
G
H
J
5
6
7
56°
52°
48°
12°E
16°
20°
24°
28°

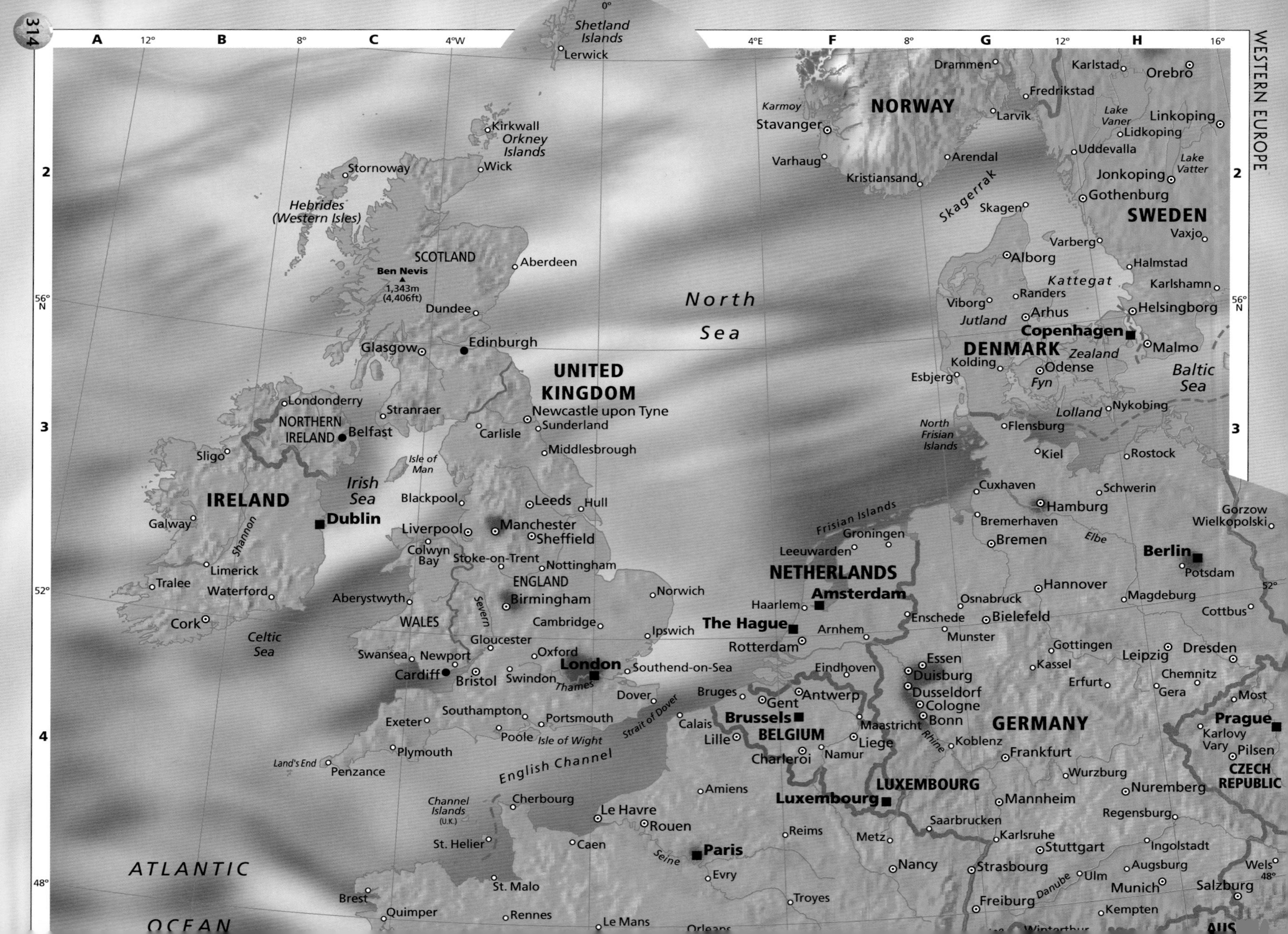

NORWAY
SWEDEN
DENMARK
UNITED KINGDOM
IRELAND
NORTHERN IRELAND
SCOTLAND
ENGLAND
WALES
NETHERLANDS
BELGIUM
LUXEMBOURG
GERMANY
CZECH REPUBLIC
North Sea
Baltic Sea
Irish Sea
Celtic Sea
English Channel
Strait of Dover
ATLANTIC OCEAN
Skagerrak
Kattegat
Shetland Islands
Orkney Islands
Hebrides (Western Isles)
Isle of Man
Isle of Wight
Channel Islands (U.K.)
North Frisian Islands
Frisian Islands
Jutland
Zealand
Fyn
Lolland
Karmoy
Land's End
Ben Nevis 1,343m (4,406ft)
Lake Vaner
Lake Vatter
Shannon
Severn
Thames
Elbe
Rhine
Seine
Danube
Lerwick
Kirkwall
Wick
Stornoway
Aberdeen
Dundee
Edinburgh
Glasgow
Stranraer
Londonderry
Belfast
Dublin
Sligo
Galway
Limerick
Waterford
Tralee
Cork
Newcastle upon Tyne
Sunderland
Middlesbrough
Carlisle
Blackpool
Leeds
Hull
Manchester
Sheffield
Liverpool
Colwyn Bay
Stoke-on-Trent
Nottingham
Birmingham
Aberystwyth
Gloucester
Cambridge
Norwich
Ipswich
Oxford
London
Swindon
Bristol
Newport
Cardiff
Swansea
Southend-on-Sea
Dover
Southampton
Portsmouth
Poole
Exeter
Plymouth
Penzance
Drammen
Larvik
Fredrikstad
Arendal
Kristiansand
Stavanger
Varhaug
Karlstad
Orebro
Linkoping
Lidkoping
Uddevalla
Jonkoping
Gothenburg
Varberg
Halmstad
Vaxjo
Karlshamn
Helsingborg
Malmo
Skagen
Alborg
Randers
Arhus
Viborg
Kolding
Esbjerg
Odense
Copenhagen
Nykobing
Cherbourg
Le Havre
Caen
Rouen
St. Helier
St. Malo
Rennes
Brest
Quimper
Le Mans
Paris
Evry
Amiens
Calais
Lille
Bruges
Gent
Brussels
Antwerp
Charleroi
Namur
Liege
Maastricht
Eindhoven
Rotterdam
The Hague
Haarlem
Amsterdam
Arnhem
Leeuwarden
Groningen
Enschede
Reims
Troyes
Metz
Nancy
Luxembourg
Saarbrucken
Strasbourg
Freiburg
Karlsruhe
Stuttgart
Ulm
Kempten
Munich
Augsburg
Ingolstadt
Regensburg
Nuremberg
Wurzburg
Mannheim
Frankfurt
Koblenz
Bonn
Cologne
Dusseldorf
Duisburg
Essen
Munster
Osnabruck
Bielefeld
Kassel
Gottingen
Erfurt
Hannover
Bremen
Bremerhaven
Cuxhaven
Hamburg
Flensburg
Kiel
Schwerin
Rostock
Magdeburg
Berlin
Potsdam
Leipzig
Dresden
Chemnitz
Gera
Cottbus
Gorzow Wielkopolski
Prague
Most
Karlovy Vary
Pilsen
Salzburg
Wels
A
12°
B
8°
C
4°W
0°
4°E
F
8°
G
12°
H
16°
2
3
4
56° N
52°
48°

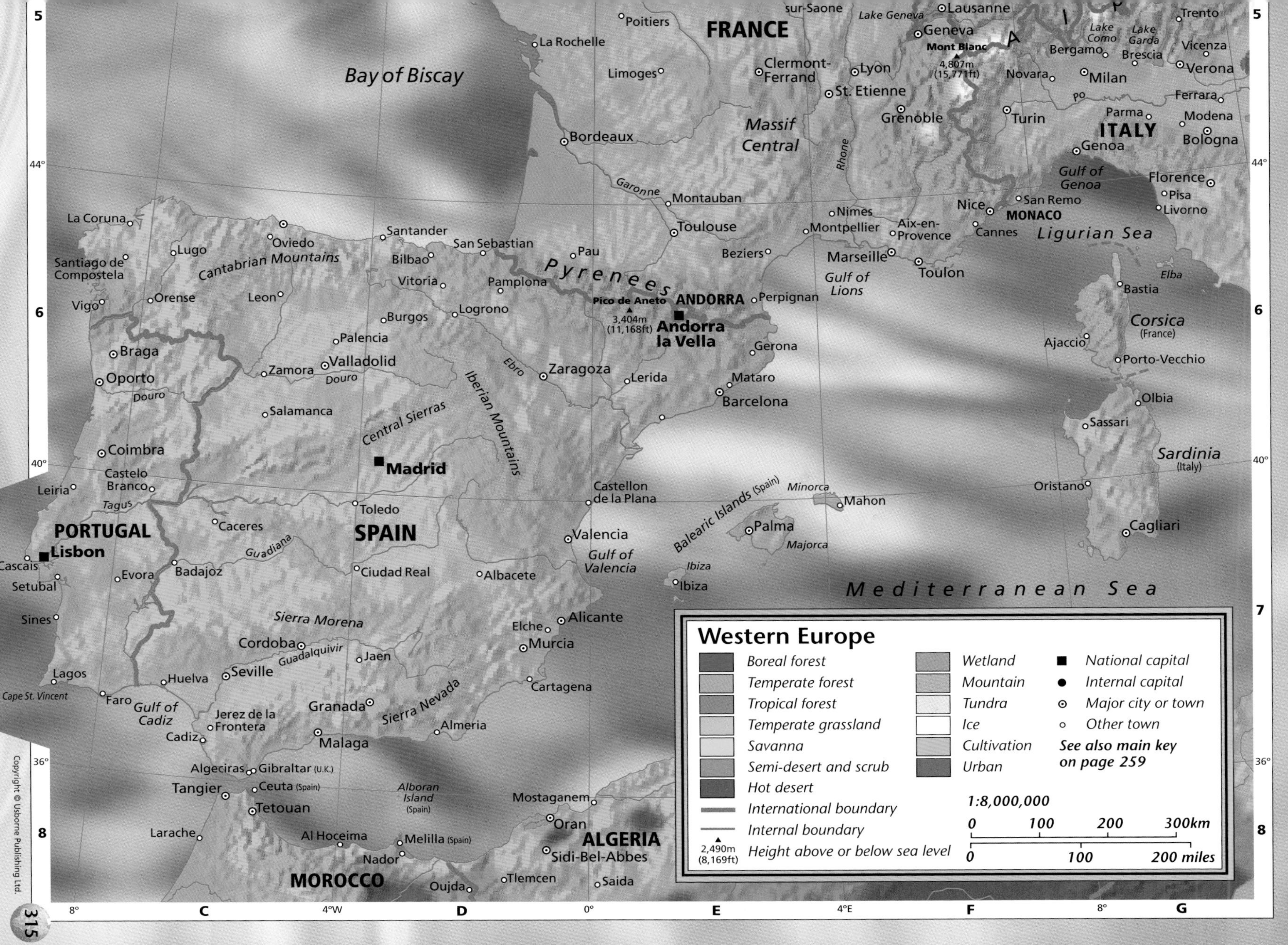

Western Europe
Boreal forest
Temperate forest
Tropical forest
Temperate grassland
Savanna
Semi-desert and scrub
Hot desert
International boundary
Internal boundary
2,490m (8,169ft) Height above or below sea level
Wetland
Mountain
Tundra
Ice
Cultivation
Urban
National capital
Internal capital
Major city or town
Other town
See also main key on page 259
1:8,000,000
0 100 200 300km
0 100 200 miles
Bay of Biscay
FRANCE
SPAIN
PORTUGAL
ITALY
ANDORRA
MONACO
MOROCCO
ALGERIA
Mediterranean Sea
Ligurian Sea
Gulf of Genoa
Gulf of Lions
Gulf of Valencia
Gulf of Cadiz
Balearic Islands (Spain)
Corsica (France)
Sardinia (Italy)
Pyrenees
Pico de Aneto 3,404m (11,168ft)
Mont Blanc 4,807m (15,771ft)
Massif Central
Cantabrian Mountains
Iberian Mountains
Central Sierras
Sierra Morena
Sierra Nevada
Madrid
Lisbon
Andorra la Vella
Alboran Island (Spain)
Gibraltar (U.K.)
Ceuta (Spain)
Melilla (Spain)
Cape St. Vincent

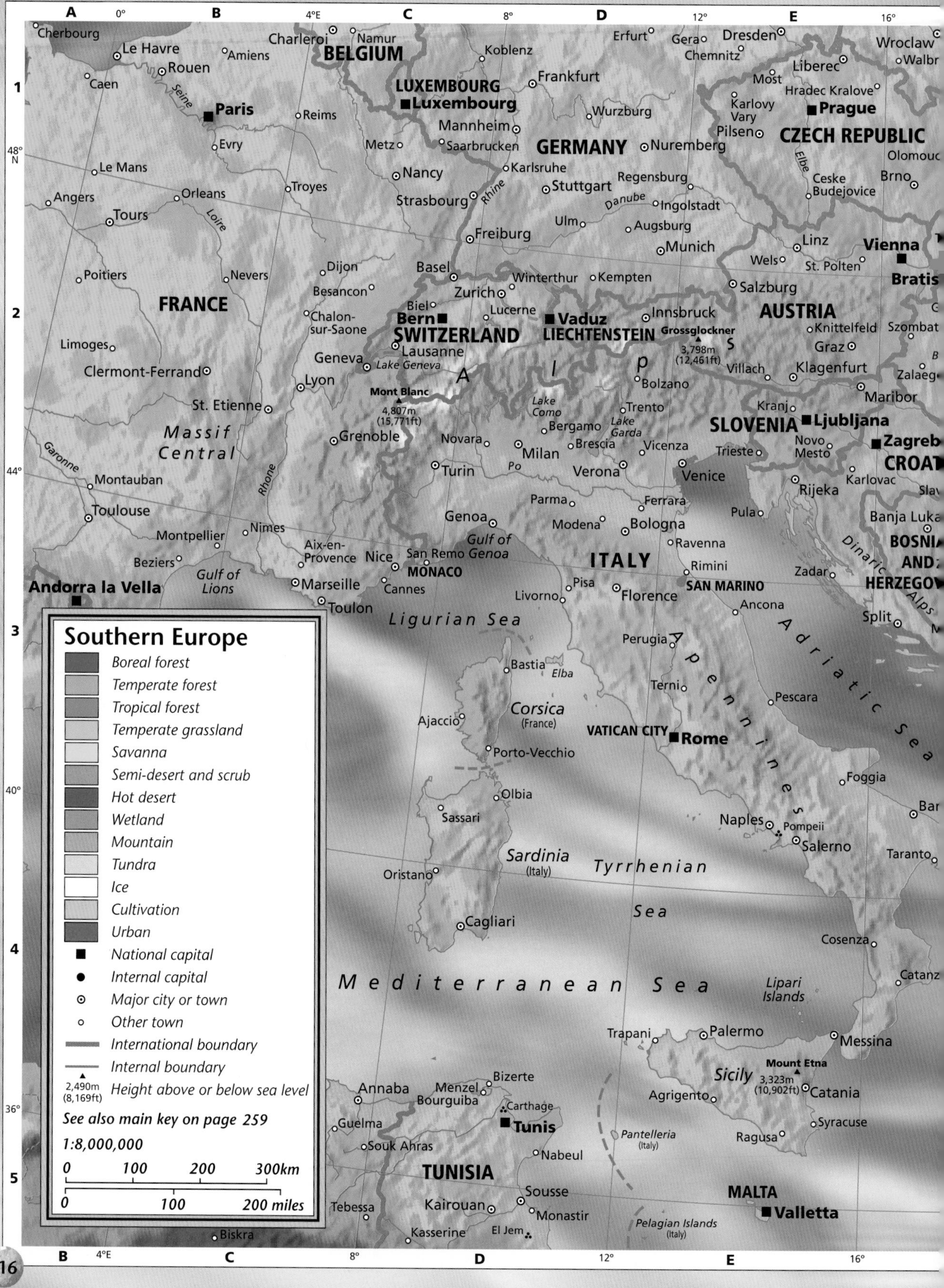
A
B
C
D
E
0°
4°E
8°
12°
16°
48° N
44°
40°
36°
1
2
3
4
5
Cherbourg
Le Havre
Amiens
Rouen
Caen
Seine
Paris
Evry
Reims
Charleroi
Namur
BELGIUM
Koblenz
LUXEMBOURG
Luxembourg
Frankfurt
Erfurt
Gera
Dresden
Chemnitz
Wroclaw
Walbr
Liberec
Most
Hradec Kralove
Karlovy Vary
Prague
Pilsen
CZECH REPUBLIC
Olomouc
Elbe
Wurzburg
Mannheim
Metz
Saarbrucken
GERMANY
Nuremberg
Le Mans
Nancy
Karlsruhe
Regensburg
Ceske Budejovice
Brno
Angers
Orleans
Troyes
Strasbourg
Rhine
Stuttgart
Danube
Ingolstadt
Tours
Loire
Ulm
Augsburg
Freiburg
Munich
Linz
Vienna
Wels
St. Polten
Bratis
Poitiers
Nevers
Dijon
Basel
Winterthur
Kempten
Salzburg
Besancon
Zurich
FRANCE
Biel
Lucerne
Innsbruck
AUSTRIA
Chalon-sur-Saone
Bern
Vaduz
Grossglockner
Knittelfeld
Szombat
Limoges
SWITZERLAND
LIECHTENSTEIN
3,798m (12,461ft)
Graz
Lausanne
A
l
p
s
Geneva
Lake Geneva
Villach
Klagenfurt
Zalaeg
Clermont-Ferrand
Lyon
Bolzano
Maribor
Mont Blanc
4,807m (15,771ft)
Lake Como
Trento
Kranj
St. Etienne
Bergamo
Lake Garda
SLOVENIA
Ljubljana
Massif Central
Grenoble
Novara
Milan
Brescia
Vicenza
Trieste
Novo Mesto
Zagreb
Garonne
Turin
Po
Verona
Venice
CROAT
Montauban
Rhone
Rijeka
Karlovac
Parma
Ferrara
Toulouse
Pula
Genoa
Modena
Bologna
Banja Luka
Montpellier
Nimes
Gulf of Genoa
Ravenna
Dinaric Alps
BOSNIA AND HERZEGOV
Aix-en-Provence
Nice
San Remo
ITALY
Beziers
MONACO
Rimini
Zadar
Gulf of Lions
Marseille
Cannes
Pisa
SAN MARINO
Andorra la Vella
Livorno
Florence
Toulon
Ancona
Ligurian Sea
Split
Perugia
Bastia
Elba
Apennines
Adriatic Sea
Terni
Pescara
Corsica (France)
Ajaccio
VATICAN CITY
Rome
Porto-Vecchio
Foggia
Olbia
Sassari
Naples
Pompeii
Salerno
Bar
Sardinia (Italy)
Tyrrhenian Sea
Taranto
Oristano
Cagliari
Cosenza
Mediterranean Sea
Lipari Islands
Catanz
Trapani
Palermo
Messina
Mount Etna
3,323m (10,902ft)
Sicily
Catania
Bizerte
Annaba
Menzel Bourguiba
Agrigento
Carthage
Guelma
Tunis
Pantelleria (Italy)
Ragusa
Syracuse
Souk Ahras
Nabeul
TUNISIA
MALTA
Sousse
Valletta
Tebessa
Kairouan
Monastir
Pelagian Islands (Italy)
Kasserine
El Jem
Biskra
Southern Europe
Boreal forest
Temperate forest
Tropical forest
Temperate grassland
Savanna
Semi-desert and scrub
Hot desert
Wetland
Mountain
Tundra
Ice
Cultivation
Urban
National capital
Internal capital
Major city or town
Other town
International boundary
Internal boundary
2,490m (8,169ft) Height above or below sea level
See also main key on page 259
1:8,000,000
0 100 200 300km
0 100 200 miles

20°
G
24°
H
28°
J
32°
K
36°
L
1
2
3
4
48° N
44°
40°
Kielce
Czestochowa
Zamosc
Lutsk
Rivne
Kiev
Lubny
Poltava
Zhytomyr
Shepetivka
Vistula
POLAND
Krakow
Tarnow
Rzeszow
Lviv
417m (1,368ft)
Bila Tserkva
Kremenchukske Reservoir
Slovyansk
Cherkasy
Kramatorsk
Kremenchuk
UKRAINE
Ternopil
Khmelnytskyy
Vinnytsya
Dniprodzerzhynsk
Dnipropetrovsk
Oleksandriya
Dnieper
Gerlachovsky stit
2,655m (8,711ft)
Dniester
Uman
Kirovohrad
Ivano-Frankivsk
Kamyanets-Podilskyy
Zaporizhzhya
Presov
Banska Bystrica
Kosice
Kryvyy Rih
Nikopol
Uzhhorod
Chernivtsi
Carpathian Mountains
Yuzhnoukrayinsk
Kakhovske Reservoir
Berdyansk
Rabnita
Miskolc
Botosani
Balti
Melitopol
Satu Mare
Suceava
MOLDOVA
Mykolayiv
Budapest
Debrecen
Baia Mare
Iasi
Chisinau
Kherson
Tiraspol
Sea of Azov
Oradea
Piatra Neamt
Tighina
Odesa
Cluj-Napoca
Bacau
Bilhorod-Dnistrovskyy
Dzhankoy
Kerch
Bekescsaba
Targu Mures
ROMANIA
Szeged
Crimea
Yevpatoriya
Feodosiya
Arad
Mount Moldoveanu
2,544m (8,346ft)
Focsani
Subotica
Sibiu
Brasov
Galati
Simferopol
Timisoara
Braila
Tulcea
Mouths of the Danube
Sevastopol
Transylvanian Alps
Buzau
Novi Sad
Ramnicu Valcea
Ploiesti
Pitesti
Belgrade
Drobeta-Turnu Severin
Bucharest
Constanta
Craiova
Danube
SERBIA
Black Sea
Ruse
Kragujevac
Dobrich
Kraljevo
Pleven
Shumen
Varna
Nis
Vratsa
Balkan Mountains
BULGARIA
Leskovac
Sliven
Niksic
Pristina
Sofia
Stara Zagora
Burgas
KOSOVO
Vranje
Plovdiv
Bosporus
Zonguldak
Kumanovo
Karabuk
Tetovo
Skopje
Blagoevgrad
Edirne
Shkoder
Corum
MACEDONIA
Istanbul
Adapazari
Tirana
Prilep
Tekirdag
Sea of Marmara
Elbasan
Bitola
Serres
Kavala
Ankara
Kirikkale
ALBANIA
Thessaloniki
Thasos
Bursa
Korce
Eskisehir
Vlore
Canakkale
Mount Olympus
2,917m (9,570ft)
Pindus Mountains
Balikesir
Kutahya
Lake Tuz
Larisa
Limnos
TURKEY
Corfu
Ioannina
Aegean Sea
Akhisar
Aksaray
Volos
Usak
Lesvos
GREECE
Manisa
Konya
Preveza
Lamia
Euboea
Skyros
Izmir
Odemis
Beysehir Lake
Chios
Isparta
Chalkida
Ephesus
Denizli
Karaman
Kefallonia
Aydin
Taurus Mountains
Patra
Peiraias
Athens
Antalya
Pyrgos
Cyclades
Alanya
Dodecanese
Gulf of Antalya
Kalamata
Rhodes
Kyrenia
Nicosia
Kythira
CYPRUS
Larnaca
Karpathos
Paphos
Limassol
Chania
Crete
Irakleio
Ierapetra
G
28°
J
32°
K
24°

African elephants in Amboseli National Park, Kenya

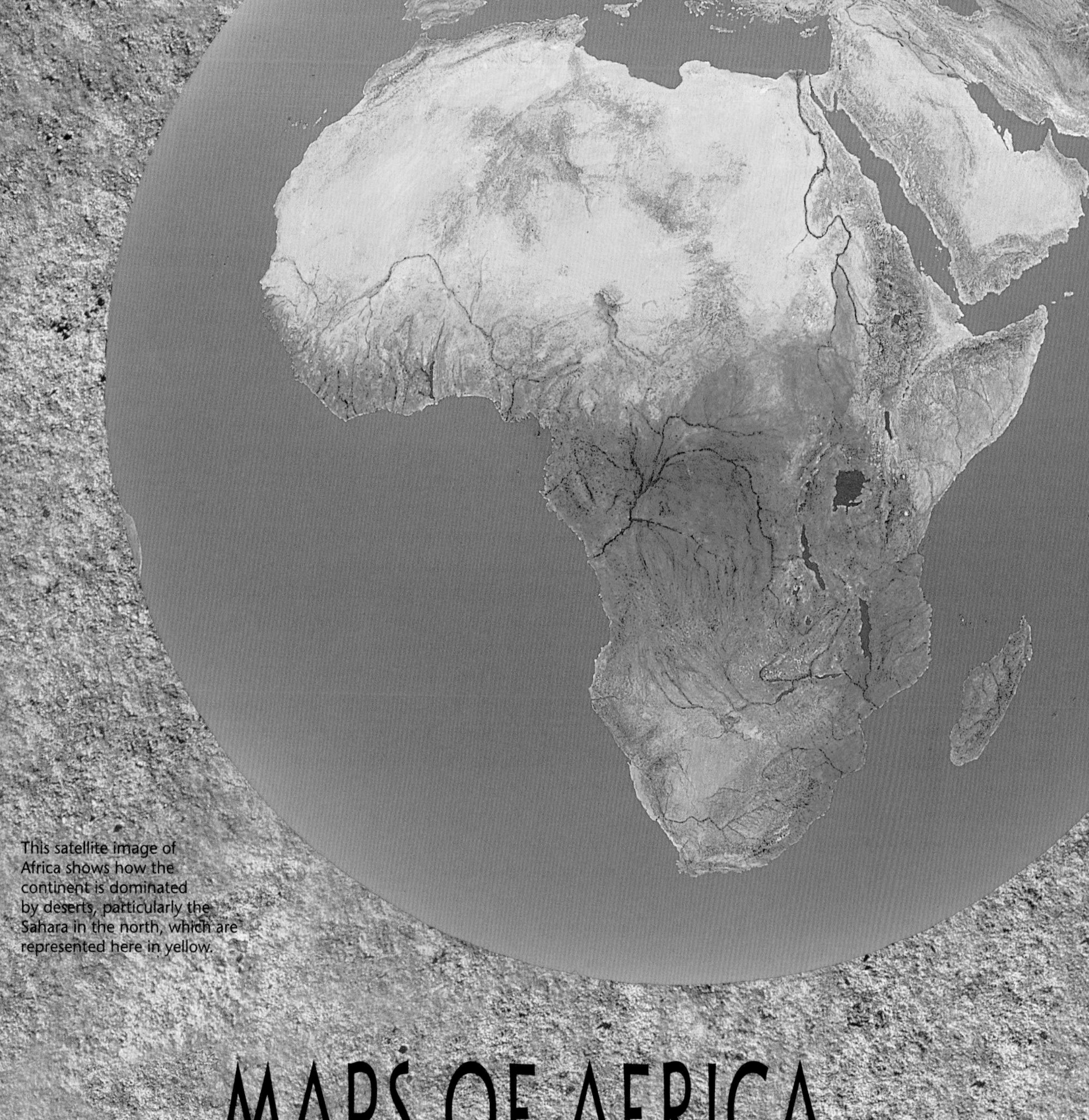

This satellite image of Africa shows how the continent is dominated by deserts, particularly the Sahara in the north, which are represented here in yellow.

MAPS OF AFRICA

Africa is the second-biggest continent and has 54 countries altogether. More than a quarter of them are landlocked, with no access to the sea except through other countries. Africa is home to the world's longest river, the Nile, and its largest desert, the Sahara. It also has vast amounts of natural resources, such as gold, copper and diamonds. Many of them have not yet begun to be used.

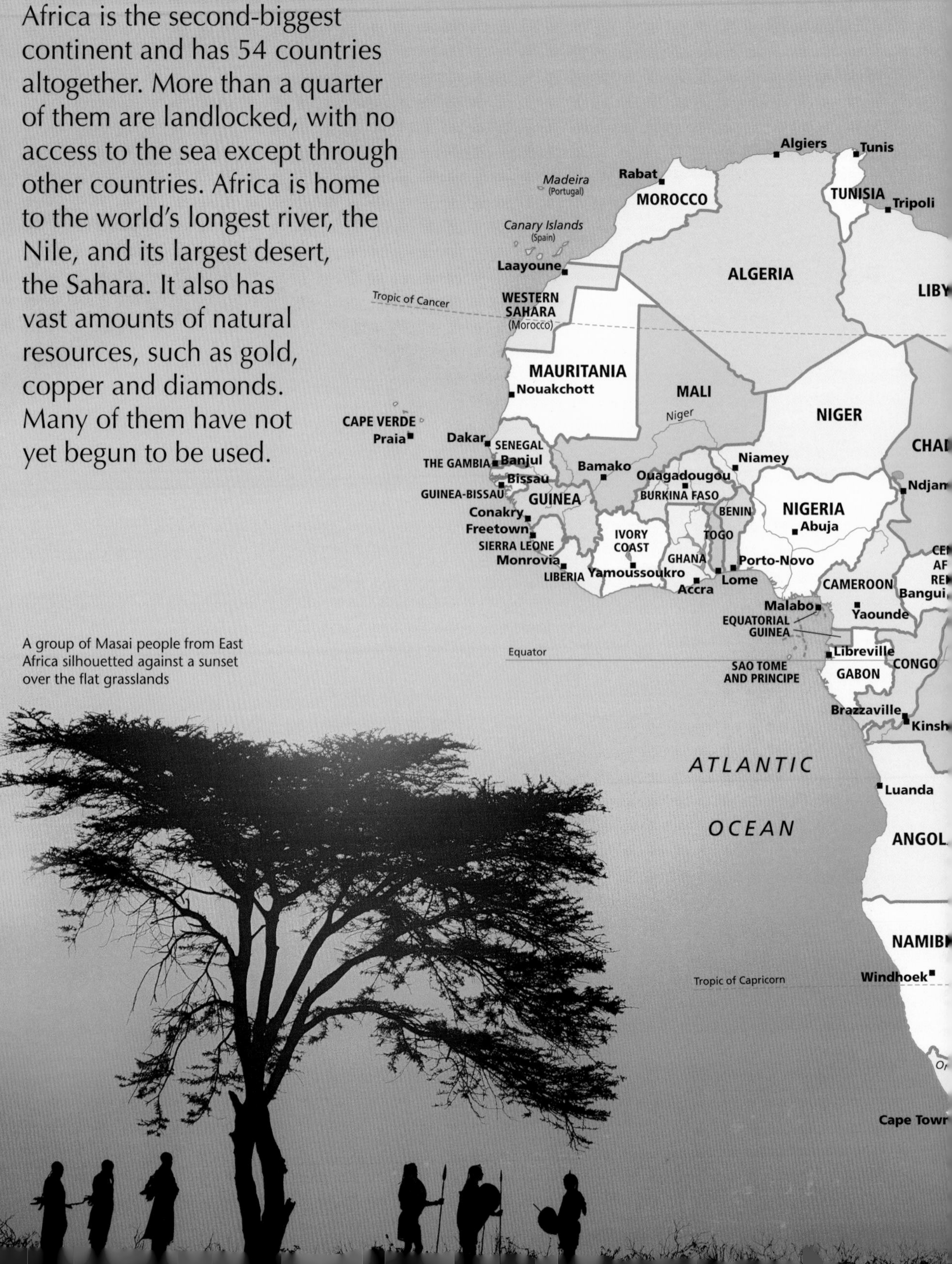

A group of Masai people from East Africa silhouetted against a sunset over the flat grasslands

The shading on this map is there to help you see clearly the different countries that make up the continent.

Facts

Total land area *30,311,690 sq km (11,703,409 sq miles)*

Total population 1.1 billion

Biggest city Cairo, Egypt

Biggest country Algeria *2,381,740 sq km (919,595 sq miles)*

Smallest country Seychelles *455 sq km (176 sq miles)*

Highest mountain Kilimanjaro, Tanzania *5,895m (19,341ft)*

Longest river Nile, running from to Burundi to Egypt *6,671km (4,145 miles)*

Biggest lake Lake Victoria, between Tanzania, Kenya and Uganda *69,484 sq km (26,828 sq miles)*

Highest waterfall Tugela Falls, on the Tugela River, South Africa *948m (3,110ft)*

Biggest desert Sahara, North Africa *9,100,000 sq km (3,513,530 sq miles)*

Biggest island Madagascar *587,713 sq km (226,917 sq miles)*

Main mineral deposits Gold, copper, diamonds, iron ore, manganese, bauxite

Main fuel deposits Coal, uranium, natural gas

A greater flamingo in the Transvaal National Park

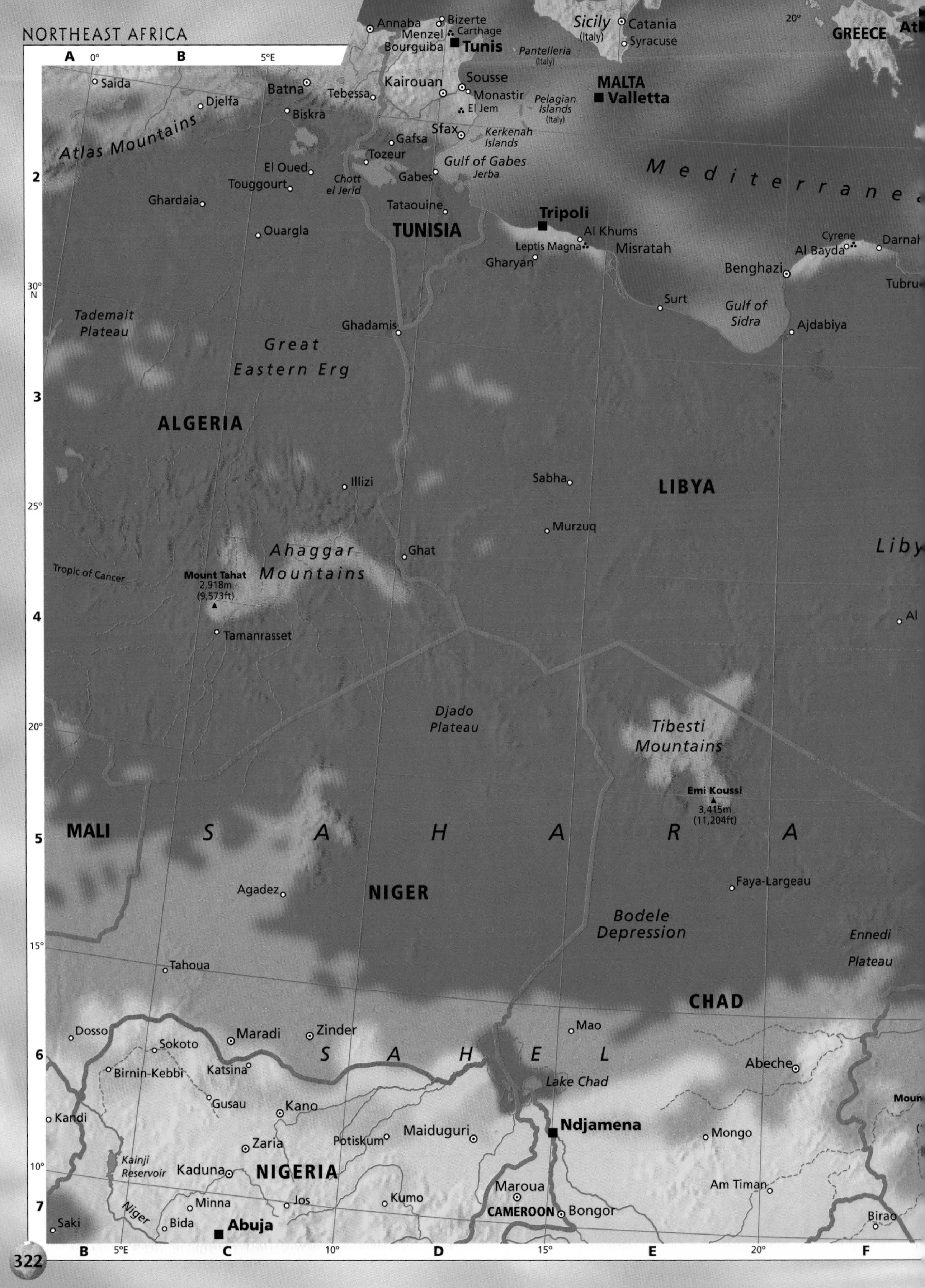
A
0°
B
5°E
Annaba
Bizerte
Menzel Bourguiba
Carthage
Tunis
Sicily
(Italy)
Catania
Syracuse
Pantelleria
(Italy)
20°
GREECE
Saida
Batna
Tebessa
Kairouan
Sousse
Monastir
El Jem
MALTA
Valletta
Pelagian Islands
(Italy)
Djelfa
Biskra
Atlas Mountains
Gafsa
Sfax
Kerkenah Islands
Tozeur
El Oued
Gulf of Gabes
Gabes
Jerba
Touggourt
Chott el Jerid
Mediterranean
Ghardaia
Tataouine
Tripoli
Ouargla
TUNISIA
Al Khums
Leptis Magna
Misratah
Gharyan
Cyrene
Al Bayda
Benghazi
Surt
Gulf of Sidra
Ajdabiya
30° N
Tademait Plateau
Ghadamis
Great Eastern Erg
ALGERIA
Illizi
Sabha
LIBYA
25°
Murzuq
Ahaggar Mountains
Ghat
Tropic of Cancer
Mount Tahat
2,918m
(9,573ft)
Tamanrasset
Djado Plateau
20°
Tibesti Mountains
Emi Koussi
3,415m
(11,204ft)
MALI
S A H A R A
Agadez
NIGER
Faya-Largeau
Bodele Depression
Ennedi Plateau
15°
Tahoua
CHAD
Dosso
Maradi
Zinder
Mao
Sokoto
S A H E L
Abeche
Birnin-Kebbi
Katsina
Lake Chad
Gusau
Kano
Kandi
Ndjamena
Maiduguri
Zaria
Potiskum
Mongo
Kainji Reservoir
Kaduna
NIGERIA
10°
Maroua
Am Timan
Minna
Jos
Kumo
Niger
Bida
Abuja
CAMEROON
Bongor
Saki
Birao
B
5°E
C
10°
D
15°
E
20°
F
2
3
4
5
6
7

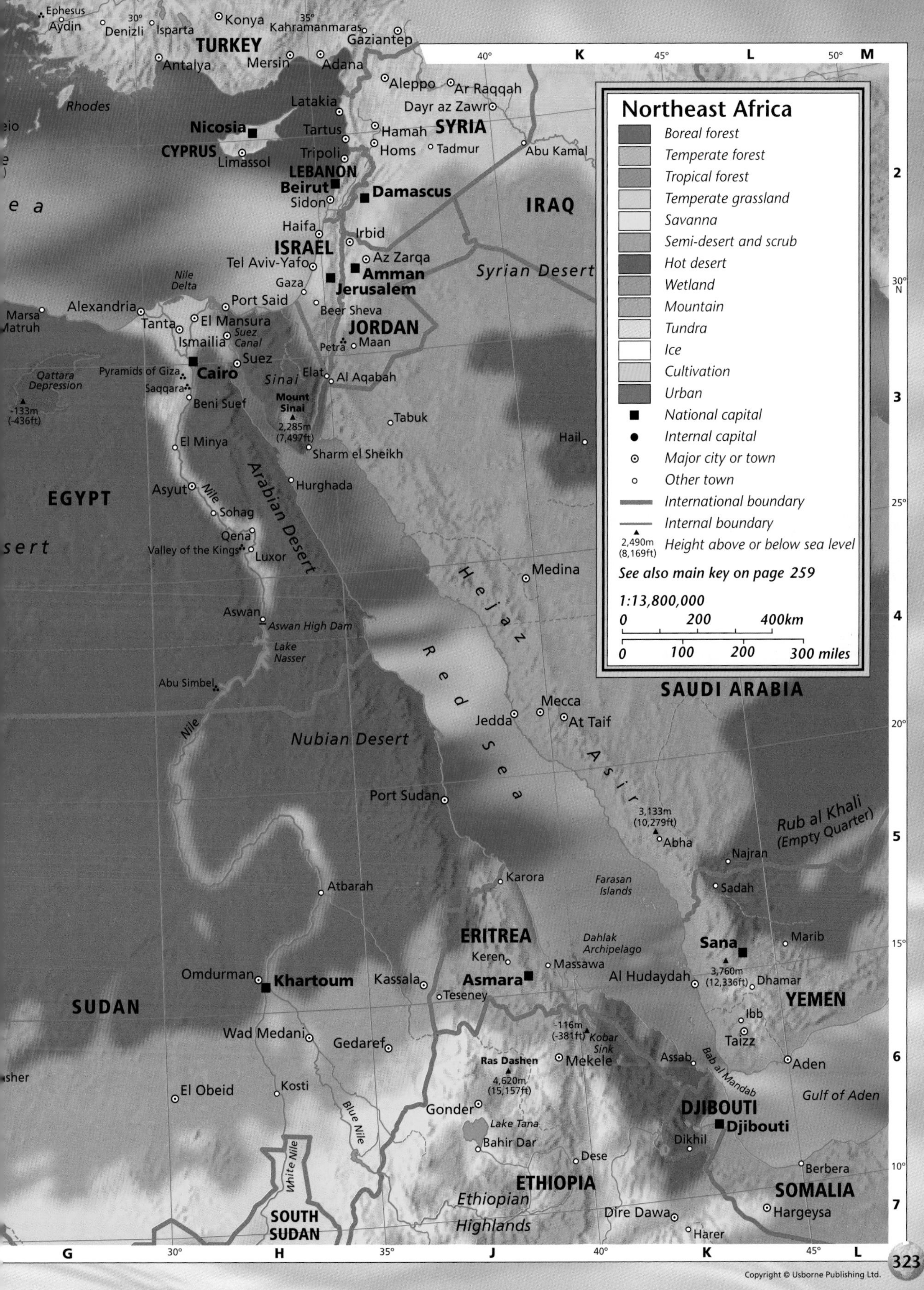
Northeast Africa
Boreal forest
Temperate forest
Tropical forest
Temperate grassland
Savanna
Semi-desert and scrub
Hot desert
Wetland
Mountain
Tundra
Ice
Cultivation
Urban
National capital
Internal capital
Major city or town
Other town
International boundary
Internal boundary
2,490m (8,169ft) Height above or below sea level
See also main key on page 259
1:13,800,000
0 200 400km
0 100 200 300 miles
TURKEY
SYRIA
CYPRUS
LEBANON
ISRAEL
JORDAN
IRAQ
EGYPT
SAUDI ARABIA
SUDAN
ERITREA
YEMEN
DJIBOUTI
ETHIOPIA
SOMALIA
SOUTH SUDAN
Ephesus
Aydin
Denizli
Isparta
Konya
Kahramanmaras
Gaziantep
Antalya
Mersin
Adana
Rhodes
Aleppo
Ar Raqqah
Latakia
Dayr az Zawr
Nicosia
Tartus
Hamah
Homs
Tadmur
Abu Kamal
Limassol
Tripoli
Beirut
Damascus
Sidon
Haifa
Irbid
Tel Aviv-Yafo
Az Zarqa
Amman
Jerusalem
Gaza
Syrian Desert
Nile Delta
Alexandria
Port Said
Beer Sheva
Marsa Matruh
Tanta
El Mansura
Suez Canal
Ismailia
Petra
Maan
Suez
Cairo
Pyramids of Giza
Saqqara
Sinai
Elat
Al Aqabah
Qattara Depression
-133m (-436ft)
Beni Suef
Mount Sinai
2,285m (7,497ft)
Tabuk
Hail
El Minya
Sharm el Sheikh
Arabian Desert
Hurghada
Asyut
Nile
Sohag
Qena
Valley of the Kings
Luxor
Medina
Hejaz
Aswan
Aswan High Dam
Lake Nasser
Red Sea
Abu Simbel
Mecca
Jedda
At Taif
Nubian Desert
Asir
Port Sudan
3,133m (10,279ft)
Abha
Rub al Khali (Empty Quarter)
Najran
Karora
Farasan Islands
Sadah
Atbarah
Dahlak Archipelago
Sana
Marib
Keren
Massawa
3,760m (12,336ft)
Omdurman
Khartoum
Kassala
Asmara
Al Hudaydah
Dhamar
Teseney
Ibb
Wad Medani
Gedaref
-116m (-381ft)
Kobar Sink
Taizz
Ras Dashen
Mekele
Assab
Bab al Mandab
Aden
4,620m (15,157ft)
El Obeid
Kosti
Gulf of Aden
Blue Nile
Gonder
Djibouti
Lake Tana
Dikhil
White Nile
Bahir Dar
Dese
Berbera
Ethiopian Highlands
Dire Dawa
Hargeysa
Harer
G H J K L M
30° 35° 40° 45° 50°
2 3 4 5 6 7
30° N
25°
20°
15°
10°

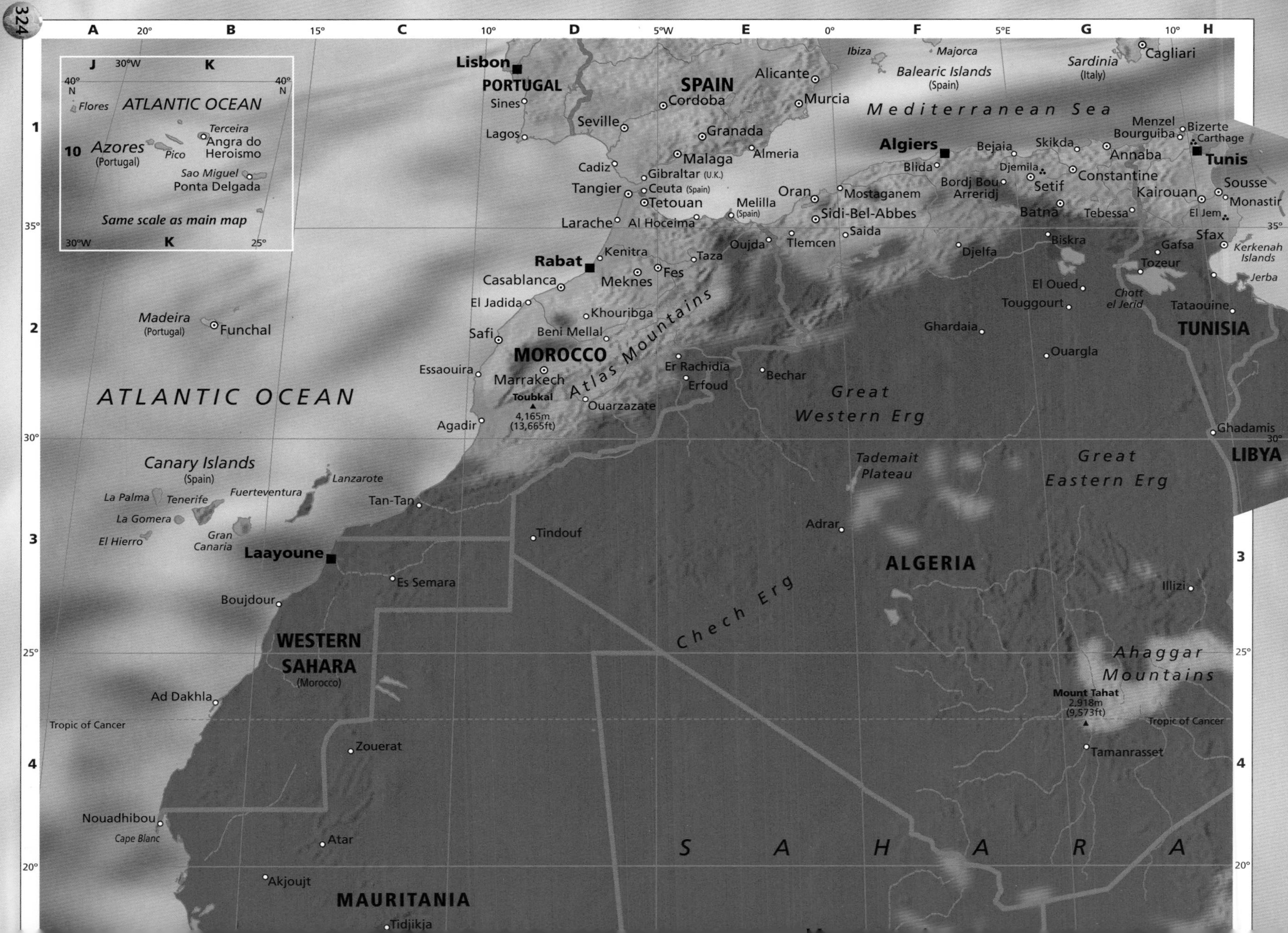
ATLANTIC OCEAN
Flores
Azores
(Portugal)
Pico
Terceira
Angra do Heroismo
Sao Miguel
Ponta Delgada
Same scale as main map
Lisbon
PORTUGAL
Sines
Lagos
SPAIN
Cordoba
Seville
Granada
Malaga
Almeria
Alicante
Murcia
Cadiz
Gibraltar (U.K.)
Ceuta (Spain)
Tangier
Tetouan
Larache
Al Hoceima
Melilla (Spain)
Ibiza
Majorca
Balearic Islands
(Spain)
Mediterranean Sea
Sardinia
(Italy)
Cagliari
Algiers
Blida
Bejaia
Djemila
Setif
Skikda
Constantine
Annaba
Bordj Bou Arreridj
Batna
Tebessa
Oran
Mostaganem
Sidi-Bel-Abbes
Saida
Tlemcen
Oujda
Menzel Bourguiba
Bizerte
Carthage
Tunis
Sousse
Kairouan
Monastir
El Jem
Sfax
Kerkenah Islands
Gafsa
Tozeur
Chott el Jerid
Jerba
Tataouine
TUNISIA
Rabat
Kenitra
Meknes
Fes
Taza
Casablanca
El Jadida
Khouribga
Beni Mellal
Safi
MOROCCO
Atlas Mountains
Marrakech
Essaouira
Toubkal
4,165m
(13,665ft)
Ouarzazate
Agadir
Er Rachidia
Erfoud
Bechar
Djelfa
Biskra
El Oued
Touggourt
Ghardaia
Ouargla
Great Western Erg
Great Eastern Erg
Ghadamis
LIBYA
Madeira
(Portugal)
Funchal
Canary Islands
(Spain)
La Palma
Tenerife
La Gomera
El Hierro
Gran Canaria
Fuerteventura
Lanzarote
Tan-Tan
Tindouf
Tademait Plateau
Adrar
Laayoune
Es Semara
Boujdour
ALGERIA
Illizi
Chech Erg
WESTERN SAHARA
(Morocco)
Ad Dakhla
Tropic of Cancer
Ahaggar Mountains
Mount Tahat
2,918m
(9,573ft)
Tamanrasset
Zouerat
Nouadhibou
Cape Blanc
Atar
Akjoujt
MAURITANIA
Tidjikja
S A H A R A

SENEGAL
THE GAMBIA
GUINEA-BISSAU
GUINEA
SIERRA LEONE
LIBERIA
IVORY COAST
BURKINA FASO
GHANA
TOGO
BENIN
NIGER
NIGERIA
SAO TOME AND PRINCIPE

St. Louis
Louga
Thies
Dara
Dakar
Kaolack
Tambacounda
Banjul
Bignona
Kolda
Ziguinchor
Bissau
Bissagos Archipelago
Boke
Kaedi
Selibabi
Kayes
Kedougou
Labe
Kindia
Conakry
Freetown
Makeni
Sefadu
Bo
Kenema
Siguiri
Kankan
Gueckedou
Zorzor
Nzerekore
1,752m (5,748ft)
Tubmanburg
Monrovia
Harper
Cape Palmas
Ayoun el Atrous
Nioro du Sahel
Kita
Niger
Bamako
Segou
Niono
Koutiala
Bougouni
Sikasso
Odienne
Man
Goundam
Mopti
San
Tougan
Black Volta
Koudougou
Bobo Dioulasso
Banfora
Korhogo
Bouna
Katiola
Bondoukou
Bouake
Yamoussoukro
Daloa
Gagnoa
Divo
Adzope
Abidjan
San Pedro
Gao
Dori
Ouahigouya
Ouagadougou
White Volta
Fada-Ngourma
Tenkodogo
Bawku
Wa
Tamale
Damongo
Wenchi
Lake Volta
Kumasi
Koforidua
Tarkwa
Cape Coast
Cape Three Points
Sekondi-Takoradi
Accra
Sokode
Abomey
Lome
Cotonou
Porto-Novo
Bight of Benin
Tillaberi
Niamey
Dosso
Kandi
Natitingou
Djougou
Parakou
Saki
Tahoua
Sokoto
Birnin-Kebbi
Kainji Reservoir
Maradi
Katsina
Gusau
Zaria
Kaduna
Minna
Bida
Abuja
Ilorin
Ogbomoso
Ibadan
Abeokuta
Lagos
Owo
Benin City
Enugu
Onitsha
Warri
Port Harcourt
Niger Delta
ATLANTIC OCEAN
Gulf of Guinea
Principe
Sao Tome
Equator

L 25°W M
ATLANTIC OCEAN
Santo Antao
Mindelo
Sal
Sao Nicolau
Boa Vista
CAPE VERDE
Sao Tiago
Maio
Fogo
Praia
15° N
11
12
Same scale as main map

15°
10°
5° N
0°
5°W
5°E
B C D E F G
6 7 8 9

Northwest Africa

Boreal forest	Wetland	■	National capital
Temperate forest	Mountain	●	Internal capital
Tropical forest	Tundra	⊙	Major city or town
Temperate grassland	Ice	○	Other town
Savanna	Cultivation		See also main key on page 259
Semi-desert and scrub	Urban		
Hot desert			
International boundary			
Internal boundary			
▲ 2,490m (8,169ft) Height above or below sea level			

1:13,800,000

0 200 400km

0 100 200 300 miles

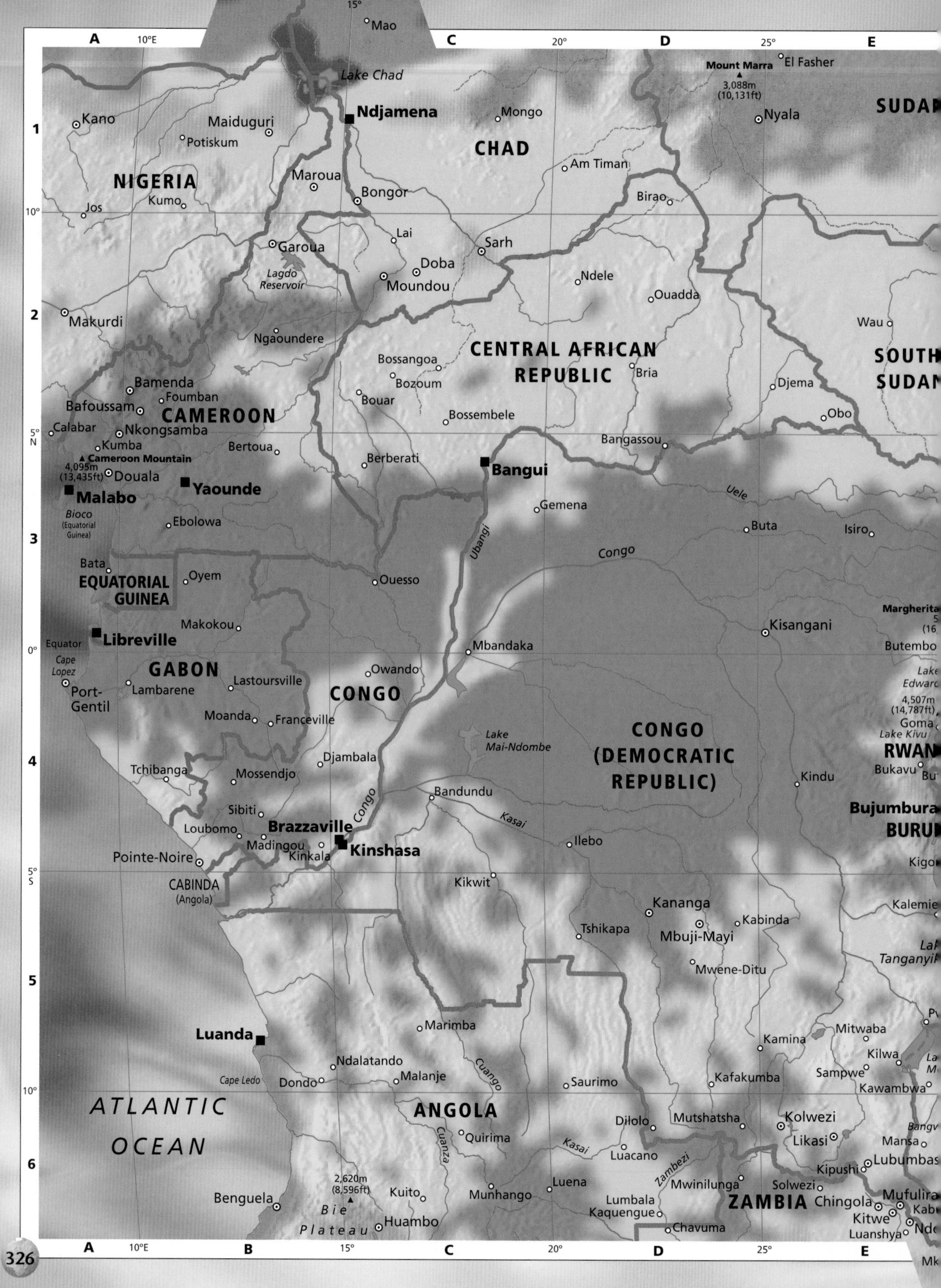

A
10°E
15°
Mao
C
20°
D
25°
E
Lake Chad
Mount Marra
3,088m
(10,131ft)
El Fasher
1
Kano
Maiduguri
Potiskum
Ndjamena
Mongo
CHAD
Nyala
SUDAN
NIGERIA
Maroua
Am Timan
Bongor
Birao
10°
Jos
Kumo
Lai
Sarh
Garoua
Doba
Moundou
Lagdo Reservoir
Ndele
Ouadda
2
Makurdi
Ngaoundere
Wau
CENTRAL AFRICAN REPUBLIC
SOUTH SUDAN
Bossangoa
Bozoum
Bouar
Bria
Djema
Bamenda
Foumban
Bafoussam
CAMEROON
Bossembele
Obo
5° N
Calabar
Nkongsamba
Kumba
Cameroon Mountain
4,095m
(13,435ft)
Douala
Bertoua
Berberati
Bangassou
Bangui
Malabo
Yaounde
Bioco
(Equatorial Guinea)
Ebolowa
Gemena
Uele
Buta
Isiro
3
Ubangi
Congo
Bata
EQUATORIAL GUINEA
Oyem
Ouesso
Margherita
Makokou
Kisangani
Libreville
Equator
0°
Mbandaka
Butembo
Cape Lopez
GABON
Owando
Lake Edward
Port-Gentil
Lambarene
Lastoursville
CONGO
4,507m
(14,787ft)
Goma
Lake Kivu
Moanda
Franceville
Lake Mai-Ndombe
CONGO (DEMOCRATIC REPUBLIC)
4
Djambala
Tchibanga
Mossendjo
Bukavu
Kindu
Bandundu
Sibiti
Bujumbura
Loubomo
Brazzaville
Kasai
Madingou
Kinkala
Kinshasa
Ilebo
Pointe-Noire
5° S
CABINDA
(Angola)
Kikwit
Kananga
Kabinda
Kalemie
Tshikapa
Mbuji-Mayi
Tanganyika
Mwene-Ditu
5
Marimba
Luanda
Kamina
Mitwaba
Ndalatando
Cuango
Kilwa
Cape Ledo
Dondo
Malanje
Saurimo
Kafakumba
Sampwe
Kawambwa
10°
ATLANTIC OCEAN
ANGOLA
Dilolo
Mutshatsha
Kolwezi
Cuanza
Quirima
Likasi
Mansa
Kasai
Luacano
6
Zambezi
Kipushi
Lubumbashi
2,620m
(8,596ft)
Mwinilunga
Solwezi
Luena
Benguela
Kuito
Munhango
Lumbala Kaquengue
ZAMBIA
Chingola
Mufulira
Kitwe
Bie Plateau
Huambo
Chavuma
Luanshya
A
10°E
B
15°
C
20°
D
25°
E

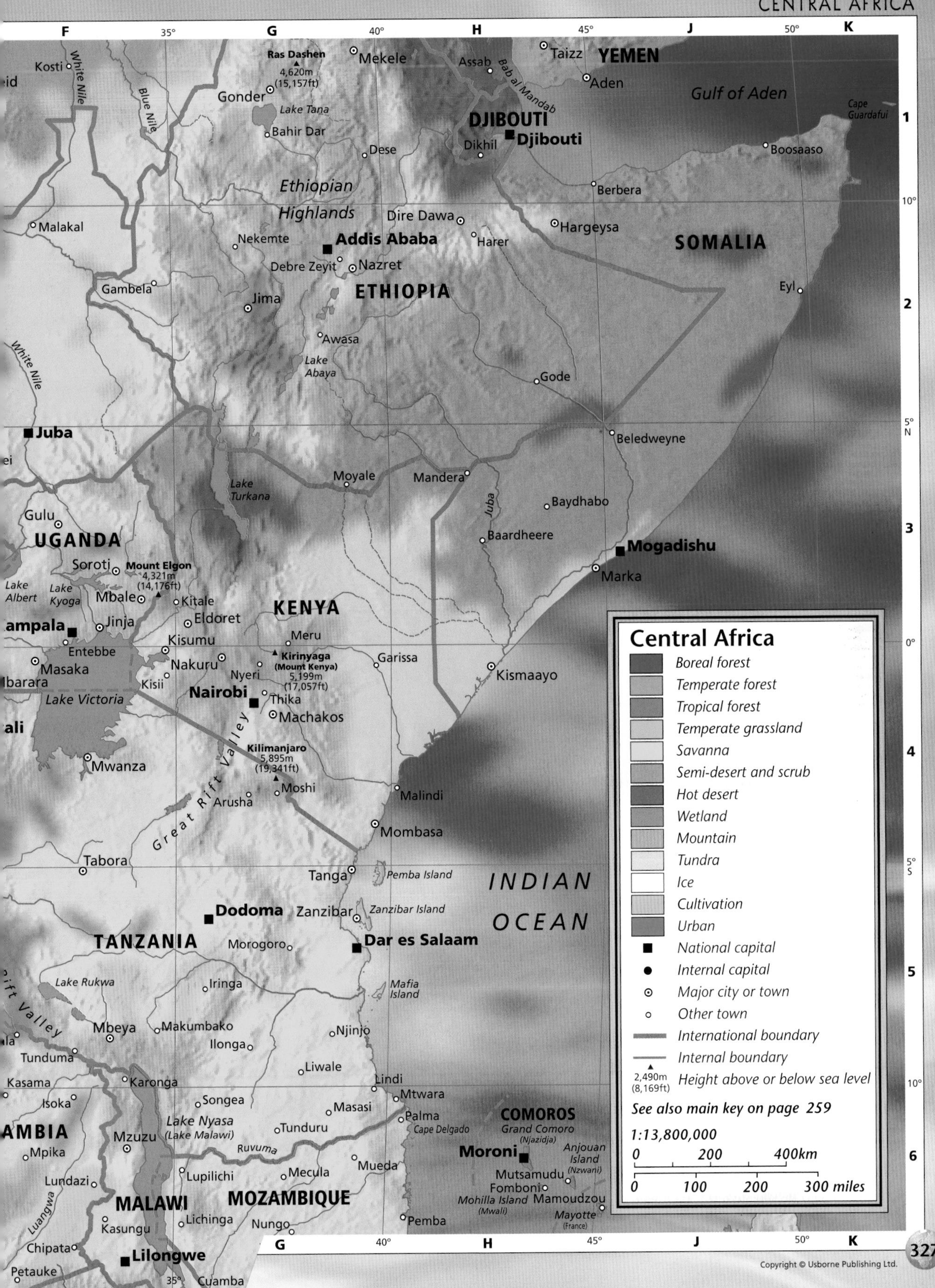

YEMEN
Taizz
Aden
Gulf of Aden
Cape Guardafui
Assab
Bab al Mandab
DJIBOUTI
Djibouti
Dikhil
Boosaaso
Berbera
Hargeysa
SOMALIA
Eyl
Ras Dashen 4,620m (15,157ft)
Mekele
Gonder
Lake Tana
Bahir Dar
Dese
Ethiopian Highlands
Dire Dawa
Harer
Addis Ababa
Nekemte
Debre Zeyit
Nazret
ETHIOPIA
Jima
Awasa
Lake Abaya
Gode
Beledweyne
Kosti
White Nile
Blue Nile
Malakal
Gambela
Juba
Lake Turkana
Moyale
Mandera
Juba
Baydhabo
Baardheere
Mogadishu
Marka
Gulu
UGANDA
Soroti
Mount Elgon 4,321m (14,176ft)
Lake Albert
Lake Kyoga
Mbale
Kitale
Eldoret
KENYA
Kampala
Jinja
Kisumu
Meru
Entebbe
Masaka
Kirinyaga (Mount Kenya) 5,199m (17,057ft)
Garissa
Nakuru
Nyeri
Kismaayo
Kisii
Nairobi
Thika
Machakos
Lake Victoria
Great Rift Valley
Kilimanjaro 5,895m (19,341ft)
Mwanza
Moshi
Arusha
Malindi
Mombasa
Tabora
Tanga
Pemba Island
INDIAN OCEAN
Dodoma
Zanzibar
Zanzibar Island
TANZANIA
Morogoro
Dar es Salaam
Lake Rukwa
Iringa
Mafia Island
Mbeya
Makumbako
Njinjo
Ilonga
Tunduma
Liwale
Kasama
Karonga
Lindi
Mtwara
Isoka
Songea
Masasi
Palma
Cape Delgado
ZAMBIA
Lake Nyasa (Lake Malawi)
Tunduru
Mzuzu
Mpika
Ruvuma
Mueda
Lundazi
Lupilichi
Mecula
Luangwa
MALAWI
MOZAMBIQUE
Kasungu
Lichinga
Nungo
Pemba
Chipata
Lilongwe
Petauke
Cuamba
COMOROS
Grand Comoro (Njazidja)
Moroni
Anjouan Island (Nzwani)
Mutsamudu
Fomboni
Mohilla Island (Mwali)
Mamoudzou
Mayotte (France)
Central Africa
Boreal forest
Temperate forest
Tropical forest
Temperate grassland
Savanna
Semi-desert and scrub
Hot desert
Wetland
Mountain
Tundra
Ice
Cultivation
Urban
National capital
Internal capital
Major city or town
Other town
International boundary
Internal boundary
2,490m (8,169ft) Height above or below sea level
See also main key on page 259
1:13,800,000
0 200 400km
0 100 200 300 miles

ANGOLA
ZAMBIA
CONGO (DEMOCRATIC REPUBLIC)
NAMIBIA
BOTSWANA
ZIMBABWE
SOUTH AFRICA
LESOTHO
SWAZILAND
ATLANTIC OCEAN
Luanda
Ndalatando
Dondo
Cape Ledo
Marimba
Malanje
Cuango
Cuanza
Quirima
Saurimo
Kasai
Luacano
Luena
Munhango
Kuito
Huambo
Benguela
Bie Plateau
Mumbue
Cangombe
Lucira
Cape St. Martha
Matala
Lubango
Namibe
Menongue
Lumbala Nguimbo
Cunene
Caiundo
Mavinga
Albino Point
Xangongo
Cuangar
Foz do Cunene
Ondangwa
Rundu
Andara
Caprivi Strip
Opuwo
Etosha Pan
Tsumeb
Okaukuejo
Otavi
Kamanjab
Namib Desert
Otjiwarongo
Kaukau Veld
Sukses
Karibib
Okahandja
Swakopmund
Walvis Bay
Windhoek
Gobabis
Rehoboth
Leonardville
Tropic of Capricorn
Kalkrand
Mariental
Gochas
Tses
Keetmanshoop
Luderitz
Seeheim
Grunau
Orange
Alexander Bay
Kenhardt
Upington
Bitterfontein
Cape Columbine
Paarl
Worcester
Cape Town
Stellenbosch
Cape of Good Hope
Cape Agulhas
Kamina
Kafakumba
Mitwaba
Pweto
Kilwa
Lake Mweru
Sampwe
Kawambwa
Mbala
Dilolo
Mutshatsha
Kolwezi
Likasi
Lake Bangweulu
Mansa
Mpika
Zambezi
Mwinilunga
Lubumbashi
Kipushi
Solwezi
Mufulira
Kabunda
Chingola
Kitwe
Ndola
Luanshya
Mkushi
Lumbala Kaquengue
Chavuma
Zambezi
Lukulu
Kabwe
Mongu
Rufunsa
Lusaka
Kafue
Cabora Bassa Reservoir
Zumbo
Kataba
Ngoma
Lake Kariba
Kariba
Chinhoyi
Bindura
Luiana
Sesheke
Zimba
Livingstone
Binga
Harare
Victoria Falls
Kamativi
Hwange
Kadoma
Okavango
Okavango Swamp
Nokaneng
Gweru
Maun
Bulawayo
Tsau
Makgadikgadi Pans (Makarikari)
Lake Ngami
Plumtree
Zvishavane
Chiredzi
Rakops
Orapa
Francistown
Selebi-Phikwe
Mamuno
Tshwane
Serowe
Messina
Mahalapye
Kang
Pietersburg
Molepolole
Mochudi
Tshane
Gaborone
Kalahari Desert
Kanye
Warmbad
Werda
Pretoria (Tshwane)
Terra Firma
Mmabatho
Krugersdorp
Benoni
Johannesburg
Springs
Molopo
Tshabong
Orkney
Standerton
Hotazel
Kroonstad
Welkom
Bethlehem
Harrismith
Tugela Falls
Ladysmith
Kimberley
Maseru
Douglas
Bloemfontein
Mafeteng
Prieska
Drakensberg
2,770m (9,088ft)
2,620m (8,596ft)
De Aar
Carnarvon
Umtata
Beaufort West
Graaff-Reinet
Cradock
Bisho
Great Karoo
East London
Groot
Grahamstown
Uitenhage
Oudtshoorn
Port Elizabeth
Cape St. Francis
15°E
20°
25°
30°
10°E
15°
10° S
15°
20°
25°
30°
A
B
C
D
E
1
2
3
4
5
6

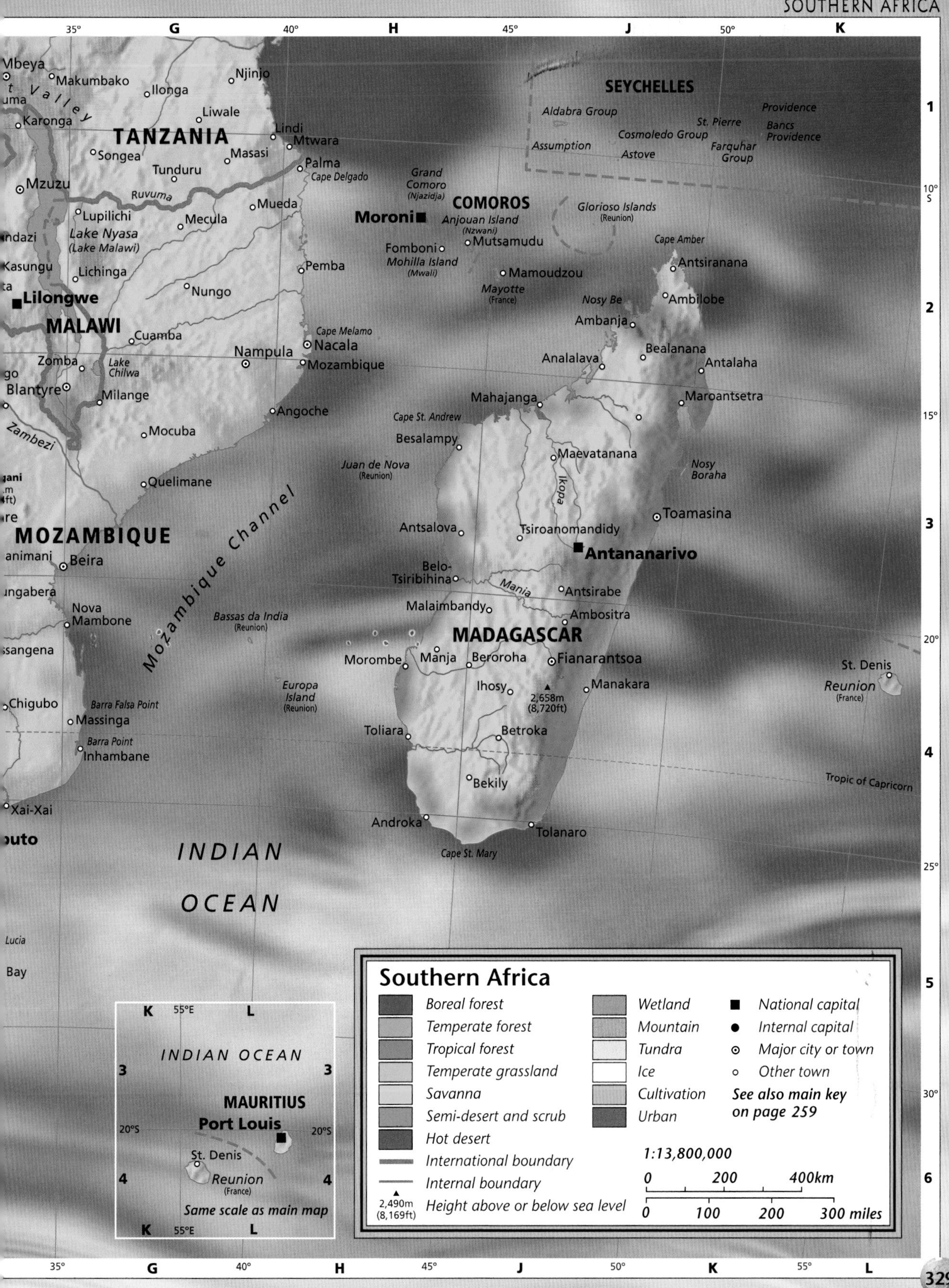
SEYCHELLES
Aldabra Group
Assumption
Cosmoledo Group
Astove
St. Pierre
Farquhar Group
Providence
Bancs Providence
TANZANIA
Mbeya
Makumbako
Ilonga
Njinjo
Liwale
Karonga
Lindi
Mtwara
Songea
Masasi
Tunduru
Palma
Cape Delgado
Mzuzu
Ruvuma
Mueda
Lupilichi
Mecula
Lake Nyasa
(Lake Malawi)
Lichinga
Kasungu
Pemba
Nungo
Lilongwe
MALAWI
Cuamba
Grand Comoro
(Njazidja)
COMOROS
Moroni
Anjouan Island
(Nzwani)
Fomboni
Mutsamudu
Mohilla Island
(Mwali)
Mamoudzou
Mayotte
(France)
Glorioso Islands
(Reunion)
Cape Amber
Antsiranana
Ambilobe
Nosy Be
Ambanja
Cape Melamo
Nacala
Nampula
Mozambique
Zomba
Lake Chilwa
Blantyre
Milange
Angoche
Zambezi
Mocuba
Quelimane
Analalava
Bealanana
Antalaha
Mahajanga
Maroantsetra
Cape St. Andrew
Besalampy
Juan de Nova
(Reunion)
Maevatanana
Nosy Boraha
Ikopa
Toamasina
MOZAMBIQUE
Mozambique Channel
Beira
Antsalova
Tsiroanomandidy
Antananarivo
Belo-Tsiribihina
Mania
Antsirabe
Nova Mambone
Malaimbandy
Ambositra
Bassas da India
(Reunion)
MADAGASCAR
Morombe
Manja
Beroroha
Fianarantsoa
Ihosy
2,658m
(8,720ft)
Manakara
St. Denis
Reunion
(France)
Chigubo
Barra Falsa Point
Massinga
Europa Island
(Reunion)
Toliara
Betroka
Barra Point
Inhambane
Bekily
Tropic of Capricorn
Xai-Xai
Androka
Tolanaro
Cape St. Mary
INDIAN OCEAN
Lucia
Bay
INDIAN OCEAN
MAURITIUS
Port Louis
St. Denis
Reunion
(France)
Same scale as main map
Southern Africa
Boreal forest
Temperate forest
Tropical forest
Temperate grassland
Savanna
Semi-desert and scrub
Hot desert
International boundary
Internal boundary
2,490m (8,169ft)
Height above or below sea level
Wetland
Mountain
Tundra
Ice
Cultivation
Urban
National capital
Internal capital
Major city or town
Other town
See also main key on page 259
1:13,800,000
0 200 400km
0 100 200 300 miles

MAPS OF THE ARCTIC AND ANTARCTICA

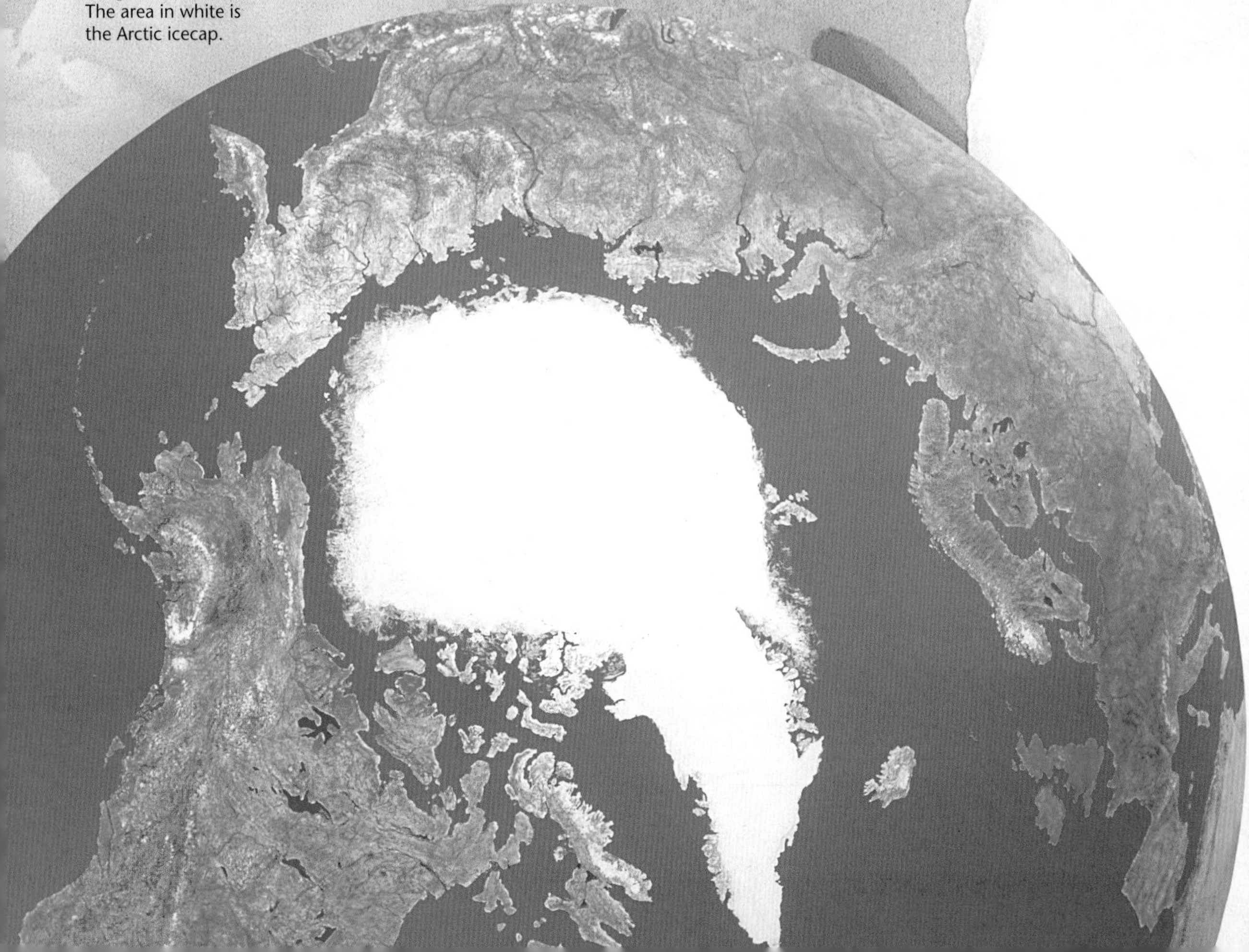

This is a satellite image of the Arctic. The area in white is the Arctic icecap.

This is a satellite image of Antarctica with its permanent white icecap.

Adelie penguins in Antarctica

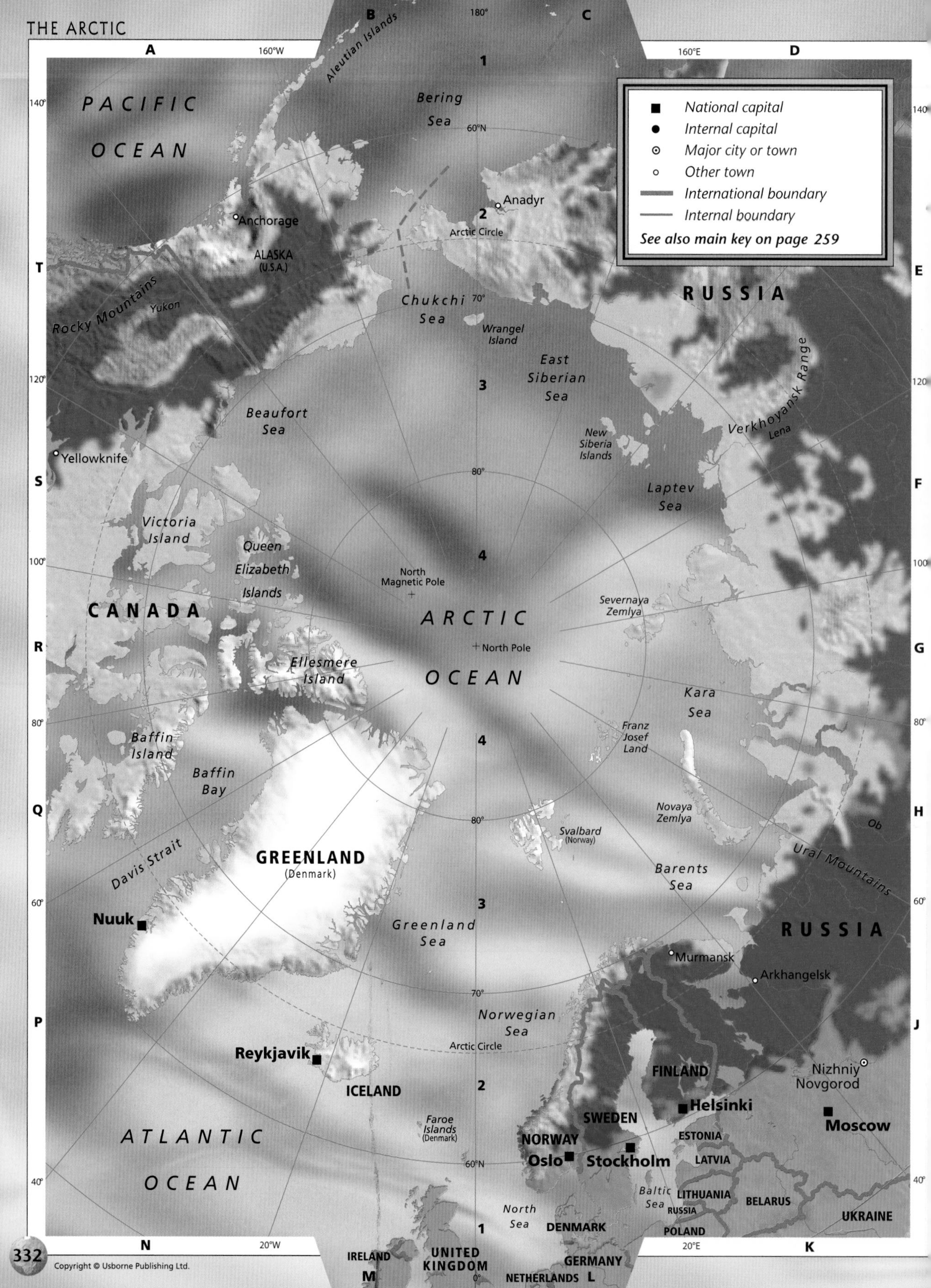

PACIFIC OCEAN
Bering Sea
Aleutian Islands
Anadyr
Anchorage
Arctic Circle
ALASKA (U.S.A.)
Rocky Mountains
Yukon
Chukchi Sea
Wrangel Island
East Siberian Sea
RUSSIA
Verkhoyansk Range
Lena
Beaufort Sea
New Siberia Islands
Yellowknife
Laptev Sea
Victoria Island
Queen Elizabeth Islands
North Magnetic Pole
CANADA
ARCTIC OCEAN
North Pole
Severnaya Zemlya
Ellesmere Island
Kara Sea
Franz Josef Land
Baffin Island
Baffin Bay
Novaya Zemlya
Svalbard (Norway)
Ob
Davis Strait
GREENLAND (Denmark)
Barents Sea
Ural Mountains
Nuuk
Greenland Sea
RUSSIA
Murmansk
Arkhangelsk
Norwegian Sea
Arctic Circle
Reykjavik
ICELAND
FINLAND
Nizhniy Novgorod
Helsinki
Moscow
Faroe Islands (Denmark)
SWEDEN
ATLANTIC OCEAN
NORWAY
Oslo
Stockholm
ESTONIA
LATVIA
Baltic Sea
LITHUANIA
BELARUS
RUSSIA
North Sea
DENMARK
POLAND
UKRAINE
IRELAND
UNITED KINGDOM
GERMANY
NETHERLANDS
National capital
Internal capital
Major city or town
Other town
International boundary
Internal boundary
See also main key on page 259

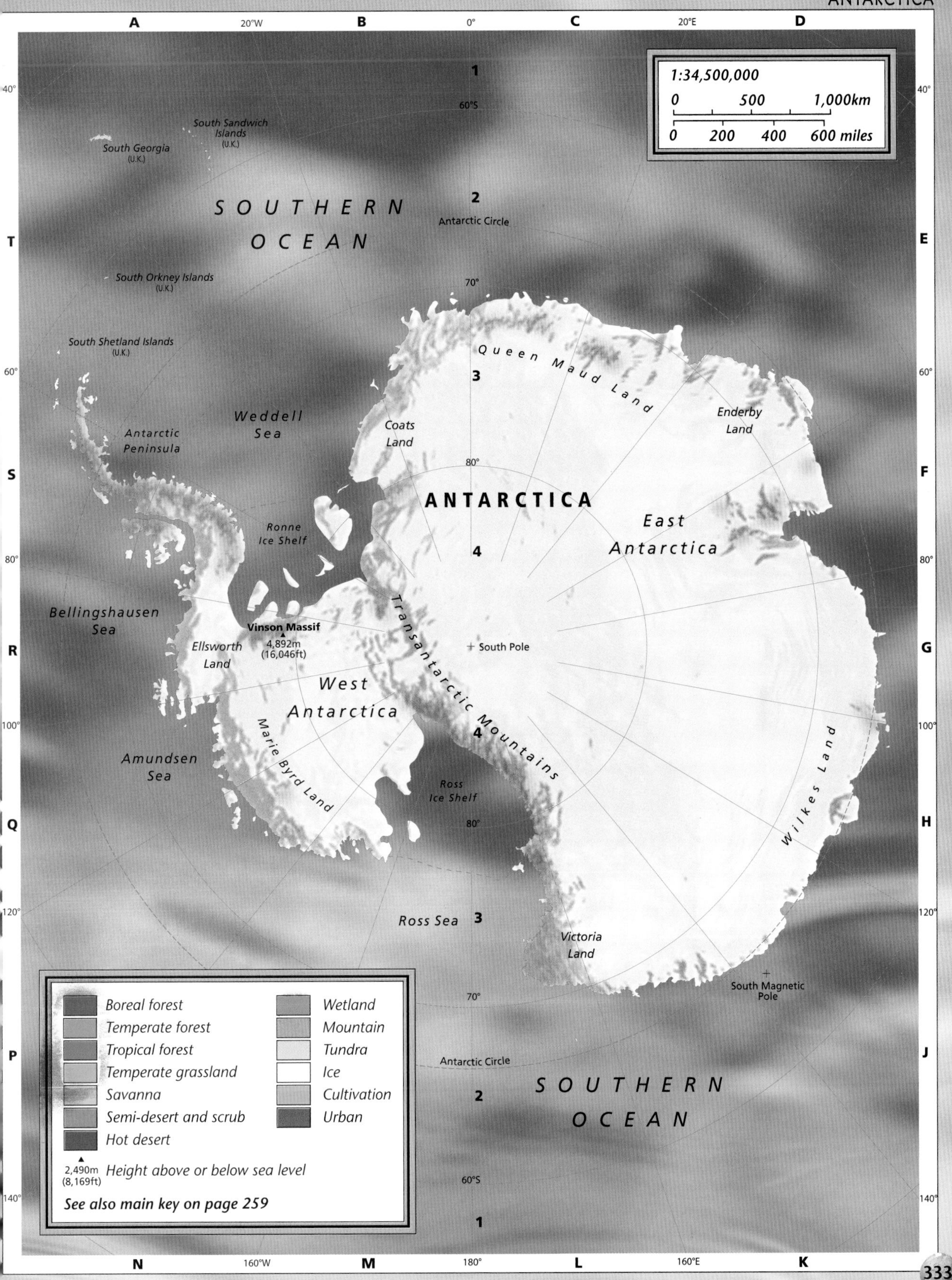
A
20°W
B
0°
C
20°E
D
1:34,500,000
0 500 1,000km
0 200 400 600 miles
60°S
South Sandwich Islands (U.K.)
South Georgia (U.K.)
SOUTHERN OCEAN
Antarctic Circle
South Orkney Islands (U.K.)
South Shetland Islands (U.K.)
70°
Queen Maud Land
Enderby Land
Coats Land
Weddell Sea
Antarctic Peninsula
80°
ANTARCTICA
East Antarctica
Ronne Ice Shelf
Bellingshausen Sea
Vinson Massif 4,892m (16,046ft)
Ellsworth Land
South Pole
Transantarctic Mountains
West Antarctica
Marie Byrd Land
Amundsen Sea
Ross Ice Shelf
Wilkes Land
Ross Sea
Victoria Land
South Magnetic Pole
Antarctic Circle
SOUTHERN OCEAN
Boreal forest
Temperate forest
Tropical forest
Temperate grassland
Savanna
Semi-desert and scrub
Hot desert
Wetland
Mountain
Tundra
Ice
Cultivation
Urban
2,490m (8,169ft) Height above or below sea level
See also main key on page 259
N
160°W
M
180°
L
160°E
K

Stalactites and stalagmites in the Cave of the Winds, Colorado Springs, U.S.A.

FACT FILE

GEOGRAPHERS AND SCIENTISTS

Geography is the scientific study of the Earth. *Geo* is Greek for "Earth", and "graphy" comes from the Greek "graphein", which means "to write". Sciences that relate to the Earth are known as Earth sciences or geosciences.

Many geographers and scientists are involved in studying different aspects of the Earth. The table below lists some of these areas of study, the scientists and geographers who study them and the area each one deals with.

Name of study	Name of scientist/geographer	What is it?
Biogeography	Biogeographer	The study of the distribution of plants and animals
Geography	Geographer	The study of the Earth's features and processes, climates, resources and the way people relate to the Earth
Historical geography	Historical geographer	The geographic study of a place or region at a specific time in the past, or the study of geographic change over a period of time
Regional geography	Regional geographer	The study of the interrelationship between human and physical geography in a particular region
Urban geography	Urban geographer	The geographical study of cities
Geology	Geologist	The study of planet Earth, what it is made of, how it formed and how it is changing
Mineralogy	Mineralogist	The study of minerals
Geomorphology	Geomorphologist	The study of landforms (the shapes and features on the Earth's surface) and the processes which cause them
Volcanology	Volcanologist	The study of volcanoes
Seismology	Seismologist	The study of earthquakes and earth tremors
Oceanography	Oceanographer	The study of seas and oceans and the seabed
Meteorology	Meteorologist	The study of the weather and weather forecasting
Climatology	Climatologist	The study of climates past and present
Ecology	Ecologist	The study of the relationship between living things (including humans) and their surroundings on Earth
Pedology	Pedologist	The study of soil, which is also often known as soil science
Cartography	Cartographer	The science of designing and making maps, and collecting the information needed to make them

These are some of the famous scientists and geographers who have contributed to our understanding of how the Earth and its processes work, and explored other aspects of geography.

al-Idrisi (c.1100–c.1165)
Arabic geographer and author who explored the Mediterranean region, created an early map of the world, and wrote a book, *The Book of Roger*, describing his travels.

Aristotle (384BC–322BC)
Greek scientist and philosopher who wrote on many subjects.He realized that the Earth was a sphere, although it took a long time for everyone to accept this. (Until about AD1500, many people still thought the world was flat.)

Darwin, Charles (1809–1882)
English scientist who developed the theory of natural selection, which argues that plant and animal species change, or evolve, over long periods of time. This theory was controversial, partly because it suggested that the Earth was much older than many people believed.

Davis, William Morris (1850–1934) American geologist and meteorologist who founded the science of geomorphology. He developed a theory of how the process of erosion forms a cycle and was famous for his detailed diagrams showing how features of the Earth's crust are formed.

Democritus (c.460BC–c.370BC)
Greek philosopher who was the first to claim that all matter was made up of tiny particles, or atoms. He also studied earthquakes, volcanoes, the water cycle and erosion.

Eratosthenes (c.276BC–c.196BC)
Greek scientist and geographer who made the first measurement of the distance around the Earth, using the stars as a guide. He was the first person to use the word *geography*.

Gould, Stephen Jay (1941–2002)
American geologist and paleontologist (person who studies fossils) who built on the theories of Charles Darwin. He wrote many popular books, such as *Wonderful Life* (1989).

Hartshorne, Richard (1899–1992)
A leading American philosopher of geography. His major work was *Perspective on the Nature of Geography*, published in 1939, in which he argued for the study of specific places and regions.

Henry the Navigator (1394–1460)
A prince of Portugal who planned and paid for many journeys of exploration to Africa. He opened a school which taught explorers how to navigate (find their way) and record their discoveries.

Herodotus (c.484BC–c.425BC)
Greek historian known as the "father of history", but also regarded as the founder of geography because he was the first person to put historical events in a geographical setting.

Humboldt, Alexander von (1769–1859)
German explorer who contributed to geography, geology, meteorology and oceanography. He explored South America and wrote *Kosmos* (The Cosmos), in 1844, describing the geography and geology of the world.

Hutton, James (1726–1797)
Scottish scientist who studied rocks and minerals, and is sometimes called "the father of geology". He said that the Earth's crust changed gradually through erosion, volcanic eruptions and other processes.

Kant, Immanual (1724–1804)
Famous German philosopher who taught physical geography.

Lyell, Sir Charles (1797–1875)
Scottish geologist who developed the theories of James Hutton. He was also a friend of Charles Darwin and his ideas helped Darwin with his theory of natural selection.

Mackinder, Sir Halford J. (1861–1947)
Leading British geographer in the early 20th century. He was head of the first university geography department in the United Kingdom.

Ptolemy (c.AD100–c.AD170)
Egyptian geographer and astronomer. He devised an early system of latitude and longitude and used it to create many maps.

Ritter, Carl (1779–1859)
German geographer who was the first professor of geography at Berlin University. He wrote his major work, the 19-volume *Erdkunde* (Earth Science), in 1817 and is seen as the founder of modern regional geography.

Strabo (c.64BC–c.AD20)
Greek historian and geographer. He wrote *Geography*, a 17-volume book which provides geographical information on the Roman Empire.

Varenius, Bernhardus (1622–1650)
Dutch geographer. He wrote a major book, *Geographia Generalis* (General Geography) in 1650, in which he was one of the first people to distinguish between physical and human geography.

Wegener, Alfred (1880–1930)
German meteorologist who claimed that the Earth's continents were once joined together in one big continent, which he named Pangaea. His theories were not widely accepted until the 1960s when they were used to develop the theory of plate tectonics.

WORLD RECORDS

Here are some of the Earth's longest rivers, highest mountains and other amazing world records. But the world is always changing; mountains wear down, rivers change shape, and new buildings are constructed. Ways of measuring things can also change. That's why you may find slightly different figures in different books.

Highest mountains	
Everest, Nepal/China	8,848m (29,029ft)
K2, Pakistan/China	8,612m (28,253ft)
Kanchenjunga, India/Nepal	8,586m (28,169ft)
Lhotse, Nepal/China	8,516m (27,940ft)
Makalu, Nepal/China	8,462m (27,762ft)
Cho Oyu, Nepal/China	8,201m (26,906ft)
Dhaulagiri, Nepal	8,167m (26,795ft)
Manaslu, Nepal	8,156m (26,759ft)
Nanga Parbat, Pakistan	8,125m (26,658ft)
Annapurna, Nepal	8,091m (26,545ft)

Longest rivers	
Nile, Africa	6,671km (4,145 miles)
Amazon, South America	6,437km (4,000 miles)
Chang Jiang (Yangtze), China	6,380km (3,964 miles)
Mississippi/Missouri, U.S.A.	6,019km (3,740 miles)
Yenisey/Angara, Russia	5,539km (3,442 miles)
Huang He (Yellow), China	5,464km (3,395 miles)
Ob/Irtysh/Black Irtysh, Asia	5,411km (3,362 miles)
Parana/River Plate, S. America	4,880km (3,032 miles)
Congo, Africa	4,700km (2,920 miles)
Amur/Shilka/Onon, Asia	4,416km (2,744 miles)

Biggest natural lakes by surface area	
Caspian Sea	386,400 sq km (149,190 sq mi)
Lake Superior	82,100 sq km (31,700 sq mi)
Lake Victoria	69,484 sq km (26,828 sq mi)
Lake Huron	59,600 sq km (23,010 sq mi)
Lake Michigan	57,800 sq km (22,317 sq mi)
Lake Tanganyika	32,600 sq km (12,590 sq mi)
Lake Baikal	31,722 sq km (12,248 sq mi)
Great Bear Lake	31,153 sq km (12,028 sq mi)
Lake Nyasa	29,600 sq km (11,430 sq mi)
Great Slave Lake	28,568 sq km (11,030 sq mi)

Deepest ocean

The Mariana Trench, part of the Pacific Ocean, is the deepest part of the sea at 10,920 meters (35,827ft) deep.

Deepest lake

Lake Baikal in Russia is the deepest lake in the world. At its deepest point it is 1,642m (5,387ft) deep.

Biggest islands	
Greenland	2,130,800 sq km (822,706 sq mi)
New Guinea	785,753 sq km (303,381 sq mi)
Borneo	748,168 sq km (288,869 sq mi)
Madagascar	587,713 sq km (226,917 sq mi)
Baffin Island	507,451 sq km (195,928 sq mi)
Sumatra	443,066 sq km (171,069 sq mi)
Honshu	225,800 sq km (87,182 sq mi)
Victoria Island	217,291 sq km (83,897 sq mi)
Great Britain	209,331 sq km (80,823 sq mi)
Ellesmere Island	196,236 sq km (75,767 sq mi)

Tallest inhabited buildings	
Burj Khalifa, Dubai	828m (2,717ft)
Mecca Royal Clock Tower Hotel	601m (1,972ft)
Taipei 101, Taipei	509m (1,670ft)
Shanghai WFC, Shanghai	492m (1,614ft)
ICC Tower, Hong Kong	484m (1,588ft)
Petronas Towers, Kuala Lumpur	452m (1,483ft)
Zifeng Tower, Nanjing	450m (1,476ft)
Willis (Sears) Tower, Chicago	442.1m (1,450ft)
Kingkey 100, Shenzhen	441.8m (1,449ft)
Guangzhou IFC, Guangzhou	437.5m (1,434ft)

Biggest cities/urban areas	
Tokyo-Yokohama, Japan	37.2 million
Jakarta, Indonesia	26.7 million
Seoul-Incheon, South Korea	22.9 million
Delhi, India	22.8 million
Shanghai, China	21.8 million
Manila, Philippines	21.2 million
Karachi, Pakistan	20.9 million
New York City, U.S.A.	20.7 million
Sao Paulo, Brazil	20.6 million
Mexico City, Mexico	20.0 million

Famous waterfalls	Height
Angel Falls, Venezuela	979m (3,212ft)
Mardalsfossen, Norway	645m (2,116ft)
Sutherland Falls, New Zealand	580m (1,903ft)
Jog Falls, India	253m (830ft)
Victoria Falls, Zimbabwe/Zambia	105m (344ft)
Iguacu Falls, Brazil/Argentina	82m (269ft)
Niagara Falls, Canada/U.S.A.	51m (167ft)

Natural disasters

Natural disasters can be measured in different ways. For example, some earthquakes score highly on the Richter scale, while others cause more destruction. The earthquakes, volcanic eruptions, floods, hurricanes and tornadoes listed here are among the most famous and destructive disasters in history.

Modern earthquakes	Richter scale	Deaths and other effects
San Francisco, U.S.A., 1906	7.8	3,000; deadliest in U.S.; Great Fire
Haiyuan, China, 1920	7.8	200,000; towns totally destroyed
Tokyo-Kanto, Japan, 1923	7.9	142,807; caused Great Tokyo Fire
Ashgabat, Turkmenistan, 1948	7.3	110,000; capital city demolished
Valdivia, Chile, 1960	9.5	2,000; strongest recorded quake
Alaska, U.S.A., 1964	9.2	128; strongest ever quake in U.S.A.
Tangshan, China, 1976	7.5	655,237; deadliest in 20th century
Indian Ocean, 2004	9.1	230,000; deadliest recorded tsunami
Haiti region, 2010	7.0	85–316,000; 1.3 million homeless
Tohoku, Japan, 2011	9.0	15,703; strongest in Japan; tsunami

Volcanic eruptions	Disastrous effects
Mount Vesuvius, Italy, AD79	Pompeii flattened; up to 20,000 died
Laki, Iceland, 1783	Huge lava flow; poison fog; famine; 9,350 died
Unzen, Japan, 1792	Over 15,000 died in landslide and tsunami
Tambora, Indonesia, 1815	92,000 people starved to death
Krakatau, Indonesia, 1883	36,500 drowned in resulting tsunami
Mount Pelee, Martinique, 1902	Nearly 30,000 people buried in ash flows
Kelut, Indonesia, 1919	Over 5,000 people drowned in hot mud
Mount St. Helens, U.S.A., 1980	Only 61 died but a large area was destroyed
Ruiz, Colombia, 1985	25,000 people died in giant mud flows
Mt. Pinatubo, Philippines, 1991	847 killed by collapsing roofs and disease

Floods	Disastrous effects
Netherlands, 1287	Storm tide broke a dam, killing 80,000
China, 1887	900,000 died after the Yellow River flooded
Johnstown, U.S.A., 1889	2,200 killed in a flood caused by rain
China, 1931	Many rivers flooded; 3.7 million people died
North Sea Flood, 1953	2,551 killed in Netherlands, UK and Belgium
Italy, 1963	Vaoint Dam overflowed; 2–3,000 killed
East Pakistan, 1970	Giant wave caused by cyclone killed 250,000
Bangladesh, 1988	1,300 died, 30m homeless in monsoon flood
Southern U.S.A., 1993	$12bn of damage after Mississippi flooded
Venezuela, 1999	Mudslides in Vargas region killed 20,066

Storms	Disastrous effects
Caribbean "Great Hurricane", 1780	Biggest-ever hurricane, killed over 20,000
Galveston Hurricane, U.S.A., 1900	Texas hit; 6–12,000 died; $100 bn of damage
Hong Kong typhoon, China, 1906	10,000 people died in this giant hurricane
Tri-State Tornado, U.S.A., 1925	Up to 700 people died across three states
Hurricane Fifi, Honduras, 1974	8,000 people died and 100,000 left homeless
Hurricane Mitch, C. America, 1998	Over 11,000 killed across Central America
Hurricane Katrina, U.S.A., 2005	Over 1,800 killed and $90 bn of damage

Amazing Earth facts

The Earth is 12,103km (7,520 miles) across. Its circumference (the distance around the Equator) is 38,022km (23,627 miles) and it is 149,503,000 km (92,897,000 miles) away from the Sun.

To make one complete orbit around the Sun, the Earth has to travel 938,900,000km (583,400,000 miles). To do this in just a year, it has to travel very fast. Because of the atmosphere surrounding the Earth, you can't feel it moving. But in fact you are zooming through space faster than any rocket.

- **Orbit speed** The Earth travels around the Sun at a speed of about 106,000kph (65,868mph).

- **Spinning speed** The Earth also spins around an axis, but the speed you are spinning at depends on where you live. Places on the Equator move at 1,600kph (995mph). New York moves at around 1,100kph (684mph). Near the poles, the spinning is not very fast at all. (You can see how this works by looking at a spinning globe.)

- **Solar System speed** The whole Solar System, including the Sun, the Earth and its moon, and the other planets and their moons, is moving at 72,400kph (45,000 mph) through the galaxy.

- **Galaxy speed** Our galaxy, the Milky Way, whizzes through the universe at a speed of 2,172,150kph (1,350,000mph).

CYCLES OF PLANET EARTH

The Earth is constantly going through repeated processes, or cycles, such as the orbit of the Earth around the Sun, the way it spins and tilts as it moves through space, the orbit of the Moon around the Earth, and the sequence of the tides.

Days and years

Days and years are created by the movement of the Earth in relation to the Sun. Here are some facts and figures about the Earth's orbit.

- One **day** is the amount of time it takes the Earth to spin around on its axis. We divide each day into 24 hours of 60 minutes each.
- The exact amount of time it takes the Earth to make one complete orbit around the Sun is 365.26 days. This is known as a **solar year**.
- Instead of having 365.26 days, a normal **year** on Earth has exactly 365 days (because this is easier for us). Every four years another day is added to make up the difference. A year with an extra day in it is called a **leap year**. The extra day is added to February, so in leap years February has 29 days instead of 28.
- Making every fourth year a leap year does not even things out exactly, so some leap years are missed. Usually, every fourth year is a leap year, such as 1988, 1992 and 1996. But century years, such as 1700, 1800 and 1900, are not leap years. However, millennium years, such as the year 2000, *are* leap years.

Calendars

A **calendar** is a system of measuring years, months, weeks and days. People don't all agree when the world began, so years cannot be measured from then. Several different calendars, mostly based on religious beliefs, are used today.

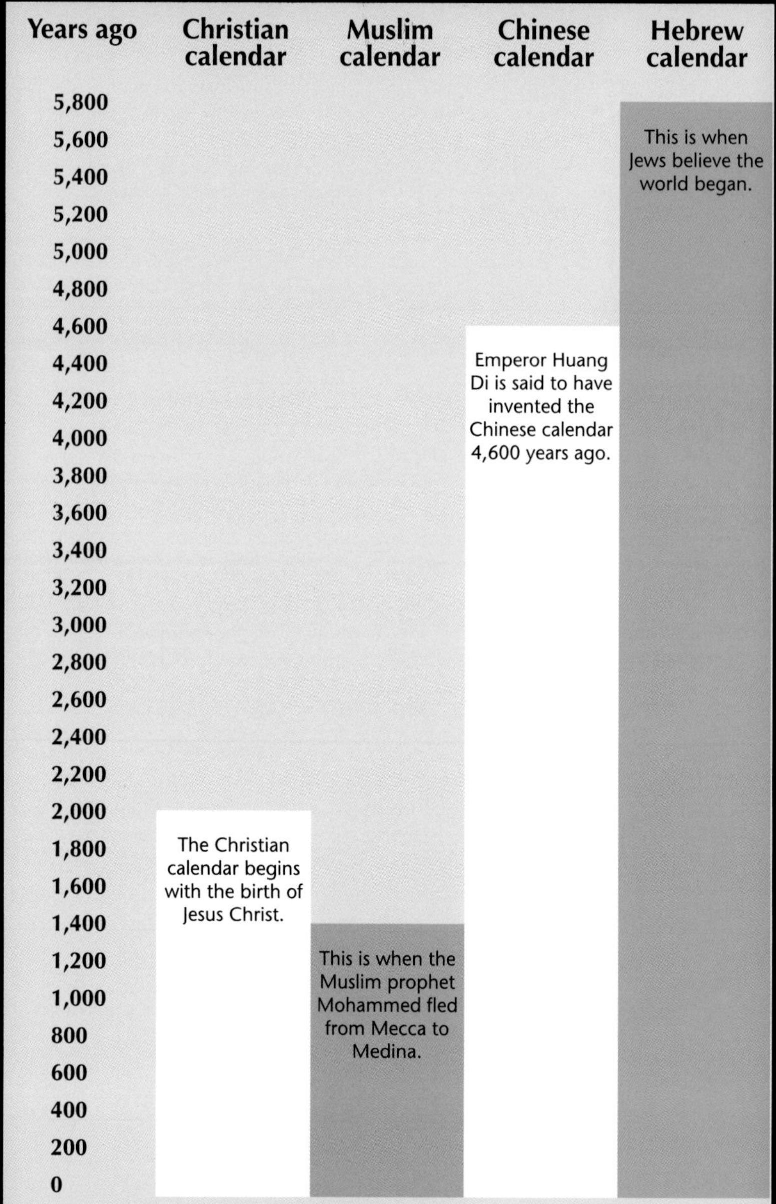

Years ago
Christian calendar
Muslim calendar
Chinese calendar
Hebrew calendar
5,800
5,600
5,400
5,200
5,000
4,800
4,600
4,400
4,200
4,000
3,800
3,600
3,400
3,200
3,000
2,800
2,600
2,400
2,200
2,000
1,800
1,600
1,400
1,200
1,000
800
600
400
200
0

This is when Jews believe the world began.

Emperor Huang Di is said to have invented the Chinese calendar 4,600 years ago.

The Christian calendar begins with the birth of Jesus Christ.

This is when the Muslim prophet Mohammed fled from Mecca to Medina.

This chart shows how many years ago the different calendars began. When the Christian calendar is on the year 2000, the Muslim calendar is on the year 1378, and so on.

The Moon

A **moon** is a ball of rock orbiting (moving around) a planet. The Earth only has one moon, but some planets have more. Saturn, for example, has at least 30 moons.

Our Moon orbits the Earth once every 27 days, 7 hours and 43 minutes. The Moon "shines" because it is reflecting light from the Sun. Whether we see a full moon, a thin crescent moon, or something in between, depends on what position the Moon is in and how much sunlight it can reflect onto the Earth. These different shapes are called the phases of the Moon.

Phases of the Moon

- A **new moon** does not shine at all. The Moon's cycle begins when the Moon is between the Earth and the Sun, so none of the light it reflects can reach the Earth.

- A **half moon** appears when the Moon has moved around and is alongside the Earth. We see half of it reflecting the Sun.

- A **full moon** is what you see when the Moon is on the opposite side of the Earth from the Sun. When the Moon is in this position, you can see sunlight reflecting off the whole of the surface facing Earth.

This diagram shows the phases of the Moon as it orbits the Earth.

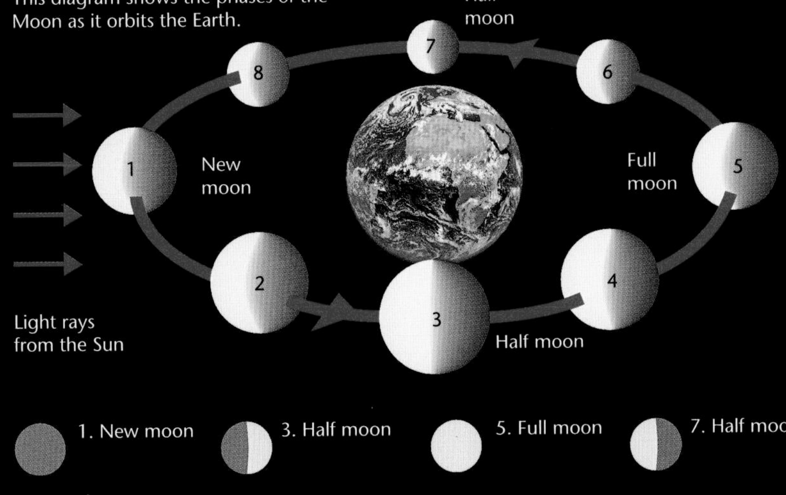

Tides

The water in the Earth's seas and oceans rises and falls twice a day. These movements are called tides, and they are caused by the gravity of the Moon.

As the Earth spins, different parts of its surface move past the Moon. The part nearest the Moon has a high tide, when the water rises as the Moon pulls it.

At the same time, a high tide also happens on the opposite side of the Earth, because of a reaction called centrifugal force, created by the way the Earth and the Moon move around each other.

While this is happening, there is a low tide on the parts of the Earth's surface that are not facing or opposite the Moon. Each part of the world has two high tides and two low tides every day.

More Moon facts

- When the Moon is moving away from the Sun and growing fuller, it is **waxing**. When it moves around toward the Sun again and seems to be getting smaller, it is **waning**.

- A **crescent moon** is between a new moon and a half moon, and looks like a crescent or C-shape.

- A **gibbous moon** is between a half moon and a full moon, and is a fat oval shape.

- A **lunar month** is the amount of time it takes the Moon to complete its cycle: 29 days, 12 hours and 44 minutes. This is longer than the orbit time, because while the Moon is making its orbit around the Earth, the Earth is moving around the Sun and so changing its own position.

- Like the Earth, the Moon spins around on its axis. It does this every 27 days, 7 hours and 43 minutes. This is exactly the same amount of time as the time it takes to travel around the Earth, which means we always see the same side of the Moon from Earth. However, we can see the other side of the Moon in pictures taken by spacecraft.

- The Moon is 3,476km (2,160 miles) across, about a quarter of the width of the Earth. Its circumference is 10,927km (6,790 miles) and its distance away from the Earth varies between 356,399 and 384,403km (221,456 and 238,857 miles). It orbits the Earth at about 3,700kph (2,300mph).

- A **month** on Earth is a period of time based on the Moon's cycle. But to make 12 months fit into a year, an average month is about 30 days long, slightly longer than a lunar month.

- A **blue moon** happens when there are two full moons within one Earth month. The second full moon of the two is called the blue moon.

TIME ZONES

When it's midday in Rio de Janeiro, it's midnight in Tokyo. This is because we divide the Earth into different time zones. Within each zone, people usually set their clocks to the same time. If you fly between two zones, you change your watch to the time of the new zone.

Dividing up time

There are 25 different time zones. They are separated by one-hour intervals and there is a new time zone roughly every 15 degrees of longitude*. The zones are measured in hours ahead of or behind Greenwich Mean Time, or GMT, which is the time at the Prime Meridian Line*.

Governments can change their countries' time zones. So, for convenience, whole countries usually keep the same local time instead of sticking to the zones exactly. For example, China could be divided into several time zones, but instead the whole country keeps the same time. A few areas, such as India, Iran and parts of Australia, use non-standard half hour deviations.

Summer time

Some countries adjust their clocks in summer. For example, in the U.K. everybody's clocks go forward one hour. This is known as Daylight Saving Time or Summer Time. It is a way of getting more out of the days by giving people an extra hour of daylight in the evening. It reduces energy use because people don't use as much electricity for lights.

Changing dates

On the opposite side of the world from the Prime Meridian Line is the International Date Line, which runs mostly through the Pacific Ocean and bends to avoid land. Places to the west of it are 24 hours ahead of places to the east. This means that if you travel east across it you lose a day and if you travel west across you gain a day.

This map shows the different times zones. The times at the top of the map tell you the time it is in the different zones when it is noon at the Prime Meridian Line. the numbers in circles tell you how many hours ahead of or behind Greenwich Mean Time an area is.

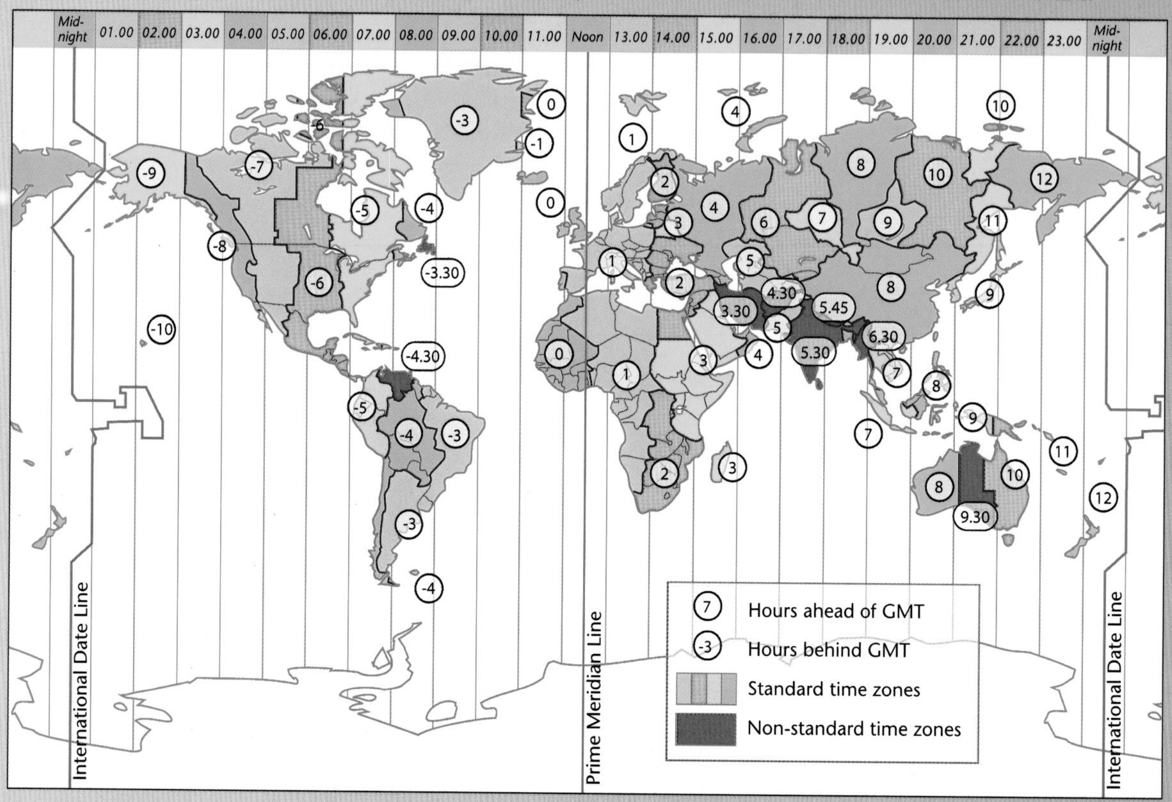

*Longitude, 250; Prime Meridian Line, 250

LOOKING AT THE STARS

On a clear night you can see a huge number of stars from Earth. If you look carefully, you will soon be able to recognize individual stars and groups of stars, known as constellations. The star maps on the following pages will show you which stars to look for.

Internet links

Go to **www.usborne.com/quicklinks** for links to websites where you can learn about how some stars and constellations got their names and much more.

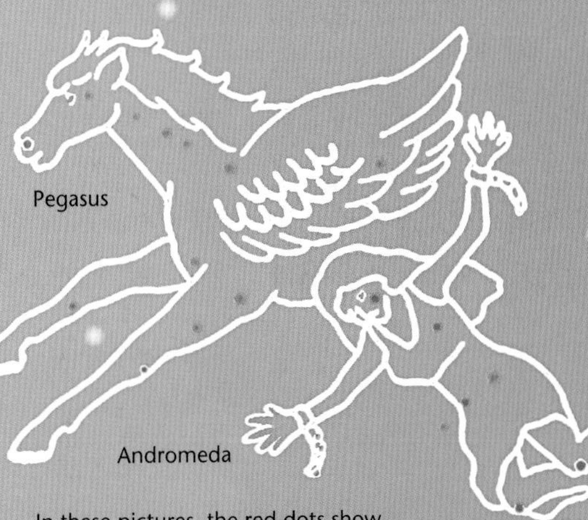

In these pictures, the red dots show the stars that make up a constellation and the white outlines show the figures they are supposed to represent.

Constellations

To make it easier to find and identify differerent stars, people divided them into constellations and gave them names, often based on characters in stories. The constellations on the star maps in this book appear in capital letters and some have been joined together with lines to make them easier to recognize.

Star maps

On the next eight pages there are star maps for each season. This is because as the Earth orbits the Sun, the part of the sky that we can see changes. In addition, many of the stars you can see from the northern hemisphere are different from the ones you can see from the southern hemisphere, so there are different maps for each of these.

You can observe the stars with your naked eye, but binoculars or a telescope like this one will make them look bigger and brighter.

Using the maps

To use the star maps, choose the right hemisphere and season and look in the direction indicated at the bottom of the map. You will find it easiest to see stars on a clear, dark night, away from city lights. You can look at them with just your naked eye or you can use binoculars or a telescope to see the fainter ones more clearly. On each pair of star maps there is a note of dates and times when the star maps will match up exactly with the night sky.

THE NIGHT SKY IN SPRING

Star maps for the northern hemisphere

The only star in the sky that doesn't seem to change its position is Polaris, in the middle of the top map. Polaris is flanked by Capella and Aldebaran on its left, and Deneb and Vega on its right.

Look out for Ursa Major (the Great Bear) overhead and Taurus (the Bull) in the west. The bright streak in the sky is the starry trail of the Milky Way.

March 15th 11:00pm
April 15th 10:00pm
May 15th 9:00pm

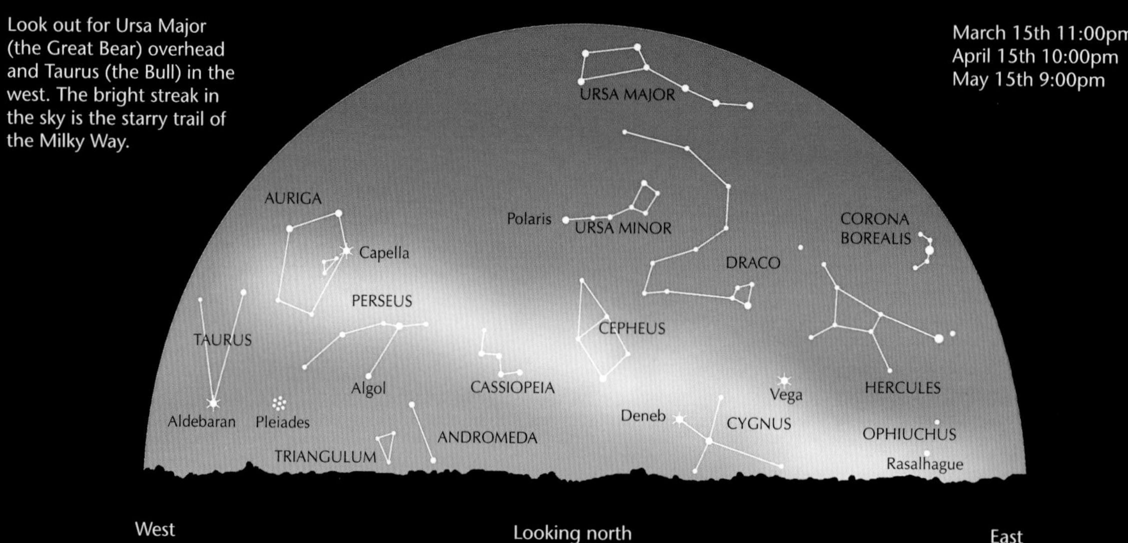

Regulus is the bright star in the middle of the sky. It is part of the constellation of Leo (the Lion).

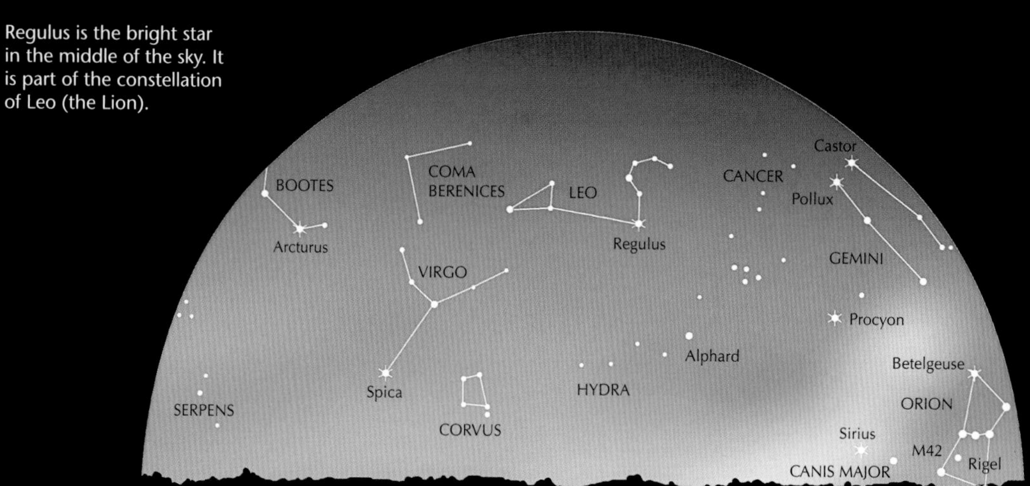

Star maps for the southern hemisphere

The most famous constellation is Crux, or the Southern Cross. It can never be seen from the northern hemisphere. Facing north, the constellations of Pegasus and Andromeda dominate the sky.

Internet links

Read tips on how to observe the night sky and how to see different constellations each month by following the website links at **www.usborne.com/quicklinks**

M31, just above the horizon, is a spiral-shaped galaxy.

September 15th 11:00pm
October 15th 10:00pm
November 15th 9:00pm

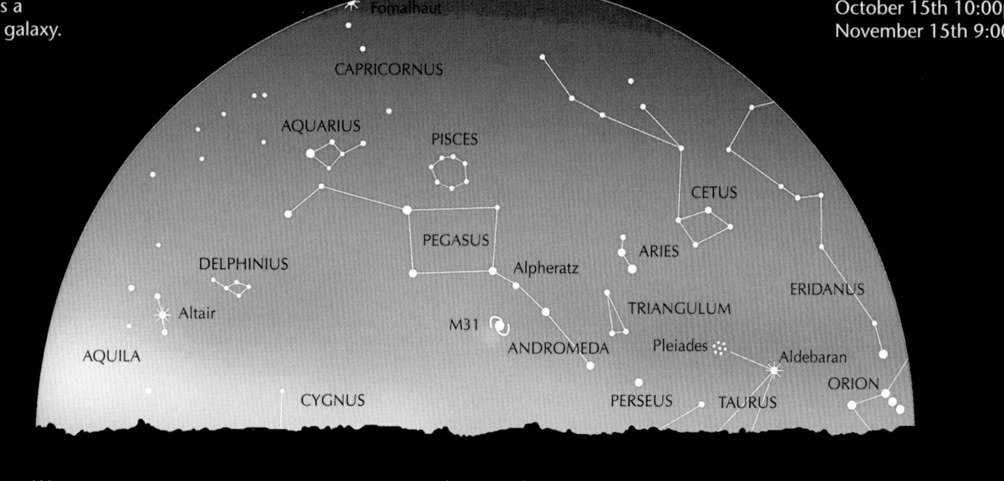

Sirius is the brightest star in the sky. Canopus is the second brightest.

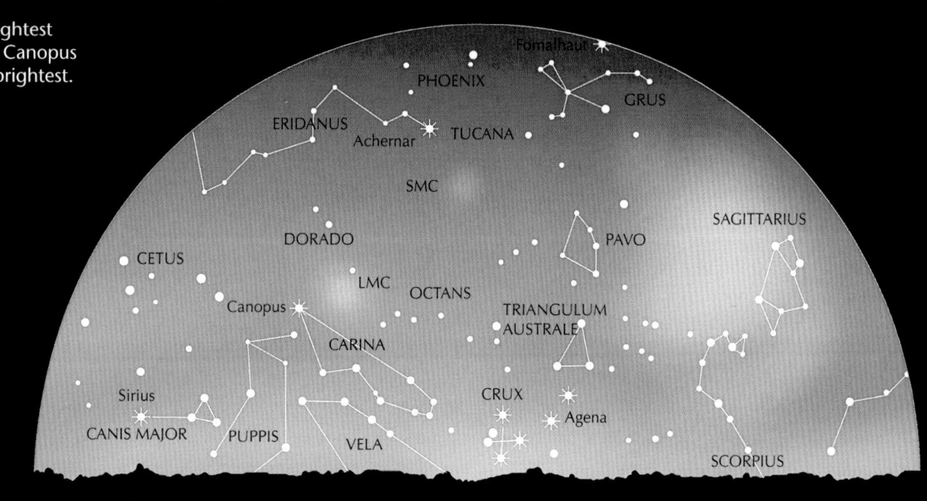

THE NIGHT SKY IN SUMMER

Maps for the northern hemisphere

The sky never really gets dark in summer, so only the brightest stars show up clearly. If the sky is clear on August 12th, stay up to watch shooting stars coming from the constellation of Pegasus.

Capella, Regulus and Deneb are the brightest stars in the sky.

June 15th 11:00pm
July 15th 10:00pm
August 15th 9:00pm

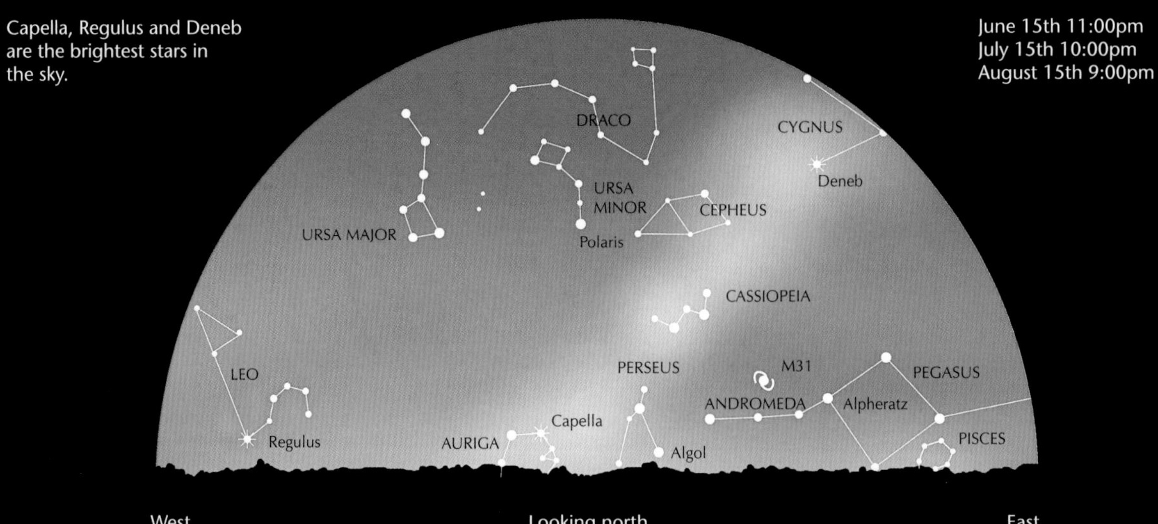

West Looking north East

Look out for Antares shining brightly above the southern horizon.

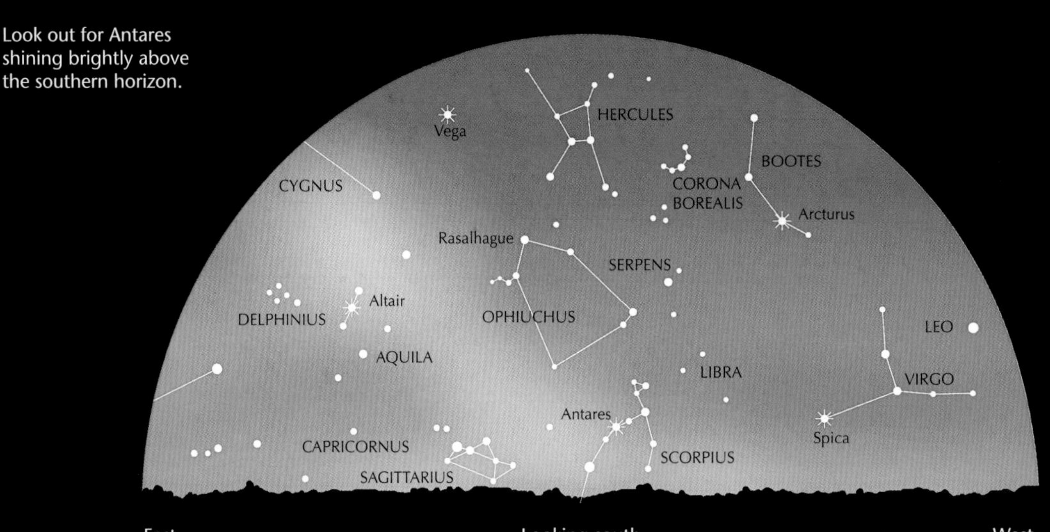

East Looking south West

Internet links

For links to websites where you can find constellation charts and star maps for each month and lots of astronomy information, too, go to **www.usborne.com/quicklinks**

Maps for the southern hemisphere

Facing north, the easiest constellations to spot are Orion and Canis Major (the Great Dog) and over to the east you can see Leo (the Lion). Sirius (the Dog Star), one of the stars in Canis Major, is the brightest star in the sky.

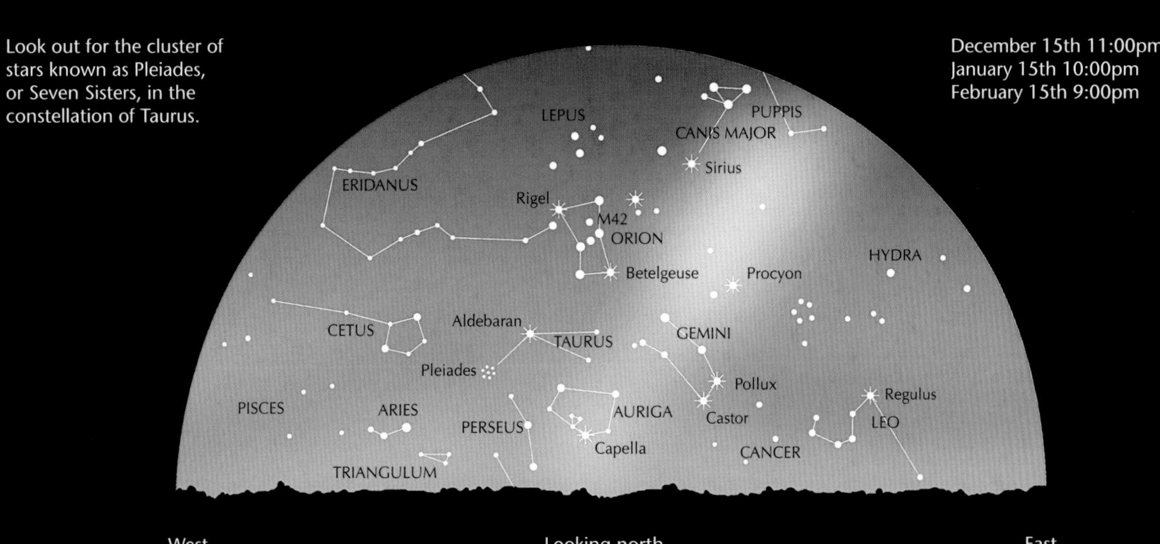

Look out for the cluster of stars known as Pleiades, or Seven Sisters, in the constellation of Taurus.

December 15th 11:00pm
January 15th 10:00pm
February 15th 9:00pm

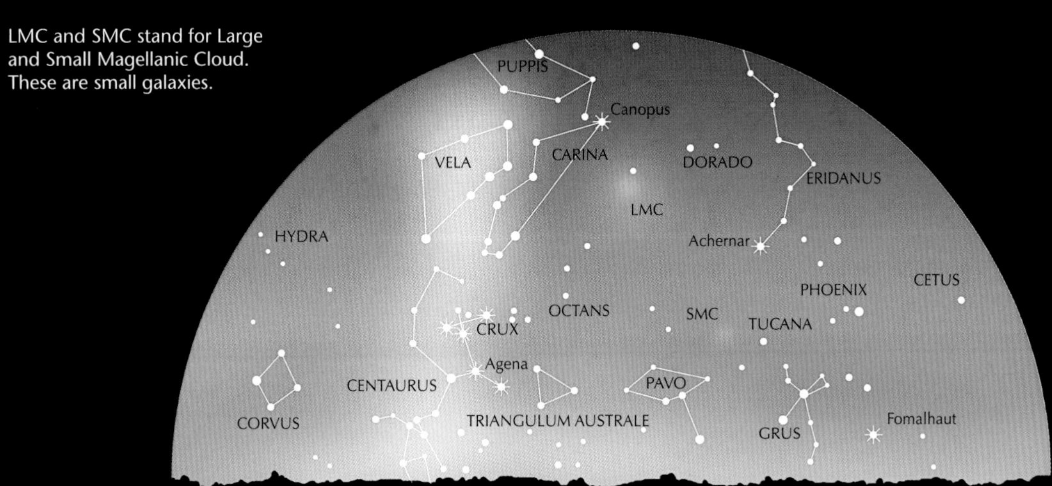

LMC and SMC stand for Large and Small Magellanic Cloud. These are small galaxies.

THE NIGHT SKY IN AUTUMN

Maps for the northern hemisphere

Facing north, look for Ursa Major, which is below Polaris and parallel with the horizon. Looking south, you should be able to see Pegasus (the Winged Horse), which has a square of stars in the middle.

In the east, the winter stars are beginning to rise, including the red star Aldebaran.

September 15th 11:00pm
October 15th 10:00pm
November 15th 9:00pm

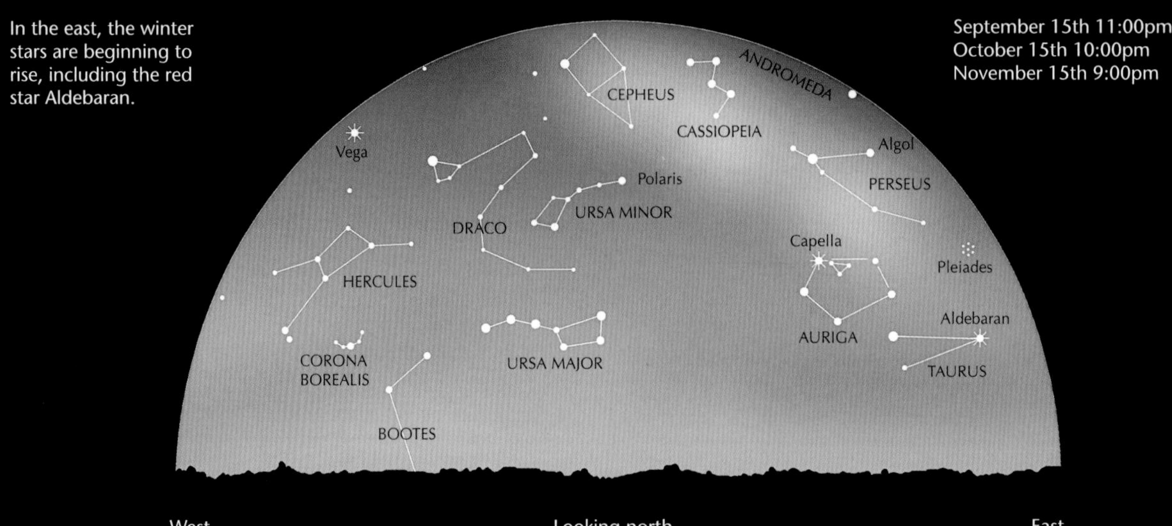

This is the best time to see M31, a huge distant galaxy. It is just visible with the naked eye, but binoculars will show it as a misty oval.

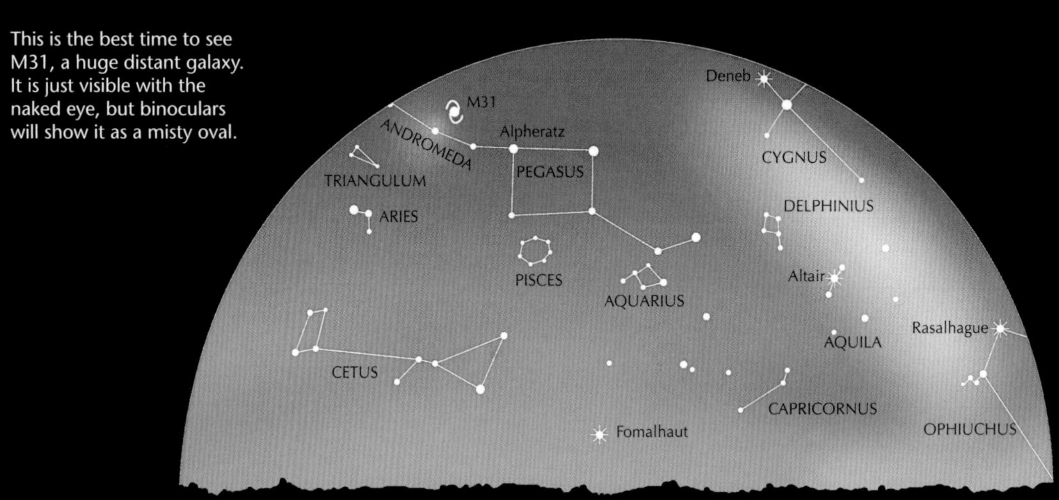

> **Internet links**
> Follow the website links at **www.usborne.com/quicklinks** to find out what to look out for in the sky on each night of autumn. You can also read about the latest astronomy discoveries and find lots of fun facts about stars, planets and space.

Maps for the southern hemisphere

Facing north, a triangle of three bright stars dominates the sky: Regulus, which is blue, yellow Arcturus and blue-white Spica. Facing south, the Milky Way crosses the sky in a wide band.

Look out for the constellations of Virgo (the Virgin) and Leo (the Lion).

March 15th 11:00pm
April 15th 10:00pm
May 15th 9:00pm

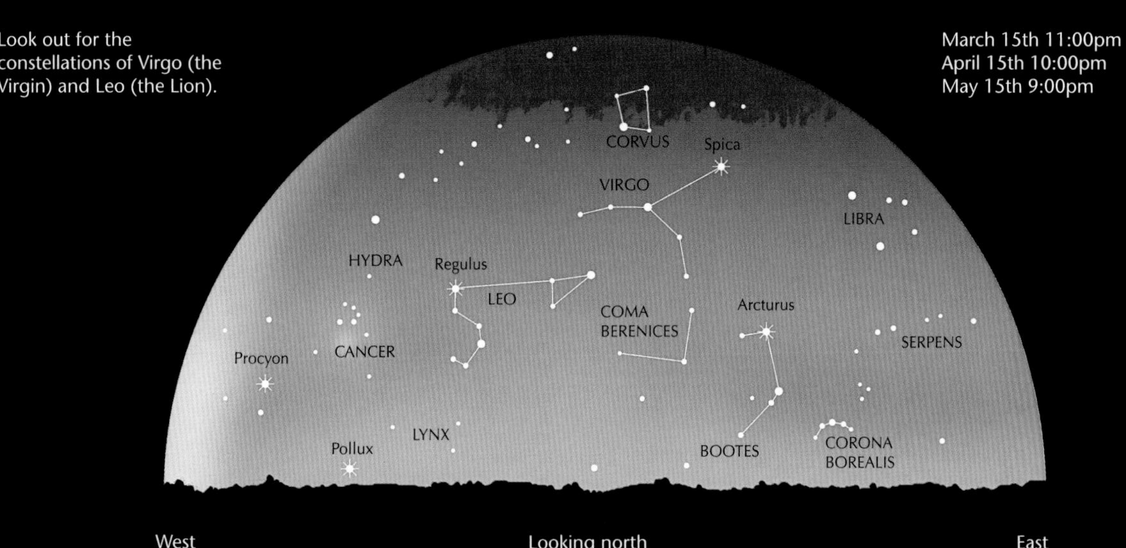

Above Crux (the Southern Cross) is Centaurus (the Centaur). A centaur was a mythical creature that was half man and half horse.

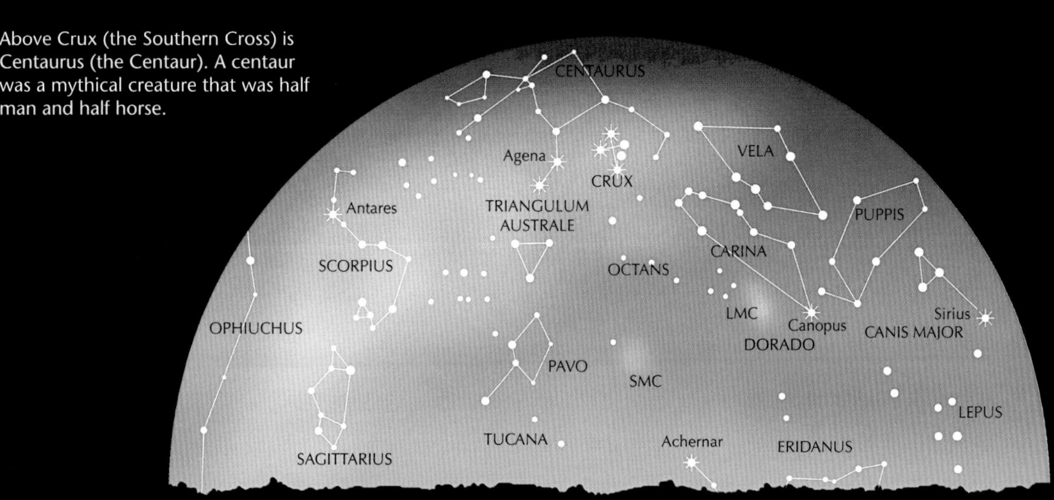

THE NIGHT SKY IN WINTER

Maps for the northern hemisphere

Winter is a good time to look for shooting stars. Set your alarm for just before dawn on December 14th to see shooting stars coming from Gemini. Looking south, you can see Orion, one of the brightest constellations.

Facing north, look for Ursa Major balancing on its tail, and Cygnus (the Swan).

December 15th 11:00pm
January 15th 10:00pm
February 15th 9:00pm

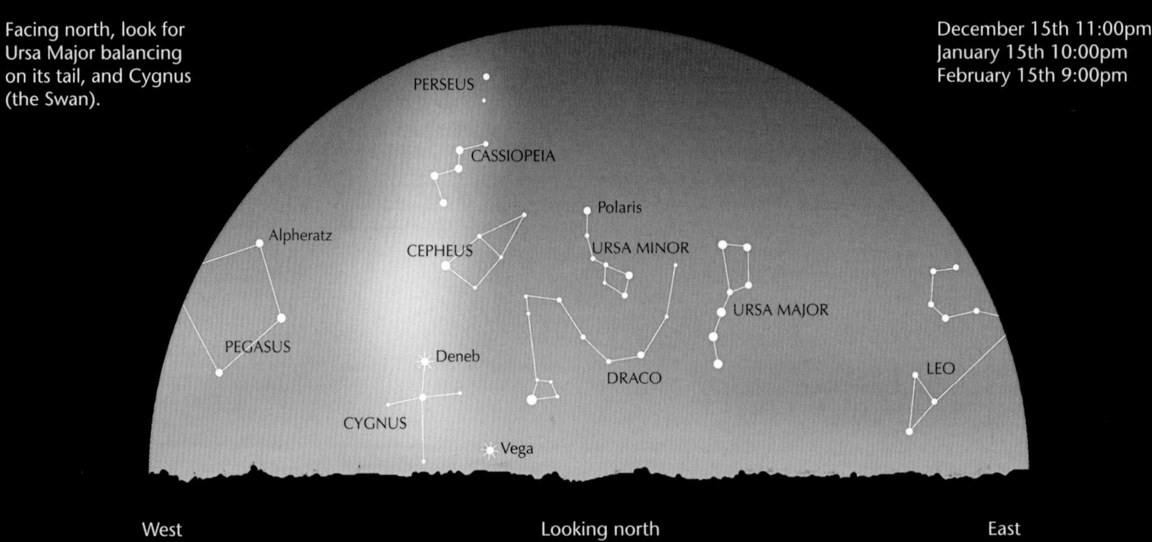

If you find the bright constellation of Orion, it will help you to locate the other constellations.

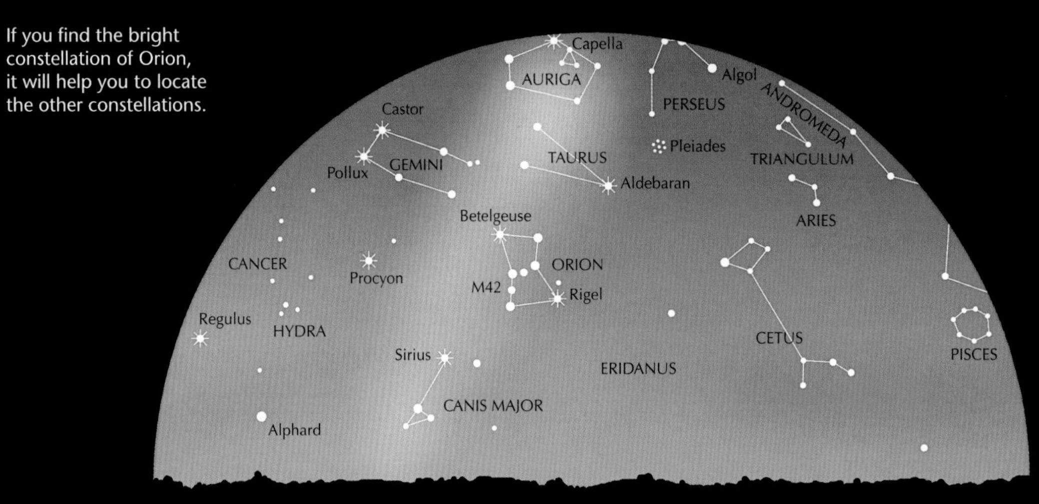

Internet links

For links to sites with articles about what you can see in the night sky in winter and tips about star gazing equipment, go to **www.usborne.com/quicklinks**

Maps for the southern hemisphere

There are plenty of bright stars to look for at this time of the year. Try to spot Deneb, Spica, Altair, Vega and Fomalhaut. The Milky Way is seen at its best, cutting the sky in half.

Look out for Ophiuchus (the Serpent Bearer), a very large group of stars, and Hercules, named after a Greek hero.

June 15th 11:00pm
July 15th 10:00pm
August 15th 9:00pm

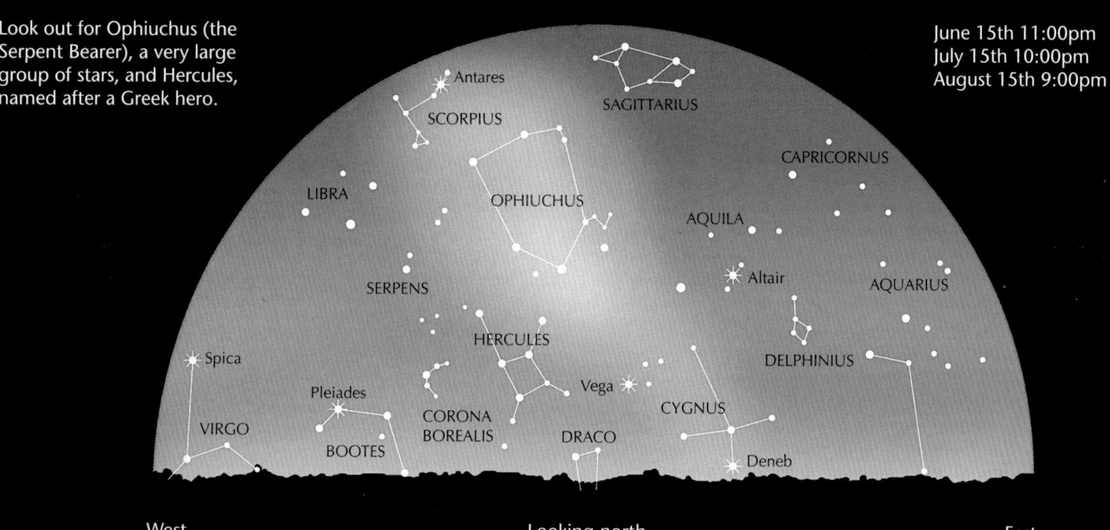

The Milky Way runs through Crux (the Southern Cross) and Centaurus (the Centaur).

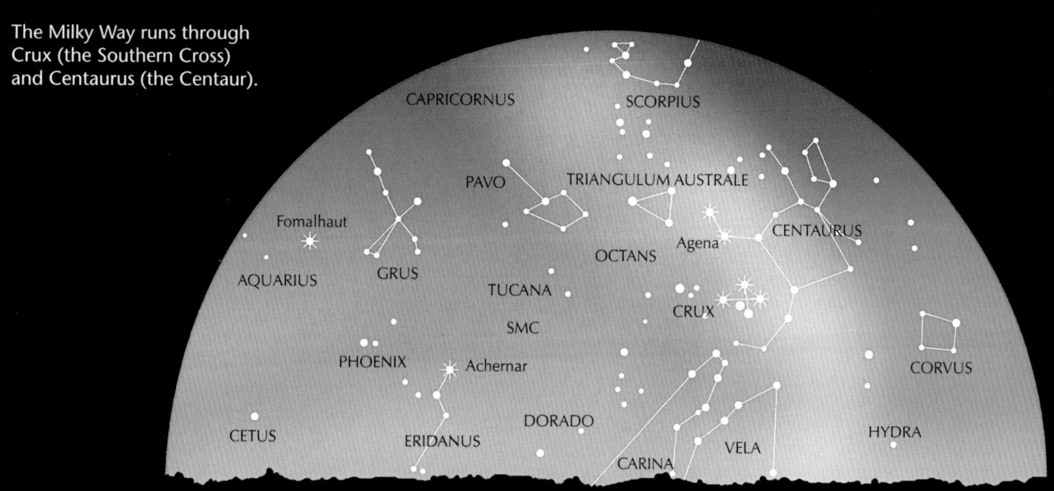

MEASUREMENTS

Measuring things – distance, area, weight, volume, time and temperature – is one of the most important parts of science. There are two main systems of measurement: metric and imperial. This page shows how each measuring system works, and also how to convert from one into the other.

Imperial

This system of measurement is very old, dating from the 12th century or even earlier. It can be hard to use because it is not based on the decimal (base 10) system which we use for numbers. Some of the units have symbols or abbreviations. For example, the symbol for an inch is ″.

Length and distance

12 inches (″) = 1 foot (′)
3 feet = 1 yard (yd)
1,760 yards = 1 mile
3 miles = 1 league

Area

144 square inches = 1 square foot
9 square feet = 1 square yard
4,840 square yards = 1 acre
640 acres = 1 square mile

Weight

16 drams (dr) = 1 ounce (oz)
16 ounces = 1 pound (lb)
14 pounds = 1 stone
2,240 pounds (160 stone) = 1 ton
2,000 pounds = 1 short ton

Volume and capacity

1,728 cubic inches = 1 cubic foot (ft^3)
27 cubic feet = 1 cubic yard (yd^3)
5 fluid ounces (fl oz) = 1 gill (gi)
20 fluid ounces = 1 pint (pt) (U.K.)
16 fluid ounces = 1 pint (U.S.)
2 pints = 1 quart (qt)
8 pints (4 quarts) = 1 gallon (gal)

Temperature

The imperial unit of temperature is one degree (°) Fahrenheit (F). The freezing point of water is 32° F and the boiling point of water is 212° F.

Metric

The metric or decimal system is based on the metre or meter, a unit of measurement which was first used in France in the 1790s. Metric units are multiples of each other by 10, 100 or 1,000. Countries around the world are gradually switching from imperial to metric. Many of the metric units have both U.S. spellings (-er) and European spellings (-re).

Length and distance

10 millimeters/millimetres (mm) = 1 centimeter/centimetre (cm)
100cm = 1 meter/metre (m)
1,000m = 1 kilometer/kilometre (km)

Area

100 square mm (mm^2) = 1 square cm (cm^2)
10,000 square cm = 1 square m (m^2)
10,000 square m = 1 hectare
1,000,000 square m = 1 square kilometer/kilometre (km^2)

Weight

1,000 grams (g) = 1 kilogram (kg)
1,000 kilograms = 1 tonne (t)

Volume and capacity

1 cubic cm (cc or cm3) = 1 milliliter/millilitre (ml)
1,000ml = 1 liter/litre (l)
1,000l = 1 cubic m (m3)

Temperature

The metric temperature unit is one degree (°) Celsius (C). Water freezes at 0°C and boils at 100° C.

Conversion tables

You can convert between metric and imperial with this table. Use a calculator to do the multiplications.

To convert	into	multiply by
cm	inches	0.394
m	yards	1.094
km	miles	0.621
grams	ounces	0.35
kilograms	pounds	2.205
tonnes	tons	0.984
square cm	square inches	0.155
square m	square yards	1.196
square km	square miles	0.386
hectares	acres	2.471
liters/litres	pints	1.76
inches	cm	2.54
yards	m	0.914
miles	km	1.609
ounces	grams	28.35
pounds	kilograms	0.454
tons	tonnes	1.016
square inches	square cm	6.452
square yards	square m	0.836
square miles	square km	2.59
acres	hectares	0.405
pints	liters/litres	0.5683

TYPES OF GOVERNMENTS

Most states have one main leader along with a parliament or assembly of politicians. The main types of governments are listed and explained below. A state can have a combination of more than one of these types of governments. For example, the United States of America is a federal republic.

Anarchy
Anarchy means a situation where there is no government. This can happen after a civil war, when a government has been destroyed and rival groups are battling to take its place.

Capitalist state
In a Capitalist or free-market state, people can own their own businesses and property, and buy services such as healthcare privately. However, most Capitalist governments also provide national health, education and welfare services.

Commonwealth
This word is sometimes used to mean a democratic republic, in which all the state's citizens are seen as having an equal interest in the functioning of the state.

Communist state
Under Communism, the state owns things like factories, farms and businesses, and provides healthcare, welfare and education for its people.

Democracy
In a democracy, the government is elected by the people, using a voting system.

Dictatorship
This is a state run by a single, unelected leader, who may use force to keep control. In a military dictatorship, the army is in power.

Federal government
In a federal system, such as that of the U.S.A., a central government shares power with a number of smaller regional governments.

Monarchy
A monarchy is a state with a king or queen. In some traditional monarchies, the monarch has complete power. A constitutional monarchy, however, also has a separate, usually democratic, government and the monarch's powers are limited.

Regional or local government
A government that controls a smaller area within a state. Some regional governments have very limited powers, and are largely directed by the central government. Others, such as the regional governments in the U.S.A., have much more power and can make their own laws.

Republic
A republic is a state with no monarch. The head of state is usually an elected president.

Revolutionary government
After a revolution, when a government is overthrown by force, the new regime is sometimes called a revolutionary government.

Totalitarian state
This is a state with only one political party, in which individuals are forced to obey the government and may also be prevented from leaving the country.

Transitional government
A government that is changing from one system to another is known as a transitional government. For example, a dictatorship may become a democracy after the dictator dies, but the transition between the systems can take several years.

GAZETTEER OF STATES

This gazetteer lists the world's 195 independent states, along with key facts about each one. In the lists of languages, the language that is most widely spoken is given first, even if it is not the official language. In the lists of religions, the one followed by the most people is also placed first. Every state has a national flag, which is usually used to represent the country abroad. A few states also have a state flag which they prefer to use instead. The state flags appear here with a dot beside them.

Afghanistan

Albania

Algeria

Andorra

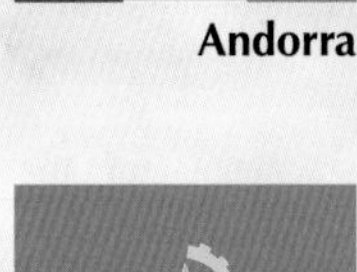
Angola

Antigua and Barbuda

• Argentina

AFGHANISTAN (Asia)
Area: 647,500 sq km (250,001 sq miles)
Population: 30,551,674
Capital city: Kabul
Main languages: Dari, Pashto
Main religion: Muslim
Government: Islamic republic
Currency: 1 afghani = 100 puls

ALBANIA (Europe)
Area: 28,748 sq km (11,100 sq miles)
Population: 3,173,271
Capital city: Tirana
Main language: Albanian
Main religions: Muslim, Albanian Orthodox
Government: democratic republic
Currency: 1 lek = 100 qintars

ALGERIA (Africa)
Area: 2,381,740 sq km (919,595 sq miles)
Population: 39,208,194
Capital city: Algiers
Main languages: Arabic, French, Berber dialects
Main religion: Sunni Muslim
Government: republic
Currency: 1 Algerian dinar = 100 centimes

ANDORRA (Europe)
Area: 468 sq km (181 sq miles)
Population: 79,218
Capital city: Andorra la Vella
Main languages: Catalan, Spanish
Main religion: Roman Catholic
Government: parliamentary democracy
Currency: 1 euro = 100 cents

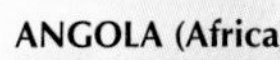

ANGOLA (Africa)
Area: 1,246,700 sq km (481,354 sq miles)
Population: 21,471,618
Capital city: Luanda
Main languages: Kilongo, Kimbundu, other Bantu languages, Portuguese
Main religions: indigenous, Roman Catholic, Protestant
Government: presidential republic
Currency: 1 kwanza = 100 centimos

ANTIGUA AND BARBUDA (North America)
Area: 443 sq km (171 sq miles)
Population: 89,985
Capital city: Saint John's
Main languages: Caribbean Creole, English
Main religion: Protestant
Government: constitutional monarchy
Currency: 1 East Caribbean dollar = 100 cents

ARGENTINA (South America)
Area: 2,766,890 sq km (1,068,302 sq miles)
Population: 41,446,246
Capital city: Buenos Aires
Main language: Spanish
Main religion: Roman Catholic
Government: republic
Currency: 1 peso = 100 centavos

ARMENIA (Asia)
Area: 29,743 sq km (11,484 sq miles)
Population: 2,976,566
Capital city: Yerevan
Main language: Armenian
Main religion: Armenian Orthodox
Government: republic
Currency: 1 dram = 100 luma

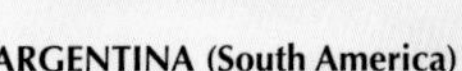

AUSTRALIA (Australasia/Oceania)
Area: 7,741,220 sq km (2,988,902 sq miles)
Population: 23,342,553
Capital city: Canberra
Main language: English
Main religion: Christian
Government: federal democratic monarchy
Currency: 1 Australian dollar = 100 cents

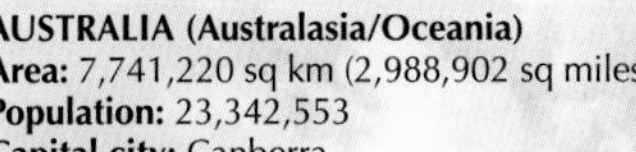

AUSTRIA (Europe)
Area: 83,870 sq km (32,382 sq miles)
Population: 8,495,145
Capital city: Vienna
Main language: German
Main religion: Roman Catholic
Government: federal republic
Currency: 1 euro = 100 cents

Armenia

Australia

Austria

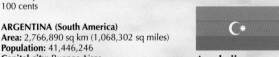

Azerbaijan

Bahamas, The

Bahrain

Bangladesh

Barbados

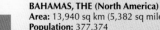

Belarus

Belgium

Belize

Benin

Bhutan

Bolivia

AZERBAIJAN (Asia)
Area: 86,600 sq km (33,436 sq miles)
Population: 9,413,420
Capital city: Baku
Main language: Azeri
Main religion: Muslim
Government: republic
Currency: 1 manat = 100 gopiks

BAHAMAS, THE (North America)
Area: 13,940 sq km (5,382 sq miles)
Population: 377,374
Capital city: Nassau
Main languages: Bahamian Creole, English
Main religion: Christian
Government: parliamentary democracy
Currency: 1 Bahamian dollar = 100 cents

BAHRAIN (Asia)
Area: 665 sq km (257 sq miles)
Population: 1,332,171
Capital city: Manama
Main languages: Arabic, English
Main religion: Muslim
Government: constitutional monarchy
Currency: 1 Bahraini dinar = 1,000 fils

BANGLADESH (Asia)
Area: 144,000 sq km (55,599 sq miles)
Population: 156,594,962
Capital city: Dhaka
Main languages: Bengali, English
Main religions: Muslim, Hindu
Government: parliamentary democracy
Currency: 1 taka = 100 poisha

BARBADOS (North America)
Area: 431 sq km (166 sq miles)
Population: 284,644
Capital city: Bridgetown
Main languages: Bajan, English
Main religion: Christian
Government: parliamentary democracy
Currency: 1 Barbadian dollar = 100 cents

BELARUS (Europe)
Area: 207,600 sq km (80,155 sq miles)
Population: 9,356,678
Capital city: Minsk
Main language: Belarusian
Main religion: Eastern Orthodox
Government: republic
Currency: 1 Belarusian ruble = 100 kopecks

BELGIUM (Europe)
Area: 30,528 sq km (11,787 sq miles)
Population: 11,104,476
Capital city: Brussels
Main languages: Dutch, French, German
Main religions: Roman Catholic, Protestant
Government: constitutional monarchy
Currency: 1 euro = 100 cents

BELIZE (North America)
Area: 22,966 sq km (8,867 sq miles)
Population: 331,900
Capital city: Belmopan
Main languages: Spanish, Belize Creole, English, Garifuna, Maya
Main religions: Roman Catholic, Protestant
Government: parliamentary democracy
Currency: 1 Belizean dollar = 100 cents

BENIN (Africa)
Area: 112,620 sq km (43,483 sq miles)
Population: 10,323,474
Capital city: Porto-Novo
Main languages: Fon, French, Yoruba, Adja
Main religions: indigenous, Christian, Muslim
Government: republic
Currency: 1 CFA* franc = 100 centimes

BHUTAN (Asia)
Area: 47,000 sq km (18,147 sq miles)
Population: 753,947
Capital city: Thimphu
Main languages: Dzongkha, Nepali
Main religions: Buddhist, Hindu
Government: constitutional monarchy
Currency: 1 ngultrum = 100 chetrum

BOLIVIA (South America)
Area: 1,098,580 sq km (424,164 sq miles)
Population: 10,671,200
Capital cities: La Paz/Sucre
Main languages: Spanish, Quechua, Aymara
Main religion: Roman Catholic
Government: republic
Currency: 1 boliviano = 100 centavos

BOSNIA AND HERZEGOVINA (Europe)
Area: 51,209 sq km (19,772 sq miles)
Population: 3,829,307
Capital city: Sarajevo
Main languages: Bosnian, Serbian, Croatian
Main religions: Muslim, Orthodox, Roman Catholic
Government: democratic federal republic
Currency: 1 marka = 100 feninga

BOTSWANA (Africa)
Area: 600,370 sq km (231,804 sq miles)
Population: 2,021,144
Capital city: Gaborone
Main languages: Setswana, Kalanga, English
Main religions: indigenous, Christian
Government: parliamentary republic
Currency: 1 pula = 100 thebe

BRAZIL (South America)
Area: 8,511,965 sq km (3,286,488 sq miles)
Population: 200,361,925
Capital city: Brasilia
Main language: Portuguese
Main religion: Roman Catholic
Government: federal republic
Currency: 1 real = 100 centavos

BRUNEI (Asia)
Area: 5,770 sq km (2,228 sq miles)
Population: 417,784
Capital city: Bandar Seri Begawan
Main languages: Malay, English, Chinese
Main religions: Muslim, Buddhist
Government: constitutional sultanate (a type of monarchy)
Currency: 1 Bruneian dollar = 100 cents

Bosnia and Herzegovina

Botswana

Brazil

Brunei

Bulgaria

Burkina Faso

Burma (Myanmar)

**CFA = Communaute Financiere Africaine*

GAZETTEER OF STATES CONTINUED:

Burundi

Cambodia

Cameroon

Canada

Cape Verde

Central African Republic

Chad

BULGARIA (Europe)
Area: 110,910 sq km (42,823 sq miles)
Population: 7,222,943
Capital city: Sofia
Main language: Bulgarian
Main religions: Bulgarian Orthodox, Muslim
Government: parliamentary democracy
Currency: 1 lev = 100 stotinki

BURKINA FASO (Africa)
Area: 274,200 sq km (105,869 sq miles)
Population: 16,934,839
Capital city: Ouagadougou
Main languages: Moore, Jula, French
Main religions: Muslim, indigenous
Government: parliamentary republic
Currency: 1 CFA* franc = 100 centimes

BURMA (MYANMAR) (Asia)
Area: 678,500 sq km (261,970 sq miles)
Population: 53,259,018
Capital city: Nay Pyi Taw
Main language: Burmese
Main religion: Buddhist
Government: military dictatorship
Currency: 1 kyat = 100 pyas

BURUNDI (Africa)
Area: 27,830 sq km (10,745 sq miles)
Population: 10,162,532
Capital city: Bujumbura
Main languages: Kirundi, French, Swahili
Main religions: Christian, indigenous
Government: republic
Currency: 1 Burundi franc = 100 centimes

CAMBODIA (Asia)
Area: 181,040 sq km (69,900 sq miles)
Population: 15,135,169
Capital city: Phnom Penh
Main language: Khmer, French
Main religion: Buddhist
Government: constitutional monarchy
Currency: 1 new riel = 100 sen

CAMEROON (Africa)
Area: 475,440 sq km (183,568 sq miles)
Population: 22,253,959
Capital city: Yaounde
Main languages: Cameroon Pidgin English, Ewondo, Fula, French, English
Main religions: indigenous, Christian, Muslim
Government: republic
Currency: 1 CFA* franc = 100 centimes

CANADA (North America)
Area: 9,984,670 sq km (3,855,103 sq miles)
Population: 35,181,704
Capital city: Ottawa
Main languages: English, French
Main religions: Roman Catholic, Protestant
Government: federal democracy
Currency: 1 Canadian dollar = 100 cents

CAPE VERDE (Africa)
Area: 4,033 sq km (1,557 sq miles)
Population: 498,897
Capital city: Praia
Main languages: Crioulo*, Portuguese
Main religions: Roman Catholic, Protestant
Government: republic
Currency: 1 Cape Verdean escudo = 100 centavos

CENTRAL AFRICAN REPUBLIC (Africa)
Area: 622,984 sq km (240,535 sq miles)
Population: 4,616,417
Capital city: Bangui
Main languages: Sangho, French
Main religions: indigenous, Christian, Muslim
Government: republic
Currency: 1 CFA* franc = 100 centimes

CHAD (Africa)
Area: 1,284,000 sq km (495,755 sq miles)
Population: 12,825,314
Capital city: N'Djamena
Main languages: Arabic, Sara, French
Main religions: Muslim, Christian, indigenous
Government: republic
Currency: 1 CFA* franc = 100 centimes

CHILE (South America)
Area: 756,950 sq km (292,260 sq miles)
Population: 17,619,708
Capital city: Santiago
Main language: Spanish
Main religions: Roman Catholic, Protestant
Government: republic
Currency: 1 Chilean peso = 100 centavos

CHINA (Asia)
Area: 9,596,960 sq km (3,705,407 sq miles)
Population: 1,385,566,537
Capital city: Beijing
Main languages: Mandarin Chinese, Yue, Wu
Main religions: Taoist, Buddhist
Government: communist republic
Currency: 1 yuan = 10 jiao

COLOMBIA (South America)
Area: 1,138,910 sq km (439,736 sq miles)
Population: 48,321,405
Capital city: Bogota
Main language: Spanish
Main religion: Roman Catholic
Government: republic
Currency: 1 Colombian peso = 100 centavos

COMOROS (Africa)
Area: 2,170 sq km (838 sq miles)
Population: 734,917
Capital city: Moroni
Main languages: Comorian*, French, Arabic
Main religion: Sunni Muslim
Government: republic
Currency: 1 Comoran franc = 100 centimes

CONGO (Africa)
Area: 342,000 sq km (132,047 sq miles)
Population: 4,447,632
Capital city: Brazzaville
Main languages: Munukutuba, Lingala, French
Main religions: Christian, animist
Government: republic
Currency: 1 CFA* franc = 100 centimes

Chile

China

Colombia

Comoros

Congo

Congo (Democratic Republic)

Costa Rica

**CFA = Communaute Financiere Africaine; Comorian = a blend of Swahili and Arabic; Crioulo = a blend of Portuguese and West African*

Croatia

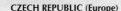

Cuba

Cyprus

Czech Republic

Denmark

Djibouti

Dominica

CONGO (DEMOCRATIC REPUBLIC) (Africa)
Area: 2,345,410 sq km (905,568 sq miles)
Population: 67,513,677
Capital city: Kinshasa
Main languages: Lingala, Swahili, Kikongo, Tshiluba, French, Kingwana
Main religions: Roman Catholic, Protestant, Kimbanguist, Muslim
Government: republic
Currency: 1 Congolese franc = 100 centimes

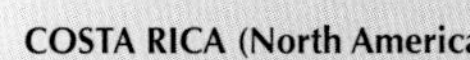

COSTA RICA (North America)
Area: 51,100 sq km (19,730 sq miles)
Population: 4,872,166
Capital city: San Jose
Main language: Spanish
Main religions: Roman Catholic, Evangelical
Government: democratic republic
Currency: 1 Costa Rican colon = 100 centimos

CROATIA (Europe)
Area: 56,542 sq km (21,831 sq miles)
Population: 4,289,714
Capital city: Zagreb
Main language: Croatian
Main religions: Roman Catholic, Orthodox
Government: republic
Currency: 1 kuna = 100 lipas

CUBA (North America)
Area: 110,860 sq km (42,803 sq miles)
Population: 11,265,629
Capital city: Havana
Main language: Spanish
Main religion: Roman Catholic
Government: communist republic
Currency: 1 Cuban peso = 100 centavos

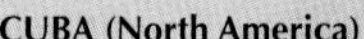

CYPRUS (Europe)
Area: 9,250 sq km (3,571 sq miles)
Population: 1,141,166
Capital city: Nicosia
Main languages: Greek, Turkish, English
Main religions: Greek Orthodox, Muslim
Government: republic with a self-proclaimed independent Turkish area
Currency: Greek Cypriot area: 1 euro = 100 cents; Turkish Cypriot area: 1 Turkish lira = 100 kurus

CZECH REPUBLIC (Europe)
Area: 78,866 sq km (30,450 sq miles)
Population: 10,702,197
Capital city: Prague
Main language: Czech
Main religion: Roman Catholic
Government: republic
Currency: 1 koruna = 100 haleru

DENMARK (Europe)
Area: 43,094 sq km (16,639 sq miles)
Population: 5,619,096
Capital city: Copenhagen
Main language: Danish
Main religion: Evangelical Lutheran
Government: constitutional monarchy
Currency: 1 Danish krone = 100 oere

DJIBOUTI (Africa)
Area: 23,000 sq km (8,880 sq miles)
Population: 872,932
Capital city: Djibouti
Main languages: Afar, Somali, Arabic, French
Main religion: Muslim
Government: republic
Currency: 1 Djiboutian franc = 100 centimes

DOMINICA (North America)
Area: 754 sq km (291 sq miles)
Population: 72,003
Capital city: Roseau
Main languages: English, French patois
Main religions: Roman Catholic, Protestant
Government: democratic republic
Currency: 1 East Caribbean dollar = 100 cents

DOMINICAN REPUBLIC (North America)
Area: 48,380 sq km (18,680 sq miles)
Population: 10,219,630
Capital city: Santo Domingo
Main language: Spanish
Main religion: Roman Catholic
Government: democratic republic
Currency: 1 Dominican peso = 100 centavos

EAST TIMOR (Asia)
Area: 15,007 sq km (5,794 sq miles)
Population: 1,132,879
Capital city: Dili
Main languages: Tetun (Tetum), Bahasa Indonesia, Portuguese
Main religions: Roman Catholic, animist
Government: republic
Currency: 1 U.S. dollar = 100 cents

ECUADOR (South America)
Area: 283,560 sq km (109,483 sq miles)
Population: 15,737,878
Capital city: Quito
Main languages: Spanish, Quechua
Main religion: Roman Catholic
Government: republic
Currency: 1 U.S. dollar = 100 cents

EGYPT (Africa)
Area: 1,001,450 sq km (386,662 sq miles)
Population: 82,056,378
Capital city: Cairo
Main language: Arabic
Main religion: Sunni Muslim
Government: transitional
Currency: 1 Egyptian pound = 100 piasters

EL SALVADOR (North America)
Area: 21,040 sq km (8,124 sq miles)
Population: 6,340,454
Capital city: San Salvador
Main language: Spanish
Main religion: Roman Catholic
Government: republic
Currency: 1 U.S. dollar = 100 cents

EQUATORIAL GUINEA (Africa)
Area: 28,050 sq km (10,830 sq miles)
Population: 757,014
Capital city: Malabo
Main languages: Fang, Bubi, other Bantu

• Dominican Republic

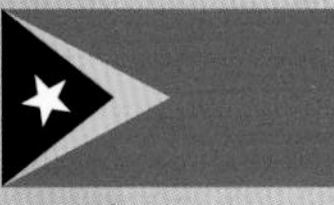

East Timor

• Ecuador

Egypt

• El Salvador

Equatorial Guinea

Eritrea

*CFA = Communaute Financiere Africaine

GAZETTEER OF STATES CONTINUED:

Estonia

Ethiopia

Federated States of Micronesia

Fiji

Finland

France

Gabon

languages, Spanish, French, Pidgin English
Main religion: Christian
Government: republic
Currency: 1 CFA* franc = 100 centimes

ERITREA (Africa)
Area: 121,320 sq km (46,842 sq miles)
Population: 6,333,135
Capital city: Asmara
Main languages: Tigrinya, Afar, Arabic
Main religions: Muslim, Coptic Christian, Roman Catholic, Protestant
Government: republic
Currency: 1 nafka = 100 cents

ESTONIA (Europe)
Area: 45,226 sq km (17,462 sq miles)
Population: 1,287,251
Capital city: Tallinn
Main languages: Estonian, Russian
Main religions: Evangelical Lutheran, Russian and Estonian Orthodox, other Christian
Government: parliamentary democracy
Currency: 1 Euro = 100 cents

ETHIOPIA (Africa)
Area: 1,127,127 sq km (435,186 sq miles)
Population: 94,100,756
Capital city: Addis Ababa
Main languages: Amharic, Tigrinya, Arabic
Main religions: Muslim, Ethiopian Orthodox, animist
Government: federal republic
Currency: 1 birr = 100 santim

FEDERATED STATES OF MICRONESIA (Australasia/Oceania)
Area: 702 sq km (271 sq miles)
Population: 103,549
Capital city: Palikir
Main languages: Chuuk, Ponapean, English
Main religions: Roman Catholic, Protestant
Government: federal republic
Currency: 1 U.S. dollar = 100 cents

FIJI (Australasia/Oceania)
Area: 18,270 sq km (7,054 sq miles)
Population: 881,065
Capital city: Suva
Main languages: Fijian, Hindustani, English
Main religions: Christian, Hindu
Government: republic
Currency: 1 Fijian dollar = 100 cents

FINLAND (Europe)
Area: 338,145 sq km (130,559 sq miles)
Population: 5,426,323
Capital city: Helsinki
Main language: Finnish, Swedish
Main religion: Evangelical Lutheran
Government: republic
Currency: 1 euro = 100 cents

FRANCE (Europe)
Area: 547,030 sq km (211,209 sq miles)
Population: 64,291,280
Capital city: Paris
Main language: French
Main religion: Roman Catholic
Government: republic
Currency: 1 euro = 100 cents

GABON (Africa)
Area: 267,667 sq km (103,347 sq miles)
Population: 1,671,711
Capital city: Libreville
Main languages: Fang, Myene, French
Main religions: Christian, animist
Government: republic
Currency: 1 CFA* franc = 100 centimes

GAMBIA, THE (Africa)
Area: 11,300 sq km (4,363 sq miles)
Population: 1,849,285
Capital city: Banjul
Main languages: Mandinka, Fula, Wolof, English
Main religion: Muslim
Government: democratic republic
Currency: 1 dalasi = 100 butut

GEORGIA (Asia)
Area: 69,700 sq km (26,911 sq miles)
Population: 4,340,895
Capital city: Tbilisi
Main languages: Georgian, Russian
Main religions: Georgian Orthodox, Muslim, Russian Orthodox
Government: republic
Currency: 1 lari = 100 tetri

GERMANY (Europe)
Area: 357,021 sq km (137,847 sq miles)
Population: 82,726,626
Capital city: Berlin
Main language: German
Main religions: Protestant, Roman Catholic
Government: federal republic
Currency: 1 euro = 100 cents

GHANA (Africa)
Area: 239,460 sq km (92,456 sq miles)
Population: 25,904,598
Capital city: Accra
Main languages: Twi, Fante, Ga, Hausa, Dagbani, Ewe, Nzemi, English
Main religions: indigenous, Muslim, Christian
Government: republic
Currency: 1 new cedi = 100 pesewas

GREECE (Europe)
Area: 131,940 sq km (50,942 sq miles)
Population: 11,127,990
Capital city: Athens
Main language: Greek
Main religion: Greek Orthodox
Government: parliamentary republic
Currency: 1 euro = 100 cents

GRENADA (North America)
Area: 344 sq km (133 sq miles)
Population: 105,897
Capital city: Saint George's
Main languages: English, French patois
Main religions: Roman Catholic, Protestant
Government: parliamentary democracy
Currency: 1 East Caribbean dollar = 100 cents

Gambia, The

Georgia

Germany

Ghana

Greece

Grenada

Guatemala

*CFA = Communaute Financiere Africaine

Guinea

Guinea-Bissau

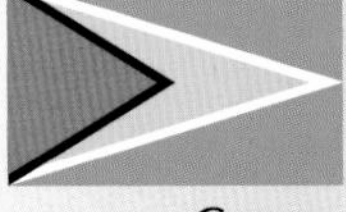

Guyana

Haiti

Honduras

Hungary

Iceland

GUATEMALA (North America)
Area: 108,890 sq km (42,043 sq miles)
Population: 15,468,203
Capital city: Guatemala City
Main languages: Spanish, Amerindian languages including Quiche, Kekchi, Cakchiquel, Mam
Main religions: Roman Catholic, Protestant, indigenous Mayan beliefs
Government: democratic republic
Currency: 1 quetzal = 100 centavos

GUINEA (Africa)
Area: 245,857 sq km (94,926 sq miles)
Population: 11,745,189
Capital city: Conakry
Main languages: Fuuta Jalon, Mallinke, Susu, French
Main religion: Muslim
Government: republic
Currency: 1 Guinean franc = 100 centimes

GUINEA-BISSAU (Africa)
Area: 36,120 sq km (13,946 sq miles)
Population: 1,704,255
Capital city: Bissau
Main languages: Crioulo*, Balante, Pulaar, Mandjak, Mandinka, Portuguese
Main religions: indigenous, Muslim
Government: republic
Currency: 1 CFA* franc = 100 centimes

GUYANA (South America)
Area: 214,970 sq km (83,000 sq miles)
Population: 799,613
Capital city: Georgetown
Main languages: Guyanese Creole, English, Amerindian languages, Caribbean Hindi
Main religions: Christian, Hindu
Government: republic
Currency: 1 Guyanese dollar = 100 cents

HAITI (North America)
Area: 27,750 sq km (10,714 sq miles)
Population: 10,317,461
Capital city: Port-au-Prince
Main languages: Haitian Creole, French
Main religions: Roman Catholic, Protestant, Voodoo
Government: republic
Currency: 1 gourde = 100 centimes

HONDURAS (North America)
Area: 112,090 sq km (43,278 sq miles)
Population: 8,097,688
Capital city: Tegucigalpa
Main language: Spanish
Main religion: Roman Catholic
Government: republic
Currency: 1 lempira = 100 centavos

HUNGARY (Europe)
Area: 93,030 sq km (35,919 sq miles)
Population: 9,954,941
Capital city: Budapest
Main language: Hungarian
Main religions: Roman Catholic, Calvinist
Government: republic
Currency: 1 forint = 100 filler

ICELAND (Europe)
Area: 103,000 sq km (39,769 sq miles)
Population: 329,535
Capital city: Reykjavik
Main language: Icelandic
Main religion: Evangelical Lutheran
Government: constitutional republic
Currency: Icelandic krona (plural: kronur)

INDIA (Asia)
Area: 3,287,590 sq km (1,269,346 sq miles)
Population: 1,252,139,596
Capital city: New Delhi
Main languages: Hindi, English, Bengali, Urdu, over 1,600 other languages and dialects
Main religions: Hindu, Muslim
Government: federal republic
Currency: 1 Indian rupee = 100 paise

INDONESIA (Asia)
Area: 1,919,440 sq km (741,100 sq miles)
Population: 249,865,631
Capital city: Jakarta
Main languages: Bahasa Indonesia, English, Dutch, Javanese
Main religion: Muslim
Government: republic
Currency: 1 Indonesian rupiah = 100 sen

IRAN (Asia)
Area: 1,648,000 sq km (636,296 sq miles)
Population: 77,447,168
Capital city: Tehran
Main languages: Farsi and other Persian dialects, Azeri
Main religions: Shi'a Muslim, Sunni Muslim
Government: Islamic republic
Currency: 10 Iranian rials = 1 toman

IRAQ (Asia)
Area: 437,072 sq km (168,754 sq miles)
Population: 33,765,232
Capital city: Baghdad
Main languages: Arabic, Kurdish
Main religion: Muslim
Government: democratic federal republic
Currency: 1 Iraqi dinar = 1,000 fulus

IRELAND (Europe)
Area: 70,280 sq km (27,135 sq miles)
Population: 4,627,173
Capital city: Dublin
Main languages: English, Irish (Gaelic)
Main religion: Roman Catholic
Government: republic
Currency: 1 euro = 100 cents

ISRAEL (Asia)
Area: 20,770 sq km (8,019 sq miles)
Population: 7,733,144
Capital city: Jerusalem
Main languages: Hebrew, Arabic
Main religions: Jewish, Muslim
Government: republic
Currency: 1 Israeli shekel = 100 agorot

ITALY (Europe)
Area: 301,230 sq km (116,306 sq miles)

India

Indonesia

Iran

Iraq

Ireland

Israel

Italy

**CFA = Communaute Financiere Africaine; Crioulo = a blend of Portuguese and West African*

GAZETTEER OF STATES CONTINUED:

Population: 60,990,277
Capital city: Rome
Main language: Italian, French, German
Main religion: Roman Catholic
Government: republic
Currency: 1 euro = 100 cents

Ivory Coast

IVORY COAST (Africa)
Area: 322,460 sq km (124,503 sq miles)
Population: 20,316,086
Capital city: Yamoussoukro
Main languages: Baoule, Dioula, French
Main religions: Christian, Muslim, animist
Government: republic
Currency: 1 CFA* = 100 centimes

Jamaica

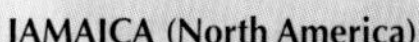

JAMAICA (North America)
Area: 10,991 sq km (4,244 sq miles)
Population: 2,783,888
Capital city: Kingston
Main languages: Southwestern Caribbean Creole, English
Main religion: Protestant
Government: parliamentary democracy
Currency: 1 Jamaican dollar = 100 cents

Japan

JAPAN (Asia)
Area: 377,835 sq km (145,883 sq miles)
Population: 127,143,577
Capital city: Tokyo
Main language: Japanese
Main religions: Shinto, Buddhist
Government: parliamentary monarchy
Currency: 1 yen = 100 sen

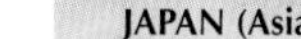

Jordan

JORDAN (Asia)
Area: 92,300 sq km (35,637 sq miles)
Population: 7,273,799
Capital city: Amman
Main languages: Arabic, English
Main religion: Sunni Muslim
Government: constitutional monarchy
Currency: 1 Jordanian dinar = 1,000 fulus

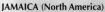

Kazakhstan

KAZAKHSTAN (Asia)
Area: 2,717,300 sq km (1,049,155 sq miles)
Population: 16,440,586
Capital city: Astana
Main languages: Kazakh, Russian
Main religions: Muslim, Russian Orthodox
Government: republic
Currency: 1 Kazakhstani tenge = 100 tiyin

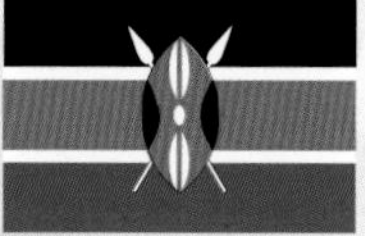
Kenya

KENYA (Africa)
Area: 582,650 sq km (224,962 sq miles)
Population: 44,353,691
Capital city: Nairobi
Main languages: Swahili, English, Kiswahili, Bantu languages
Main religions: Christian, indigenous
Government: republic
Currency: 1 Kenyan shilling = 100 cents

Kiribati

KIRIBATI (Australasia/Oceania)
Area: 811 sq km (313 sq miles)
Population: 102,351
Capital city: Bairiki
Main languages: Gilbertese, i-Kiribati, English
Main religions: Roman Catholic, Protestant
Government: republic
Currency: 1 Australian dollar = 100 cents

Kosovo

KOSOVO (Europe)
Area: 10,887 sq km (4,203 sq miles)
Population: 1,815,606
Capital city: Pristina
Main languages: Albanian, Serbian, Bosnian, Turkish
Main religion: Muslim, Serbian Orthodox, Roman Catholic
Government: republic
Currency: 1 euro = 100 cents

Kuwait

KUWAIT (Asia)
Area: 17,820 sq km (6,880 sq miles)
Population: 3,368,572
Capital city: Kuwait City
Main languages: Arabic, English
Main religion: Muslim
Government: constitutional monarchy
Currency: 1 Kuwaiti dinar = 1,000 fulus

Kyrgyzstan

KYRGYZSTAN (Asia)
Area: 198,500 sq km (76,641 sq miles)
Population: 5,547,548
Capital city: Bishkek
Main languages: Kyrgyz, Russian, Uzbek
Main religions: Muslim, Russian Orthodox
Government: republic
Currency: 1 Kyrgyzstani som = 100 tyiyn

Laos

LAOS (Asia)
Area: 236,800 sq km (91,429 sq miles)
Population: 6,769,727
Capital city: Vientiane
Main languages: Lao, French, English
Main religions: Buddhist, animist
Government: communist republic
Currency: 1 new kip = 100 at

Latvia

LATVIA (Europe)
Area: 64,589 sq km (24,938 sq miles)
Population: 2,050,317
Capital city: Riga
Main languages: Latvian, Russian
Main religions: Lutheran, Roman Catholic, Russian Orthodox
Government: republic
Currency: 1 euro = 100 cents**

Lebanon

LEBANON (Asia)
Area: 10,400 sq km (4,015 sq miles)
Population: 4,821,971
Capital city: Beirut
Main languages: Arabic, French, English
Main religions: Muslim, Christian
Government: republic
Currency: 1 Lebanese pound = 100 piasters

Lesotho

LESOTHO (Africa)
Area: 30,355 sq km (11,720 sq miles)
Population: 2,074,465
Capital city: Maseru
Main languages: Sesotho, English, Zulu, Xhosa
Main religions: Christian, indigenous
Government: constitutional monarchy
Currency: 1 loti = 100 lisente

LIBERIA (Africa)
Area: 111,370 sq km (43,000 sq miles)

**CFA = Communaute Financiere Africaine; **From 2014, replacing Latvian lats and santims*

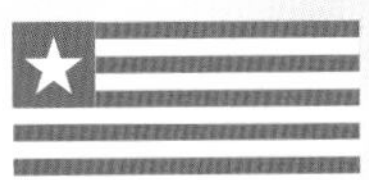

Liberia

Libya

Liechtenstein

Lithuania

Luxembourg

Macedonia

Madagascar

Population: 4,294,077
Capital city: Monrovia
Main languages: Kpelle, English, Bassa
Main religions: indigenous, Christian, Muslim
Government: republic
Currency: 1 Liberian dollar = 100 cents

LIBYA (Africa)
Area: 1,759,540 sq km (679,362 sq miles)
Population: 6,201,521
Capital city: Tripoli
Main languages: Arabic, Italian, English
Main religion: Sunni Muslim
Government: emerging democratic republic
Currency: 1 Libyan dinar = 1,000 dirhams

LIECHTENSTEIN (Europe)
Area: 160 sq km (62 sq miles)
Population: 36,925
Capital city: Vaduz
Main languages: German
Main religion: Roman Catholic
Government: constitutional monarchy
Currency: 1 Swiss franc = 100 centimes

LITHUANIA (Europe)
Area: 65,300 sq km (25,212 sq miles)
Population: 3,016,933
Capital city: Vilnius
Main languages: Lithuanian, Polish, Russian
Main religions: Roman Catholic, Lutheran, Russian Orthodox
Government: parliamentary democracy
Currency: 1 Lithuanian litas = 100 centas

LUXEMBOURG (Europe)
Area: 2,586 sq km (998 sq miles)
Population: 530,380
Capital city: Luxembourg
Main languages: Luxembourgish, German, French
Main religion: Roman Catholic
Government: constitutional monarchy
Currency: 1 euro = 100 cents

MACEDONIA (Europe)
Area: 25,333 sq km (9,781 sq miles)
Population: 2,107,158
Capital city: Skopje
Main languages: Macedonian, Albanian
Main religions: Macedonian Orthodox, Muslim
Government: republic
Currency: 1 Macedonian denar = 100 deni

MADAGASCAR (Africa)
Area: 587,040 sq km (226,657 sq miles)
Population: 22,924,851
Capital city: Antananarivo
Main languages: Malagasy, French, Cotiers
Main religions: indigenous beliefs, Christian
Government: republic
Currency: 1 ariary = 5 iraimbilanja

MALAWI (Africa)
Area: 118,480 sq km (45,745 sq miles)
Population: 16,362,567
Capital city: Lilongwe
Main languages: Chichewa, English, Chinyanja
Main religions: Protestant, Roman Catholic, Muslim
Government: republic
Currency: 1 Malawian kwacha = 100 tambala

MALAYSIA (Asia)
Area: 329,750 sq km (127,317 sq miles)
Population: 29,716,965
Capital city: Kuala Lumpur
Main languages: Bahasa Melayu, English, Chinese dialects, Tamil
Main religions: Muslim, Buddhist, Daoist
Government: constitutional monarchy
Currency: 1 ringgit = 100 sen

MALDIVES (Asia)
Area: 300 sq km (116 sq miles)
Population: 345,023
Capital city: Male
Main languages: Maldivian, English
Main religion: Sunni Muslim
Government: republic
Currency: 1 rufiyaa = 100 laari

MALI (Africa)
Area: 1,240,000 sq km (478,767 sq miles)
Population: 15,301,650
Capital city: Bamako
Main languages: Bambara, Fulani, Songhai, French
Main religion: Muslim
Government: republic
Currency: 1 CFA* franc = 100 centimes

MALTA (Europe)
Area: 316 sq km (122 sq miles)
Population: 429,004
Capital city: Valletta
Main languages: Maltese, English
Main religion: Roman Catholic
Government: democratic republic
Currency: 1 euro = 100 cents

MARSHALL ISLANDS (Australasia/Oceania)
Area: 181 sq km (70 sq miles)
Population: 52,634
Capital city: Majuro
Main languages: Marshallese, English
Main religion: Protestant
Government: republic
Currency: 1 U.S. dollar = 100 cents

MAURITANIA (Africa)
Area: 1,030,700 sq km (397,955 sq miles)
Population: 3,889,880
Capital city: Nouakchott
Main languages: Arabic, Wolof, French
Main religion: Muslim
Government: Islamic republic
Currency: 1 ouguiya = 5 khoums

MAURITIUS (Africa)
Area: 2,040 sq km (788 sq miles)
Population: 1,244,403
Capital city: Port Louis
Main languages: Mauritius Creole French, French, Hindi, Bhojpuri, Urdu, Tamil, English
Main religion: Hindu, Christian, English
Government: parliamentary democracy
Currency: 1 Mauritian rupee = 100 cents

Malawi

Malaysia

Maldives

Mali

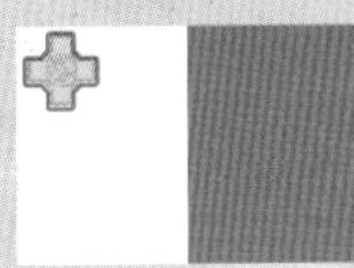

Malta

Marshall Islands

Mauritania

**CFA = Communaute Financiere Africaine*

GAZETTEER OF STATES CONTINUED:

Mauritius

MEXICO (North America)
Nationality: Mexican
Area: 1,972,550 sq km (761,606 sq miles)
Population: 122,332,399
Capital city: Mexico City
Main languages: Spanish, Mayan, Nahuatl
Main religion: Roman Catholic, Protestant
Government: federal republic
Currency: 1 new Mexican peso = 100 centavos

Mexico

MOLDOVA (Europe)
Area: 33,843 sq km (13,067 sq miles)
Population: 3,487,204
Capital city: Chisinau
Main languages: Moldovan, Russian, Gagauz
Main religion: Eastern Orthodox
Government: republic
Currency: 1 Moldovan leu = 100 bani

Moldova

MONACO (Europe)
Area: 1.95 sq km (0.75 sq miles)
Population: 37,831
Capital city: Monaco
Main languages: French, Monegasque, Italian
Main religion: Roman Catholic
Government: constitutional monarchy
Currency: 1 euro = 100 cents

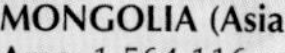

MONGOLIA (Asia)
Area: 1,564,116 sq km (603,909 sq miles)
Population: 2,839,073
Capital city: Ulan Bator
Main language: Khalkha Mongol
Main religion: Tibetan Buddhist Lamaist
Government: republic
Currency: Mongolian tugrik

Monaco

MONTENEGRO (Europe)
Area: 14,026 sq km (5,415 sq miles)
Population: 621,383
Capital city: Podgorica
Main language: Serbian, Montenegrin
Main religion: Orthodox Christian, Muslim
Government: republic
Currency: 1 euro = 100 cents

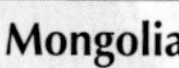
Mongolia

MOROCCO (Africa)
Area: 446,550 sq km (172,414 sq miles)
Population: 33,008,150
Capital city: Rabat
Main languages: Arabic, Berber, French
Main religion: Muslim
Government: constitutional monarchy
Currency: 1 Moroccan dirham = 100 centimes

Montenegro

MOZAMBIQUE (Africa)
Area: 801,590 sq km (309,496 sq miles)
Population: 25,833,752
Capital city: Maputo
Main languages: Makua, Tsonga, Portuguese, Emskhuwa, Xichangana
Main religions: indigenous, Christian, Muslim
Government: republic
Currency: 1 metical = 100 centavos

Morocco

NAMIBIA (Africa)
Area: 825,418 sq km (318,696 sq miles)
Population: 2,303,315
Capital city: Windhoek
Main languages: Afrikaans, German, English
Main religions: Christian, indigenous
Government: republic
Currency: 1 Namibian dollar = 100 cents

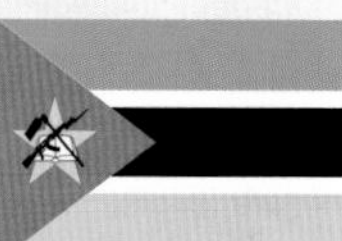
Mozambique

NAURU (Australasia/Oceania)
Area: 21 sq km (8 sq miles)
Population: 10,051
Capital: Yaren
Main languages: Nauruan, English
Main religion: Christian
Government: republic
Currency: 1 Australian dollar = 100 cents

Namibia

NEPAL (Asia)
Area: 147,181 sq km (56,827 sq miles)
Population: 27,797,457
Capital city: Kathmandu
Main languages: Nepali, Maithili
Main religions: Hindu, Buddhist
Government: federal republic
Currency: 1 Nepalese rupee = 100 paisa

Nauru

NETHERLANDS (Europe)
Area: 41,526 sq km (16,033 sq miles)
Population: 16,759,229
Capital cities: Amsterdam, The Hague
Main language: Dutch
Main religion: Protestant, Roman Catholic
Government: constitutional monarchy
Currency: 1 euro = 100 cents

NEW ZEALAND (Australasia/Oceania)
Area: 268,680 sq km (103,738 sq miles)
Population: 4,505,761
Capital city: Wellington
Main languages: English, Maori
Main religion: Christian
Government: parliamentary democracy
Currency: 1 New Zealand dollar = 100 cents

Nepal

NICARAGUA (North America)
Area: 129,494 sq km (49,998 sq miles)
Population: 6,080,478
Capital city: Managua
Main language: Spanish
Main religion: Roman Catholic, Protestant
Government: republic
Currency: 1 gold cordoba = 100 centavos

Netherlands

NIGER (Africa)
Area: 1,267,000 sq km (489,191 sq miles)
Population: 17,831,270
Capital city: Niamey
Main languages: Hausa, Djerma, French
Main religion: Muslim
Government: republic
Currency: 1 CFA* franc = 100 centimes

New Zealand

NIGERIA (Africa)
Area: 923,768 sq km (356,669 sq miles)
Population: 173,615,345
Capital city: Abuja
Main languages: Hausa, Yoruba, Igbo, English, Fulani
Main religions: Muslim, Christian, indigenous
Government: federal republic
Currency: 1 naira = 100 kobo

Nicaragua

**CFA = Communaute Financiere Africaine*

Niger

Nigeria

North Korea

Norway

Oman

Pakistan

Palau

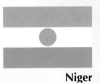

NORTH KOREA (Asia)
Area: 120,540 sq km (46,541 sq miles)
Population: 24,895,480
Capital city: Pyongyang
Main language: Korean
Main religions: Buddhist, Confucian
Government: authoritarian socialist
Currency: 1 North Korean won = 100 chon

NORWAY (Europe)
Area: 323,802 sq km (125,021 sq miles)
Population: 5,042,671
Capital city: Oslo
Main language: Norwegian
Main religion: Evangelical Lutheran
Government: constitutional monarchy
Currency: 1 Norwegian krone = 100 oere

OMAN (Asia)
Area: 212,460 sq km (82,031 sq miles)
Population: 3,632,444
Capital city: Muscat
Main languages: Arabic, English, Baluchi
Main religion: Muslim
Government: monarchy
Currency: 1 Omani rial = 1,000 baiza

PAKISTAN (Asia)
Area: 803,940 sq km (310,403 sq miles)
Population: 182,142,594
Capital city: Islamabad
Main languages: Punjabi, Sindhi, Urdu, English
Main religion: Muslim
Government: federal republic
Currency: 1 Pakistani rupee = 100 paisa

PALAU (Australasia/Oceania)
Area: 458 sq km (177 sq miles)
Population: 20,918
Capital city: Melekeok
Main languages: Palauan, English, Philipino
Main religions: Christian, Modekngei
Government: democratic republic
Currency: 1 U.S. dollar = 100 cents

PANAMA (North America)
Area: 78,200 sq km (30,193 sq miles)
Population: 3,864,170
Capital city: Panama City
Main languages: Spanish, English
Main religions: Roman Catholic, Protestant
Government: democracy
Currency: 1 balboa = 100 centesimos

PAPUA NEW GUINEA (Australasia/Oceania)
Area: 462,840 sq km (178,704 sq miles)
Population: 7,321,262
Capital city: Port Moresby
Main languages: Tok Pisin, Hiri Motu, English
Main religions: Christian, indigenous
Government: parliamentary democracy
Currency: 1 kina = 100 toea

PARAGUAY (South America)
Area: 406,750 sq km (157,047 sq miles)
Population: 6,802,295
Capital city: Asuncion
Main languages: Guarani, Spanish
Main religion: Roman Catholic
Government: republic
Currency: 1 guarani = 100 centimos

PERU (South America)
Area: 1,285,220 sq km (496,226 sq miles)
Population: 30,375,603
Capital city: Lima
Main languages: Spanish, Quechua, Aymara
Main religion: Roman Catholic
Government: republic
Currency: 1 nuevo sol = 100 centimos

PHILIPPINES (Asia)
Area: 300,000 sq km (115,831 sq miles)
Population: 98,393,574
Capital city: Manila
Main languages: Tagalog, English, Ilocano, Cebuano
Main religion: Roman Catholic
Government: republic
Currency: 1 Philippine peso = 100 centavos

POLAND (Europe)
Area: 312,679 sq km (120,726 sq miles)
Population: 38,216,635
Capital city: Warsaw
Main language: Polish
Main religion: Roman Catholic
Government: democratic republic
Currency: 1 zloty = 100 groszy

PORTUGAL (Europe)
Area: 92,391 sq km (35,672 sq miles)
Population: 10,608,156
Capital city: Lisbon
Main language: Portuguese
Main religion: Roman Catholic
Government: democratic republic
Currency: 1 euro = 100 cents

QATAR (Asia)
Area: 11,437 sq km (4,416 sq miles)
Population: 2,168,673
Capital city: Doha
Main languages: Arabic, English
Main religion: Muslim
Government: monarchy
Currency: 1 Qatari riyal = 100 dirhams

ROMANIA (Europe)
Area: 237,500 sq km (91,699 sq miles)
Population: 21,698,585
Capital city: Bucharest
Main languages: Romanian, Hungarian, German
Main religion: Romanian Orthodox
Government: republic
Currency: 1 leu = 100 bani

RUSSIA (Europe and Asia)
Area: 17,075,200 sq km (6,592,772 sq miles)
Population: 142,833,689
Capital city: Moscow
Main language: Russian
Main religions: Russian Orthodox, Muslim
Government: federal government
Currency: 1 ruble = 100 kopeks

Panama

Papua New Guinea

Paraguay

• Peru

Philippines

Poland

Portugal

GAZETTEER OF STATES CONTINUED:

Qatar

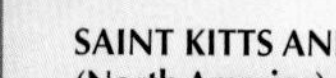

Romania

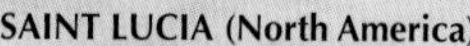

Russia

Rwanda

Saint Kitts and Nevis

Saint Lucia

Saint Vincent and the Grenadines

RWANDA (Africa)
Area: 26,338 sq km (10,169 sq miles)
Population: 11,776,522
Capital city: Kigali
Main languages: Kinyarwanda, French, English, Swahili
Main religions: Roman Catholic, Protestant, Adventist
Government: republic
Currency: 1 Rwandan franc = 100 centimes

SAINT KITTS AND NEVIS (North America)
Area: 261 sq km (101 sq miles)
Population: 54,191
Capital city: Basseterre
Main language: English
Main religions: Protestant, Roman Catholic
Government: constitutional monarchy
Currency: 1 East Caribbean dollar = 100 cents

SAINT LUCIA (North America)
Area: 616 sq km (238 sq miles)
Population: 182,273
Capital city: Castries
Main languages: French patois, English
Main religion: Roman Catholic, Protestant
Government: parliamentary democracy
Currency: 1 East Caribbean dollar = 100 cents

SAINT VINCENT AND THE GRENADINES (North America)
Area: 389 sq km (150 sq miles)
Population: 109,373
Capital city: Kingstown
Main languages: English, French patois
Main religions: Protestant, Roman Catholic
Government: parliamentary democracy
Currency: 1 East Caribbean dollar = 100 cents

SAMOA (Australasia/Oceania)
Area: 2,944 sq km (1,137 sq miles)
Population: 190,372
Capital city: Apia
Main languages: Samoan, English
Main religion: Christian
Government: constitutional monarchy
Currency: 1 tala = 100 sene

SAN MARINO (Europe)
Area: 61 sq km (24 sq miles)
Population: 31,448
Capital city: San Marino
Main language: Italian
Main religion: Roman Catholic
Government: republic
Currency: 1 euro = 100 cents

SAO TOME AND PRINCIPE (Africa)
Area: 1,001 sq km (386 sq miles)
Population: 192,993
Capital city: Sao Tome
Main languages: Crioulo* dialects, Portuguese
Main religion: Christian
Government: republic
Currency: 1 dobra = 100 centimos

SAUDI ARABIA (Asia)
Area: 2,149,690 sq km (830,000 sq miles)
Population: 28,828,870
Capital city: Riyadh
Main language: Arabic
Main religion: Muslim
Government: monarchy
Currency: 1 Saudi riyal = 100 halalah

SENEGAL (Africa)
Area: 196,190 sq km (75,749 sq miles)
Population: 14,133,280
Capital city: Dakar
Main languages: Wolof, French, Pulaar
Main religion: Muslim
Government: democratic republic
Currency: 1 CFA* franc = 100 centimes

SERBIA (Europe)
Area: 77,474 sq km (29,913 sq miles)
Population: 9,510,506
Capital city: Belgrade
Main language: Serbian, Hungarian
Main religion: Serbian Orthodox, Roman Catholic, Muslim
Government: republic
Currency: 1 Serbian dinar = 100 para

SEYCHELLES (Africa)
Area: 455 sq km (176 sq miles)
Population: 92,838
Capital city: Victoria
Main language: Seselwa, English
Main religion: Roman Catholic
Government: republic
Currency: 1 Seychellois rupee = 100 cents

SIERRA LEONE (Africa)
Area: 71,740 sq km (27,699 sq miles)
Population: 6,092,075
Capital city: Freetown
Main languages: Mende, Temne, Krio, English
Main religions: Muslim, indigenous, Christian
Government: republic
Currency: 1 leone = 100 cents

SINGAPORE (Asia)
Area: 693 sq km (268 sq miles)
Population: 5,411,737
Capital city: Singapore
Main languages: Chinese, Malay, English, Tamil
Main religions: Buddhist, Muslim
Government: parliamentary republic
Currency: 1 Singapore dollar = 100 cents

SLOVAKIA (Europe)
Area: 48,845 sq km (18,859 sq miles)
Population: 5,450,223
Capital city: Bratislava
Main languages: Slovak, Hungarian
Main religion: Roman Catholic, Protestant
Government: parliamentary democracy
Currency: 1 euro = 100 cents

SLOVENIA (Europe)
Area: 20,273 sq km (7,827 sq miles)
Population: 2,071,997
Capital city: Ljubljana

Samoa

• San Marino

Sao Tome and Principe

Saudi Arabia

Senegal

Serbia

Seychelles

**CFA = Communaute Financiere Africaine; Crioulo = a blend of Portuguese and West African*

Sierra Leone

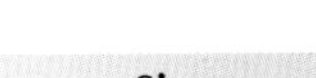

Singapore

Slovakia

• Slovenia

Solomon Islands

Somalia

South Africa

Main language: Slovenian
Main religion: Roman Catholic
Government: democratic republic
Currency: 1 euro = 100 cents

SOLOMON ISLANDS (Australasia/Oceania)
Area: 28,450 sq km (10,985 sq miles)
Population: 561,231
Capital city: Honiara
Main languages: Solomon pidgin, Kwara'ae, To'abaita, English
Main religion: Christian
Government: parliamentary democracy
Currency: 1 Solomon Islands dollar = 100 cents

SOMALIA (Africa)
Area: 637,657 sq km (246,201 sq miles)
Population: 10,495,583
Capital city: Mogadishu
Main languages: Somali, Arabic, Oromo
Main religion: Sunni Muslim
Government: federal parliamentary republic
Currency: 1 Somali shilling = 100 cents

SOUTH AFRICA (Africa)
Area: 1,219,912 sq km (471,011 sq miles)
Population: 52,776,130
Capital cities: Pretoria, Cape Town, Bloemfontein
Main languages: Zulu, Xhosa, Afrikaans, Pedi, English, Tswana, Sotho, Tsonga, Swati, Venda, Ndebele, Isi Zulu, Isi Xhosa
Main religions: Christian, indigenous
Government: republic
Currency: 1 rand = 100 cents

SOUTH KOREA (Asia)
Area: 98,480 sq km (38,023 sq miles)
Population: 48,508,972
Capital city: Seoul
Main language: Korean
Main religions: Christian, Buddhist
Government: republic
Currency: 1 South Korean won = 100 jeon

SOUTH SUDAN (Africa)
Area: 619,745 sq km (239,285 sq miles)
Population: 11,296,173
Capital city: Juba
Main languages: English, Arabic, Dinka, Nuer, Bari, Zande, Shilluk
Main religions: indigenous, Christian, Islam
Government: federal democratic republic
Currency: 1 South Sudanese pound = 100 piastres

SPAIN (Europe)
Area: 504,750 sq km (194,885 sq miles)
Population: 46,926,963
Capital city: Madrid
Main languages: Castilian Spanish, Catalan
Main religion: Roman Catholic
Government: constitutional monarchy
Currency: 1 euro = 100 cents

SRI LANKA (Asia)
Area: 65,610 sq km (25,332 sq miles)
Population: 46,926,963
Capital cities: Colombo, Sri Jayewardenepura Kotte
Main languages: Sinhala, Tamil, English
Main religions: Buddhist, Hindu, Muslim
Government: republic
Currency: 1 Sri Lankan rupee = 100 cents

SUDAN (Africa)
Area: 1,844,797 sq km (712,280 sq miles)
Population: 37,964,306
Capital city: Khartoum
Main languages: Arabic (official), English (official), Nubian, Ta Bedawie, Fur
Main religions: Sunni Muslim
Government: federal republic
Currency: 1 Sudanese pound = 100 piastres

SURINAME (South America)
Area: 163,270 sq km (63,039 sq miles)
Population: 539,276
Capital city: Paramaribo
Main languages: Sranang Tongo, Dutch, English
Main religions: Hindu, Christian, Muslim
Government: republic
Currency: 1 Surinamese dollar = 100 cents

SWAZILAND (Africa)
Area: 17,363 sq km (6,704 sq miles)
Population: 1,249,514
Capital cities: Mbabane, Lobamba
Main languages: Swati, English
Main religions: Christian, indigenous, Muslim
Government: monarchy
Currency: 1 lilangeni = 100 cents

SWEDEN (Europe)
Area: 449,964 sq km (173,732 sq miles)
Population: 9,571,105
Capital city: Stockholm
Main language: Swedish
Main religion: Lutheran
Government: constitutional monarchy
Currency: 1 Swedish krona = 100 oere

SWITZERLAND (Europe)
Area: 41,290 sq km (15,942 sq miles)
Population: 8,077,833
Capital city: Bern
Main languages: German, French, Italian
Main religions: Roman Catholic, Protestant
Government: federal republic
Currency: 1 Swiss franc, franken or frano = 100 centimes, rappen or centesimi

SYRIA (Asia)
Area: 185,180 sq km (71,498 sq miles)
Population: 21,898,061
Capital city: Damascus
Main languages: Arabic, Kurdish
Main religions: Muslim, Christian
Government: republic
Currency: 1 Syrian pound = 100 piastres

TAJIKISTAN (Asia)
Area: 143,100 sq km (55,251 sq miles)
Population: 8,207,834
Capital city: Dushanbe
Main languages: Tajik, Russian

South Korea

South Sudan

• Spain

Sri Lanka

Sudan

Suriname

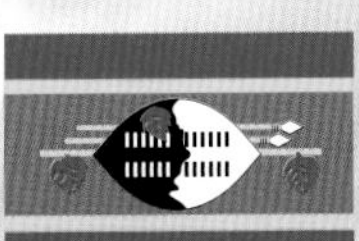

Swaziland

*CFA = *Communaute Financiere Africaine*

GAZETTEER OF STATES CONTINUED:

Sweden

Switzerland

Syria

Tajikistan

Tanzania

Thailand

Togo

Main religion: Sunni Muslim
Government: republic
Currency: 1 somoni = 100 dirams

TANZANIA (Africa)
Area: 945,087 sq km (364,900 sq miles)
Population: 49,253,126
Capital cities: Dar es Salaam, Dodoma
Main languages: Swahili, English, Sukuma
Main religions: Christian, Muslim, indigenous
Government: republic
Currency: 1 Tanzanian shilling = 100 cents

THAILAND (Asia)
Area: 514,000 sq km (198,457 sq miles)
Population: 67,010,502
Capital city: Bangkok
Main languages: Thai, English, Chaochow
Main religion: Buddhist
Government: constitutional monarchy
Currency: 1 baht = 100 satang

TOGO (Africa)
Area: 56,785 sq km (21,925 sq miles)
Population: 6,816,982
Capital city: Lome
Main languages: Mina, Ewe, Kabye, French
Main religions: indigenous, Christian, Muslim
Government: republic
Currency: 1 CFA* franc = 100 centimes

TONGA (Australasia/Oceania)
Area: 748 sq km (289 sq miles)
Population: 105,323
Capital city: Nukualofa
Main languages: Tongan, English
Main religion: Christian
Government: constitutional monarchy
Currency: 1 pa'anga = 100 seniti

TRINIDAD AND TOBAGO (North America)
Area: 5,128 sq km (1,980 sq miles)
Population: 1,341,151
Capital city: Port-of-Spain
Main languages: English, French, Spanish, Hindi
Main religions: Christian, Hindu
Government: parliamentary democracy
Currency: 1 Trinidad and Tobago dollar = 100 cents

TUNISIA (Africa)
Area: 163,610 sq km (63,170 sq miles)
Population: 10,996,515
Capital city: Tunis
Main languages: Arabic, French
Main religion: Muslim
Government: republic
Currency: 1 Tunisian dinar = 1,000 millimes

TURKEY (Europe and Asia)
Area: 780,580 sq km (301,384 sq miles)
Population: 74,932,641
Capital city: Ankara
Main language: Turkish
Main religion: Muslim
Government: democratic republic
Currency: 1 Turkish lira = 100 kurus

TURKMENISTAN (Asia)
Area: 488,100 sq km (188,456 sq miles)
Population: 5,240,072
Capital city: Ashgabat (Ashkhabad)
Main languages: Turkmen, Russian
Main religion: Muslim
Government: republic
Currency: 1 Turkmen new manat = 100 tenge

TUVALU (Australasia/Oceania)
Area: 26 sq km (10 sq miles)
Population: 9,876
Capital city: Funafuti
Main languages: Tuvaluan, English
Main religion: Congregationalist
Government: constitutional monarchy
Currency: 1 Tuvaluan dollar or 1 Australian dollar = 100 cents

UGANDA (Africa)
Area: 236,040 sq km (91,136 sq miles)
Population: 37,578,876
Capital city: Kampala
Main languages: Luganda, English, Swahili
Main religion: Christian, Muslim, indigenous
Government: republic
Currency: 1 Ugandan shilling = 100 cents

UKRAINE (Europe)
Area: 603,700 sq km (233,090 sq miles)
Population: 45,238,805
Capital city: Kiev
Main languages: Ukrainian, Russian
Main religion: Ukrainian Orthodox
Government: republic
Currency: 1 hryvnia = 100 kopiykas

UNITED ARAB EMIRATES (Asia)
Area: 83,600 sq km (32,278 sq miles)
Population: 9,346,129
Capital city: Abu Dhabi
Main languages: Arabic, English
Main religion: Muslim
Government: federation
Currency: 1 Emirati dirham = 100 fulus

UNITED KINGDOM (Europe)
Area: 244,820 sq km (94,526 sq miles)
Population: 63,136,265
Capital city: London
Main language: English
Main religions: Anglican, Roman Catholic
Government: constitutional monarchy
Currency: 1 British pound = 100 pence

UNITED STATES OF AMERICA (North America)
Area: 9,826,630 sq km (3,794,083 sq miles)
Population: 320,050,716
Capital city: Washington D.C.
Main language: English
Main religions: Protestant, Roman Catholic
Government: federal republic
Currency: 1 U.S. dollar = 100 cents

URUGUAY (South America)
Area: 176,220 sq km (68,039 sq miles)
Population: 3,407,062
Capital city: Montevideo
Main language: Spanish
Main religion: Roman Catholic
Government: republic
Currency: 1 Uruguayan peso = 100 centesimos

Tonga

Trinidad and Tobago

Tunisia

Turkey

Turkmenistan

Tuvalu

Uganda

Ukraine

United Arab Emirates

United Kingdom

United States of America

Uruguay

Uzbekistan

Vanuatu

UZBEKISTAN (Asia)
Area: 447,400 sq km (172,742 sq miles)
Population: 28,934,102
Capital city: Tashkent
Main languages: Uzbek, Russian
Main religions: Muslim, Eastern Orthodox
Government: republic
Currency: 1 Uzbekistani sum = 100 tiyin

VANUATU (Australasia/Oceania)
Area: 12,200 sq km (4,710 sq miles)
Population: 252,763
Capital city: Port Vila
Main languages: Bislama, French, English
Main religion: Christian
Government: republic
Currency: 1 vatu = 100 centimes

VATICAN CITY (Europe)
Area: 0.44 sq km (0.17 sq miles)
Population: 799
Capital city: Vatican City
Main languages: Italian, Latin
Main religion: Roman Catholic
Government: led by the Pope
Currency: 1 euro = 100 cents

VENEZUELA (South America)
Area: 912,050 sq km (352,144 sq miles)
Population: 30,405,207
Capital city: Caracas
Main language: Spanish
Main religion: Roman Catholic
Government: federal republic
Currency: 1 bolivar = 100 centimos

VIETNAM (Asia)
Area: 329,560 sq km (127,244 sq miles)
Population: 91,679,733
Capital city: Hanoi
Main languages: Vietnamese, French, English, Khmer, Chinese
Main religion: Buddhist
Government: communist state
Currency: Vietnamese dong

YEMEN (Asia)
Area: 527,970 sq km (203,850 sq miles)
Population: 24,407,381
Capital city: Sana
Main language: Arabic
Main religion: Muslim
Government: republic
Currency: 1 Yemeni rial = 100 fulus

ZAMBIA (Africa)
Area: 752,614 sq km (290,586 sq miles)
Population: 14,538,640
Capital city: Lusaka
Main languages: Bemba, Tonga, Nyanja, English, Kaonda, Lozi, Lunda, Luvale
Main religions: Christian, Muslim, Hindu
Government: republic
Currency: 1 Zambian kwacha = 100 ngwee

ZIMBABWE (Africa)
Area: 390,580 sq km (150,804 sq miles)
Population: 14,149,648
Capital city: Harare
Main languages: Shona, Ndebele, English
Main religions: Christian, indigenous
Government: republic
Currency: 1 Zimbabwean dollar = 100 cents

The United Nations

The United Nations (U.N.) is an organization which aims to bring countries together to work for peace and development. Of the world's 195 states, 193 are members of the U.N. Those that don't belong are Kosovo and the Vatican City.

Internet links

For links to websites with flags, facts, maps, quizzes, and more information about the U.N., go to www.usborne.com/quicklinks

Ban Ki-moon, the Secretary-General of the U.N., shakes hands with Hillary Clinton, the Secretary of State of the U.S.A.

Vatican City

Venezuela

Vietnam

Yemen

Zambia

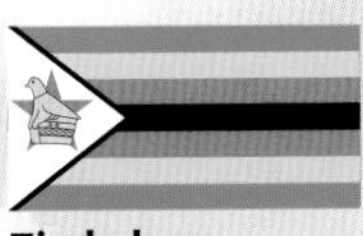

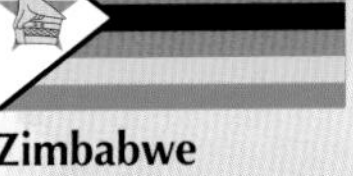

Zimbabwe

GLOSSARY

This glossary explains some of the words you may come across when reading about the Earth and its peoples. Words in *italic type* have their own entry elsewhere in the glossary.

ablation zone The lower end of a *glacier*, where the ice melts and flows into streams and rivers, or into the sea.

abyssal plain A huge, flat expanse of seabed that forms most of the ocean floor.

accumulation zone The top of a *glacier*, where snow falls and is gradually compacted into ice.

acid rain Rain containing dissolved chemicals from polluted air. The chemicals make the water acidic, which means it can eat away at rock and damage plant life.

active volcano An active volcano is one which might *erupt* at any time.

adaptation The way a plant or animal *species* develops over time to suit its *habitat*.

aid Any kind of help, especially that given by one country to another. The help can be money, food, equipment or expert help from teachers and engineers.

animism The belief that plants, stones and other natural objects have living souls or spirits.

anticyclone An area of high *atmospheric pressure*, which pushes winds outward. It is the opposite of a *cyclone*.

apartheid A system, such as the one used in South Africa until 1994, which separates people according to their race.

aquifer A layer of *porous* rock which can hold water and carry it along under the ground.

arable Arable land is suitable for growing crops (plants). Arable farming means crop farming.

archipelago A group of islands.

asteroid A small rock that *orbits* the Sun. There are thousands of asteroids in the part of the *Solar System* known as the Asteroid Belt.

atmosphere A layer of gases that surrounds the Earth and some other planets and stars.

atmospheric pressure The force the *atmosphere* exerts on Earth. It can change according to how warm the air is and how high you are above sea level.

atom A tiny particle. All *elements* are made up of atoms.

aurora Flickering lights, caused by *magnetic* particles from the Sun, that sometimes appear in the sky near the poles. The lights in the north are named the aurora borealis and those in the south are the aurora australis.

axis An imaginary line running through the middle of the Earth, from the *North Pole* to the *South Pole*, around which the Earth spins.

bacterium (plural: **bacteria**) A tiny *organism* found in the soil, in the air, and in plants and animals.

bedrock The solid layer of rock that lies underneath the soil, covering the Earth's surface.

biome An area with a *climate* that supports a particular range of plants and animals. For example, deserts, mountains and seas are all biomes.

black smoker A kind of *hydrothermal vent* which churns out black water containing many dissolved minerals. The minerals gradually build up around the vent, forming a chimney.

border A line separating political or geographical areas, especially countries. Borders are drawn up by governments and can change over time.

camouflage Patterns or features, that help plants and animals to look like their backgrounds and avoid being seen. For example, a tiger's stripes blend in with long grass.

canopy The thick upper layer of leaves and branches in a rainforest.

carnivore An animal or plant that feeds on animals.

caste An inherited class, also known as *Jati*, in traditional Indian *culture*.

census An official count of the number of people in a country. Other information, such as age, sex and occupation, may also be noted in a census.

central business district (CBD) The main business area of a city, where most of the stores, banks and offices are found.

chlorofluorocarbon (CFC) Any of various chemicals that are thought to damage the layer of *ozone* in the Earth's *atmosphere*.

chlorophyll A green chemical in plants which enables them to convert sunlight into food.

civilization The process of human development from small prehistoric groups to complex human societies with cities, governments, laws and communication systems.

civil war A war between people of the same country.

climate The typical or average weather conditions in a particular region.

colonization The process of establishing a settlement or settlements in another country. It may involve imposing a new *culture*, language or religion.

comet A chunk of dirty ice mixed with dust and grit which travels around the *Sun*.

compass A device containing a *magnetic* needle that points to the *North Pole*. A compass is used to find your direction.

conservation Protecting and preserving *environments,* including the plants, animals and buildings that form a part of them, and trying to reduce the damage caused to them by *pollution*.

constellation A group of *stars* that form a recognizable pattern.

continent One of the Earth's major land masses.

continental crust Part of the Earth's *crust* that forms land masses. Continental crust is made mostly of a rock called granite and similar light rocks.

continental shelf A wide shelf of seabed that surrounds most land masses, making the sea much shallower near the land than it is in the middle of the oceans.

continental slope The steep slope leading from the edge of the *continental shelf* down to the deeper seabed.

coral reef A structure made up of the skeletons of small sea animals called coral polyps. A reef builds up gradually as old polyps die and new ones grow on top.

core The central part of the inside of the Earth, which scientists think is made of the metals iron and nickel.

Coriolis effect The effect of the spinning of the Earth, which forces winds and *currents* into a spiral.

creole A language formed from a European language and another language. The word creole can also be used to describe a person who is descended from Europeans and another ethnic group.

crevasse A crack in a *glacier*.

crop rotation Changing the crop grown on a particular piece of land each year, to give the soil the opportunity to recover.

crust The Earth's solid outer layer. It consists of *continental crust* which forms the land, and *oceanic crust* which forms the seabed.

culture The way of life of a group of people. It includes their customs, hobbies, food, fashions and beliefs.

current A body of water or air which moves in a definite direction, often through a stiller surrounding body. For example, the Gulf Stream is a current that carries warm water across the Atlantic Ocean from the Caribbean to northern Europe.

cyclone An area of low *atmospheric pressure* where winds rotate inward.

debris Any kind of loose rock, mud or other matter – such as the rocks carried along by a *glacier*, or the material carried and deposited by a flowing river.

deforestation Reducing or removing forests by cutting down or burning trees. Soil is washed away more easily in deforested areas.

degree One 360th of a circle. Degrees are used with *latitude* and *longitude* to measure distance on the Earth's surface. One degree is one 360th of the distance around the Earth.

delta A fan-shaped system of streams, created when a river splits up into many smaller branches and deposits *debris* as it nears the sea.

deposition Dropping or leaving behind rocks or other *debris*.

desertification The process of non-desert land becoming desert.

development The improvement of a country's industry, wealth and standard of living.

DNA Material, like a set of "coded instructions", in living *organisms* that contains the information they need to function and develop.

dormant volcano A volcano that is temporarily inactive, but could *erupt* in the future. The word dormant means "sleeping".

drumlin A small hill formed from *debris* deposited by a moving *glacier*, lengthened in the direction of the movement of the glacier to form an oval shape.

dyke A barrier built at the coast to stop the sea from flooding the land at high *tide*.

ecosystem A living system that includes a group of plants and animals and the *habitat* they live in.

ecotourism A type of tourism that aims to protect the environment, for example by charging tourists to visit nature reserves to spot wildlife.

element A substance, such as iron, oxygen or silicon, made of one type of *atom*. There are over a hundred elements on Earth.

El Niño A weather phenomenon that sometimes makes part of the Pacific Ocean get much warmer than normal, causing severe storms.

emergent A tree that rises above the main *canopy* in a rainforest.

emigration Movement from one country to settle in another.

environment Surroundings, including the landscape, living things and the *atmosphere*.

Equator An imaginary line around the middle of the Earth, exactly halfway between the *North Pole* and the *South Pole*.

erratic A large boulder that has been deposited by a *glacier* and is left standing away from its source.

eruption The ejection of *lava*, rocks, hot ash and gases from a volcano.

estuary A wide channel that forms where a river joins the sea.w

ethnic group A group of people who share things like language, *culture* and religion, and who often live together in the same area.

Eurasia The continent of Europe and Asia.

evolution The gradual development of plants and animals, over many generations, to fit in better with their *habitats*.

exfoliation A process which involves shedding layers. When a rock exfoliates, its outer layers peel off like the layers of an onion. This is caused by changes in temperature, which make rock shrink and expand.

export A product sent abroad to be sold.

extinction The death of a *species* of plant or animal.

fallow Fallow land is farmland that is being left to rest and recover between crops.

famine A widespread shortage of food, which can lead to starvation and the spread of diseases.

Far East The most easterly countries of Asia, especially China and Japan.

fault A crack in the Earth's *crust*.

fault creep The gradual movement of two pieces of the Earth's *crust* along a *fault*.

fertile Fertile land is land that is good for growing plants. Fertile also means able to reproduce.

fertilizer A substance, such as manure, that contains *nitrates* and other chemicals and is put on land to make it more *fertile*.

fold mountains A mountain range formed by the Earth's *crust* buckling up into folds when the *plates* of the crust push together.

food chain A sequence showing which *species* eat which.

food web A network of *food chains* showing which *species* eat each other in an *ecosystem*.

footloose industry An industry that does not have to locate near its raw materials, either because it hardly uses any, or because the raw materials it does use are light and easy to transport. Also known as light industry.

fossil The shape or remains of a plant or animal that died long ago, hardened and preserved in rock.

fossil fuel A fuel, such as coal, oil or gas, made from the compressed bodies of plants and animals that died many years ago.

freeze-thaw action The action of water that seeps into cracks in rocks and then freezes, which makes it expand. This expansion forces the cracks apart, so they gradually get bigger.

fungus (plural: **fungi**) A type of *organism*, including mushrooms, that is similar to a plant but has no leaves or flowers.

galaxy A huge group of stars and planets. There are millions of galaxies in the universe.

genetically modified food Food crops which have been genetically changed. This may be to make them grow faster or resist frost or pests.

genetic engineering Changing the *DNA* of plants and animals to benefit medicine, farming and industry. In farming, for example, scientists can create new plant species which work better as crops.

geostationary Moving in such a way as to remain above the same point on the Earth's surface. For example, geostationary *satellites* orbit the Earth at the same speed as the Earth spins, so they always stay above the same part of the Earth.

geyser A spring that discharges water and steam, heated up inside the Earth, in bursts.

glacial valley A deep U-shaped valley carved by a flowing *glacier*, left behind after the glacier melts.

glacier A mass of ice that flows very slowly downhill.

globalization The organization of industry on a worldwide scale.

global warming The gradual warming-up of the Earth's atmosphere, possibly due to the *greenhouse effect*.

gorge A deep, narrow valley, shaped by a river gradually cutting down into the land it flows across.

gravity The pulling force that holds the *atmosphere* and objects in place on the Earth and stops them from floating out into space.

greenhouse effect The effect of certain gases in the *atmosphere* which trap heat from the Sun, causing the Earth to heat up.

greenhouse gas A gas, such as carbon dioxide, which contributes to the *greenhouse effect*.

gross national product (GNP) The total value of the goods and *services* produced by a nation over a year.

groundwater Water that has soaked into the ground and is stored inside *porous* rock.

habitat The place where an animal or plant *species* lives.

hanging valley A valley found high up the side of a *glacial valley*. Hanging valleys once contained mini-glaciers that flowed into a large glacier. When glaciers melt, hanging valleys are left behind, high up the mountainside.

heat expansion The increase in size of many substances, such as wood or rock, as they get warmer.

heavy industry An industry, such as ship-building, that uses heavy raw materials and needs large machines.

hemisphere Half of the Earth.

herbivore An animal that eats plants.

horizon A layer in soil. It is also the line where you can see the land meeting the sky when you look into the distance.

hot spot An area of the Earth's *crust* where *magma* breaks through and forms a volcano.

hot spring See **thermal spring.**

Human Development Index A system developed by the United Nations for measuring the standard of living in different countries.

humidity The amount of water contained in the air.

humus The part of soil that makes it *fertile*. Humus is made from rotted plant and animal matter.

hunter-gatherer Someone who survives by hunting animals and collecting wild plants, instead of by farming.

hydroelectric power (HEP) Power created from the energy of flowing water.

hydrothermal vent A hole in the seabed, through which a *thermal spring* emerges. See also **black smoker**.

Ice age A period when the Earth was much colder than average. There have been several major Ice ages since the Earth began.

iceberg A huge chunk of a *glacier* that has broken off into the sea.

ice sheet A sheet of ice covering a large area, such as the ice that covers Antarctica. An ice sheet is a type of large *glacier* which flows outward from the middle.

igneous rock Rock formed when *magma* escapes from inside the Earth, and then cools and hardens.

immigration Movement of people into a new country, usually to settle there permanently.

impermeable Not allowing water to pass through.

import A product or service brought into a country from another country.

indigenous Originating naturally in an area. Indigenous people are the people who first lived in a particular place.

infrared A type of energy that *radiates* from hot things. It is invisible to the human eye, but can be detected by infrared cameras.

intensive farming A type of farming that involves using chemicals and technology to increase *yield*.

interglacial A period of time within an *Ice age* when the climate gets slightly warmer for a while.

International Date Line An imaginary line on the Earth's surface, to the east of which the date is one day earlier than to the west. It runs on the opposite side of the world to the *Prime Meridian Line* at 180° of *longitude*, except where it bends to avoid time change in populated areas.

irrigation The artificial watering of land to help grow crops.

isobar A line that links points with the same *atmospheric pressure*. The isobars on a weather map show patterns of atmospheric pressure.

isthmus A narrow strip of land connecting two larger land areas. For example, Central America is an isthmus connecting North and South America.

landslide A sudden slippage of rocks and soil down a hillside, usually caused by heavy rain or earthquakes.

latitude A measurement of how many *degrees* a place is north or south of the *Equator*. Lines of latitude are imaginary lines around the Earth, parallel to the *Equator*.

lava Hot molten rock which bursts or flows out of volcanoes. Lava also sometimes seeps out of holes in the ground, called vents.

leap year A year every four years that has 366 days instead of 365. The extra day is added in February, to make February 29th.

less developed country (LDC) A poor country which has not yet been industrialized and has low standards of living.

lithosphere The outer layers of Earth, made up of the *crust* and upper *mantle*.

longitude A measurement of how many *degrees* a place is east or west of the *Prime Meridian Line*. Lines of longitude are imaginary lines that run around the Earth from north to south.

magma Hot, molten rock inside the Earth.

magnet An object that has magnetic force, an invisible force that attracts iron and steel. The ends of a magnet are known as its poles.

magnetic poles The Earth is like a giant *magnet*, and the ends of this magnet are called the magnetic poles. They move gradually over time, and are not in exactly the same place as the geographic *North Pole* and *South Pole*.

malaria A disease, affecting millions of people, which is spread by insects called mosquitoes.

mantle The thick layer of rock under the Earth's *crust*. Some of it is solid and some is *magma*.

manufacturing industry Industry, such as ship-building or clothes-making, that involves making new products.

matriarchy A system in which women are the most powerful members of families and of society.

meander A bend or long loop in a river. Meanders form when rivers flow across gently sloping land.

Mediterranean A type of *climate* that has warm winters and hot summers, and is good for growing many types of crops. It is named after the region around the Mediterranean Sea, but is also found in other parts of the world.

megacity A name for a city that has more than ten million people.

mestizo A Spaniard or Portuguese person of mixed origin, especially with Native American ancestors.

metamorphic rock Rock that has been changed by heat or pressure. For example, when a rock called shale is squashed, it hardens into a type of metamorphic rock called slate.

meteoroid Dust or a small chunk of rock which *orbits* the *Sun*.

Middle East An area of Asia between the Red Sea and Persian Gulf, as well as Israel, Jordan, Syria, Lebanon, Iraq and Iran.

migration Moving from one place to another. Many animals migrate each season to find food.

Milky Way The *galaxy* of which the *Sun* and *Solar System* are a part. It can often be seen as a broad band of light in the night sky.

mineral A non-living substance found in the Earth, such as salt, iron, diamond or quartz.

missionary A member of a group sent by a religious body to do religious or social work in another country.

molecule Two or more *atoms* bonded together.

monsoon A strong seasonal change in the weather that affects certain parts of Asia. Monsoon regions have three seasons – a long, cool, dry season, a hot, humid season and a rainy season.

moon A natural *satellite* which *orbits* a *planet*. The Earth has one moon which orbits it once a month.

moraine Boulders, clay and other *debris* left behind by a *glacier*.

more developed country (MDC) A wealthy country with well-developed industry and a high standard of living.

national park An area of natural beauty protected by law from building and development.

native Belonging to a particular place.

natural selection The theory that those animals and plants that are best suited to their *environment* are the most likely to survive.

newly industrialized country (NIC) A country that has recently increased its wealth and standard of living through the development of modern industry.

New World A phrase used to mean North, Central and South America. The term was first applied by European explorers.

niche A particular plant or animal *species'* place in an *ecosystem*.

nitrate Any of a group of chemicals found in soil that helps plants grow.

nomad Someone who has no permanent home and travels around to make a living. Many nomads herd animals.

northern hemisphere The half of the Earth that lies north of the *Equator*.

North Pole The most northern point on the Earth, and one end of the *axis* the Earth spins around.

nuclear power Energy produced by splitting *atoms* of a *radioactive element* called uranium.

oasis A *fertile* area in a desert, supplied by water from an *aquifer*.

oceanic crust Part of the Earth's *crust* that forms the seabed. Oceanic crust is made mostly of a rock called basalt.

oceanic ridge A raised ridge on the seabed, caused by the *plates* of the Earth's *crust* pulling apart and *magma* pushing up in between.

oceanic trench A deep trench in the seabed that forms where one *plate* pushes underneath another.

official language The language of a country that is spoken at work, at school and in government. The official language may be different from the language spoken in homes or with friends, and is not always the language spoken by the majority of the population.

omnivore An animal that eats both meat and plants. Omnivore means "everything-eater".

orbit The path of an object as it travels around, or orbits, another.

ore Rock containing metal that can be extracted.

organic farming A type of farming that doesn't use artificial chemicals and methods.

organic food Food produced by organic farming that contains no artificial chemicals.

organism A living thing, such as a plant, animal or *bacterium*.

outback The remote bush country of Australia.

outcrop An area of land where part of a rock formation reaches the surface.

oxbow lake A curved lake left behind when a river *meander* gets cut off from the rest of the river.

ozone A type of oxygen in which each *molecule* contains three oxygen *atoms* instead of two.

ozone layer A layer of *ozone* in the Earth's *atmosphere*, from 20 to 50km (12 to 30 miles) above the Earth's surface, which protects the Earth from the *Sun's* rays. The ozone layer may be being damaged by *chlorofluorocarbons*, or *CFCs*.

Pangaea The name scientists give to a huge continent that they think once existed on Earth. It gradually broke up to form the *continents* we have today.

passport An official document issued by the government of a country to a person who belongs to that country. A passport can allow travel to foreign countries, act as an identity card and give its owner the right to re-enter his or her *native* country.

pastoral farming A type of farming that involves raising and breeding animals.

patriarchy A system in which men are the most powerful members of families and of society.

peninsula A long piece of land that sticks out into the sea.

permafrost A layer of the ground that is permanently frozen.

photosynthesis A chemical process in plants, which converts sunlight into food.

pidgin A language made up of elements of two or more languages to help groups who speak different languages communicate.

pilgrimage A journey to a sacred place.

planet A celestial body that *orbits* a *star*. For example, Earth and Mars are planets which orbit the *Sun*.

plate One of the large pieces of *lithosphere* that make up the Earth's surface layer.

plate tectonics The theory that *plates* gradually move around and rub against each other.

poles The *North Pole* and the *South Pole*, the coldest points of the Earth and those that are farthest away from the *Equator*.

pollution Waste or dirt, such as exhaust from cars, that builds up faster than it can be broken down.

population The number of people living in a particular place.

porous Able to soak up water. Porous rock can soak up water like a sponge and store it underground.

port A town or city where ships can load and unload.

precipitation Rain, snow, hail or any other water falling from the sky.

precision farming A type of farming that uses the latest science and technology to grow crops more efficiently.

primary industry An industry that takes raw materials from the Earth. Mining and fishing are primary industries.

Prime Meridian Line An imaginary line that runs from north to south through Greenwich, England, at zero *degrees* of *longitude*. The time along the Prime Meridian Line is called Greenwich Mean Time.

projection A representation of the Earth's surface on a flat map.

quaternary industry An industry, such as accountancy, in which information is bought and sold.

radar A system that detects objects such as clouds by sending out radio waves and collecting the signals that bounce back. Radar stands for **RA**dio **D**etecting **A**nd **R**anging.

radiation Energy, such as light, heat or *radioactive* particles, that radiates (flows outward) from an energy source. For example, the *Sun* radiates light and heat.

radioactive A substance that gives out *radiation*. Radioactive substances, such as uranium, give off particles which can be harmful.

refugee A person who has fled from their country to escape some danger or problem.

remote sensing Recording information from a long distance away; for example, measuring sea temperatures from a *satellite*.

reservation An area of public land set aside for a special purpose. For example, in North America European settlers forced Native Americans to live on reservations.

rift valley A valley formed on land where two *plates* of the Earth's *crust* pull away from each other.

Ring of Fire A group of volcanoes and *faults* that forms a huge ring in the Pacific Ocean.

satellite An object that *orbits* a *planet*. Many satellites are built to do particular jobs, such as monitoring the weather.

scale The size of a map in relation to the area it represents. If a map's scale is 1:100, 1cm on the map represents 100cm of the area shown.

secondary industry An industry, such as building or making cloth in a factory, that makes things out of raw materials.

sedimentary rock Rock made up of particles of sand, mud and other *debris* that have settled on the seabed and been squashed down to form hard rock.

selective breeding Developing plants and animals by choosing those with good qualities for farming.

service industry An industry, such as banking or waitressing, that involves people doing or supplying something for other people. See also **tertiary industry**.

settlement A collection of homes forming a community.-

sewage Waste and dirty water from sinks and bathrooms.

shaman A religious leader who is believed to have magical powers.

shanty town A makeshift town on the outskirts of a city where people build their own homes out of waste materials.

shifting agriculture A system of farming in which people clear a small area of forest to use as farmland. After a few years, they move on to another area.

site The place where a *settlement* has been built.

situation A *settlement's* position in the surrounding area, such as in a gap in a range of hills.

smog A mixture of smoke and fog. Also a general word for *pollution*.

Solar System The *Sun* and the *planets, satellites* and other objects that *orbit* it.

solar year The amount of time it takes the Earth to *orbit* the *Sun* once. A solar year is 365.26 days.

sonar A method of bouncing sounds off objects and measuring the results in order to make maps. Sonar is used to map the seabed.

southern hemisphere The half of the Earth that lies south of the *Equator*.

South Pole The most southern point on the Earth, and one end of the *axis* the Earth spins around.

species (plural: **species**) A type of plant, animal or other living thing.

stalactite A column of stone hanging down inside a cave, made by water dripping from the roof and depositing dissolved minerals.

stalagmite A tower of stone rising from the ground in a cave, made by water dripping onto the floor and depositing dissolved minerals.

star A huge ball of burning gas in space. The *Sun*, in the middle of our *Solar System*, is a star.

state An area of land that has its own government, laws and money. It can also mean one of a number of regional governments forming a federation under a central government, as in the U.S.A.

stoma (plural: **stomata**) One of the tiny holes in the leaves of plants. A stoma allows gases and water in and out. See also **transpiration**.

stratum (plural: **strata**) A layer of rock.

subduction zone An area of the seabed where one *plate* of the Earth's *lithosphere* plunges beneath another, forming a deep trench.

submersible A small submarine used by scientists to explore the oceans and the seabed.

Sun The medium-sized *star* that lies in the middle of our *Solar System*.

temperate A type of *climate* that is mild and damp.

terrace One of a series of large steps dug into hillsides to hold soil and water in place for farming.

tertiary industry An industry, such as teaching or banking, that provides services for others.

thermal spring A flow of water heated by underground rocks that emerges on the Earth's surface. Also known as a hot spring.

tidal wave A type of very large wave. *Tsunamis* are not tidal waves, as they are caused by underwater volcanoes or earthquakes and have nothing to do with tides.

tide The daily rise and fall of the sea, caused by the Moon's *gravity*.

time zone A region where the same standard time is used.

topsoil The rich, uppermost layer of soil. It contains *humus* and *organisms* that make it *fertile*.

transpiration A process where water that has been sucked in through a plant's roots travels up to the leaves, and transpires, or evaporates, through the *stomata*.

treeline The height up a mountain above which there are no more trees (because it is too cold and windy for them to survive).

tributary A river that flows into a bigger river, instead of into the sea.

tropics The warm, wet areas on either side of the *Equator,* between the Tropic of Cancer and the Tropic of Capricorn.

tsunami A giant wave made by an earthquake, landslide or volcanic activity on the seabed causing the water to make waves.

tundra A type of land, found in the Arctic, where a layer of the ground is permanently frozen.

turbine A machine that converts turning power (such as the spinning of a waterwheel) into electricity.

ultraviolet (UV) A type of invisible *radiation* from the Sun which can cause skin damage.

understorey The level of a rainforest where small trees and plants grow, between the *canopy* and the forest floor.

urbanization An increase in the number of people living in towns and cities rather than in the countryside.

visa A stamp on a *passport* from the government of a country which shows that the owner is allowed to travel through that country for a fixed period of time.

water table The top level of *groundwater* that is stored in underground rock.

yield The amount of food or other produce that is grown on a particular piece of land.

MAP INDEX

This is an index of the places and features named on the maps. Each entry consists of the following parts: the name (given in bold type), the country or region within which it is located (given in italics), the page on which the name can be found (given in bold type), and the grid reference (also given in bold type). For some names, there is also a description explaining what kind of place it is – for example a country, internal administrative area (state or province), national capital or internal capital. To find a place on a map, first find the map indicated by the page reference. Then use the grid reference to find the square containing the name or town symbol. See page 251 for help with using the grid.

a

b

d

e

f

g

h

O

P

t

U

GENERAL INDEX

In this index, words that have a lot of page numbers may have a number in **bold** to show where to find the main explanation. The maps are listed in a separate index on pages 376–389.

g

h

i

t

ACKNOWLEDGEMENTS

Every effort has been made to trace the copyright holders of the material in this book. If any rights have been omitted, the publishers offer to rectify this in any subsequent edition, following notification. The publishers are grateful to the following organizations and individuals for their contributions and permission to reproduce material (t=top, m=middle, b=bottom, l=left, r=right, SPL=Science Photo Library):
Cover © DYNAMIC EARTH IMAGING/SPL; **p1** © Jason Hosking/Corbis **p2–3** © Eastcott Momatiuk/Digital Vision/Getty Images; **p4–5** © Digital Vision; **p6–7** © Digital Vision; **p6** (tr) Jeremy Gower; **p8–9** © Digital Vision; **p10 (bl)** Courtesy of SOHO/Extreme Ultraviolet Imaging Telescope (EIT) consortium. SOHO is a project of international cooperation between ESA and NASA; (ml) NASA/Johns Hopkins University Applied Physics Laboratory/Carnegie Institution of Washington; (m + tr) JPL/NASA; (mr) © Digital Vision; **p11** (l + tr) © Digital Vision; (tl + mr) NASA/U.S. Geological Survey; (tm) NASA; (tr) Alan Stern (Southwest Research Institute), Marc Buie (Lowell Observatory), NASA and ESA; (br) WFI, European Southern Observatory; **p12** (bl) © Digital Vision; (tr) © Digital Vision; **p13** (tr) © Digital Vision; (r) Courtesy Canadian Space Agency © 2001; **p14** (l) © Dave G. Houser/CORBIS; (r) © Digital Vision; (b) Jeremy Gower; **p14–15** (t) © Digital Vision; **p15** (m, bm + b) © Digital Vision; **p16** (bl) Jeremy Gower; (mr + br) © Digital Vision; **p17** (t) Chris Lyon; (tr) Gary Bines; (b) SPL/© Simon Fraser; **p18–19** Gary Bines/© Digital Vision; **p19** (tl) Jeremy Gower; (bm) Chris Lyon; (mr) Andy Burton; (br) Howard Allman; p20 (m) Guy Smith; (b) Jeremy Gower; **p20–21** (t) Jeremy Gower; **p21** (b) © Galen Rowell/CORBIS; (tr) Guy Smith; (mr) © Yann Arthus-Bertrand/CORBIS; **p22–23** (b) G.S.F Picture Library © Dr. B. Booth; **p22** Mike Freeman; **p23** Mike Freeman; **p24** (bl) © Kevin Fleming/CORBIS; (tr) Jeremy Gower; **p25** (l) Mike Freeman and SPL/© Roberto de Gugliemo; (tr) SPL/Rosenfeld Images Ltd; (br) © Dorothy Burrows, Eye Ubiquitous/CORBIS; **p26** (bl) © Digital Vision; **p26–27** © Digital Vision; **p27** (tr) © Digital Vision; (br) Laura Fearn; **p28** (b) © Ken Wilson, Papilio/CORBIS; (t) © Robert Pickett/CORBIS; **p29** (tl) Andrew Beckett; (b) © Bob Rowan, Progressive Image/CORBIS; (tr) © Michael Boys/CORBIS; **p30** (t) © Richard Hamilton Smith/CORBIS; (b) © Eric Crichton/CORBIS; **p31** (b) Still Pictures/© Alan Watson; (tm) © Dean Conger/CORBIS; (tr) © Ancient Art and Architecture; **p32–33** © John Farmer, Cordaiy Photo Library Ltd/CORBIS; **p33** (tr) Jeremy Gower; (br) © Robert Holmes/CORBIS; **p34–35** (b) © Layne Kennedy/CORBIS; **p34** (t) Jeremy Gower; **p35** (tl) © Richard A. Cooke/CORBIS; (br) © Wolfgang Kaehler/CORBIS; **p36–37** © Douglas Peebles/CORBIS; **p38** (bl + m) Jeremy Gower; (br) Chris Shields; **p38–39** (m) G.S.F Picture Library © Dr. B. Booth; **p39** (br) Chris Shields; **p40** (main) © Digital Vision; (bl, tr + br) Jeremy Gower; **p41** (bl) © Digital Vision; (r) © SuperStock; **p42–43** © Michael T. Sedam/CORBIS; **p42** (tr) Jeremy Gower; **p43** (tl) © Ralph White/CORBIS; (br) Still Pictures/© D. Drain; **p44** (bl) Jeremy Gower; **p44–45** © Amos Nachoum/CORBIS; **p45** (b) © Douglas Peebles/CORBIS; (tr) G.S.F. Picture Library © Solarfilm A; **p46** (bl) © Philip James Corwin/CORBIS; **p46–47** G.S.F. Picture Library © Univ. California; **p48–49** © Chien-Min Chung/In Pictures/Corbis; **p48** (tr) © Grant Smith/CORBIS; **p49** (t) Photo courtesy of Kinemetrics Inc.; (r) Peter Bull; **p50** (main) © Kevin Shafer/CORBIS; (ml, bl + br) Jeremy Gower; **p51** Jeremy Gower; **p52** (t) Jeremy Gower; (b) © Roger Rossmeyer/CORBIS; **p53** (bl) Warren Photographic/Jane Burton; (r) © Richard Cummins/CORBIS; **p54** (b) Jeremy Gower; (tr) © Costas Syrolakis; **p55** (b) Still Pictures/© UNEP/Foto; (tr) Jeremy Gower; **p56–57** © Lawson Wood/CORBIS; **p58** (bl + tr) © Digital Vision; (br) Ian Jackson; **p59** (ml) Shuttle Views of the Earth: Geology from Space. Compiled by Pat Jones, courtesy of LPI; (b) © Digital Vision; (tr) Frans Lanting/Tony Stone Images; **p60** (bl) © David Muench/CORBIS; (tr) © NASA/CORBIS; **p60–61** (b) © John and Dallas Heaton/CORBIS; **p61** (tl + br) Jeremy Gower; **p62** (m) © Charles and Josette Lenars/CORBIS; (tr) Rex Features/Mansell Collection; **p63** (tl) © Michael T. Sedam/CORBIS; (b) © Philip James Corwin/CORBIS; (tr) © Charles and Josette Lenars/CORBIS; **p64** (b) Jeremy Gower; (m) Evian Natural Mineral Water; (tr) Photography courtesy of The Strathmore Mineral Water Company; **p65** (b) © Macduff Everton/CORBIS; (tr) © Richard Hamilton Smith/CORBIS; **p66–67** © Neil Rabinovitz/CORBIS; **p66** (bl) Chris Lyon; **p67** (tm) Jeremy Gower; (mr) Ralph A. Clevenger/CORBIS; **p68–69** (background) © Digital Vision; **p68** (ml) Laura Fearn; (bl) Chris Lyon; (mr) Shaun Egan/Tony Stone Images; **p69** (b) © Digital Vision; (tr) © Anthony Bannister, ABPL/CORBIS; **p70** (tl) © Lawson Wood/CORBIS; (m) SPL/Dr. Ken McDonald; (b) © Amos Nachoum/CORBIS; **p71** (tl) © Digital Vision; (b) © Digital Vision; (tr) Peter Dennis; **p72–73** © Michael S. Yamashita/CORBIS; **p72** (ml + tr) © Michael S. Yamashita/CORBIS; **p73** (tl) © Charles O'Rear/CORBIS; (br) © Digital Vision; **p74–75** © Steve Kaufman/CORBIS; **p76–77** (background) © Craig Aurniss/CORBIS; **p76** (l) © Michael Yashmita/CORBIS; (tr) Ian Jackson; **p77** (m) Ian Jackson; (tm) © Digital Vision; (br) © Wolfgang Kaehler/CORBIS; **p78–79** (background) Shuttle Views of the Earth: Clouds from Space. Compiled by Pat Jones, courtesy of LPI; **p78** (bl) Peter Dennis; (tr) SPL/Scott Camazine; **p79** (tl + tr) Shuttle Views of the Earth: Clouds from Space. Compiled by Pat Jones, courtesy of LPI; (ml) © Wolfgang Kaehler/CORBIS; (bl) © Digital Vision; **p79** (tr margin) SPL/Scott Camazine; (br) Ian Jackson; **p80–81** Glen Alison/Tony Stone Images; **p80** (bl) Shuttle Views of the Earth: Clouds from Space. Compiled by Pat Jones, courtesy of LPI; **p81** (tr) Fortean Picture Library/Werner Burger; **p82–83** John Lund/Tony Stone Images; **p82** (b) Guy Smith; (tr) Shuttle Views of the Earth: Clouds from Space. Compiled by Pat Jones, courtesy of LPI; **p84–85** © Michael S. Yamashita/CORBIS; **p84** (tr) Shuttle Views of the Earth: Geology from Space. Compiled by Pat Jones, courtesy of LPI; **p85** (ml + tr) © Digital Vision; **p86** (b) Robert H. Pearson, Canada; (tr) © Brian and Cherry Alexander; **p87** (l) Will and Deni McIntyre/Tony Stone Images; (tr) Seymour Snowman Sun Protection Campaign, NSW Cancer Council and NSW Health Department; (br) © Peter Turnley/CORBIS; **p88** (bl) © Digital Vision; (tr) SPL/Magrath/Folsom; **p88–89** SPL/Pekka Parviainen; **p89** (m) Fortean Picture Library/Llewellyn Publications; (tr) © Alamy and E. Vicens/CORBIS; **p90–91** (t) © Digital Vision; (b) © NASA **p90** (t) © Digital Vision; **p91** (tr) International Weather Productions; **p92–93** © Scott T. Smith/CORBIS; **p94–95** © George Hall/CORBIS; **p94** (tl) © Digital Vision; (ml) © Jonathan Blair/CORBIS; (bl) NASA; (b) © Digital Vision; **p95** (tr) SPL/NASA; **p96–97** (background) Shuttle Views of the Earth: Oceans from Space. Compiled by Pat Jones and Gordon Wells, courtesy of LPI; **p96** (b) SPL/NASA; **p97** (t) SPL/Los Alamos National Laboratory; (bl) Shuttle Views of the Earth: Oceans from Space. Compiled by Pat Jones and Gordon Wells, courtesy of LPI; **p98** (bl) © Karl Switak, ABPL/CORBIS; (m) Peter Bull; (tr) SPL/Dr. Jeremy Burgess; **p99** (tl) Still Pictures/Nick Cobbing; (b) Peter Bull; (r) © Chinch Gryniewicz, Ecoscene/CORBIS; **p100** (m) SPL/PLI; **p100–101** (t) © Dewitt Jones/CORBIS; **p101** (bl) © Paul A. Souders/CORBIS; (br) © Digital Vision; **p102–103** © Vince Streano/CORBIS; **p102** (bl) © Digital Vision; (tr) © Ron Boardman, FLPA/CORBIS; **p103** (t) © Wolfgang Kaehler/CORBIS; **p104–105** © Digital Vision; **p104** (t) SPL/Arc Science Simulations; **p105** (bl) © Digital Vision; (tr) Still Pictures/© Kevin Schafer; **p106–107** © Michael and Patricia Fogden/CORBIS; **p108** (tl, mr + bm) © Digital Vision; (br) © Ron Boardman, FLPA/CORBIS; **p109** (t) © Digital Vision; (bl) Howard Allman; (r) © Galen Rowell/CORBIS; **p110** (ml) Ian Jackson; (b) Chris Shields; **p110–111** © Stuart Westmoreland/CORBIS; **p111** (tr + mr) Ian Jackson; (mr) Jeremy Gower; (b) Ian Jackson; **p112** (ml) © Tom Brakefield/CORBIS; (tr) Ian Jackson; (br) David Wright; **p113** © Digital Vision; **p114–115** © Digital Vision; **p114** (b) © Digital Vision; **p115** (ml) Still Pictures/Michael Viard; (tr) © Digital Vision; (br) Ian Jackson; **p116–117** © Reinhard Eisele/CORBIS; **p116** (b) Nicola Butler; **p117** (bl, m + mr) Ian Jackson; (tr) © Digital Vision; **p118–119** © Buddy Mays/CORBIS; **p118** (tr) Nicola Butler; **p119** (t) © Buddy Mays/CORBIS; (mr) Ian Jackson; (br) © Anthony Bannister, ABPL/CORBIS; **p120–121** © Kit Kittle/CORBIS; **p120** (bl) Jeremy Gower; **p121** (ml) Yann Layma/Tony Stone Images; (tr) SPL/David Scharf; **p122–123** © Christine Osborne/CORBIS; **p122** (m) © Jeremy Horner/CORBIS; (tr) Nicola Butler; **p123** (mr) Ian Jackson; **p124** (b) © Gail Mooney/CORBIS; (tr) Nicola Butler; **p125** (tr) Still Pictures/Carlos Guarita; (ml) Richard Passmore/Tony Stone Images; (mb) Still Pictures/Carlos Guarita; **p126** (ml) Nicola Butler; (r) © Stuart Westmoreland/CORBIS; **p127** (tl) © Ron Watts/CORBIS; (tr) © Stuart Westmoreland/CORBIS; (br) © George MacCarthy/CORBIS; **p128–129** (background) © Digital Vision; **p128** (m) NOAA; (b) © Digital Vision; **p129** (m) © Digital Vision; (b) Ian Jackson; **p130–131** © Galen Rowell/CORBIS; **p130** (tr) © David Muench/CORBIS; **p131** (tr) © William A. Bake/CORBIS; (br) © Catherine Karnow/CORBIS; **p132–133** © Yann Arthus-Bertrand/CORBIS; **p134–135** © Keren Su/CORBIS; **p134** (m) Ian Jackson; (tr) Fiona Patchett and Laura Fearn; p135 (tl) © W. Wayne Lockwood, M.D./CORBIS; (mr) Ian Jackson; **p136** (bl) Ian Jackson; (br) Rachel Lockwood; (mr) Ian Jackson; **p137** (t) © Richard Hamilton Smith/CORBIS; (bl) Ian Jackson; (br) © Digital Vision; **p138–139** (t) SPL/Voker Steger, PETER ARNOLD INC.; (b) © Jans Peter Lahall/Robert Harding; **p138** (m) Stephen Moncrieff; **p139** (tr) SPL/Ed Young/AGSTOCK; **p140–141** (b) © Hans **p140** (tr) Ron Giling/Robert Harding; **p141** (m) Craig Asquith; **p142–143** © Nathan Benn/CORBIS; **p143** (t) © Mark Edwards/Robert Harding; (b) © Steve Raymer/CORBIS;

p144–145 © Marc Garanger/CORBIS; **p144** (tr) © Digital Vision; **p145** (bl) © Liba Taylor/CORBIS; (tr) © Morton Beebe/CORBIS; **p146–147** © Bob Krist/CORBIS; **p146** (tr) Stephen Moncrieff; **p147** (tr) Ron Giling/Robert Harding; **p148** (l) Harmut Schwarzbach/Robert Harding; **p149** (tl) Shehzad Noorani/Robert Harding; (br) © Bob Krist/CORBIS; **p150–151** © Digital Vision; **p150** (r) Thomas Raupach/Robert Harding; **p151** (bl) © Richard Cummins/CORBIS; **p152** (bl) © Peter Turnley/CORBIS; (tr) © Hartmut Schwarzbach/Robert Harding; **p152–153** Bruce Coleman Collection/Jules Cowan; **p154** (l) Harmut Scharzbach/Robert Harding; (tr) Photo courtesy of Boeing Satellite Systems; **p155** (tl) © Nik Wheeler/CORBIS; (br) Jean Luc & F. Ziegler/Robert Harding; **p156** Wateraid/Jim Holmes; **p157** (t) Greenpeace/Borstelman; (b) Greenpeace/Morgan; **p158–159** © Phil Schermeister/CORBIS; **p160–161** © Craig Aurness/CORBIS; **p160** (tr) © Gunter Marx Photography/CORBIS; **p161** (tr) © Joseph Sohm; Chromo Sohm Inc./CORBIS; **p162** (background) © Ron Watts/CORBIS; (bl) © Flip Schulke/CORBIS; **p162–163** (t) © Kevin Fleming/CORBIS; **p163** (bl) © Douglas Peebles/CORBIS; (r) © Digital Vision; **p164** (m) © Marc Muench/CORBIS; (tr) © Gunter Marx/CORBIS; (br) © Lowell Georgia/CORBIS; **p165** (tr) © Michael Lewis/Bruce Coleman; (br) © Galen Rowell/CORBIS; **p166** (tr) © Gianni Dagli Orti/CORBIS; (b) Howard Allman; **p167** © Charles Josette Lenars/CORBIS; **p168** (bl) © Robert Francis/Eye Ubiquitous/Hutchison; (tr) © Bill Gentile/CORBIS; **p169** (t) Howard Allman; (b) © Danny Lehman/CORBIS; **p170** (l + tr) Howard Allman; **p171** (r) © Philip Gould/CORBIS; **p172–173** © Jeremy Horner/CORBIS; **p174–175** Brian Vikander/CORBIS; **p170–171** © Bob Krist/CORBIS; **p174** (tr) Galen Rowell/CORBIS; **p175** (r) © Annie Griffiths Belt/CORBIS; **p176–177** (t) © Jeremy Horner/CORBIS; (b) © Jeremy Horner/Eye Ubiquitous/Hutchison; **p176** (bl) © Pablo Corral V/CORBIS; **p177** (br) © Sarah Errinton/Eye Ubiquitous/Hutchison; **p178–179** © The Purcell Team/CORBIS; **p178** (bl) © Wolfgang Kaehler/CORBIS; (tr) © Estate of Jesco Von Puttamer/Eye Ubiquitous/Hutchison; **p179** (tr) © Luiz Claudio Marigo/Bruce Coleman; **p180–181** © Edward Parker/Eye Ubiquitous/Hutchison; **p180** (b) © S. Molins/Eye Ubiquitous/Hutchison; (tr) © Jeremy Horner/Eye Ubiquitous/Hutchison; **p181** (tr) © Inge Yspeert/CORBIS; **p182–183** (background) © Bruce Coleman/Nicholas Devore; **p182** (bl) © Will and Deni McIntyre/Tony Stone Images; **p183** (b) © Diego Lezama Orezzoli/CORBIS; (tr) © Edward Parker/Eye Ubiquitous/Hutchison; **p184–185** © Abbie Enock,Travel Ink/CORBIS; **p184** (tr) © Bettman/CORBIS; **p185** (tr) © Dennis Degnan/CORBIS; **p186–187** © Earl and Nazima Kowall/CORBIS; **p188–189** © Jack Fields/CORBIS; **p188** (tl) Michael S. Yamashita/CORBIS; **p189** (tl) © Adam Woolfitt/CORBIS (br) © Charles and Josette Lenars/CORBIS; **p190–191** (background) © John Cancalosi/Bruce Coleman; **p190** (b) © Roger Ressmeyer/CORBIS; (tr) © Patrick Ward/CORBIS; **p191** (tl) © Australian Picture Library/CORBIS; (br) © Charles and Josette Lenars/CORBIS; **p192–193** © Gerald S. Cubitt/Bruce Coleman; **p192** (tr) © Robert Francis/Eye Ubiquitous/Hutchison; **p193** (t) © Doug Armand/Tony Stone Images; (br) © Pacific Stock/Bruce Coleman; **p194** (b) © Isabella Tree/Eye Ubiquitous/Hutchison; **p195** (tl) © Chris Rainier/CORBIS; (br) © Fritz Prenzel/Bruce Coleman; **p196–197** © Pacific Stock/Bruce Coleman; **p196** (bl) © Pacific Stock/Bruce Coleman; (tr) © Jan Butchofsky-Houser/CORBIS; **p197** (tr) © Jack Fields/CORBIS; **p198–199** © Steve Raymer/CORBIS; **p200–201** © Keren Su/CORBIS; **p200** (bl) © Neil Rabinowitz/CORBIS; **p201** (tm) © Bob Krist/CORBIS; (b) © Wolfgang Kaehler/CORBIS; **p202–203** © Alain Compost/Bruce Coleman; **p202** (bl) © Isabella Tree/Eye Ubiquitous/Hutchison; **p203** (ml) © Kenneth Fischer/Bruce Coleman; (r) © Robin Constable/Eye Ubiquitous/Hutchison; **p204–205** (background) © Digital Vision **p204** (b) © Dave Saunders/Tony Stone Images; (tr) © Charles and Josette Lenars/CORBIS; **p205** (tl) © Staffan Widstrand/Bruce Coleman; (br) © Christina Dodwell/Eye Ubiquitous/Hutchison; **p206–207** © Estate of B. Gerard/Eye Ubiquitous/Hutchison; **p206** (bl) © Dave G. Houser/CORBIS; (tr) © Nik Wheeler/CORBIS; **p207** (bl) © Dean Conger/CORBIS; (r) © Kevin Schafer/CORBIS; **p208** (l) © Wally McNamee/CORBIS; (tr) © Peter Turnley/CORBIS; p209 (tl) © Christine Osborne/CORBIS; (b) © Kevin R. Morris/CORBIS; **p210–211** (background) © Wolfgang Kaehler/CORBIS; **p210** (b) © Michael MacIntyre/Eye Ubiquitous/Hutchison; (tr) © David Cliverd/Eye Ubiquitous/Hutchison; **p211** (bl) © Jeremy Horner/Eye Ubiquitous/Hutchison; (tr) © Catherine Karnow/CORBIS; **p212–213** © Gerald S. Cubitt/Bruce Coleman; **p212** (bl) © Pacific Stock/Bruce Coleman; (tr) © Paul Almasy/CORBIS; **p213** (br) © Alain Compost/Bruce Coleman; **p214** (bl) © Ric Ergenbright/CORBIS; **p214–215** (t) © SuperStock; (b) © John Dakers, Eye Ubiquitous/CORBIS; **p215** (r) © Yoshikazu Tsuno/AFP/Getty Images; **p216–217** © Fulvio Roiter/CORBIS; **p218–219** (background) © Larry Lee Photography/CORBIS; **p218** (l) © Gianni Dagli Orti/CORBIS; **p219** (tl) © DPA Deutche Press-Agentur/DPA/Press Association Images; (r) ANGEL OF THE NORTH (1998) by Antony Gormley, steel, 22 x 54 x 2.20m, © Courtesy of the artist and Jay Jopling/White Cube, London. Photographer Graeme Peacock, courtesy of Gateshead Metropolitan Borough Council; **p220** (tl) Howard Allman; **p220–221** © Hans Wolf/The Image Bank/Getty Images; **p221** (t) © Todd Gipstein/CORBIS; (r) © Pete Saloutos/CORBIS; **p222** (b) © Rethly Akos; (tr) © Greenpeace/Shirly; **p223** © Franz-Marc Frei/CORBIS; **p224–225** © Jan Jordan; **p224** (bl) © J.F.Causse/Tony Stone Images; (tr) © Les Gibbon; Cordaiy Photo Library Ltd./CORBIS; **p225** (r) © Brian and Cherry Alexander; **p226** (tr) Photo © European Parliament; (b) © Powerstock Zefa; **p227** (tl) © European Communities; (tr) © European Communities; (b) © Peter Turnley/CORBIS; **p228** © Bettman/CORBIS; **p229** (tl) © Catherine Karnow/CORBIS; (br) © Nik Wheeler/CORBIS; **p230–231** © Charles and Josette Lenars/CORBIS; **p232–233** Glen Christian/Robert Harding; **p233** (tr) © Karen Tweedy-Holmes/CORBIS; (br) © David Reed/CORBIS; **p234–235** © Adrian Arbib/CORBIS; **p234** (tr) © Margaret Courtney-Clarke/CORBIS; **p235** © Daniel Lainé/CORBIS; **p236–237** © Christine Osborne/CORBIS; **p236** (bl) © J.Wright/Eye Ubiquitous/Hutchison; (tr) Ian Jackson; **p237** (b) © Roger Wood/CORBIS; **p238–239** (b) © Sarah Errington/Eye Ubiquitous/Hutchison; **p238** (l) © Mary Jellife/Eye Ubiquitous/Hutchison; **p239** (tl) © Daniel Lainé/CORBIS; (tr) © Sarah Errington/Eye Ubiquitous/Hutchison; **p240** (tr) © Digital Vision; (b) © Kevin Fleming/CORBIS; **p241** © David Brinicombe/Eye Ubiquitous/Hutchison; **p242–243** © Nevada Wier/CORBIS; **p242** (bl) © Peter Turnley/CORBIS; (tr) Ian Jackson; **p243** (tr) © Chris Hellier/CORBIS; (b) © Peter Johnson/CORBIS; **p244–245** (background) © Sarah Errington/Eye Ubiquitous/Hutchison; **p244** (l) © Bruce Coleman Inc.; **p245** (bl) © Crispin Hughes/Eye Ubiquitous/Hutchison; (tl) © CORBIS; (r) © Contemporary African Art Collection Limited/CORBIS; **p246–247** © Digital Vision; **p248** (ml) Stephen Moncrieff; (bl) © Air Photographics, Inc., CNOVS-969-20; (tr) © Digital Vision; **p249** (t, bm + br) European Map Graphics Ltd; **p250** (b) Stephen Moncrieff; (tr) © Dan Guravich/CORBIS; **p251** (bl) European Map Graphics Ltd; (tr) © W. Perry Conway/CORBIS; **p252–253** (background) © Digital Vision; **p252** (mr) PHOTO ESA; **p253** (tl) © NERC Satellite Station, University of Dundee www.sat.dundee.ac.html; (br) SPL/European Space Agency; **p254** (b) © Christopher Cormack/CORBIS; **p255** Stephen Moncrieff/Craig Asquith; **p256–257** © Raymond Gehman/CORBIS; **p256** (tr) © Owen Franken/CORBIS; **p257** (tr) © Adam Woolfitt/CORBIS; **p258–259** European Map Graphics Ltd; **p264–265** © Thomas D. Mangelsen/Robert Harding; **p264** (b) © SPL/Julian Baum and David Angus; **p266–267** © Richard Cummins/CORBIS; **p267** (br) © W. Perry Conway/CORBIS; **p274–275** © John Cancalosi/Robert Harding; **p275** © SPL/Julian Baum and David Angus; **p276–277** © Galen Rowell/CORBIS; **p277** (tr) © Darren Maybury, Eye Ubiquitous/CORBIS; **p282–283** © Amos Nachoum/CORBIS; (t) © SPL/Worldsat International; **p284–285** © Pascal Kobeh/Robert Harding; **p285** (br) © Bates Littlehales/CORBIS; **p290** SPL/ © Tom Van Sant; **p290–291** © Chase Swift/CORBIS; **p292–293** © Michael S. Yamashita/CORBIS; **p293** (br) © Keren Su/CORBIS; **p306–307** © S. Dalton/NHPA/Photoshot; **p306** © SPL/Julian Baum and David Angus; **p308–309** © Digital Vision **p309** (r) Agripicture/© Peter Dean; **p318–319** © Tim Harris/Minden Pictures/Corbis; **p319** SPL/Julian Baum and David Angus; **p320–321** © Tom Brakefield/CORBIS; **p321** (br) © Nigel T. Davis, Gallo Images/CORBIS; **p330–331** © Digital Vision; **p330** (b) SPL/Julian Baum and David Angus; **p331** (tr) SPL/ Julian Baum and David Angus; **p334–335** © David Muench/CORBIS; **p336–337** (background) © Digital Vision; **p338–339** (background) © Digital Vision; **p341** (m) Susannah Owen/© Digital Vision; **p342** (b) Craig Asquith; **p343** (ml) Peter Bull; (b) Howard Allman; **p344–351** Mike Olley; **p352–353** (background) © Digital Vision; **p354–367** © Courtesy CIA; (background) © Digital Vision; **p367** (b) UN Photo by Mark Garten; **p368–375** (background) © Digital Vision Maps based on data distributed by the EROS Data Center Distributed Active Archive Center (EDC DAAC), located at the U.S. Geological Survey's EROS Data Center in Sioux Falls, South Dakota.

This edition updated by Phil Clarke and Michael Hill • Managing editor: Felicity Brooks • Managing designer: Stephen Wright • Cover design: Michael Hill
Digital image processing: John Russell and Mike Olley • Picture research: Ruth King

With thanks to: Jos Poels, flag consultant; Matthew Preston, Lecturer in Politics, Wadham College, Oxford; Stuart Atkinson, astronomy consultant; Ruth Brocklehurst; Alice Pearcey; Katie Daynes.
 This edition first published in 2013 by Usborne Publishing Ltd, 83–85 Saffron Hill, London EC1N 8RT, England. www.usborne.com UE. First published in America in 2002. This edition first published in America in 2013.